Reinventing
Civil Society

Reinventing Civil Society

The Emerging Role of Faith-Based Organizations

Cynthia Jackson-Elmoore
Richard C. Hula
Laura A. Reese

Routledge
Taylor & Francis Group

LONDON AND NEW YORK

To our spouses, Ambrose, Catherine, and Gary, for
endless friendship, love, and support;
we give honor, respect, and thanks to our parents.

First published 2011 by M.E. Sharpe

Published 2015 by Routledge
2 Park Square, Milton Park, Abingdon, Oxon OX14 4RN
711 Third Avenue, New York, NY 10017, USA

Routledge is an imprint of the Taylor & Francis Group, an informa business

Library of Congress Cataloging-in-Publication Data

Jackson-Elmoore, Cynthia, 1965–
Reinventing civil society : the emerging role of faith-based organizations / by Cynthia Jackson-
Elmoore, Richard C. Hula, and Laura A. Reese.
    p. cm.
Includes bibliographical references and index.
ISBN 978-0-7656–1040–9 (hardcover : alk. paper) — ISBN 978-7656-1041-6 (pbk. : alk. paper)
    1. Low-income housing—Government policy—United States. 2. Low-income housing—
Michigan. 3. Nonprofit organizations—Michigan. 4. Faith-based human services—United
States—Evaluation. 5. Civil society—United States. I. Hula, Richard C., 1947–
II. Reese, Laura A. (Laura Ann), 1958– III. Title.

HD7287.96.U6J33 2011
363.5'83—dc22   2010040644

ISBN 13: 9780765610416 (pbk)
ISBN 13: 9780765610409 (hbk)

Contents

List of Tables, Figures, and Appendices

Tables

Figures

Maps

Appendices

Preface

There is a time for everything and a season for every activity. The time has come for this book examining the role of the faith community in housing, politics, and urban policy. What started as a search for knowledge quickly became a labor of love fueled by our passion to know what difference faith makes in local communities, particularly as it impacts low-income housing opportunities. This book would not be possible without the hardworking individuals found in both secular and faith-based organizations who strive daily to provide low-income housing and associated services. We are indebted to their efforts both as scholars and citizens. We are thankful for the willingness of many of them to participate in this research.

Without question, Harry Briggs, Executive Editor at M.E. Sharpe, deserves recognition for amazing patience and commitment to this project: thank you. We are also appreciative of the invaluable assistance that Elizabeth Granda, Associate Editor at M.E. Sharpe, provided through the publication process. Assistance from the Community Economic Development Association of Michigan (CEDAM) was critical to many aspects of this project. We appreciate CEDAM's support over the years; Angie Gaabo and Emily Dooer were particularly instrumental in ensuring access to data and background information. We are grateful for the expertise that our editor, Anna Kirkwood Graham, demonstrated in finalizing the manuscript.

Many people and entities contributed to the completion of this book. For example, the project was launched with monetary support from the Michigan State University Community Vitality Program funded by the Michigan Agricultural Experiment Station and the Office of the Provost. The book also benefited from insights offered by colleagues at conferences of the Urban Affairs Association (UAA) and American Political Science Association (APSA), as well as by the White House Faith-Based and Community Initiative Conference on Research, Outcomes, and Evaluation.

Two faculty colleagues merit special recognition for their selfless assistance with this project. Sarah Reckhow conducted the social network analysis, providing network maps and consultation on related methodology. She also graciously reviewed material in Chapter 9 to ensure that our interpretations and discussion were accurate and reflective of the analyses she performed. Gary Sands served as a consultant on housing in general and the landscape of Michigan nonprofit housing providers in particular, and prepared and provided guidance on developing the Venn diagrams based on data from the Nonprofit Housing Provider Survey. A cadre of graduate students, research technicians, undergraduates, and support staff at Michigan State University assisted in various stages of the project. They include Rebecca Bromley, Moushumi Choudhury, Davia Cox Downey, Elie Durkee, Kathryn Durkee, Susan Durkee, Monaca Eaton, Jessica Faist-Witt, Gabriela Frask, Mark Nicol, Erin Sergison, Boaz Were, Edward Woloch, and Minting Ye.

We especially appreciate the support, understanding, and encouragement that our families provided during the completion of this work and provide in all endeavors of our lives. Our personal networks of support from friends, faith communities, and colleagues were accessed more times than we can count over the years. We are grateful and thankful that we have strong social and community ties that enable us to do the work that we love.

Portions of Chapters 2, 4, and 6–8 (as they relate to the 2003 survey conducted by the Community Economic Development Association of Michigan) appeared in Richard Hula, Cynthia Jackson-Elmoore, and Laura Reese (2008), "The Emerging Role of Faith-Based Organizations in the Low-Income Housing Market," pages 103–146 in *Innovations in Effective Compassion: Compendium of Research Papers Presented at the Faith-Based and Community Initiatives Conference on Research, Outcomes, and Evaluation,* edited by Pamela Joshi, Stephanie Hawkins, and Jeffrey Novey, and prepared for the U.S. Department of Health and Human Services, Office of the Assistant Secretary for Planning and Evaluation, the Center for Faith-Based and Community Initiatives.

Part I

Introduction

1

Faith-Based Nonprofits and the Civil Society

There is a great deal of popular and scholarly interest in the service activities of faith-based organizations. Often these activities have an explicitly political component as faith-based institutions seek to modify public policy. Such efforts can generate significant controversy, an outcome not difficult to understand. There is, first of all, the broad constitutional debate as to the proper relationship between church and state. Although faith-based organizations have long been active in the American political process, a strong ambivalence toward such activity persists. Moreover, the issues taken up by faith-based organizations often represent core cleavages in society. Questions about morality, civil rights, and education are almost certain to spawn intense debate. Thus, when faith-based organizations lobby for particular public policies or support political candidates, they are clearly taking on a public or expressly political role in American society.

A large body of research has explored the impact and role of religion in the political sphere. What has not been systematically explored, certainly not in the academic arena, is the role of faith-based organizations (FBOs) in the provision of public services. To the extent that public service provision—be it housing, education, child care, or job training—involves public funding, substitutes for the public provision of goods and services, and implies decisions about who gets what services and how services are allocated, it too constitutes an inherently political role for faith-based organizations.

Faith-based organizations are important actors in the American political system through their role as producers and distributors of publicly supported goods and services. Indeed, FBOs engage in a bewildering number of production activities.[1] Examples range from traditional food and emergency support programs, to running publicly supported schools, to implementing job training and economic development efforts. There is a long tradition of faith-based organizations providing social services to members of their community. At times these efforts have received considerable public support. At other times public subsidy has been minimal. This role received a great deal of attention in the administration of President George W. Bush, which was committed to expanding federal support for faith-based and community organizations willing to deliver a variety of social services. A similar commitment to faith-based organizations has been embraced by the administration of President Barack Obama. It is likely that interest in these organizations as service providers will continue to increase since both major national parties endorse the concept.

The expanded interest in the civic role of faith-based organizations is part of a broader overall shift in American politics. Put simply, Americans have become extraordinarily cynical about the overall capacity of all public institutions, and are increasingly looking to the private sector as a means to reach public goals. There are a variety of explanations for the decline in citizen confidence. Many cite the apparent failure of a number of large-scale social initiatives such as the War on Poverty in the 1960s and the military disaster in Viet Nam in the 1970s as contributing to a loss of citizen confidence. More current issues such as the U.S. involvements in Iraq and Afghanistan and questions about the motivations behind them have done little to boost public trust in government. Moreover, citizen cynicism has been strongly reinforced in the political rhetoric of politicians and other opinion leaders. Certainly what once seemed to be an inevitable expansion of traditional public sector institutions in the United States now seems far from inevitable even given expansions in the early tenure of the Obama administration. What is perhaps most noteworthy is that skepticism about the utility of government cuts across ideological and partisan lines. Consider the position articulated by Bill Clinton and Al Gore (1992, 22–23):

> We can no longer afford to pay more for—and get less from—our government. The answer for every problem cannot always be another program or more money. It is time to radically change the way the government operates—to shift from the top down bureaucracy to entrepreneurial government that empowers citizens and communities to change our country from the bottom up. We must reward people and ideas that work and get rid of those that don't.

While much contemporary political rhetoric is framed in relatively straightforward antigovernment terms, actual institutional and policy changes have been much more complex. Indeed, it is not clear that citizen discontent in fact translates into demands for dramatic reductions in public services. For example, in 1976 a plurality (44 percent) of survey respondents indicated that they would prefer a larger government that provided more service. Forty-two percent indicated a preference for a smaller government providing fewer services. In 2008 the number of citizens preferring a smaller government increased to 50 percent. Nevertheless, 45 percent of the sample continued to endorse the notion of a larger government with more services (Roper Center 2007).

While there is popular ambivalence about the proper scope of government, there seems little question that there is broad support for reconsidering how government should do its work. Nor can there be any serious doubt that restructuring has occurred. Perhaps the two most important trends have been a decentralization of political authority to state and local governments and a commitment to utilizing private sector institutions to implement policy choices. Initially the emphasis on the private sector focused on market institutions and forces.[2] More recently, however, attention has been directed at nonprofit organizations and, in particular, faith-based organizations as important sources of institutional reform. Perhaps no element of this change has been more controversial than efforts to engage faith-based organizations in the production and provision of public goals. Unfortunately the ensuing debate has largely been framed in ideological rather than empirical terms.

The evaluation of publicly funded faith-based services is further obscured by the fact that the minimal academic literature on faith-based community development efforts and a somewhat greater body of research on social service provision do not inform each other. There is even less research on how faith-based efforts compare to governmental activities. It appears, or is widely assumed, that many faith-based organizations engage in a variety of service provision and community development activities. Still, much understanding of faith-based service provision comes from the popular news media. While such "accounts offer important pieces of a story . . . the literature about them [FBOs] tends to be scattered, disjointed, and descriptive rather than conceptual or analytical" (Thomas and Blake 1996, 136); little has changed since this assessment. In sum, there is a dearth of academic literature on the nature, extent, and effects of faith-based service provision, and what limited research exists tends to be fragmented and case study in nature. While the popular media has often favorably reported on model cases of faith-based service provision, there have yet to be rigorous evaluations of such efforts; there is little understanding of the nature and political implications of such service provision; and the impacts on church and state separation have not been fully and explicitly explored.

The complexity and breadth of faith-based political activity including service provision make it difficult to generalize about such behavior. This difficulty is compounded by the fact that much of the available literature is anecdotal, argumentative, and generally atheoretical. While public debate on the appropriate role of faith-based organizations has been extensive and often quite heated, resolution of key issues has been difficult due to a lack of reliable data on what faith-based organizations do and how they do it. Indeed, the information base for secular nonprofits is hardly any better. This book imposes some order on the existing literature by reviewing and assessing what is known about the public service activities of FBOs and posing and testing opposing models of sacred service provision in the public sphere.[3]

Organization and Research Questions

Four broad kinds of "policy behaviors" serve as an organizing framework. While the book focuses largely on service delivery and policy advocacy activities in the areas of housing and community development, they are framed within the context of the larger political roles of faith-based and community-based institutions. It is important to note that these distinctions are not as clear-cut as they are often depicted in the literature. The first two examples of "policy behaviors" include what are generally considered overt political behavior:

- *Electoral Politics:* Activity that involves the recruitment and support of candidates for elective public office. Specific strategies include voter mobilization, financial support, and issue mobilization.
- *Policy Advocacy:* Activities that focus on efforts to influence policy makers to support specific policy positions. Examples include both traditional lobbying strategies and public mobilization.

These activities are targeted directly at the political system. There is typically a perceived link between organizational activity and a desired policy outcome.

Other interactions with the political system can be seen as targeted at implementation of decisions already taken. These include:

- *Service Delivery:* Activities that involve the provision of specific goods and services to a targeted population. These activities can be undertaken with or without publicly provided resources.
- *Community and Economic Development:* Activities that focus on efforts to implement programs to substantially restructure the local economic, social, or political system. These activities also can be undertaken with or without publicly provided resources.

Some argue that engagement in policy implementation is not really political activity. This view is, of course, reminiscent of early claims in public administration that it is possible to separate political and administrative issues. The popular support given this view is indicated by the variety of institutional structures that have been created with the aim of shielding administrators from "politics." Examples range from civil service regulations to city and county manager positions at the local level.

While the image of program administration free of politics continues to have popular appeal, an enormous amount of empirical scholarship has documented that such a vision is naive. At a minimum, service providers make a number of decisions that impact who will receive what services. Such decisions are almost never explicitly mandated in program legislation or administrative rules (Lipsky 1980). In addition to the discretion of direct service providers, it is clear that implementation units inevitably become advocates for programs and budgets within their jurisdictions (Needleman and Needleman 1974; Knott and Miller 1987; Niskanen 1994; Henig et al. 2003).

It should be stressed that the overt electoral activities of faith-based organizations are not the focus of the current study. There is a large body of literature examining the political role of religion, faith-based organizations, congregations, and, particularly, African American churches (see, for example, Brown and Wolford 1984; Gurin et al.

1989; Brown and Brown 2003; Fitzgerald et al. 2005). While a critical and interesting line of research, what has been far less examined, and less transparent, are the political dynamics of service provision by such organizations. Faith-based nonprofits have been providing social services for decades and were receiving public funding long before the political visibility of the Bush administration's Office of Faith-Based and Community Initiatives. Yet the outcomes and implications of this role and the integration of faith-based organizations in the governing fabric of communities has surprisingly not been the target of as extensive a body of research. For this reason, and because of the presumed connections among service provision, politics, and governing, these areas are the focus here (Hula et al. 2007).

The following, while not exhaustive, provide a sense of the nature of the central research questions addressed:

- How do faith-based and secular social service efforts compare, complement each other, and interact?
- What types of housing and community development activities are faith-based institutions pursuing?
- Are the same types of organizations (faith-based and secular nonprofits) active in housing and community development activities? Are they financed in a similar manner?
- What clienteles are served by faith-based and secular community organizations?
- How are faith-based services financed and organized? What is the extent of public sector funding? How does it affect the nature and extent of service activities?
- What is the extent of collaboration among faith-based organizations, other nonprofits, and local governmental institutions in service provision?
- Does the provision of public services appear to correlate with or lead to greater integration of FBOs in local governing processes?

The ultimate aim of the work is to focus directly on the political implications of faith-based service provision. In short, do sacred organizations provide services any differently than secular ones? Does increasing faith-based service provision have any impact on governing the civil society?

Conceptual Models

Two opposing conceptual models are posed to answer the primary research questions. First, resistance to providing public funding to FBOs has revolved around several distinct claims. Some argue that public institutions simply do a better or more equitable job at providing services than private agencies.[4] A second concern is that FBOs will take over the policy arena and interject morality wars into local politics. Hence, they will not limit their activity to service delivery, but rather cross over into political/policy realms. As a corollary, there is a presumed danger that FBOs will use their public funding to provide services to a narrow group of clients potentially delimited by sect, race, lifestyle, or ethnicity. Ultimately there is concern that FBOs will either allow government to step out of traditional service provision roles, edge out other nonprofit providers, or both, reducing service options and narrowing clients served. Finally, some have argued that public funding represents a threat to the institutional integrity of the FBO itself in that efforts to secure public funding may distort internal priorities of the organization and dilute the contribution of faith (Henig et al. 2003). The role of faith-based service provision, in light of these concerns, is modeled in Figure 1.1.

Arguments in favor of providing funding to FBOs maintain that FBOs will largely just continue to provide services, perhaps more services or to more and/or different populations. The underlying beliefs that drive FBOs are seen as a positive mechanism leading to better outcomes. It is hoped that FBOs will provide services more effectively because of the power of faith, the commitment of volunteers and staff, and the knowledge of and proximity to communities served (Figure 1.2). This view is rooted in the politics/administration dichotomy, positing that FBOs are implementing public policy decisions more effectively than government providers, but nothing more—at least in a governing sense.

These arguments differ in their contention about whether funding FBOs provides a mechanism for linkages to policy networks and ultimately the political processes of public policy making. The central question is: Is there a linear progression from services to policy? Do some organizations focus directly on policy activity as opposed to service delivery and vice versa? Do some organizations provide services and eschew policy activities? Is it possible that FBOs do not themselves engage in explicit policy activity but that their mere presence encourages or inspires policy makers to consider alternative policy strategies? In short, how tight or inherent are the links between service provision and governance?

Figure 1.1 presents the elements of logic that are defined here as arguments against funding FBOs to provide public services. Overall, the concern is that public funding of FBOs will give them greater power within the governing system— through the entrée of public funding and service provision—affecting who gets what services and, ultimately, public policy. The argument begins with a comparison of different types of nongovernmental service providers; in this case, more traditional nonprofits as well as the more specialized class of FBOs. These providers vary along dimensions other than faith, of course: geographic location, experience, size, budget, and staff, for example. These factors, along with faith, will probably affect the nature of services provided. According to this argument, however, the faith variable should have the greatest impact on the quality and quantity of services provided. More important, it should affect the nature of clients served. Concerns have been expressed in both the popular and academic literatures that FBOs would limit clients to those of their own faith or would discriminate on the basis of race, ethnicity, or lifestyle factors.

9

Figure 1.1 The Anti-FBO Argument: Service Delivery Activity Leads to Political or Policy Engagement by FBOs

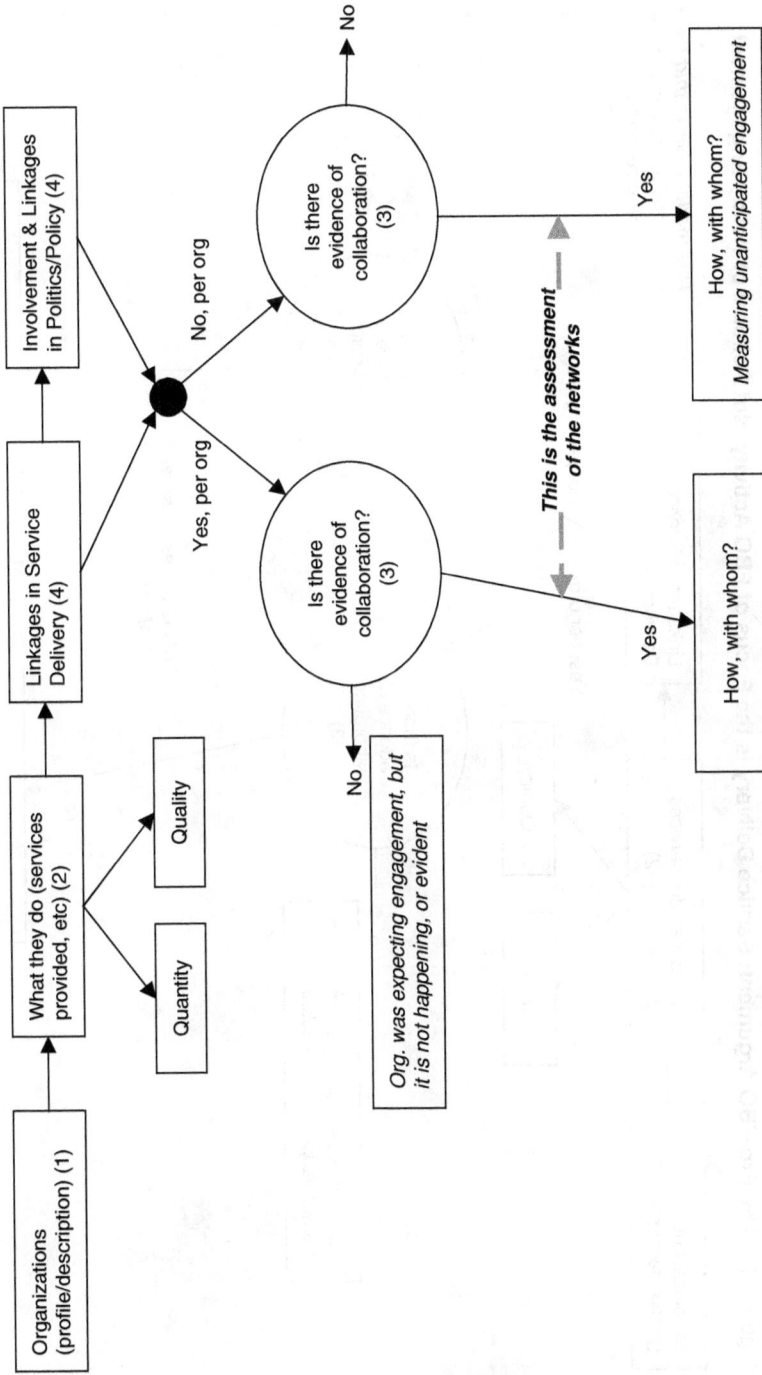

10

Figure 1.2 **The Pro-FBO Argument: Service Delivery Is the Focus of FBO Activity, Not Political or Policy Engagement**

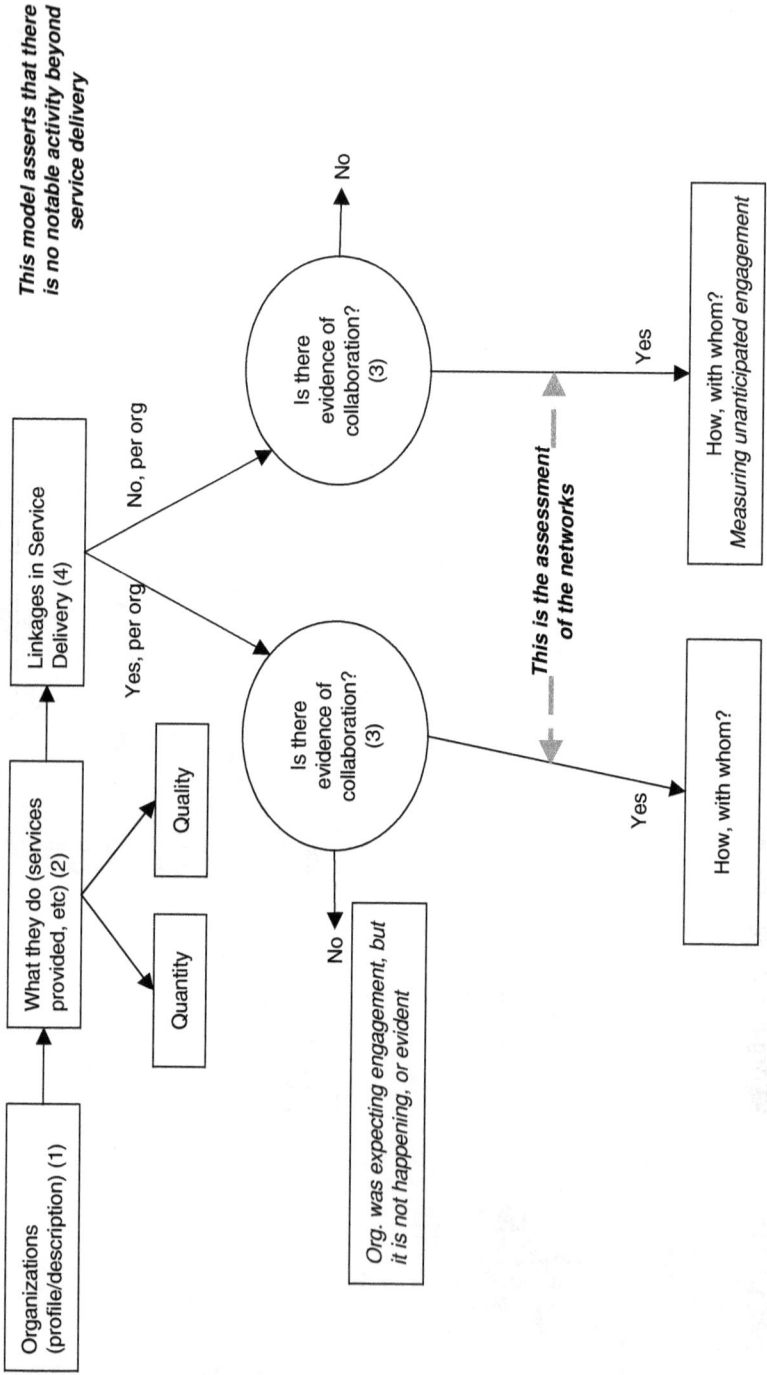

This model asserts that there is no notable activity beyond service delivery

Organizations (profile/description) (1)

What they do (services provided, etc) (2)

Quantity

Quality

Linkages in Service Delivery (4)

Yes, per org

No, per org

Is there evidence of collaboration? (3)

Is there evidence of collaboration? (3)

No

Yes

No

Yes

Org. was expecting engagement, but it is not happening, or evident

How, with whom?

How, with whom?
Measuring unanticipated engagement

This is the assessment of the networks

The connections between the nature of the nonprofit provider and services provided are inherently interesting and have been the subject of previous research (Livezey et al. 1996; Goggin and Orth 2002; Hula et al. 2007). What happens after, or as a result of, service provision has not been explored. It is logical to expect that linking FBOs into the public sphere through funding, service contracts, and oversight will open the door for them to have a greater role in the public policy and governing processes more generally. In short, the linkages with the public sphere engendered by providing services lead to more substantive roles in political and policy processes. Again, the central point of the argument in Figure 1.1 is that public funding of religious nonprofits provides a link to the public policy process that may well lead to a greater role for religious actors in governing and policy making. If this is indeed the case, then there would probably be significant impacts on the nature of clients served, public access to services, and even greater attention to religious and morality-based interests in public policy.

Obviously, individual nonprofits do not provide services alone. There are other actors—public, private for-profit, and nonprofit organizations—that provide similar services or different elements of the same service. In addition, citizen, neighborhood, and community groups are also involved in service provision and coproduction. Thus, nonprofits provide services in a networked environment. This network can be collaborative, competitive, or fragmented. These realities are illustrated in the two collaboration circles under the main path diagram and are discussed in the next section of this chapter on collaboration, partnerships, and networks.

A more sanguine view of faith-based service provision is portrayed in Figure 1.2 and largely supports arguments for public funding of such services. The two arguments are the same through the service linkage box. However, the underlying assumption here is that there are no inherent connections between the service provision role and later influence in the political process. In short, FBOs are publicly funded, they provide services to populations in need—perhaps more effectively because of their faith foundation—and they enhance the overall ability of government to ensure that social services are provided. Service provision does not necessarily imply that FBOs are interested in, or will move into, greater roles in the governing process.

Collaboration, Partnerships, Networks

Central to both models is the issue of collaboration or service networks. Organizations, whether sacred, governmental, or secular nonprofit, are unlikely to provide services in a vacuum. Most social services are provided by a variety of actors—sometimes in collaboration, others in conflict. Gray (1989, 5) defines collaboration as "a process through which parties who see different aspects of a problem can constructively explore their differences and search for solutions that go beyond their own limited vision of what is possible." Similarly, Chrislip and Larson (1994, 5) assert that collaboration is a "mutually beneficial relationship between two or more parties who work toward common goals by sharing responsibility, authority, and accountability for achieving results." It is useful to note that collaboration is often imposed by the constraints of the political process itself. For example, political leaders can seldom simply impose their policy preferences. Political success is reached only through a process of identifying partners and creating coalitions. This is typically true for implementation efforts, as well (Stone 1985, 1989).

The nature of low-income housing provision suggests that collaboration is indeed an ingredient essential to success. Results from a 1998 survey conducted by the National Civic League suggest that, on a national level, there is a fair degree of collaboration between cities and community-based organizations for the provision of affordable housing and homeless assistance (Rich et al. 1998).[5] With respect to poverty reduction and urban revitalization, city officials and representatives of community-based organizations both noted that early collaboration was a key to success. This included collaborating to: (1) identify community needs; (2) include key stakeholders in the process; (3) develop a project or program concept; and/or (4) identify and secure funding. Collaboration has been noted as a way to build consensus, develop strategic approaches to problem solving, and provide opportunities to achieve long-term, sustainable accomplishments. Collaboration for housing services also presents an opportunity for organizations to share resources, avoid costly duplication, and think broadly and systematically about community housing assets and needs.

It is possible that different types of nonprofit providers have varying propensities to collaborate or compete. As noted in Figure 1.1, if there is evidence of collaboration with other actors it is important to explore whether the presence of the network serves to enhance the political or policy role of the nonprofits involved. It is also important to assess whether particular network configurations increase the power of nonprofits in the policy process. If there is no evidence of collaboration, is it because nonprofits are competing or simply acting alone in a fragmented environment? Lack of collaboration should limit the policy role of nonprofits and also reduce service benefits (in effectiveness and efficiency) that would emanate from collaborative work.

If service delivery and not political or policy engagement is the focus of organizational activity, as depicted in Figure 1.2, then collaboration among nonprofit providers similarly allows for more efficient and effective service provision but does not increase the power of the religious network in public policy making. This argument does not imply that religious actors do not participate in the political process. Rather it acknowledges that there are variations among faith-based actors: some will focus on political processes, some will focus on service provision and service to communities, and some will do both. What it does suggest is that service provision is not inherently a vehicle for political participation or a role in the governing process.

A central focus of this study is the extent and degree to which there is collaboration among and between faith-based and community organizations, other nonprofits, and/

Figure 1.3 **Collaboration**

		Is there evidence of collaboration?	
		Yes	No
Does organization indicate that it collaborates with other organizations?	Yes	*Assessment of network relationships.* The organization said it was collaborating and there was evidence to support the claim. • How the organization(s) are collaborating and with whom. • Collaboration for service delivery only. • Collaboration for political/policy purposes only. • Collaboration for service delivery *and* collaboration for political/policy purposes.	Organization said it was collaborating but there is little to no evidence to support the claim. • No service delivery collaboration. • No collaboration for political/policy reasons.
	No	*Assessment of network relationships.* This captures unanticipated collaboration. The organization said that it did not collaborate, but there is contrary evidence to suggest that they do. • How the organization(s) are collaborating and with whom. • Collaboration for service delivery only. • Collaboration for political/policy purposes only. • Collaboration for service delivery and collaboration for political/policy purposes.	Organization indicated that it was not collaborating and survey data support the claim. There is no evidence of collaborating for service delivery or for political/policy purposes. In short, the organization does not appear to be collaborating at all.

or the government in providing services (Figure 1.3). Of particular interest are the networks within which organizations collaborate, with whom they collaborate, and for what reasons (see Figures 1.1 and 1.2 also). Again, understanding these networks is critical to the extent that the presence of networks or particular types of networks can enhance the role of faith-based actors in the political process. Figure 1.3 provides an overview of the network assessment conducted in the book. First, perceptions of collaboration are compared to the reality of collaboration. Then the nature, scope, and extent of collaboration activities are assessed. For example, is there any evidence of collaboration at all? When there is collaboration, what types of entities are working together and for what purpose: service delivery, political/policy activities, or both? Do faith-based organizations tend to collaborate only with each other, thus maintaining a separation between church and state? Or do various types of nonprofits collaborate, thus blurring the sacred-secular boundaries? Finally, how great is the presence of local government in service networks? Does the funding of nonprofits appear to allow government to step out of service provision (a substitution effect) or do public actors continue to be active participants (an enhancement effect)?

Organization of the Book

The book is divided into four parts. Part I provides an overview of the research and key questions, highlights common themes and arguments in the scholarly and popular literature, and describes the methodological approach for the study, and discusses the history of nonprofit housing in Michigan, which serves as the database for this study. Part II focuses on the debate over the role and effectiveness of the nonprofit sector. Of particular interest is the viability of the sector as it relates to faith-based and community-based organizations. Select experiences from around the United States are examined, along with issues of capacity, focusing on the nature of housing providers, along with organizational and financial considerations. Part III details data and findings on the role and effectiveness of the nonprofit sector in Michigan. Key issues include the nature and extent of and satisfaction with housing provision, as well as the scope and extent of nonprofit community involvement in services outside of the housing arena. Part IV highlights impacts, implications, and conclusions. Of particular note are the collaborations, partnerships, and networks for low-income housing provision and the political and policy dimensions of nonprofit activity in the housing arena.

Notes

1. The terms "provision" and "production" of public services are used interchangeably throughout the book. Technically, nonprofits produce services provided via government funding. The literature typically refers to nonprofit or faith-based service provision, so the more common vernacular is employed here.

2. For example, some interesting reform efforts in the 1980s attempted to introduce "market forces" within government bureaucracies (Hula 1988). For a very influential popular discussion of such efforts see Osborne and Gaebler (1992).

3. It is useful to study faith-based organizations, particularly since they make up such an important segment of the service delivery community (Kearns et al. 2005). The discussion of the extent and nature of religiosity and distinct delineations along a continuum of faith-saturated to secular is left to others (Jeavons 1998; Smith and Sosin 2001; Search for Common Ground 2002; Ebaugh et al. 2003; Sider and Unruh 2004). The literature is in basic agreement that organizations vary on a continuum where some are more religious than others. The term "faith-based organizations" in this book includes collaborations of congregations or religious organizations, as well as organizations based on religious principles that operate independently of congregations. The specific focus is those organizations involved in service delivery in the housing arena. This research also includes secular organizations that function independently or in cooperation with religious organizations.

4. There are, of course, a variety of justifications for this claim. They range from simple economic efficiency to accountability.

5. City officials and executive directors of community-based organizations in cities with populations of at least 50,000 were surveyed by mail (Rich et al. 1998).

References

Brown, R.E., and Monica Wolford. 1984. Religious Resources and African American Political Action. *National Political Science Review* 4:30–48.

Brown, R. Khari, and Ronald E. Brown. 2003. Faith and Works: Church-Based Social Capital Resources and African American Political Activism. *Social Forces* 82:617–641.

Chrislip, David D., and Carl E. Larson. 1994. *Collaborative Leadership: How Citizens and Civic Leaders Can Make a Difference.* San Francisco: Jossey-Bass.

Clinton, Bill, and Al Gore. 1992. *People Come First.* New York: Times Books.

Ebaugh, Helen R., Paula Pipes, Janet S. Chafetz, and Martha Daniels. 2003. Where's the Religion? Distinguishing Faith-Based From Secular Social Service Agencies. *Journal for the Scientific Study of Religion* 42 (3):411–426.

Fitzgerald, Scott T., and Ryan E. Spohn. 2005. Pulpits and Platforms: The Role of the Church in Determining Protest among Black Americans. *Social Forces* 84 (2):1015–1049.

Goggin, Malcolm L., and Deborah A. Orth. 2002. *How Faith-Based and Secular Organizations Tackle Housing for the Homeless.* Albany, NY: Rockefeller Institute of Government.

Gray, Barbara. 1989. *Collaborating: Finding Common Ground for Multiparty Problems.* San Francisco: Jossey-Bass.

Gurin, Patricia, Shirley Hatchett, and James S. Jackson. 1989. *Hope and Independence: Blacks' Response to Electoral and Party Politics.* New York: Russell Sage Foundation.

Henig, Jeffrey R., Thomas T. Holyoke, Natalie Lacireno-Paquet, and Michele Moser. 2003. Privatization, Politics, and Urban Services: The Political Behavior of Charter Schools. *Journal of Urban Affairs* 25 (1):37–54.

Hula, Richard C. 1988. *Market-Based Public Policy.* London: Macmillian.

Hula, Richard C., Cynthia Jackson-Elmoore, and Laura Ann Reese. 2007. Mixing God's Work and the Public Business: A Framework for the Analysis of Faith-Based Service Delivery. *Review of Policy Research* 24(1):67–89.

Jeavons, Thomas H. 1998. Identifying Characteristics of "Religious" Organizations: An Exploratory Proposal. In *Sacred Companies: Organizational Aspects of Religion and Religious Aspects of Organization,* ed. N.J. Demerath III et al., 79–95. New York: Oxford University Press.

Kearns, Kevin, Chisung Park, and Linda Yankoski. 2005. Comparing Faith-Based and Secular Community Service Corporations in Pittsburgh and Allegheny County, Pennsylvania. *Nonprofit and Voluntary Sector Quarterly* 34(2):206–231.

Knott, Jack H., and Gary J. Miller. 1987. *Reforming Bureaucracy: The Politics of Institutional Choice.* Englewood Cliffs, NJ: Prentice-Hall.

Lipsky, Michael. 1980. *Street-Level Bureaucracy: Dilemmas of the Individual in Public Services.* New York: Russell Sage Foundation.

Livezey, Lowell W., Elfriede Wedam, and Larry L. Greenfield. 1996. Survey of Religious, Social Service and Community Organizations in Metropolitan Chicago. www.thearda.com.

Needleman, Martin L., and Carolyn Emerson Needleman. 1974. *Guerrillas in the Bureaucracy: The Community Planning Experiment in the United States.* New York: Wiley.

Niskanen, William A. 1994. *Bureaucracy and Public Economics.* Aldershot, Hants, England and Brookfield, VT: Edward Elgar.

Osborne, David, and Ted Gaebler. 1992. *Reinventing Government: How the Entrepreneurial Spirit Is Transforming the Public Sector.* Reading, MA: Addison-Wesley.

Rich, Michael, Michael Giles, and Emily Stern. 1998. *Collaborating to Reduce Poverty.* Washington, DC: National League of Cities.

Roper Center Public Opinion Archives. 2007. Confidence in Institutions. June. www.ropercenter.uconn.edu/data_access/tag/Congressgrsource.html.

Search for Common Ground. 2002. *Finding Common Ground: 29 Recommendations of the Working Group of Human Needs and Faith-Based and Community Initiatives.* Washington, DC: Search for Common Ground.

Sider, Ronald J., and Heidi Rolland Unruh. 2004. Typology of Religious Characteristics of Social Service and Educational Organizations and Programs. *Nonprofit and Voluntary Sector Quarterly* 33(1):109–134.

Smith, Steven Rathgeb, and Michael R. Sosin. 2001. The Varieties of Faith-Related Agencies. *Public Administration Review* 61(6):651–670.

Stone, Clarence N. 1985. Efficiency versus Social Learning: A Reconsideration of the Implementation Process. *Policy Studies Review* 4(3):484–496.

———. 1989. *Regime Politics: Governing Atlanta, 1946–1988.* Lawrence: University Press of Kansas.

Thomas, June M., and Reynard N. Blake. 1996. Faith-Based Community Development and African-American Neighborhoods. In *Revitalizing Urban Neighborhoods,* ed. W.D. Keating, N. Krumholtz, and P. Star, 131–143. Lawrence: University Press of Kansas.

2

Nonprofit Housing Provision

Themes and Arguments

A range of social, cultural, political, and market dynamics have altered the organizational and institutional landscapes of U.S. urban centers. Impacts have varied from service delivery arrangements to governing systems. Fundamental questions have been raised about what the government should do and how it should do it. Faith-based organizations (FBOs) have become particularly important actors in the political process through their traditional role as producers and distributors of publicly supported goods and services. The role of FBOs received increased emphasis because of the Charitable Choice provision of the Personal Responsibility and Work Opportunity Reconciliation Act of 1996 (PRWORA P.L.104–193 [1996]) and the commitment during the administration of President George W. Bush to expanding federal support for more and different types of FBOs willing to deliver a variety of social services (Twombly 2002). States have also embraced more variety in faith-based service provision. Such decisions have an impact on who gets what services and how those services are allocated, thus constituting an inherently political role for FBOs.

FBOs are of interest because they are involved in the provision of a number of social services—including housing, education, child care, and health—and there is evidence to suggest that partnerships between the faith community and government can enhance service delivery (Shirley 2001). FBOs also engage in a range of community development, economic development, and community organizing activities (Roozen et al. 1984; Walker 1993; Wineburg 1996; Cnaan et al. 1999; Reese and Shields 1999; Reese 2004). Table 2.1 highlights a variety of service arenas in which the government, FBOs, secular nonprofits, and private for-profit organizations engage. Housing is particularly interesting and important for a number of reasons. For instance, it is a service that FBOs have a long history of providing. Some FBOs use their experiences in the housing arena as a springboard to other community and economic development activities including job and entrepreneurial training and business incubation and consultation (Lincoln and Mamiya 1990; La Barbera 1992; Hodgkinson and Weitzman 1993; Heim 1995; Cisneros 1996; Reese and Shields 1999, 2000).

Brick-and-mortar construction as well as rehabilitation of single- and multi-family home ownership and rental properties are typical activities in the housing arena. Housing developers also become involved in a number of other services

---

Table 2.1

Examples of Service Areas and Corresponding Programs

Service categories	Examples of programs
Housing	Construction, rehabilitation, management
Economic development	Commercial ventures, industrial development, entrepreneurial training or small business incubation, banking/credit union
Social services	Job counseling, training and placement, day care provision, financial counseling or investment clubs, homeless and poor people services, counseling/programs for families, drug and alcohol abuse
Education (adults)	Computer literacy, literacy, GED, functional English translation, tutoring
Health services	Health fairs/screenings, blood drives/organ donation, health education, medical or dental clinic, drug and alcohol prevention, health insurance programs, maternity programs, nutrition programs
Community organizing	Meeting space provision, holiday celebrations or fairs, community security, organizing around issues, interfaith/interdenominational collaboration, mobilization, voter registration, recreational programs, neighborhood cleanup/improvement
Youth development	Day care (preschool), charter or private school, programs for gang members, youth offenders or runaways, mentoring, after-school and weekend programs, skill development, job training, tutoring/literacy, summer programs
Senior citizen services	Transportation, day care, visitation, meals, exercise, health care, other assistance

Source: Botchwey (2007, 41).

---

that assist individuals and families and ultimately support neighborhoods (Hoch 2000; Cnaan 2001). These projects can include home-ownership counseling services, rental and furniture assistance, employment training, and educational services, among others. Many nonprofit organizations, faith-based and secular, undertake this holistic approach to housing by providing services that address needs beyond basic shelter (Housing Plus Services 2002, 2006; Cohen et al. 2004); this is typically referred to as "housing plus."[1] Table 2.2 highlights a few national examples of programs that can be categorized as housing plus. Two key principles underlying housing plus services are the beliefs that (Cohen et al. 2004, 516):[2]

- Housing and services should be integrated to enhance the social and economic well-being of residents and to build healthy communities.
- Services should maximize use of existing resources, avoid duplication, and expand the economic, social, and political resources available to residents.

Table 2.2

Types of National Housing Plus Programs

Program	Authorization[a]	Purpose	Budget (2010)
Family Self-Sufficiency (FSS)	National Affordable Housing Act of 1990, P.L. 101–625	Assist low-income families in becoming economically independent	$60 million
Resident Opportunities and Self-Sufficiency (ROSS)	The Consolidated Appropriations Act 2008, P.L. 110–161	Assist low-income families in finding services and becoming economically independent	$50 million[b]
HOPE VI	1993 Appropriations Act, P.L. 102–389	Improve seriously distressed public housing and encourage economic independence	$200 million[c]
Jobs-Plus	Omnibus Consolidated Recessions and Appropriations Act of 1996, P.L. 104–134	Reduce unemployment and increase wages of low-income tenants	N/A[d]
HUD Neighborhood Networks	Appropriations bill FY2001, HUD, P.L. 106–37	Support creation of service learning centers in HUD properties	N/A[e]

Sources: Bratt (2008) and HUD (2008, 2009, 2010).

[a] Additional public laws may also impact the authorization of these programs.

[b] In FY10, HUD put funding into salaries for staff working with family and elderly program, rather than directly funding service delivery associated with ROSS type activities (HUD 2009, I-12).

[c] In 2003, 9% of total HOPE VI funds had been allocated to services. HOPE VI was allocated $99 and $100 million in FY07 and FY08, respectively. The program was determined to have exceeded its goal to demolish more than 100,000 of the worst U.S. public housing units. In addition, the Office of Management and Budget's program assessment and rating tool (PART) revealed that the HOPE VI program was ineffective and more costly in comparison to other programs (HUD 2008, K-1). HUD's Choice Neighborhoods Initiative was intended to build upon previous HOPE VI effort to revitalize severely distressed public housing (HUD 2009, N-1).

[d] Part of HUD's moving to work initiative.

[e] Neighborhood network centers are not funded through federal grants; instead they rely on local resources, foundations, corporations, individual donations, business profits, user fees, and in-kind contributions. Practice has been to absorb any federal costs associated with the initiative through the Public Housing Capital Fund, without establishing a specific set-aside (HUD 2008, F-15).

The reality that some organizations choose to adopt the housing plus services or a holistic approach to housing is not surprising. There is a logical connection between housing and other social service activities since housing activities have the capacity to build other types of community social capital (Hays 2002). Faith-based housing activity predates and underpins most other social service provision, and there is sufficient activity in the housing arena to ensure both potential variability and adequate sample size (Goggin and Orth 2002). This chapter begins with a discussion of political, market, social, and other contextual factors that have helped shape the nature of faith-based involvement in urban housing and that contribute to the expansion of housing provision to other types of community development. Key themes from the popular press and existing research literature are highlighted in the context of the study's main research objectives.

Background

Faith-based and secular organizations have a long and established history of social service delivery (de Toqueville 1969; Netting 1984; Wineburg 1992; Hodgkinson and Weitzman 1993). In the mid-1970s, there was a renewed interest in alternative service delivery arrangements that might prove more efficient, responsive, and personal than the existing government infrastructure. In the 1980s, the discussion focused on the relative value of privatization and efforts to encourage private market actors to assume service delivery responsibilities typically reserved for the government (Hula 1988; Gormley 1991; National Performance Review 1993; Jackson 1994; Savas 2000). There was a subsequent effort to engage nonprofit organizations as alternative private and public service producers, particularly for housing. The common argument is that like other mediating institutions (e.g., family, neighborhood, schools), secular and faith-based nonprofits provide a unique promise and possibility that is not evident in other alternatives for local service delivery (Berger and Neuhaus 1977).

National, regional, state, and local nonprofits continue to gain ascendency in the housing arena today. Wylde (1986) argues that the federal government engages in partnerships with local nonprofits to build and maintain housing because most national organizations would not assume the responsibility for providing affordable housing. It is also possible that real estate developers and national nonprofits alike may be less willing to partner with the federal government to provide affordable housing because of a perceived threat of political entanglement. As a result, nonprofit developers may be the only entities willing to provide low-income housing (Wright 1981; Koschinsky 1998). Community-based nonprofit organizations are often hailed as useful for localized, innovative housing provision, particularly since they create an avenue for small-scale individualized development (Rubin 1993). They are also viewed as necessary players in the housing arena and key to successful neighborhood revitalization. Much of this confidence and preference for community-based organizations is tied to their ability to address the sensitivities of human or social services while attending to the complexity and technicalities of physical development (Walker, 1993). Increasingly, the argument is made that faith-based organizations may have a similar capacity to meet special housing needs.

Two competing forces account for governmental and societal acceptance of nonprofits in service delivery and other typical government roles: the increasingly negative view of government and its capacity, coupled with the generally positive view of the ability of nonprofit organizations. Variations on these themes are evident in U.S. social policy passed in the late twentieth and early twenty-first centuries at the federal, state, and local levels, and across the judicial, legislative, and executive branches of government. A 1988 U.S. Supreme Court ruling essentially declared that FBOs can engage in social service delivery (*Bowen v. Kendrick* 1988). Since that time, scholars and practitioners have argued that government funding of faith-based service delivery generally helps stabilize funding in the sector (Wineburg 1993; National Commission on Civic Renewal 1998).

Government partnerships with nonprofit organizations for service delivery are long-standing. The 1990s gave rise to new levels of interest and commitment, however, particularly at the federal level. For example, passage of the Personal Responsibility and Work Opportunity Reconciliation Act of 1996 (P.L. 104–193 [1996]) or PRWORA, and in particular Charitable Choice, provided an opportunity for FBOs to compete on a more level playing field for federal funding for service delivery. The Center for Community and Interfaith Partnerships was established under the administration of President Bill Clinton by the U.S. Department of Housing and Urban Development (HUD) in 1997. In 2001, President George W. Bush issued two executive orders (no. 13199 and no. 13198), establishing the White House Office of Faith-Based and Community Initiatives and five centers for these initiatives in five federal agencies.[3] In March 2004, HUD issued a final rule to implement Executive Order 13279 (see note 3) within the confines of HUD programs and policies. This particular final rule, set within the framework of con-stitutional church-state guidelines, indicates that faith-based organizations should be able to compete for federal funding on equal footing with other organizations (HUD 2004). In February 2009, President Barack Obama reaffirmed the nation's commitment to community and faith-based initiatives by signing Executive Order 13498—which amended Executive Order 13199—to establish the White House Office and President's Advisory Council of Faith-Based and Neighborhood Part-nerships.[4] As President Obama noted:

> Faith-based and other neighborhood organizations are vital to our Nation's ability to address the needs of low-income and other underserved persons and communities. The American people are key drivers of fundamental change in our country, and few institutions are closer to the people than our faith-based and other neighborhood organizations. It is critical that the Federal Government strengthen the ability of such organizations and other nonprofit providers in our neighborhoods to deliver services effectively in partnership with Federal, State, and local governments and with other private organizations. (Obama 2009, 1)

Similarly, local governments have partnered with the faith-based community and built on long-standing traditions and commitment to service offered by FBOs. According to a survey conducted by the U.S. Conference of Mayors, by 2001, at least 121 mayors had created offices of faith-based community initiatives, appointed liaisons to the faith community, or both, and another 37 mayors were planning to appoint liaisons in the future (U.S. Conference of Mayors 2001). Building on this momentum and the national movement, the U.S. Conference of Mayors made a commitment to continue to work with President George W. Bush to assist faith- and community-based efforts in cities throughout the country (ibid.). In 2004, a new Mayors Center for Faith-Based and Community Initiatives was launched to "to inform, educate and train mayors, city-designated faith-based liaisons, and other public servants on how to best engage the faith community for more effective partnerships and service" (U.S. Conference of Mayors 2004, 4). These and other actions signaled support across all levels and branches of government for an expanded role for FBOs in society.

Role of the Nonprofit Sector in the Provision of Housing and Related Services

What is the role of the nonprofit sector and of faith-based organizations, in particular, in housing, and how has it evolved? Figure 2.1 highlights some of the key national events impacting faith-based and community-based organizations' evolving role in housing provision. The involvement of nonprofit organizations in the housing arena can be traced to the establishment of settlement houses and cooperatives for working families in the late 1800s and early 1900s (Birch and Gardner 1981; Keating et al. 1990). Nineteenth-century historical ties notwithstanding, considerable efforts in the twentieth century provide a framework for nonprofit involvement in housing development and housing services. One example is the Ford Foundation's Gray Areas pilot program with programmatic and operating funds for community development organizations addressing issues in low-income communities (Zdenek 1987; Milofsky 1988; Smith and Lipsky 1993). Growing momentum for community-based action set the stage for government initiatives to formalize the role of nonprofits in the housing arena.

The federal Section 202 program, established in 1959, provided a mechanism for nonprofit organizations to develop affordable housing for elderly and disabled populations. Federal legislation passed in the 1960s and 1970s also facilitated nonprofit involvement in housing development. Examples include Section 221(d)(3) and 236 below-market-interest-rate programs; the Office of Economic Opportunity and the Model Cities Program, which were supportive of housing development corporations; the 1966 Special Impact Amendment to the Economic Opportunity Act, which officially led to the creation of community development corporations (CDCs); Title IV of the 1974 Community Services Act, which authorized considerable funding for CDCs; and Title VI of the Housing and Community Develop-

Figure 2.1   **Overview of Select National Events and Activities Influencing Nonprofit Organization Involvement in the Housing Arena**

Late 1800s– Early 1900s	Settlement houses and cooperatives for families
1959	Federal Section 202 program (affordable housing, housing for disabled, elderly)
1961	National Housing Act, Section 221(d)(3)—below-market-interest-rate Mortgages (funding to sponsors, including nonprofits)
1962–1967	Ford Foundation Gray Areas pilot program
1966	Special impact amendment to the 1964 Economic Opportunity Act (creation of community development corporations [CDCs]) Demonstration Cities and Metropolitan Development Act (Model Cities Program)
1968	Housing and Urban Development Act (Section 236 program)
1974	Community Services Act—Title IV Housing Act (Section 8)
1978	Housing and Community Development Amendments (Congregate Housing Act, Neighborhood Reinvestment Corporation established)
Mid-1970s– 1980s	Widespread interest in privatization, particularly in housing, with increasing focus on nonprofits
1980s	Federal housing assistance decreased; number of community-based housing providers increased.
1986	Low-Income Housing Tax Credit (LIHTC) enacted under the Tax Reform Act of 1986.
1988	*Bowen v. Kendrick*—U.S. Supreme Court decision affirming faith-based organization involvement in service delivery
1990	Renewed interest in nonprofit service provision, growth in CDCs and housing production by CDCs National Affordable Housing Act of 1990 and Family Self-Sufficiency Program Cranston-Gonzalez National Affordable Housing Act of 1990[a]
1996	Charitable Choice Component of Personal Responsibility and Work Opportunity Reconciliation Act Low-Income Housing Tax Credit (LIHTC) became permanent through amendments to the tax code.
1997	Multifamily Assisted Housing Reform and Affordability Act (MAHRA)
2001	Executive orders established Faith-based and Community Initiative (FBCI) and the first five centers to coordinate FBCI activity.[b]
2002	President Bush issued Executive Order 13279, which instructed agencies to develop policies/rules to ensure that faith-based organizations received equal treatment, protection, and access to federal funding.
2004	HUD developed a rule to implement Executive Order 13279 to enable faith-based and community organizations to compete for federal funding on equal footing with other organizations.

(continued)

Figure 2.1 *(continued)*

2009	President Obama issued Executive Order 13498, reconfiguring and expanding the White House initiatives to engage the nonprofit sector in an array of social service and global issues.

Note: This overview is intended to be illustrative and not exhaustive.

[a] This is also referred to as the HOME Investment Partnership Act. One of the purposes of this act is to "extend and strengthen partnerships among all levels of government and the private sector, including for-profit and nonprofit organizations, in the production and operation of housing affordable to low-income and moderate-income families" (P.L. 101–625).

[b] See Note 4 for information on additional centers that were created since 2001.

---

ment Amendments of 1978, which created a national nonprofit organization, the Neighborhood Reinvestment Corporation to, among other things, help establish neighborhood housing services programs (Keyes 1971; Mayer 1984). Similarly, several federal demonstration programs, eventually folded into the Community Development Block Grant program, provided considerable opportunities for CDCs in the housing arena. Congress continued to pass legislation to encourage the development of affordable housing throughout the twentieth century. At the start of the twenty-first century, the federal, state, and local governments in the United States continued to look to the nonprofit sector to alleviate considerable housing pressures, particularly in the low-income and affordable-housing markets (Bishop 1991; Goetz 1992; Vidal 1992; Bratt et al. 1994).

In addition to national trends and authorizing policies, several state-specific events and policy-related actions occurred in Michigan to pave the way for faith-based engagement in the housing arena (see Figure 2.2). The Michigan Housing Facilities Act of 1933 authorized local governments to buy, construct, maintain, rehabilitate, repair, or provide financing for housing. The Neighborhood Enterprise Zone Act of 1992 was designed to improve the housing stock in distressed Michigan communities by providing tax incentives for the development and rehabilitation of residential housing and encouraging owner-occupied housing and new investment in communities that might otherwise be neglected. In March 2005, Governor Jennifer Granholm (D) issued Executive Order 2005–6 to establish the Governor's Office of Community and Faith-Based Initiatives.[5] Granholm described the office as a "bridge designed to physically connect faith based and community nonprofit organizations to people and resources in State Government" (Granholm 2007, p. 1). In 2006, the Michigan legislature passed a law that allowed nonprofit organizations to hold property for a designated amount of time without a tax burden, to provide an opportunity to rehab the housing for low-income individuals and families. As noted in the bill analysis:

> There are a number of charitable community organizations working to increase home ownership in Michigan by providing homes to families that otherwise could not afford to buy one, usually for the cost of building or restoring the homes. Sometimes

these groups hold the property for months or years while the homes are being built or refurbished and suitable owners are found. During this time, the charitable housing organizations are responsible for paying taxes on the property. Nonprofit housing organizations do not have large budgets, usually relying heavily on donated labor and materials, and the expense of paying property taxes is often significant for them. (Senate Fiscal Agency 2007, 1)

In 2008, a series of laws were passed that authorized funding for a variety of housing options and partnerships with eligible nonprofit organizations to meet the state's goal of improving the quality and quantity of the housing stock available for low- and moderate-income individuals.

These federal, state, and local trends suggest a willingness and desire within government to partner with FBOs for the delivery of public services. Some of the fascination with, and willingness for, expansion of the involvement of FBOs in social service delivery in general and housing in particular stems from anecdotes and long-held beliefs and assumptions about the faith community. For example, there is an underlying belief that FBOs have the human and social capital, if not the financial resources, to design, implement, nurture, and sustain community development efforts (Hacala 2001). A key assumption regarding FBOs and service delivery is that if adequate financial resources are deployed, FBOs may become even more active partners in the service delivery arena (Briggs 2004). There is also an inherent trust in FBOs, linked to a general belief that secular nonprofits and faith-based organizations have a unique set of strengths and resources that facilitate their work in the housing field. Some of the key assets of secular and faith-based nonprofits are noted below (Rubin 1993; Bratt et al. 1994; Vidal 1995; Chaves and Tsitsos 2001); they

- are cultural anchors within the community;
- tend to be trusted by their communities;
- can access both human and financial capital;
- have the capacity for relatively quick implementation;
- are able to customize programs and services to address local conditions;
- are capable of providing and creating leadership within the community; and
- can reach individuals and communities that might not otherwise be served.

The Housing Arena

The 1960s gave rise to community development corporations (CDCs) to combat the social ills of poverty, revitalize local communities, and provide some measure of community participation and control. In many instances, efforts launched by CDCs were the only visible action for housing, human services, and business development (Mayer 1984; Powell 1987; Zdenek 1987; Keating et al. 1990). Although many of the early organizations are no longer in existence, new CDCs continue to emerge. Increasing pressure for a community

Figure 2.2   **Select Events and Activities Influencing Nonprofit Organization Involvement in the Michigan Housing Arena**

1898	General Property Tax Law (section 211.7kk) defines eligible nonprofit housing property[a]
1917	Housing Law of Michigan
1933	Housing Facilities Act. Allowed localities to create housing commissions.
1966	Michigan State Housing Development Authority (MHSDA) Act (Section 8 defined) (Designation of subsidiary nonprofit housing corporations) (Addressed state's low-income housing tax credit)
1981	Michigan Economic and Social Opportunity Act
1992	Neighborhood Enterprise Zone Act. Provided for the development and rehabilitation of residential housing. Michigan HOME program connected to the 1990 federal Home Investment Partnership Act developed at MSHDA.[b]
1999	Urban Homesteading in Single-Family Public Housing Act
2003	Executive order to establish the governor's office of Community and Faith-based Initiatives.
2004	Michigan Housing and Community Development Fund (MHCDF) Act. Established programs concentrating efforts in downtowns, neighborhoods, and affordable and supportive housing (no funding authorized, repealed 2008).
2005	Executive order established Governor's Office of Community and Faith-Based Initiatives.
2006	Public Act 612 of 2006, providing for tax exemption on eligible nonprofit housing (with a two-year window for occupancy by a low-income resident).
2007	Michigan Legislature passed the FY 2008 budget with a $2.2 million appropriation for MHCDF.
2008	Several laws passed dealing with financing for low-income housing and partnerships between local governments and nonprofit housing providers.

Note: This overview is intended to be illustrative and not exhaustive.

[a]"Eligible nonprofit housing property" means a single-family dwelling or duplex owned by a charitable nonprofit housing organization, which intends to transfer ownership of the unit to a low-income person after construction or renovation is completed; the housing is to be used as that low-income person's principal residence. "Low-income person" means a person with a family income of not more than 80 percent of the statewide median gross income who is eligible to participate in the charitable nonprofit housing organization's program based on criteria established by that organization (General Property Tax Act, 1893).

[b]Representative of Michigan State Housing Development Authority, personal interview, February 2009.

voice, combined with the privatization movement, created additional pathways for nonprofit involvement in the housing arena (Boyte and Riessman 1986; Hodgkinson and Lyman 1989).

From one perspective, it can be argued that the introduction of Charitable Choice legislation and President George W. Bush's faith-based initiatives were simply two more federal efforts to enlarge opportunities for nonprofit organizations. The caveat is, of course, that a different type of nonprofit was potentially gaining access. Although FBOs have been subsumed broadly within the nonprofit realm, these latter federal initiatives specifically reached out to faith communities, acknowledging the general importance of community-based organizations. Research by Ellen and Voicu (2006) suggests that there is indeed a role for nonprofit organizations to play in housing services, since city investment in the rehabilitation of rental housing by both for-profit and nonprofit organizations produces positive spillover effects. Although for-profit developers may generate greater impacts than nonprofits, the outcomes of nonprofit housing are likely to remain stable over time. This suggests that both types of development are important in the housing market; as such, there should be viable avenues for nonprofit organizations to compete effectively in the housing arena.

There are a variety of roles that secular and faith-based nonprofit organizations can assume in housing services. Examples include producing housing units, providing auxiliary or wraparound housing services, building political support for affordable housing, and engaging in broader community development activities (Briggs 2004).[6] Table 2.3 highlights ways in which nonprofit organizations can be involved in the production of housing units.

Housing Production

CDCs, in particular, are key organizations in the local housing market. Their activities include providing housing for a variety of special needs populations including the elderly, people with disabilities, HIV/AIDS patients, and substance abusers. In addition to providing housing and economic development services (e.g., job creation and industrial and small-business development),[7] CDCs engage in home-ownership counseling, community organizing, and a range of social services (Walker 1993). There has been a proliferation of CDCs since the 1960s. This is especially true for CDCs established by and within the faith community.

By the early 1990s, 2 percent of the CDCs engaged in housing production were producing 25 percent of the sector's housing units. Nearly 50 percent of the CDCs accounted for fewer than 8 percent of units placed in production by the sector. Between 1988 and 1990, 1.7 percent of CDCs produced over 200 housing units, 2.7 percent of CDCs produced between 101 and 200 units, 5.7 percent produced 51 to 100 units, 14.5 percent produced 26 to 50 units, 26.5 percent produced between 11 and 25 units, and 48.7 percent produced up to 10 housing units (Figure 2.3) (Walker 1993).

Table 2.3

Select Dimensions of Housing Unit Production, by Nonprofit Organizations

Dimension	Example
Legal/Financial Arrangement	• Owner-developer • General partner • Limited partner
Level of Development	• New unit creation • Unit rehabilitation (substantial, moderate, light) • Repair
Type of Unit	• Owner-occupied • Single-family rental property (1–4 units) • Multifamily rental property (medium- or large-scale building) • Cooperative
Institutional Relationships (Partnerships/Cooperation)	• Public sector • Financial institutions • Nonprofit organizations
Extent of Involvement	• Ad hoc (project-by-project) • Ongoing program management

Source: Walker (1993).

Figure 2.3   **Percentage of Community Development Corporations Producing Housing Units between 1988 and 1990**

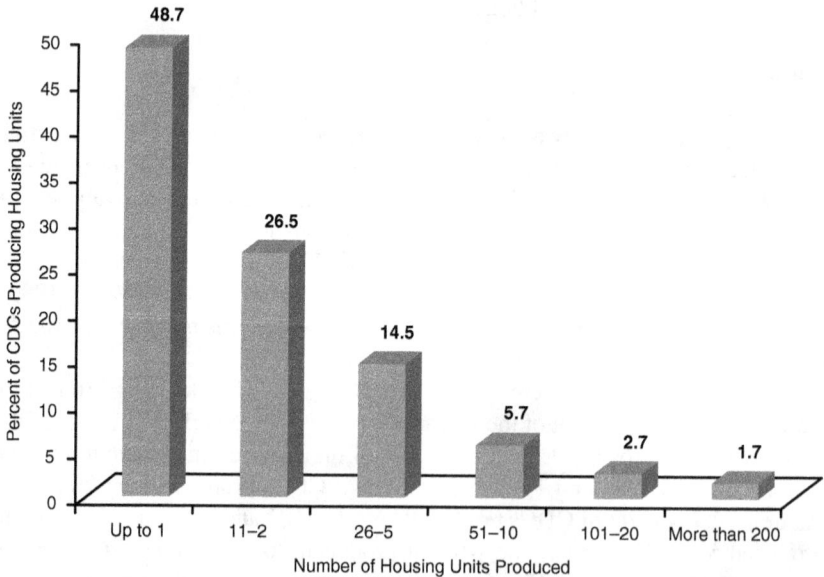

Source: Walker (1993).

A survey conducted by the National Conference for Community Economic Development (NCCED) in the late 1990s determined that out of 3,600 CDCs, nearly 14 percent (500) were faith based (NCCED 1999). CDCs produced 650,000 housing units, according to the 1998 housing survey. An estimated 109,000 of those housing units were produced by faith-based organizations, accounting for approximately 17 percent of all units produced by nonprofit community organizations at that time (NCCED 1999; Fannie Mae Foundation 2001; NCCED 2005).[8] Table 2.4 highlights the growth in the number of CDCs and the proportion of faith-based CDCs engaging in the housing arena. By 2005, over 1.2 million housing production units were attributed to CDCs. At that time there were 4,600 CDCs in the United States, 25 percent of which were faith based (NCCED 2005).[9] This represented growth both in the number of CDCs and in the proportion of faith-based organizations engaging in community development. Although once concentrated in the urban centers of northeastern and central states, by the early twenty-first century CDCs were equally dispersed across the United States, with representation in rural areas and small cities as well as the traditional urban core (Walker 1993; National Alliance of Community Economic Development Associations [(NACEDA)] 2007). This geographic distribution suggests an increased presence of CDCs and a corresponding opportunity for faith-based and secular involvement in housing services.

Breadth and Scope of Service Delivery: Populations Served

FBOs have been engaging in housing-related activities for decades, from the provision of temporary shelters for the homeless to shelter subsidies and advocacy efforts. The growth of government funding of housing activities led to greater involvement of the nonprofit sector as a whole in the housing arena. In addition to temporary housing, faith-based and secular nonprofits have been involved in services and activities for rental housing and home ownership, as well as housing for targeted populations such as the elderly and disabled.

The 1996 National Survey of Homeless Assistance Providers and Clients found that 85 percent of the homeless assistance programs available at the time were offered by nonprofit agencies (see Figure 2.4) (Burt et al. 1999). The data also revealed that 60 percent of all available housing programs for the homeless (e.g., emergency, transitional, and permanent housing, and voucher programs) were provided by secular nonprofit organizations and 26 percent by faith-based organizations. Likewise, secular nonprofits provided 55 percent and faith-based organizations 34 percent of other housing-related services and activities for the homeless, including drop-in centers, financial and housing assistance programs, outreach activities, and other programs (Burt et al. 1999). The involvement of nonprofit organizations with housing for the homeless has continued into the twenty-first century. For example, in 2005, 13 percent of CDCs provided emergency shelter and 25 percent provided transitional housing (NCCED 2005).

Table 2.4

Community Development Corporation Proliferation and Housing Production, 1998 and 2005

	1998	2005
Number of CDCs	3,600	4,600
Percent faith-based CDCs	14%	25%
Housing units produced by CDCs	650,000	1.2 million

Source: Fannie Mae Foundation 2001; NCCED 1999, 2005.

Figure 2.4   **Delivery of Homeless Assistance Programs by Sector, 1996**

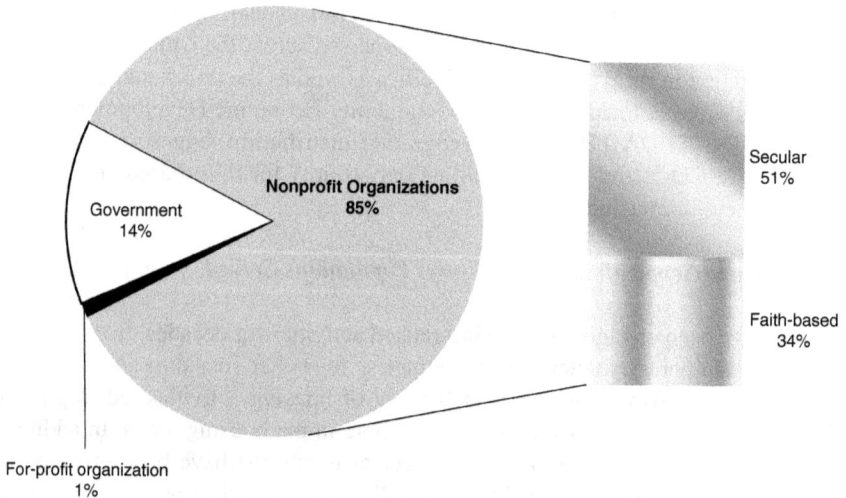

Source: Burt et al. (1999).

One of the perceived benefits of nonprofit involvement in housing is that these providers will serve populations that would otherwise go without service or be underserved. In 2005, CDCs were reporting that they served low-income and poor individuals and communities (NCCED 2005). Similarly, low-income housing tax credit (LIHTC) units owned by nonprofit organizations between 1995 and 2005 had a higher incidence of location in census tracts characterized by a high proportion of poverty, nonwhite populations, female-headed households, and renter-owned housing than did the total population of LIHTC units (Climaco et al. 2007). Non-profits have also tended to be more involved in developing multifamily units and in serving a variety of special needs populations. They are, in short, working in and with the most distressed communities and populations.

Organizational Considerations

There is a good deal of speculation in both the academic and popular literatures that secular and faith-based nonprofit organizations differ on many basic organizational characteristics. Reported findings remain mixed, however. For example, some studies have demonstrated that there are few to no discernable differences between the management capacity, organizational strategies, and service delivery activities of faith-based and secular organizations, although these organizations may differ with respect to their use of volunteers and reliance on government funding (Ebaugh et al. 2003; Kearns et al. 2005). To be certain, the nonprofit housing sector is diverse on a number of dimensions, including organizational and program characteristics, number and types of housing units produced, and level and sources of funding (Walker 1993; NCCED 1999, 2005). A number of factors can affect the extent and nature of FBOs' housing and other community service activities, including age, size, financial status, and location of the organization (Lincoln and Mamiya 1990; Hall 1992; La Barbera 1992; Chang et al. 1994; Devita et al. 1999; Reese and Shields 2000; Chaves and Tsitsos 2001).[10] For example, older, larger, and more financially stable FBOs, often located in urban centers, have been more likely to engage in service delivery. An interesting question is whether these same factors are applicable to participation in the low-income and affordable housing arena.

Organizational Staffing

CDCs and other community-based organizations can range in staff size from fewer than ten to well over 1,100 employees, making it difficult to compare capacity across organizations (NACEDA 2007). In 1990, the median staff size of CDCs nationally was seven paid employees (Walker 1993). In 2005, CDCs were reported to have a median staff size of seven full-time and three part-time staff and five volunteers (NCCED 2005). Similar staff sizes have also been noted for other types of faith-based and secular human service agencies (Clerkin and Grønbjerg 2007). In a study of homeless service delivery, Ebaugh et al. (2003) found that faith-based and secular organizations both employed fewer than 50 paid staff and relied on a combination of volunteers and paid staff. In this instance, FBOs were twice as likely to rely on volunteers compared to secular organizations, which had a 0.89:1 ratio of volunteers to paid staff (Ebaugh et al. 2003).

Research generally suggests that FBOs rely more heavily on volunteers and have a lower proportion of their budget covered through government funding than do their secular counterparts (Hodgkinson and Weitzman 1993; Cnaan 1997; Printz Platnick 1998; Chaves 2002; Monsma 2002; Twombly 2002; Kearns et al. 2005; Ebaugh et al. 2006). The considerable range in organizational size, coupled with variable staffing patterns, makes it difficult to compare capacity across organizations. Some of the research shows a connection among paid staffing, use of volunteers, and percentage of government funding; nonprofit organizations that receive more government funding tend to rely more on paid staff for critical organizational functions, and less on volunteers (Salamon 1987a, 1987b; VanTil 1988; Smith and Lipsky 1993).

Organizational Funding

Nonprofit funding received increasing attention in the academic literature toward the end of the twentieth century (e.g., Salamon 1987a, 1998; VanTil 1988; Grønbjerg 1993; Crittenden 2000; Ebaugh et al. 2005a, 2005b). Even so, there was little empirical research on how faith-based social service organizations, particularly housing service providers, were funded (Jeavons 1994; Twombly 2002). Despite all of the controversy around Bush's faith-based initiatives, there remained a dearth of empirical evidence on: (1) characteristics of FBOs that receive government funding; (2) attitudes toward government funding; (3) networks and collaboration among organizations receiving government funding; as well as (4) the issue of whether government funding caused mission creep or restricted an organization's service capacity or social and political activism.

Research demonstrated that, in general, large social service agencies (measured in terms of assets) tended to receive the largest share of government funding and to rely heavily on such funding. Organizations receiving government funding also tended to provide more and varied programs (Smith and Lipsky 1993; Grønbjerg and Smith 1999; Twombly 2002; Farnsley 2003; Ebaugh et al. 2005a). Within the housing arena, the more funding sources a nonprofit organization had, the greater the number of housing units produced by the organization (Walker 1993). Some research, however, indicated that receiving government funding could cause an organization to feel constrained in determining who it would serve and the breadth and depth of its housing services (Goetz 1992). This highlighted the need to diversify the stream of funding and ensure that there were multiple partners for an array of housing and other programmatic priorities. Faith-based and secular organizations have indeed relied on a variety of funding sources, including government, banks, foundations, individuals, and a range of other secular agencies and religious organizations (Walker 1993). In general, FBOs tended to rely more heavily on religious sources for funding, while secular agencies tended to rely more heavily on government and secular sources (Burt et al. 1999; Twombly 2002; Ebaugh et al. 2003; Monsma 2003).

Church-state issues related to public funding of faith-based initiatives through such mechanisms as Charitable Choice have been a topic of interest for both scholars and practitioners. Monsma (2002) provided a framework for understanding how church-state relations might be structured to allow for viable partnerships in service provision. These models—libertarian, statist, and pluralist—address, in a practical sense, the question posed by Dionne and Chen (2001, 15), "How can sacred places serve civic purposes?" The libertarian approach places FBOs in the position of supplementary or back-up provider of social services, filling gaps left by government-provided services in a relatively uncoordinated manner. This model of faith-based service provision has few church-state implications since public funding would be limited, with the two spheres operating separately. The statist model places the government in the primary role of providing services and closely regulating service provision. Here, the separation of church and state is carefully maintained, the duality protected by limited public funding and government strictures on the amount of religion tied to services. Monsma (2002) posited the pluralist approach as the most promising. In this model,

> government is *extensive*. It has a society-wide role to play in coordinating societal efforts to achieve the public interest that touches on every other societal structure. But, government is not intensive. It ought to seek to coordinate, help, and empower the other social structures, never to supplant and replace them. (p. 8, italics in original)

Key in this argument was the notion that public funding of faith-based initiatives was most viable through such a pluralist model where government, sacred, and secular organizations worked together to provide services. Evidence suggests that this was both practical and realistic since there already were extensive partnerships among government, secular, and faith-based service providers, with organizations sharing referrals, program expertise, and information. Several trends had emerged throughout the twentieth century, demonstrating the viability of the pluralist model for church-state relations (Chaves and Tsitsos 2001; Monsma 2002):

- Government funding for service contractors continued to favor public, for-profit, or secular nonprofit service providers. These providers tended to be larger and better staffed and generally provided a wider array of services. This suggests that faith-based provision of services was not at a point where it stood alone as an alternative to government service provision (and may never be).
- Faith-based providers maintained basic elements of religious content even when funded publicly; those faith-based providers that most fully integrated religion and service delivery were the least likely to be publicly funded, however.
- Faith-based providers offered more life-oriented services and fewer content-oriented services, making them a complement to and not a substitute for governmental efforts.
- Those FBOs receiving public money did not feel that they had to compromise their religious values and goals. Rather, the most frequent complaint was the extensive paperwork associated with receiving public funding.
- There were already established partnerships among government, secular, and faith-based service providers, with organizations sharing referrals, program expertise, and information.

Other research suggested that state and/or federal funding for service provision by FBOs might have had some negative impacts. For example, governmental guidelines and regulations appear to have placed increased burdens on FBOs, shifting their priorities away from clients and increasing bureaucracy (Netting 1984; Sherman 1995; Monsma 2003). This effect may have been exacerbated in situations where there was a value conflict between the sacred and secular missions of such organizations (La Barbera 1992). Concerns were raised that reliance on government funding might diminish flexibility, creativity, and institutional and religious autonomy (Nichols 1988; Smith and Lipsky 1993; Jeavons 1994; Monsma 1996).[11] Furthermore, there was concern that such funding might cause faith organizations to shift away from the religious foundations that, theoretically, make their service delivery uniquely effective. The available evidence is conflicting; some studies indicated that it was possible for faith-based organizations to maintain purity and clarity in their organizational mission and goals while receiving government funding (Garland 1992; Monsma 1996), while others indicated that nonprofit organizations, particularly FBOs, that received government funding were heavily influenced in both their mission and activities or feared that receiving government funding would jeopardize or diminish their religious missions (DiMaggio and Powell 1991; Smith and Lipsky 1993; Chaves 1999; Smith and Sosin 2001).

These challenges and conflicts could have been mitigated if FBOs were not solely responsible for service delivery, but rather acted as a broker or catalyst to bring together other local leaders, organizations, and forces (Cisneros 1996). FBOs may have facilitated government participation in neighborhood social service and development initiatives (McKnight and Kretzmann 1993). Where the impact of government funding may have been most noticeable was with regard to networking activity. Guo (2007) found that nonprofit organizations that relied on government funding were less likely to develop governing boards with strong community representation. This in turn might have impacted the ability of those organizations to network adequately with other individuals and organizations in the community.

Capacity Building and Technical Assistance

Twombly (2002) found that large faith-based and secular social service agencies have very similar expenditures and may also share a similar administrative approach when supplying social services. Cnaan et al. (1999, 26) similarly argue that "the uniqueness of religious-based social services as opposed to secular services is not always clear. Some [FBOs] have become an arm of the government and disassociated from their religions origins." One thing is clear: faith-based service providers have to balance tensions among multiple entities, including government, faith communities, other service providers, and recipients of services (Netting 1984).

Briggs (2004) argues that with careful attention to capacity building and access to the prerequisite political support, money, and other key resources, FBOs should be as capable as, if not more capable than, other organizations (e.g., public, for-profit, secular nonprofit) in serving the needs of a community.[12] In order to maximize the ability of faith-based organizations to contribute to solving U.S.

social problems, housing key among them, it is necessary to provide resources and opportunities to engage in capacity building (Sider 2000). There is an established institutional support network to help nonprofit organizations confront some of the largest challenges in the wholesale production of affordable housing (Table 2.5). This institutional network includes government agencies, nonprofit intermediaries, foundations, financial institutions, educational institutions, consultants, and trade associations (Vidal 1992; Schwartz et al. 1996; Yin 1998; Silverman 2001; Frisch and Servon 2006).

Faith-based and secular nonprofit organizations have noted a number of obstacles to their involvement in the housing arena, including financing and organizational capacity issues, such as training and technical assistance and general operating support (Vidal 1992; Walker 1993). Building organizational capacity and providing timely and adequate technical assistance to nonprofit organizations are essential to their ability to provide services in a systematic and sustained manner. Although government organizations may have the skill sets and resources to provide technical assistance, nonprofit organizations that perceive that requesting assistance will jeopardize future funding options will be reluctant to seek support from the government (Mitchell et al. 2002). Fortunately, there are a variety of sources of technical assistance for nonprofit organizations, including universities, consulting firms, and other private organizations. Even so, some organizations may be less than forthcoming about their limitations, making them unlikely to request and receive necessary technical assistance. For example, Bratt and Rohe (2005) found that some CDCs involved in housing services were reluctant to acknowledge capacity problems because of a fear that doing so would negatively impact their chances of receiving funding. The extent to which organizational capacity can be developed depends largely on the willingness of an organization to seek and obtain necessary assistance.

Partnerships and Collaboration

Briggs (2004) maintains that FBOs are strategically positioned to help organize stakeholders and frame issue agendas, work effectively with others, join and leave coalitions as dictated by the goal to be accomplished, and be active service delivery partners with government entities, businesses, secular nonprofits, and other organizations in the faith community. This makes collaboration for service provision both a viable and natural activity. Collaboration is a complex construct (Gray 1989; Wood and Gray 1991; Grell and Gappert 1993; Chrislip and Larson 1994) that has been defined as:

- "[A] process through which parties who see different aspects of a problem can constructively explore their differences and search for solutions that go beyond their own limited vision of what is possible" (Gray 1989, 5).
- "[A]n organizational and interorganizational structure in which resources,

---

Table 2.5

Organizational Challenges to Providing Affordable Housing

Classification of challenge	Examples
Predevelopment Costs	• Feasibility studies • Legal, engineering, and architecture fees • Purchase of development rights
Development Financing	• Equity capital • Mortgage • Gap financing (e.g. Low-income Housing Tax Credit, the Enterprise Foundation)
Organizational Capacity	• Training and technical assistance • General operating support (e.g. state and local governments, universities, foundations)

Source: Schwartz et al. (1996).

---

power, and authority are shared and people are brought together to achieve a common goal that could not be accomplished by a single entity, individual, or organization independently" (Colby and Murrell 1998, 191).

- "[A] mutually beneficial relationship between two or more parties who work toward common goals by sharing responsibility, authority, and accountability for achieving results" (Chrislip and Larson 1994, 5).

Thus collaboration is referred to alternatively as a process, a structure, or a relationship for pooling resources to accomplish a common goal.

Regardless of size, many organizations providing housing, related services, or both find it necessary to partner with a variety of funding sources including banks, national nonprofit intermediaries (e.g., Local Initiatives Support Corporation [LISC], Enterprise Community Partners, NeighborWorks America), government entities, foundations, corporations, and individuals. Keyes (1996) argues that devolution forces local nonprofits to establish new collaborative networks with other organizations in order to preserve and support housing projects and initiatives in the face of declining resources. For example, housing developers may find it necessary to supplement the low-income housing tax credit (LIHTC) with other funding sources.[13] These financial arrangements alone do not define the landscape of partnerships and collaboration for housing provision and other service delivery activity, however. Research demonstrates that nonprofit organizations that partner with funding organizations; federal, state, and/or local government; and national foundations have a higher capacity to achieve goals, particularly in the housing arena (Saidel 1991; Schwartz et al. 1996; Nye and Glickman 2000; Glickman and Servon 2003).

Collaborating early and frequently appears to be an important factor in succeeding in the process. Key activities include collaborating to identify community needs, including key stakeholders, developing a project or program concept, and identifying and securing funding. Organizations may choose to collaborate for any number of reasons, including enhancing their ability to influence policy decisions, creating or expanding capacity to deliver public goods and services, and strengthening their individual and collective capacity to address community-wide issues (Chaskin et al. 2001). Collaboration allows organizations to increase effectiveness and impact service delivery by creating mechanisms to: (1) build effective and representative boards; (2) retain program staff in the face of uneven funding levels; (3) share expertise and other resources; (4) avoid duplication; (5) create linkages to disenfranchised constituencies; and (6) forge political alliances (Takahashi and Smutny 2001; Mitchell et al. 2002, 627–628).

Collaboration makes sense under several circumstances (London 1995), such as when:

- Several stakeholders are interdependent and have a vested interest in the problem(s).
- Stakeholders are not necessarily organized in any systematic way.
- There is disparity of resources for dealing with the problems among stakeholders.
- Stakeholders have different levels of expertise and access to information about the problem(s).
- The problems are characterized by technical complexity.
- Incremental or unilateral efforts to deal with the problem(s) typically produce less than satisfactory solutions.
- Existing processes for addressing problems have proved insufficient.

Collaboration is also noted as providing a way to build consensus, develop strategic approaches to problem solving, and provide opportunities to achieve long-term, sustainable accomplishments. Examples of other benefits of collaboration between government and nonprofit organizations (faith-based or secular) include (Gray 1989; Winer and Ray 1997; Rich et al. 1998, p.194):

- Public officials gain better understanding of community needs.
- Partners gain better understanding of each other's capacity.
- Activities are better aligned with community priorities.
- Activities are more effective at achieving goals.
- Activities are more comprehensive.
- Atmosphere of mutual trust is created.
- Large-scale activities can be undertaken.
- FBOs and CBOs gain access to government's technical resources.
- Larger pool of funding is available.

Government and nonprofit officials also note barriers to effective collaboration, particularly for community-based organizations (CBOs). Many of these barriers have the potential to inhibit collaboration between the government and FBOs. Limited local government funding for service delivery activities is a common theme. Additionally, CBOs view local governments as having an excessive need to maintain control, being overly bureaucratic, and maintaining a local political environment that is not generally supportive of the CBOs' efforts to engage in service delivery efforts (Rich et al. 1998). It has also been noted that the missions, goals, and intended beneficiaries of potential collaborators may be distinct enough to cause some hesitation or unwillingness to work together. Similarly, funding sources and other external conditions may make it difficult for potential collaborators to work together, even when there is an earnest desire to do so (Mitchell et al. 2002; Guo 2007). Potential barriers to collaboration notwithstanding, the increased role of faith-based and community-based organizations in service delivery in general and housing in particular is probably attributable to the emergence and expansion of networking, partnering, and collaborating activities within and across sectors (Clavel et al. 1997; Gittell and Vidal 1998; Liu and Stroh 1998; McDermott 2004).

Markers of Success

Extant research suggests several characteristics of successful nonprofit organizations (Table 2.6). Among other things, these organizations tend to be older and have stable funding sources, flexible resources, programs and services that are relevant to the constituency being served, strong ties to government, and a demonstrated willingness and ability to coordinate and cooperate with other service providers (McCann and Selsky 1984; Knauft et al. 1991; Vidal 1992; Provan and Milward 1995). The extent of success that a nonprofit organization that provides housing and other services experiences depends to some extent on the strength and nature of the interactions and intersections between organizational cooperation and collaboration, service quality, and the existing political and financial environment in the state and community within which it operates (Evans 1998; Binder 2007). Similarly, Bratt and Rohe (2004) note that housing production by CDCs is most successful when the organization is fully integrated into the local network of fiscal and policy support, particularly since being part of an interwoven network provides opportunities to gain assistance in setting goals and achieving outcomes. The same could be said for almost any nonprofit engaged in housing.

In order to influence policy, these organizations ultimately need broad-based community support, a flexible policy agenda, the ability to be politically connected yet remain autonomous, and to operate in the public domain (Hula et al. 1997). Research also demonstrates that success is partially predicated on the ability of an organization both to produce clear results that are of value to the community and to sustain itself over time (Hula and Jackson-Elmoore, 2001). Although age is often cited as a precursor to success, this may not hold when it comes to housing, at least not once organizations have survived beyond a certain number of

Table 2.6

Characteristics and Capacities of Effective Nonprofit Organizations

- Stable funding
- Clearly articulated mission and goals
- Experienced executives (combined with effective and committed board)
- Skilled employees and competent managerial leadership
- Adequate space and equipment
- Sound fiscal practices
- Programs and/or services relevant to the constituency being served
- Effective fiscal development programs
- Flexible resources
- Ability to adjust to environmental demands (innovation and adaptation)
- Clear and visible history of commitment to constituencies
- Strong ties to government officials
- Demonstrated willingness and ability to coordinate/cooperate with other service providers

Sources: McCann and Selsky (1984), Knauft et al. (1991), and Provan and Milward (1995).

years. Some research suggests that there is relatively little distinction in housing production capacity among CDCs over five years of age. This could indicate that these organizations have the ability to get up to speed and become factors in the housing arena relatively quickly (Walker 1993). Of course, the ability to compete and remain viable will be tied to issues of overall organizational capacity. It is similarly argued that organizational capacity is a factor in nonprofit-government collaboration, particularly as it relates to housing development. This suggests that issues of capacity building are central to an understanding of the potential of all nonprofits to fill increasing service delivery roles, especially in the area of housing, which has many market dimensions.

Political and Policy Considerations

In addition to direct service delivery, many nonprofit organizations become socially and/or politically active in relation to specific needs of their clients and in policy areas associated with their programs (Smith and Lipsky 1993; Walker 1993; Grønbjerg and Smith 1999). The evidence is mixed on the association between government funding and social or political activism for faith-based organizations (Goetz 1992). For example, for several years following the passage of the Charitable Choice provision in the Personal Responsibility and Work Opportunity Reconciliation Act of 1996, FBOs feared that receiving government funding would restrict their ability to advocate for social issues (Netting 1982; Rose-Ackerman 1983; Reid 1999). Some organizations became more active precisely because of access to funding and a desire to influence the nature and extent of constraints associated with government funding (Lipsky and Smith, 1990; Rubin, 1993). Chaves et al. (2004) found a positive relationship between government funding and political activism. Similarly, Ebaugh et al. (2006, 2269) found that faith-based social service coalitions that had a "strong public persona as faith-based" were more likely to get involved in social activism. Coalitions that were more outwardly directed toward service delivery and interaction with individuals were less inclined to be politically active, however.

It has been argued that reliance on government funding and integration into the market and housing infrastructure effectively co-opted some CDCs and other nonprofit organizations. The result of this co-optation was that the organizations ceased to effectively represent and advocate for their constituencies and the associated neighborhoods that necessitated their founding (Gittell 1980; Lauria 1982, 1986; Stoecker 1994). The case of CDCs' (and other nonprofit organizations') withdrawal from political action and lack of political effectiveness may have been overstated, however (Goetz 1992). For one thing, development activities in and of themselves represent a form of empowerment, creating greater assets and increasing political efficacy and, potentially, political access for communities and residents. In essence, rather than CDCs' advocating for social change, their engagement in development results in social change (Rubin 1993; Lauria 1997). With respect to more traditional advocacy efforts, CDCs do undertake efforts to influence public and private actors outside of their local community, as well as local citizens, regardless of funding sources (Goetz 1992).[14] Although CDCs may at times choose to avoid formal policy statements, they do nonetheless engage in public debate on a range of issues, including housing.

Whether engaging in direct or indirect advocacy, CDCs are also active on behalf of both community interests and their own survival (Table 2.7). What is less clear is whether CDCs and other nonprofit organizations involved in the housing arena have gained sufficient political clout and access to impact state and local politics on behalf of their constituencies and for housing policy in general. Research by Goetz (1992) suggests that CDCs may enjoy unprecedented access to government officials, particularly at the local level, and therefore have greater entrée to policy making. Other researchers contend, however, that a range of community-based organizations have an active role to play in policy for low-income and affordable housing (Rubin 2000; Marwell 2004).

In summary, existing literature clearly points to connections among public funding, organizational capacity, and collaborative networks in enabling and enhancing the housing and social service provision roles of nonprofit organizations. Research is somewhat mixed, however, regarding sacred and secular differences in organizational capacity, funding patterns, propensity to collaborate, and nature of service outputs. Existing literature also suggests important connections among public funding, service provision, and policy influence for nonprofits. Several questions about these relationships remain insufficiently explored:

Table 2.7

Examples of Advocacy Undertaken by CDCs and Other Nonprofits

Type of advocacy[a]	Efforts/Actions	Empowerment results
Externally based advocacy	• Influencing public/private decision makers • Changing, maintaining resources controlled by nonprofit organizations	Entire community is empowered by greater access to decision makers and resources
Internally based advocacy	• Community organizing • Mobilizing tenants • Enhancing political capacity of neighborhood organizations	Individual community members are empowered
Organizational survival advocacy[b]	• Lobbying for programs that serve their organizations • Lobbying for support of their own development projects	Organizational position and/or resources are preserved or enhanced
Community interest advocacy	• Lobbying for programs or resources that support a general thematic or programmatic area	Community needs are addressed

Source: Goetz (1992).

[a]These forms of advocacy are not mutually exclusive and indeed CDCs (and other nonprofit organizations) can and do engage in multiple types.

[b]Organizational advocacy is not included in the scope of this particular research effort.

- Do capacity and funding attributes affect the propensity of service nonprofits to move into or strengthen their public policy roles?
- How important are collaborative networks in making the service–policy influence connections?
- Do specific types of networks enhance the civic and policy roles of nonprofits?
- Are particular types of nonprofits more prone to become active in policy arenas? Or are particular service profiles, for example housing plus services, more likely to enhance engagement with the policy process?
- Are there differences between sacred and secular nonprofits in their desire for and success in translating service activity into political and policy influence?
- Do the service activities of faith-based nonprofits provide an entrée into the local civic arena, giving these organizations a place in urban governing regimes?

In short, more detail is needed in understanding how, when, and if nonprofits and FBOs in particular become a greater part of civil society.

Notes

This literature review is based on a systematic examination of scholarly, government, and industry-related sources relative to keywords generated by the investigators a priori. Keywords focused on faith-based housing, faith-based service delivery, nonprofit organizations, and variations of these themes. Peer-reviewed journal articles were identified by a computerized search of scholarly literature databases (e.g., Web of Science, Social Sciences Citation Index). Additional background information was obtained from government publications and databases available through the Internet (e.g., statistical abstracts, census data, and government survey data) and survey data available online or through direct contact with nonprofit organizations engaged in the housing industry.

1. Holistic development is the process of building the community through physical and social programs; nonprofits often barter the construction to get support for social programs (Rubin 1994).

2. See Cohen et al. (2004) for a discussion of eleven principles for the design and implementation of housing plus services programs.

3. Issued on January 29, 2001, Executive Order 13199 established the White House Office of Faith-Based and Community Initiatives. That same day, Executive Order 13198 created Centers for Faith-Based and Community Initiatives in the Offices of the Attorney General, the Secretary of Education, the Secretary of Labor, the Secretary of Health and Human Services, and the Secretary of Housing and Urban Development. On December 12, 2002, President George W. Bush issued Executive Order 13280 creating two additional Centers for Faith-Based and Community Initiatives in the offices of the Secretary of Agriculture and the Administrator of the Agency for International Development, and Executive Order 13279 requiring equal protection for faith-based and community organizations. Three new Centers for Faith-Based and Community Initiatives were created by Executive Order 13342 on June 1, 2004, in the Small Business Administration, the Department of Commerce, and the Department of Veterans Affairs. The eleventh Center for Faith-Based and Community Initiatives was created in the Department of Homeland Security on March 7, 2006, by Executive Order 13397.

4. President Obama focused on the role that these organizations can play in helping the nation's economic recovery as well as in (1) addressing issues facing women and children and teen mothers; (2) encouraging responsible fatherhood, and (3) fostering interfaith dialogues around the world.

5. The office was renamed the Governor's Office of Faith-Based and Neighborhood Partnerships to mirror the federal office instituted in 2009 under President Obama.

6. Building political support includes activities such as political advocacy, grassroots organizing, and building coalitions with other organizations.

7. Between 1994 and 2005, CDCs increasingly engaged in commercial and industrial development in communities as well as economic and business development, taking a holistic view of the needs of a neighborhood and city (NCCED 2005). Examples of business development activities have included owning or developing a business, making equity investments in businesses, providing technical assistance, and providing entrepreneurial training (Reese and Shields 1999).

8. Using similar data from 1991, Walker (1993) estimated that by 1990, CDCs (no distinction between sacred and secular) had accounted for 15 percent of all housing units produced. For the 1995 data, Habitat for Humanity accounted for another 30,000 units, resulting in over 31 percent of housing units produced being attributed to the faith community.

9. The 2005 survey included additional questions to provide more context on faith-based CDCs (NCCED 2005).

10. The research also indicates that denomination, theology, pastoral characteristics, pastoral initiative, extent of political activities, and being located in a census tract with low educational attainment affect community service activities.

11. Some organizations avoided working with any level of government due to concerns about secular and sacred conflicts (Reese and Shields 2000). Interestingly enough, research on faith-based providers indicted that while fear of government entanglement was high, a primary reason that more faith-based service providers had not received public funding was that they had applied for funding and been turned down (Monsma 2002).

12. Briggs (2004) adds the caveat that FBOs need to have the capacity to navigate issues key to the separation of church and state debate, as well as to work toward gaining and articulating clarity between religious/congregational imperatives and service delivery obligations.

13. The need to supplement tax credits became particularly intense in the U.S. and global economic recession in the first decade of the twenty-first century.

14. Marwell (2004) notes that many community organizations may simply choose to limit their political involvement to activities associated with electing representatives who will be more likely to support allocating resources to community development.

References

Berger, Peter L., and Richard J. Neuhaus. 1977. *To Empower People: The Role of Mediating Structures in Public Policy.* Washington, DC: American Enterprise Institute for Public Policy Research.

Binder, Amy. 2007. For Love and Money: Organizations' Creative Responses to Multiple Environmental Logics. *Theory and Society* 36(6): 547–571.

Birch, Eugenie L., and Deborah S. Gardner. 1981. The Seven Percent Solution: A Review of Philanthropic Housing, 1870–1910. *Journal of Urban History* 7:403–438.

Bishop, Catherine M. 1991. *Building on Success: A Report on State Capacity-Building Programs Targeted to Nonprofit Housing Developers.* Washington, DC: National Support Center for Low-Income Housing.

Botchwey, Nisha D. 2007. The Religious Sector's Presence in Local Community Development. *Journal of Planning Education and Research* 27:36–48.

Bowen v. Kendrick. 1988. 487 U.S. 589.

Boyte, Harry Chatten, and Frank Riessman. 1986. *The New Populism: The Politics of Empowerment.* Philadelphia: Temple University Press.

Bratt, Rachel G. 2008. Viewing Housing Holistically: The Resident-Focused Component of the Housing-Plus Agenda. *Journal of the American Planning Association* 74(1): 100–110.

Bratt, Rachel G., Langley C. Keyes, Alex Schwartz, and Avis C. Vidal. 1994. *Confronting the Management Challenge: Affordable Housing in the Nonprofit Sector.* New York: Community Development Research Center.

Bratt, Rachel G., and William M. Rohe. 2004. Organizational Changes among CDCs: Assessing the Impacts and Navigating the Challenges. *Journal of Urban Affairs* 26(2): 197–220.

———. 2005. Challenges and Dilemmas Facing Community Development Corporations in the United States. *Community Development Journal* 42(1): 63–78.

Briggs, Xavier de Souza. 2004. Faith and Mortar: Religious Organizations and Affordable Housing Strategy in Urban America. In *Building the Organizations that Build Communities,* ed. Roland V. Anglin, 43–54. Washington, DC: U.S. Department of Housing and Urban Development.

Burt, Martha R., Laudan Y. Aron, Toby Douglas, Jesse Valente, Edgar Lee, and Britta Iwen. 1999. Homelessness: Programs and the People They Serve, Summary Report. Findings of the National Survey of Homeless Assistance Providers and Clients. Washington, DC: Urban Institute.

Chang, Patricia M.Y., David R. Williams, Ezra E.H. Griffith, and John Young. 1994. Church-Agency Relationships in the Black Community. *Nonprofit and Voluntary Sector Quarterly* 23(2):91–105.

Chaskin, Robert J., Prudence Brown, Sudhir Venkatesh, and Avis Vidal. 2001. *Building Community Capacity.* New York: Aldine De Gruyter.

Chaves, Mark. 1999. Religious Congregations and Welfare Reform: Who Will Take Advantage of "Charitable Choice"? *American Sociological Review* 64(6): 836–846.

———. 2002. Religious Organizations: Data Resources and Research Opportunities. *American Behavioral Scientist* 45(10): 1523–1549.

Chaves, Mark, Laura Stephens, and Joseph Galaskiewicz. 2004. Does Government Funding Suppress Nonprofits' Political Activity? *American Sociological Review* 69:292–316.

Chaves, Mark, and W. Tsitsos. 2001. Congregations and Social Services: What They Do, How They Do It, and With Whom. *Nonprofit and Voluntary Sector Quarterly* 30(4): 660–683.

Chrislip, David D., and Carl E. Larson. 1994. *Collaborative Leadership: How Citizens and Civic Leaders Can Make a Difference.* San Francisco: Jossey-Bass.

Cisneros, Henry G. 1996. *Higher Ground: Faith Communities and Community Building.* Washington, DC: U.S. Department of Housing and Urban Development.

Clavel, Pierre, Jessica Pitt, and Jordan Yin. 1997. The Community Option in Urban Policy. *Urban Affairs Review* 32(4): 435–458.

Clerkin, Richard M., and Kirsten A. Grønbjerg. 2007. The Capacities and Challenges of Faith-Based Human Service Organizations. *Public Administration Review* 67(1): 115–126.

Climaco, Carissa, Joshua Cox, and Meryl Finkel. 2007. *HUD National Low-Income Housing Tax Credit (LIHTC) Database, Projects Placed in Service through 2005.* Cambridge, MA: Abt Associates.

Cnaan, Ram A. 1997. Social and Community Involvement of Religious Congregations Housed in Historic Religious Properties: Findings from a Six-City Study. Final Report to Partners for Sacred Places. Philadelphia: University of Pennsylvania.

———. 2001. Philadelphia Census of Congregations and Their Involvement in Social Service Delivery. *Social Service Review* 75:559–580.

Cnaan, Ram A., Robert J. Wineburg, and Stephanie C. Boddie. 1999. *The Newer Deal: Social Work and Religion in Partnership.* New York: Columbia University Press.

Cohen, Carol S., Elizabeth Mulroy, Tanya Tull, Catherine White, and Sheila Crowley. 2004. Housing Plus Services: Supporting Vulnerable Families in Permanent Housing. *Child Welfare* 83(5): 509–528.

Colby, Suzanne M., and W. Murrell. 1998. Child Welfare and Substance Abuse Services: From Barriers to Collaboration. In *Substance Abuse, Family Violence, and Child Welfare: Bridging Perspectives,* ed. R.L. Hampton, B. Senatore, and T.P. Gullotta, 188–219. Thousand Oaks, CA: Sage.

Crittenden, William F. 2000. Spinning Straw into Gold: The Tenuous Strategy, Funding, and Financial Performance Linkage. *Nonprofit and Voluntary Sector Quarterly* 29:164–182.

de Toqueville, Alexis. 1969. *Democracy in America.* New York: Harper and Row. (Orig. pub. 1835).

Devita, Carol J., Tobi J.Printz Platnick, and Eric C. Twombly. 1999. *Findings from the Survey of Community Services of Faith-Based Organizations in New Jersey.* Washington, DC: Center for Nonprofits and Philanthropy, Urban Institute.

DiMaggio, Paul J., and Walter W. Powell. 1991. *The New Institutionalism in Organizational Analysis.* Chicago: University of Chicago Press.

Dionne, E.J., and M.H. Chen. 2001. When the Sacred Meets the Civic: An Introduction. In *Sacred Places, Civic Purposes: Should Government Help Faith-Based Charity?* ed. E.J. Dionne and M.H. Chen, 1–16. Washington, DC: Brookings.

Ebaugh, Helen Rose, Janet Saltzman Chafetz, and Paula Pipes. 2005a. Faith-Based Social Service Organizations and Government Funding: Data from a National Survey. *Social Science Quarterly* 86(2): 273–292.

———. 2005b. Funding Good Works: Funding Sources of Faith-Based Social Service Coalitions. *Nonprofit and Voluntary Sector Quarterly* 34(4): 448–472.

———. 2006. Where's the Faith in Faith-Based Organizations? Measures and Correlates of Religiosity in Faith-Based Social Service Coalitions. *Social Forces* 84(4): 2259–2272.

Ebaugh, Helen Rose, Paula Pipes, Janet Saltzman Chafetz, and M. Daniels. 2003. Where's the Religion? Distinguishing Faith-Based from Secular Social Service Agencies. *Journal for the Scientific Study of Religion* 42(3): 411–426.

Ellen, Ingrid Gould, and Ioan Voicu. 2006. Nonprofit Housing and Neighborhood Spillovers. *Journal of Policy Analysis and Management* 25: 31–52.

Evans, Richard. 1998. Tackling Deprivation on Social Housing Estates in England: An Assessment of the Housing Plus Approach. *Housing Studies* 13(5): 713–726.

Fannie Mae Foundation. 2001. *Facts about the Role of Faith-Based Organizations in Providing Affordable Housing and Financial Services in American Communities.* Washington, DC: Fannie Mae.

Farnsley, Arthur E. 2003. *Rising Expectations: Urban Congregations, Welfare Reform, and Civic Life.* Bloomington: Indiana University Press.

Frisch, Michael, and Lisa Servon. 2006. CDCs and the Changing Context for Urban Community Development: A Review of the Field and the Environment. *Community Development: Journal of the Community Development Society* 27(4): 88–108.

Garland, Diana R. 1992. *Church Social Work: Helping the Whole Person in the Context of the Church.* Botsford, CT: North American Christians in Social Work.

Gittell, Marilyn. 1980. *Limits to Citizen Participation: The Decline of Community Organizations.* Beverly Hills, CA: Sage.

Gittell, Ross J., and Avis Vidal. 1998. *Community Organizing: Building Social Capital as a Development Strategy.* Thousand Oaks, CA: Sage.

Glickman, Norman J., and Lisa J. Servon. 2003. By the Numbers: Measuring Community Development Corporation Capacity. *Journal of Planning Education and Research* 22:240–256.

Goetz, Edward G. 1992. Local Government Support for Nonprofit Housing: A Survey of U.S. Cities. *Urban Affairs Quarterly* 27(3): 420–435.

Goggin, Malcolm L., and Deborah A. Orth. 2002. *How Faith-Based and Secular Organizations Tackle Housing for the Homeless.* Albany, NY: Rockefeller Institute of Government.

Gormley, William T. 1991. *Privatization and Its Alternatives.* Madison: University of Wisconsin Press.

Granholm, Jennifer. 2007. Office of Community and Faith-Based Initiatives. http://www.michigan.gov/outreach/0,1607,7--203--112869--,00.html.

Gray, Barbara. 1989. *Collaborating: Finding Common Ground for Multiparty Problems.* San Francisco: Jossey-Bass.

Grell, Jan, and Gary Gappert. 1993. The New Civic Infrastructure: Intersectoral Collaboration and the Decision-Making Process. *National Civic Review* 82(2): 140–148.

Grønbjerg, Kirsten A. 1993. *Understanding Nonprofit Funding: Managing Revenues in Social Services and Community Development Organizations.* San Francisco: Jossey-Bass.

Grønbjerg, Kirsten A., and Steven Rathgeb Smith. 1999. Nonprofit Organizations and Public Policies in the Delivery of Human Services. In *Philanthropy and the Nonprofit Sector in a Changing America,* ed. Thomas Ehrlich, 139–172. Bloomington: Indiana University Press.

Guo, Chao. 2007. When Government Becomes the Principal Philanthropist: The Effects of Public Funding on Patterns of Nonprofit Governance. *Public Administration Review* 67(3): 458–473.

Hacala, Joseph R. 2001. Faith-Based Community Development: Past, Present, Future. *America* 184:15–17.

Hall, Peter Dobkin. 1992. *Inventing the Nonprofit Sector.* Baltimore, MD: Johns Hopkins University Press.

Hays, R. Allen 2002. Habitat for Humanity: Building Social Capital through Faith Based Service. *Journal of Urban Affairs* 24:247.

Heim, S. Mark. 1995. God's Long Shot in the Inner City: A Vision of Church-Based Economic Development. *Christian Century,* 680–682.

Hoch, Charles. 2000. Sheltering the Homeless in the US: Social Improvement and the Continuum of Care. *Housing Studies* 15(6): 865–876.

Hodgkinson, Virginia A., and Richard W. Lyman. 1989. *The Future of the Nonprofit Sector: Challenges, Changes, and Policy Considerations.* San Francisco: Jossey-Bass.

Hodgkinson, Virginia A., and Murray S. Weitzman. 1993. *From Belief to Commitment: The Community Service Activities and Finances of Religious Congregations in the United States.* Washington, DC: Independent Sector.

Housing Plus Services Committee of the National Low-income Housing Coalition. 2002. *Housing Plus Services Typology.* www.nlihc.org/doc/typology.pdf.

———. 2006. *Housing Plus Services Principles for Program Design and Implementation.* www.nlihc.org/doc/principles.pdf.

HUD. *See* U.S. Department of Housing and Urban Development.

Hula, Richard C. 1988. *Market-Based Public Policy.* London: Macmillian.

Hula, Richard C., and Cynthia Jackson-Elmoore. 2001. Nonprofit Organizations as Political Actors: Avenues for Minority Incorporation. *Policy Studies Review* 18(4): 27–52.

Hula, Richard C., Cynthia Y. Jackson, and Marion Orr. 1997. Urban Politics, Governing Nonprofits, and Community Revitalization. *Urban Affairs Review* 32(4): 459–489.

Jackson, Cynthia Y. 1994. *Production and Financing Choices for Municipal Services: Contracting and Franchising.* Los Angeles: University of Southern California.

Jeavons, Thomas H. 1994. *When the Bottom Line Is Faithfulness: Management of Christian Service Organizations.* Bloomington and Indianapolis: Indiana University Press.

Kearns, Kevin, Chisung Park, and Linda Yankoski. 2005. Comparing Faith-Based and Secular Community Service Corporations in Pittsburgh and Allegheny County, Pennsylvania. *Nonprofit and Voluntary Sector Quarterly* 34(2): 206–231.

Keating, Dennis W., Keith P. Rasey, and Norman Krumholz. 1990. Community Development Corporations in the United States: Their Role in Housing and Urban Redevelopment. In *Government and Housing: Developments in Seven Countries,* ed. Willem van Vliet and Jan van Weesep, 206–218. Newbury Park, CA: Sage.

Keyes, Langley C. 1971. The Role of Nonprofit Sponsors in the Production of Housing. In Papers submitted to the U.S. House Committee on Banking and Currency, Subcommittee on Housing Panels on Housing Production, Housing Demand, and Developing a Suitable Living Environment. 92nd Cong., 1st Sess., Pt. 1:159–181. Washington, DC: GPO.

———. 1996. Networks and Nonprofits: Opportunities and Challenges in an Era of Federal Devolution. *Housing Policy Debate* 7:201.

Knauft, E. Burt, Renee A. Berger, and Sandra T. Gray. 1991. *Profiles of Excellence.* San Francisco: Jossey-Bass.

Koschinsky, Julia. 1998. Challenging the Third Sector Housing Approach: The Impact of Federal Policies (1980–1996). *Journal of Urban Affairs* 20(2): 117–135.

La Barbera, Priscilla A. 1992. Enterprise in Religious-Based Organizations. *Nonprofit and Voluntary Sector Quarterly* 21:51–67.

Lauria, Mickey. 1982. Selective Urban Redevelopment: A Political Economic Perspective. *Urban Geography* 3(3): 224–239.

———. 1986. The Internal Transformation of Community-Controlled Implementation Organizations. *Administration and Society* 17(4): 387–410.

———. 1997. *Reconstructing Urban Regime Theory: Regulating Urban Politics in a Global Economy.* Thousand Oaks, CA: Sage.

Lincoln, C. Eric, and Lawrence H. Mamiya. 1990. *The Black Church in the African American Experience.* Durham, NC: Duke University Press.

Lipsky, Michael, and Steven Rathgeb Smith. 1990. Nonprofit Organizations, Government and the Welfare State. *Social Science Quarterly* 104(4): 625–648.

Liu, Y. Thomas, and Robert C. Stroh. 1998. Community Development Intermediary Systems in the United States: Origins, Evolution, and Functions. *Housing Policy Debate* 9(3): 575–594.

London, Scott. 1995. Collaboration and Community. Pew Partnership for Civic Change. www.scottlondon.com/reports/ppcc.html.

Marwell, Nicole P. 2004. Privatizing the Welfare State: Nonprofit Community-Based Organizations as Political Actors. *American Sociological Review* 69(2): 265–291.

Mayer, Neil S. 1984. *Neighborhood Organizations and Community Development: Making Revitalization Work.* Washington, DC: Urban Institute Press.

McCann, Joseph E., and John Selsky. 1984. Hyperturbulence and the Emergence of Type 5 Environments. *Academy of Management Review* 9(3): 460–470.

McDermott, Mark. 2004. National Intermediaries and Local Community Development Corporations: A View from Cleveland. *Journal of Urban Affairs* 26(2): 171–176.

McKnight, John L., and John P. Kretzmann. 1993. *Building Communities from Inside Out: A Path Toward Finding and Mobilizing Community Assets.* Evanston, IL: Center for Urban Affairs and Policy Research, Northwestern University.

Milofsky, Carl. 1988. Scarcity and Community: A Resource Allocation Theory of Community and Mass Society Organizations. In *Community Organizations: Studies in Resource Mobilization and Exchange,* ed. Carl Milofsky, 16–21. New York: Oxford University Press.

Mitchell, Roger E., Paul Florin, and John F. Stevenson. 2002. Supporting Community-Based Prevention and Health Promotion Initiatives: Developing Effective Technical Assistance Systems. *Health Education and Behavior* 29(5): 620–639.

Monsma, Stephen V. 1996. *When Sacred and Secular Mix: Religious Nonprofit Organizations and Public Money.* Lanham, MD: Rowman and Littlefield.

———. 2002. Faith-Based Organizations as Partners with Government in Providing Welfare to Work Services. Paper presented at the American Political Science Association Annual Conference, Boston.

———. 2003. Nonprofit and Faith-Based Welfare-to-Work Programs. *Society* (January/February): 13–18.

National Alliance of Community Economic Development Associations (NACEDA). 2007. Community Development Fact Sheet. Arlington, VA: NACEDA.

National Commission on Civic Renewal. 1998. *A Nation of Spectators: How Civic Disengagement Weakens America and What We Can Do About It.* College Park, MD: The National Commission on Civil Renewal.

National Congress for Community Economic Development (NCCED). 1999. *Coming of Age: Trends and Achievements of Community-Based Development Organizations.* Washington, DC: NCCED.

———. 2005. Reaching New Heights. Trends and Achievements of Community-Based Development Organizations. 5th National Community Development Census. Washington, DC: NCCED.

National Performance Review. 1993. *Creating a Government that Works Better and Costs Less: Report of the National Performance Review: The Gore Report on Reinventing Government.* Washington, DC: Times Books.

Netting, F. Ellen. 1982. Secular and Religious Funding of Church-Related Agencies. *Social Service Review* 56(4): 586–604.

———. 1984. Church-Related Agencies and Social Welfare. *Social Service Review* (September): 404–420.

Nichols, J. Bruce. 1988. *The Uneasy Alliance: Religion, Refugee Work, and U.S. Foreign Policy.* New York: Oxford University Press.

Nye, Nancy, and Norman J. Glickman. 2000. Working Together: Building Capacity for Community Development. *Housing Policy Debate* 11(1): 163–198.

Obama, Barack. 2009. Executive Order no. 13498. Washington, DC.

Powell, Walter W., ed. 1987. *The Nonprofit Sector: A Research Handbook.* New Haven, CT: Yale University Press.

Printz Platnick, T.J. 1998. Faith-Based Service Providers in the Nation's Capitol: Can They Do More? Public Policy Brief, Charting Civil Society, no. 2, April. Washington, DC: Urban Institute.

Provan, Keith G., and H. Brinton Milward. 1995. A Preliminary Theory of Interorganizational Network Effectiveness: A Comparative Study of Four Community Mental Health Systems. *Administrative Science Quarterly* 40(2): 1–33.

Reese, Laura A. 2004. A Matter of Faith: Urban Congregations and Economic Development. *Economic Development Quarterly* 18(1): 50–66.

Reese, Laura A., and Gary Shields. 1999. Economic Development Activities of Urban Religious Institutions. *International Journal of Economic Development* 2:165–199.

———. 2000. Faith-Based Economic Development. *Policy Studies Review* 17(2/3): 84–103.

Reid, Elizabeth J. 1999. Nonprofit Advocacy and Political Participation. In *Nonprofits and Government: Collaboration and Conflict,* ed. Elizabeth T. Boris and C. Eugene Steuerle, 291–325. Washington, DC: Urban Institute Press.

Rich, Michael, Michael Giles, and Emily Stern. 1998. *Collaborating to Reduce Poverty.* Washington, DC: National League of Cities.

Roozen, D.A., W. McKinney, and J.W. Carroll. 1984. *Varieties of Religious Presence: Mission in Public Life.* New York: Pilgrim Press.

Rose-Ackerman, Susan. 1983. Unintended Consequences: Regulating the Quality of Subsidized Daycare. *Journal of Policy Analysis and Management* 3:14–30.

Rubin, Herbert J. 1993. Understanding the Ethos of Community-Based Development: Ethnographic Description for Public Administrators. *Public Administration Review* 53(5): 428–437.

———. 1994. There Aren't Going to Be Any Bakeries Here If There Is No Money to Afford Jellyrolls: The Organic Theory of Community-based Development. *Social Problems* 41(3): 401–424.

———. 2000. *Renewing Hope within Neighborhoods of Despair: The Community-Based Development Model.* Albany: State University of New York Press.

Saidel, Judith R. 1991. Resource Interdependence: The Relationship between State Agencies and Nonprofit Organizations. *Public Administration Review* 51(6): 543–553.

Salamon, Lester M. 1987a. Of Market Failure, Government Failure, and Third-Party Government: Toward a Theory of Government-Nonprofit Relations in the Modern Welfare State. *Journal of Voluntary Action Research* 16(1–2): 29–49.

———. 1987b. Partners in Public Service: The Scope and Theory of Government-Nonprofit Relations. In *The Nonprofit Sector: A Research Handbook,* ed. Walter W. Powell, 99–117. New Haven, CT: Yale University Press.

———. 1998. *America's Nonprofit Sector: A Primer.* 2d ed. New York: Foundation Center.

Savas, Emanuel S. 2000. *Privatization and Public-Private Partnerships.* New York: Chatham House.

Schwartz, Alex, Rachel G. Bratt, Avis C. Vidal, and Langley C. Keyes. 1996. Nonprofit Housing Organizations and Institutional Support: The Management Challenge. *Journal of Urban Affairs* 18(4): 389–407.

Senate Fiscal Agency. 2007. Bill Analysis. Nonprofit Housing—Tax Exemption. S.B. 65-Enrolled. Lansing, MI: Senate Fiscal Agency.

Sherman, Amy L. 1995. Cross Purposes: On Religious Charities in Michigan. *Policy Review* (Fall): 58–63.

Shirley, Dennis L. 2001. Faith-based Organizations, Community Development, and the Reform of Public Schools. *Peabody Journal of Education* 76(2): 222–240.

Sider, Ron J. 2000. Maximizing the Contribution of Faith-Based Organizations to Solve Today's Most Urgent Social Problems. *Social Work and Christianity* 27(1): 71–79.

Silverman, Robert Mark. 2001. Neighborhood Characteristics, Community Development Corporations and the Community Development Industry System: A Case Study of the American Deep South. *Community Development Journal* 36(3): 234–245.

Smith, Steven Rathgeb, and Michael Lipsky. 1993. *Nonprofits for Hire: The Welfare State in the Age of Contracting.* Cambridge, MA: Harvard University Press.

Smith, Steven Rathgeb, and Michael R. Sosin. 2001. The Varieties of Faith-Related Agencies. *Public Administration Review* 61(6): 651–670.

Stoecker, Randy. 1994. *Defending Community: The Struggle for Alternative Redevelopment in Cedar-Riverside.* Philadelphia: Temple University Press.

Takahashi, Lois M., and Gayla Smutny. 2001. Collaboration among Small, Community-Based Organizations: Strategies and Challenges in Turbulent Environments. *Journal of Planning Education and Research* 21(2): 141–153.

Twombly, Eric. 2002. Religious versus Secular Human Service Organizations: Implications for Public Policy. *Social Science Quarterly* 83(4): 947–961.

U.S. Conference of Mayors. 2001. Proclamation: Mayoral Acknowledgement and Support of Faith-Based and Community Initiatives 69th Annual Conference. http://www.usmayors.org/69thAnnualMeeting/proclamation.pdf.

———. 2004. Mayors Launch New Center for Faith-Based and Community Initiatives. http://www.usmayors.org/72ndWinterMeeting/faithbased_012104.pdf.

U.S. Department of Housing and Urban Development. 2004. Equal Participation of Faith-Based Organizations: Final Rule. http://edocket.access.gpo.gov/2004/pdf/04–15677.pdf.

———. 2008. Congressional Justification for 2009 Estimates: Public and Indian Housing. http://hud.gov/offices/cfo/reports/2009/cjs/pih1.pdf.

———. 2009. Congressional Justification for 2010 Estimates: Public and Indian Housing. http://hud.gov/offices/cfo/reports/2010/cjs/pih2010.pdf.

———. 2010. FY 2011 Budget. http://hud.gov/budgetsummary2011/budget-authority-by-prog.pdf.

VanTil, Jon.1988. *Mapping the Third Sector: Voluntarism in a Changing Social Economy.* New York: Foundation Center.

Vidal, Avis C. 1992. *Rebuilding Communities: A National Study of Urban Community Development Corporations.* New York: New School for Social Research, Community Development Research Center.

———. 1995. Reintegrating Disadvantaged Communities into the Fabric of Urban Life: The Role of Community Development. *Housing Policy Debate* 6:169–230.

Walker, Christopher. 1993. Nonprofit Housing Development: Status, Trends, Prospects. *Housing Policy Debate* 4(3): 339–414.

Wineburg, Robert J. 1992. Local Human Services Provision by Religious Congregations: A Community Analysis. *Nonprofit and Voluntary Sector Quarterly* 23(Summer): 107–118.

———. 1993. Social Policy, Community Service Development, and Religious Organizations. *Nonprofit Management and Leadership* 3(3): 283–297.

———. 1996. An Investigation of Religious Support of Public and Private Agencies in One Community in an Era of Retrenchment. *Journal of Community Practice* 3(2): 35–56.

Winer, Michael, and Karen Ray. 1997. *Collaboration Handbook: Creating, Sustaining, and Enjoying the Journey.* St. Paul, MN: Amherst H. Wilder Foundation.

Wood, Donna J., and Barbara Gray. 1991. Toward a Comprehensive Theory of Collaboration. *Journal of Applied Behavioral Science* 27(2): 139–162.

Wright, Gwendolyn. 1981. Preserving Homes and Promoting Change. *The Antioch Review* 39(4): 457–475.

Wylde, Kathryn. 1986. Partnerships for Housing. *Proceedings of the Academy of Political Science* 36(2): 111–121.

Yin, Jordan S. 1998. The Community Development Industry System: A Case Study of Politics and Institutions in Cleveland, 1967–1997. *Journal of Urban Affairs* 20(2): 137–157.

Zdenek, Robert. 1987. Community Development Corporations. In *Beyond the Market and the State: New Directions in Community Development,* ed. Severyn T. Bruyn and James Meehan, 112–127. Philadelphia: Temple University Press.

3

Understanding the Policy Role of Faith-Based Organizations

Nonprofit organizations (both faith-based and secular) play an important role in the production and distribution of low-income housing in the United States. This fact illustrates an important feature of American political society and supports the common view that Americans have a strong distrust of government. Citizens often prefer to substitute private institutions for public agencies even when activities are publicly financed. There can be little doubt that public cynicism is higher in the United States than almost any other industrial nation. As a result, citizens are less likely to be guaranteed access to basic goods and services such as health care and housing through public institutions. This rejection and distrust of public institutions within the housing market has stimulated the development of nonprofit (and even some for-profit) organizations that significantly aid efforts to address the shortfalls of a private housing market.

Faith-based housing providers operate in a complex system of public and private institutions. It is unlikely that one can understand the behavior and performance of any one set of institutions within this system without having some sense of the overall context in which they work. This network is extraordinarily complicated and messy. Like most other goods of value, housing is largely allocated through private sector markets. However, private and nonprofit organizations are active on the margins of the private housing market where market failure is most likely to occur. These margins are typically defined by special needs populations who for a variety of reasons are disadvantaged by low disposable income. Lack of income is, of course, associated with a variety of factors such as physical disabilities, old age, and racial and ethnic discrimination. Both faith-based and secular nonprofit organizations play a critical role in efforts to provide housing to these populations (Cnaan 2006).

The Public Sector Context

While hostility toward and mistrust of government are nothing new in American politics, popular reports in the early twenty-first century suggest that they have reached extraordinary proportions. Commentators point to numerous national surveys indicating a sharp decline in overall respect for and trust in American political institutions. For example, Table 3.1 reports some of the results of a 2007 national

Table 3.1

Distrust of National Public Institutions

Question: "I am going to read a list of institutions in American society. Would you tell me how much confidence you, yourself, have in each one—a great deal, quite a lot, some, or very little?"

Institution	A great deal of confidence
Presidency	12%
Supreme Court	14%
Congress	4%

Source: Roper Center (2008).

survey measuring levels of confidence in the president, the Supreme Court, and Congress. Confidence in the first two is quite low and an even smaller percentage of respondents express a good deal of confidence in Congress. All told, these numbers are cause for concern.

Attitudes of Michigan citizens toward government have been regularly measured by the Institute for Public Policy and Social Research (IPPSR) at Michigan State University. Since 1994 IPPSR has conducted a quarterly public opinion survey, the State of the State Survey (SOSS). Between 1995 and 2009, Michigan citizens were asked eleven times whether they trusted the federal and state governments "almost always," "sometimes," "seldom," or "almost never." The question was asked about local government nine times. Figure 3.1 highlights the percentage of the population that reported trusting government "almost all the time." Figure 3.2 depicts the percentage of the population reporting trust in the government at least "sometimes."[1]

Figure 3.1 and Figure 3.2 present a fascinating picture of popular attitudes toward government in the state of Michigan. Citizens expressed remarkably little faith in any level of government. Between 1995 and 2009 an average of only 21 percent of Michigan's residents reported that they trusted the federal government "most of the time."[2] The average level of trust was slightly higher for state government (27 percent) and significantly higher for local government (40 percent), but in no case did the percentage rise to half the population. Figure 3.2 shows that, on average, 71 percent of respondents reported trusting the federal government at least "some of the time." This means that on average 25 percent of the population "hardly ever" or "never" trusted the federal government. State government was trusted by 80 percent of the population "some of the time," and local government by 82 percent. Again this means that almost 20 percent of the population "hardly ever" or "never" trusted state or local government.

In addition to showing high levels of overall citizen alienation, Figure 3.1 and Figure 3.2 reveal that trust levels, while always relatively low, are quite volatile. This is particularly the case with attitudes toward the federal government. In

Figure 3.1   **Percent Respondents Expressing High Trust in Federal, State, and Local Government in Michigan, 1994–2006**

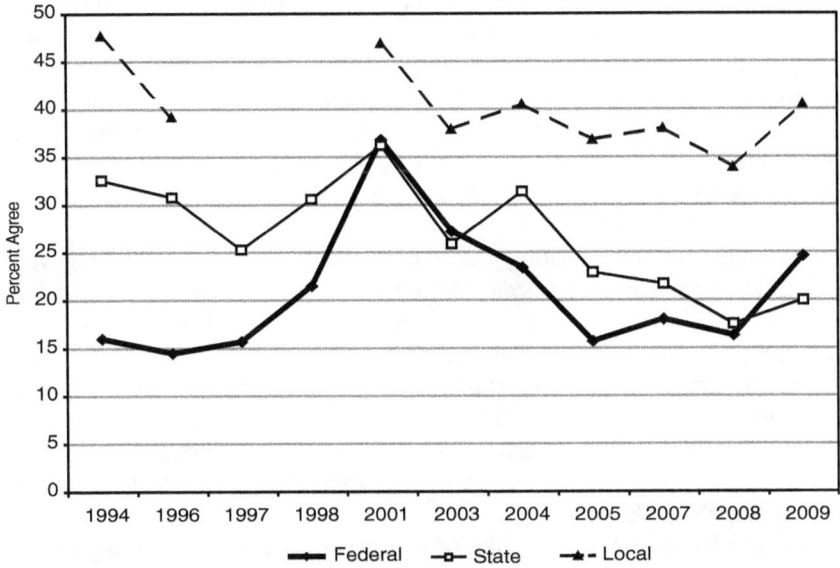

Source: IPPSR (2009).

Figure 3.2   **Percent Respondents Expressing Moderate Trust in Federal, State, and Local Government in Michigan, 1994–2006**

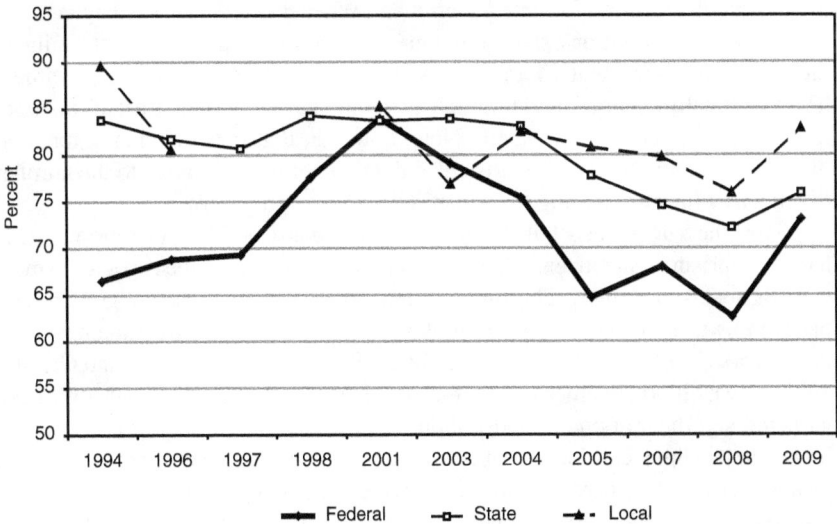

Source: IPPSR (2009).

1994, slightly more than 16 percent of the population claimed to trust the federal government "most of the time." By 2001 this had increased to around 37 percent. After 2001, this percentage began to decline once again. By 2007 the percentage of citizens trusting the federal government "most of the time" had dropped to around 18 percent. After 2007, trust began to rise slightly so that, by 2009, 25 percent of the population claimed they trusted the federal government "most of the time." The proportion of the population expressing trust in the federal government "some of the time" increased from 67 percent in 1994 to almost 84 percent in 2001. This percentage declined after 2001 to 63 percent in 2008. The year 2009 saw an increase to just over 73 percent.

A similar pattern of volatility can be observed for both state and local government. The trend for trust in state and local government, however, is more of a gradual, long-term decline. The percentage of citizens expressing trust in state government "most of the time" dropped from 33 percent in 1994 to 20 percent in 2009. The percentage of citizens expressing some trust in state government dropped from 84 percent in 1994 to 76 percent in 2009. Those who trusted local government "most of the time" declined from 48 percent in 1994 to 41 percent in 2009, and those who trusted local government "at least some of the time" declined from 89 percent in 1994 to 83 percent in 2009.

Figures 3.1 and 3.2 also show that Michigan citizens expressed varying levels of trust for different levels of government. The data support the common assertion that Americans generally prefer or at least trust government closest to them. Figure 3.1 shows that citizens were much more likely to "usually trust" local government than the federal government. This pattern is replicated in Figure 3.2, which combines respondents who usually and sometimes trusted government. It is interesting to note the intermediate pattern for state government. When the SOSS survey began to ask government trust questions, state government tended to have levels of trust similar to those of local government. More recently, however, public trust in state government has dramatically declined. By 2009 state government was "usually trusted" no more often than the federal government. Note, however, that fewer citizens expressed the view that they "sometimes trusted" federal government relative to the number of citizens who were willing to "sometimes" trust state government.

Given the widespread public ambivalence toward political institutions, it is hardly surprising that citizens often feel that government lacks the capacity to meet existing social challenges. This ongoing concern about the efficacy of government has led to widespread calls for a rethinking of how American government should do its work (Hanke and Academy of Political Science 1987; Osborne and Gaebler 1992; Savas 2000). Numerous alternatives have been suggested, but two have garnered significant popular and political support. The first alternative emerged in the 1980s with a call for decentralization of federal responsibilities to state and local governments. There have also been widespread calls for increased privatization to directly engage private market actors in the production and distribution of publicly financed goods and services (see, for example, Hula 1988; Gormley 1991;

and Jackson 1994). Both trends have had the indirect effect of increasing the role of the nonprofit sector in the production and distribution of a variety of publicly financed goods.

The Role of the Voluntary Association in America

Many observers have commented on the extraordinarily well-developed set of associations and voluntary groups in the United States that sometimes take on roles similar to those of government. Examples here include not only faith-based organizations, but also other nonprofit and voluntary associations. Alexis de Tocqueville recognized this American penchant for nongovernmental associations in the nineteenth century:

> Americans of all ages, all conditions, all minds constantly unite. Not only do they have commercial and industrial associations in which all take part, but they also have a thousand other kinds: religious, moral, grave, futile, very general and very particular, immense and very small; Americans use associations to give fêtes, to found seminaries, to build inns, to raise churches, to distribute books, to send missionaries to the antipodes; in this manner they create hospitals, prisons, schools. Finally, if it is a question of bringing to light a truth or developing a sentiment with the support of a great example, they associate. Everywhere that, at the head of a new undertaking, you see the government in France and a great lord in England, count on it that you will perceive an association in the United States. (de Toqueville 1969)

The complexity of America's nonprofit world is staggering. A 2008 report issued by the Urban Institute documents that 1.4 million nonprofits were registered with the IRS in 2005. Of the total, 63 percent were registered as 501(c)(3) public charities. In 2006, $295 billion was contributed to nonprofits. In that same year almost 27 percent of adults in the United States reported volunteering over 12.9 billion hours (Blackwood et al. 2008).

Public charities include organizations that are active in the arts, education, health care and human services, and housing. Such organizations make up the bulk of what most observers think of as the nonprofit sector. Charitable organizations include the estimated 350,000 religious congregations in the country. Note, however, that religious congregations are not required to register (approximately 50 percent of these organizations do register). Faith-based organizations are clearly an important component of this associational mix. Unfortunately there is little verifiable information as to what concrete impact such organizations have in the United States. Indeed, there is little verifiable data available on how much activity is taking place or even the number of active organizations that exist. Ironically, past regulations, which sought to separate secular and faith-based activities by exempting religious institutions from taxation or even formal registration, make it extraordinarily difficult to evaluate claims about how and whether such organizations are conducting the public's business.

A limited number of empirical studies do provide some evidence of the scope and impact of religiously affiliated nonprofit groups. One important source of information is the National Congregations Study (NCS). The NCS is an ongoing national survey effort to gather information about the basic characteristics of America's congregations. The first wave of the NCS took place in 1998; Wave II was fielded in 2006–2007 (Chaves 1998; Chaves and Anderson 2008).[3] The study was repeated in order to track both continuity and change among American congregations. Data collection was done in conjunction with the General Social Survey (GSS). In both 1998 and 2006, the GSS asked respondents who attend religious services to name their religious congregation, thus generating a nationally representative sample of religious congregations. National Congregations Study researchers then contacted each of the congregations and interviewed someone, usually a clergyman, who was familiar with the congregation (Chaves et al. 2009).

Table 3.2 provides an overview of social welfare activities of the nation's congregations. The data show that congregations are in fact active in various service activities targeted to individuals and families outside the congregation. In 1998, almost 57 percent of all reporting congregations claimed to be involved in at least one such social service project. In 2006–2007 that increased to 65 percent. With regard to housing, in 1998, about 32 percent of the congregations indicated that they sponsored or participated in activities related to home building, repair or maintenance, Habitat for Humanity, and/or day shelters. Similarly, 5 percent indicated that they provided furniture, household items, and money for rent or utilities (Chaves 1998). There is also evidence that many congregations seek some sort of external funding for these projects. In 1998, just over 10 percent of reported projects (10.6 percent) depended at least in part on funding external to the congregation. This proportion was almost exactly the same as reported in 2006–2007 (10.7 percent). Only about 2.6 percent of all congregations reported obtaining government funding in 1998. This percentage increased a bit, to 4 percent, in 2006–2007. Note, however, there is strong and consistent interest in obtaining public funds (47.3 percent in 1998 and 47.2 percent in 2006–2007). Explicit policies against accepting public funds are relatively uncommon (16.2 percent of all 1998 congregations, and 16.0 percent in 2006–2007).

The "estimated number" reported in Table 3.2 for each survey year is an estimate of the total number of congregations in the United States responding positively to each of the questions listed in the table. It is simply the sample percentage response in each survey year multiplied by the estimated total number of congregations in the nation. Obviously this estimate is a crude one, but it does give some measure of the magnitude of activity of religious congregations in social services. In 1998, for example, the NCS estimates that over 197,000 congregations were active in projects targeted to nonmember recipients. The 2006–2007 survey suggests that that number has risen to over 225,000 active congregations. More than 37,000 congregations had programs or initiatives that relied on financial resources external to the congregation. In 1998, 2.6 percent of all congregations reported receiving

Table 3.2

Congregations and Social Services

	1998		2006–2007	
	Percent yes	Estimated number	Percent yes	Estimated number
Congregations engaged in human service projects to help people outside their congregations	56.5%	197,750	64.9%	227,500
Congregations sponsored or participated in home building, repair, maintenance, and related bricks and mortar activities[a]	32.1%	112,350	b	b
Congregations sponsored or participated in provision of furniture, household items, or money for rent	5.1%	17,850	b	b
Congregation projects supported by outside funds	10.6%	37,100	10.7%	37,450
Outside funds received from government for project	2.6%	9,100	4.0%	14,000
Congregation would like to apply for government money for social services programs	47.3%	165,550	47.2%	165,200
Policy against receiving public funds	16.2%	56,700	16.0%	56,000

Source: National Congregation Study (Chaves, 1998).

[a]In 1998, 17% of the congregations sponsored or participated in Habitat for Humanity Projects, while approximately 13% did so in 2006–2007; this is in addition to the percentage noted above.

[b]Data from the 2006–2007 wave were not scheduled to be released until July 2009. Subsequent to that combined data files were released and not all of the data were presented in the same format (Chaves and Anderson, 2008).

government funding. By 2006–2007 that had increased to 4 percent. Finally, it should be noted that there seems to be a potential for much greater activity, given that just over 47 percent of all congregations indicated an interest in obtaining public funding for social service projects (Chaves 1998).

There exist several empirical efforts to map the actual services provided by religious organizations. Ram Cnaan (2006) and his associates have attempted to provide a comprehensive picture of social services provided by religious congregations in one large city through the Philadelphia Census of Congregations (PCC). The PCC is an ambitious effort to catalogue demographic characteristics and programmatic efforts of all religious congregations in the city of Philadelphia. The PCC strongly supports the aggregate data presented in Table 3.2 and shows that Philadelphia congregations are quite active in providing social services to their communities. As is indicated in the national aggregate data, much of this effort is without any public subsidy. Cnaan argues that such activity is a natural outgrowth of the mutual support system that characterizes religious congregations. In Philadelphia, engagement in social services seems to hold across the religious spectrum. Moreover, Cnaan argues that often these efforts are not isolated activities, but rather are part of a complex interrelated set of activities across a wide range of congregations.

Perhaps the most provocative finding reported by Cnaan (2006) is simply the importance of religiously based social services in the social welfare system of the city. Religious congregations in Philadelphia appear to provide a substantial social safety net. Based on the Philadelphia data, Cnaan concludes:

> Most basic needs such as food and immediate shelter are provided by congregations. They may not be able to replace public mental health or child welfare services that are outside their domain. However, their services, which are often short-term, emergency-based, and segmented, taken together are a major part of the American welfare system.
>
> To be a needy person in America without access to local congregations is a most frightening prospect. One needs to look at what congregations are giving and not at what they can provide in order to appreciate the magnitude of congregation-based care. (Cnaan 2006, 278–279)

The Religion in Urban America Program (RUAP) has conducted several surveys in metropolitan Chicago to explore efforts by religious organizations to address urban issues. A 1996 survey targeted all the identifiable religious, social service, and community organizations in the Chicago metropolitan area.[4] The survey presented further evidence of an active and complex network of religiously based organizations contributing to an American social safety net. For example, these organizations engaged in an array of activities related to jobs and economic insecurity (25.7 percent) and urban government (5.8 percent). The majority (70 percent) of the Chicago nonprofit organizations responding to the survey indicated that service delivery was their most important programmatic and service-related role (Livezey

Table 3.3

Ties between Chicago Social Service Provider Organizations and Religious Institutions

Organizational ties	Percent
Formal link to religious body	36.1%
Has specific religious identity but independent of formal religious body	19.1%
Not religious organization but cooperates with religious organization	7.9%
Not a religious organization and not related to religious organizations or based on religious values	36.8%

$N = 327$
Source: Religion in Urban America Program (Livezey et al., 1996).

et al. 1996).[5] Table 3.3 shows that over 36 percent of the region's nongovernmental social service agencies have direct ties to a formal religious institution. Only 37 percent of all service providers claimed to be purely secular—that is, they were not a religious organization, were not related to a religious organization, and were not based on religious values.

An important finding in the 1996 RUAP survey of Chicago social service providers is that religiously oriented institutions are much more likely to receive public funding to support their programming than one might assume by looking only at the national congregational data presented in Table 3.2. Figure 3.3 shows that although only about 4.2 percent of congregations in Chicago reported receiving public funding, just under 50 percent of all of that city's nongovernmental social service providers reported government funds as a major source of support. It is also interesting to note that for over 50 percent of these organizations, some sort of religious funding remained an important source of support. Such support can include direct congregational subsidy (31.9 percent); city, metropolitan area, or state religious bodies (15.2 percent); or national religious bodies (7.7 percent). These data offer convincing evidence (at least for this metropolitan region) that there is a great deal of commingling of public and religious efforts to provide social services. Moreover, there is no reason to expect that Chicago is unique in this respect.

Nonprofit social service providers in Chicago also report working with an array of other organizations, including religious organizations, social service or community organizations, and state agencies. The Chicago nonprofit social service providers tend to be less connected to businesses, banks and corporations, civic organizations, neighborhood organizations, and local government agencies (Figure 3.4). Even so, these organizations network with others in order to carry out their missions and functions. Figure 3.5 highlights various reasons that nonprofit social service providers in Chicago network with other organizations. Chicago area nonprofits network for the purposes of giving and receiving services, advice, and funding. The most commonly cited reasons for connecting to and networking

Figure 3.3   **Major Funding Sources for Chicago's Nongovernmental Social Service Providers**

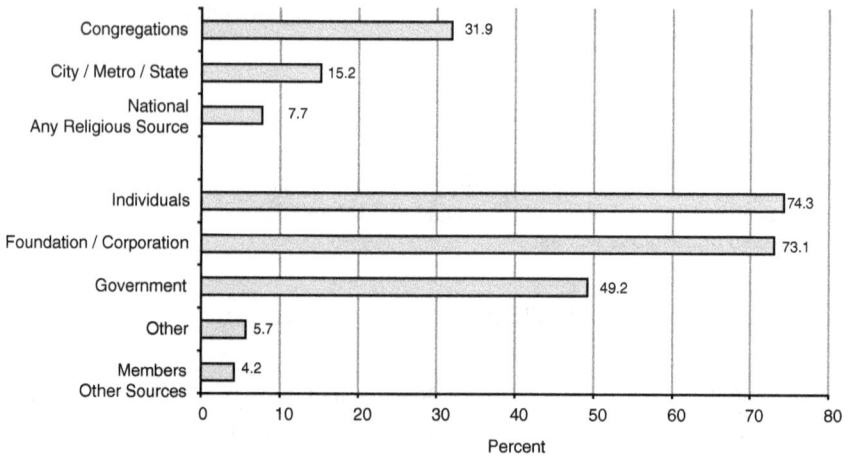

Source: Religion in Urban America Program (Livezey et al. 1996).

Figure 3.4   **Organizations Connected to Chicago's Nongovernmental Social Service Providers**

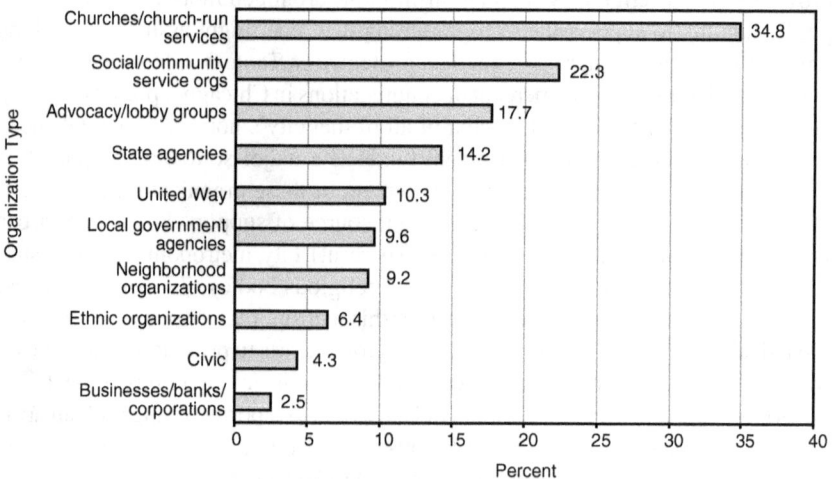

Source: Religion in Urban America Program (Livezey et al. 1996).

with other organizations are to deliver services (62 percent), to provide advice or consultation (54 percent), and to pool resources (46 percent).

Another survey conducted by the RUAP in 1994 examined Chicago's religious congregations.[6] This congregational study provides a snapshot of the range of activities in which area congregations were involved. An overview of these find-

Figure 3.5   **Chicago's Nongovernmental Social Service Providers' Rationale for Networking**

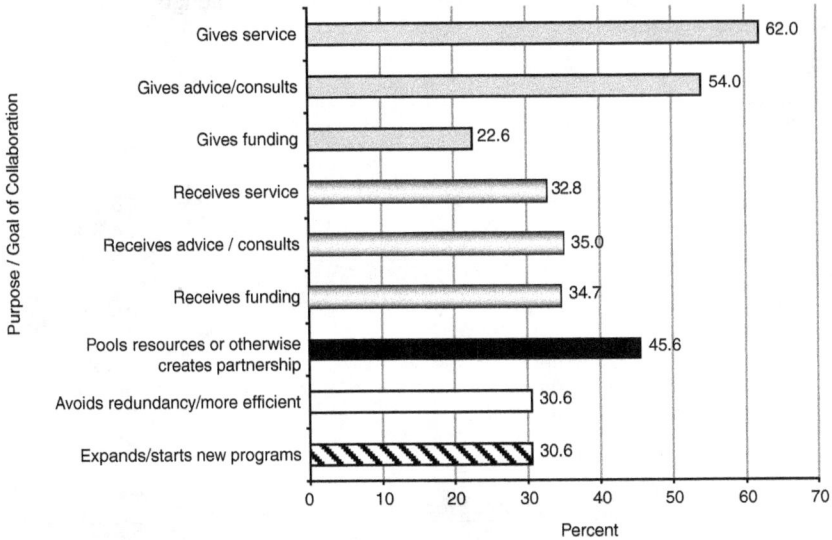

Source: Religion in Urban America Program (Livezey et al. 1996).

ings is presented in Table 3.4 and Figure 3.6. These data confirm that religious organizations (at least in the Chicago area) are active over a wide range of issues. They also reconfirm that religious organizations engage in housing-related activities and view shelter as a particularly important priority.

The 1994 survey of Chicago religious congregations demonstrates that those that engage in housing undertake other social and economic activities in their communities, including providing temporary shelter and food as well as offering services to people in need of employment. Approximately 70–90 percent of the congregations engaged in housing also offered services to people in need of employment (72.2 percent), shelter (69.8 percent), and/or food (88.9 percent). Similarly, about 46 percent of the congregations engaged in housing were also active on land use and zoning issues, and nearly 60 percent were involved with job training and job placement activities (see Tables 3.5 and 3.6).

The Chicago-based survey indicates that religious congregations collaborate with an array of organizations across the public, for-profit, and nonprofit sectors. At least 60 percent of the religious congregations reported working with community organizations, social service agencies, and/or other religious organizations (Figure 3.7). This is similar to the experiences of other (faith-based and secular) nonprofit social service providers in Chicago (Livezey et al. 1996). The religious congregations that engaged in housing-related activities also reported similar collaboration patterns (Table 3.7). For instance, congregations engaged

Table 3.4

Social Welfare and Economic Activities Reported by Chicago Area Congregations

	Percent
Activity	
Employment	30.8%
Shelter	49.3%
Food	75.1%
Immigration problems	34.3%
Other	25.9%
Public Issue	
Land use/zoning	9.6%
Housing	29.6%
Job training and/or placement	26.3%
Neighborhood anticrime issues	46.0%
Issues affecting the elderly	35.8%
Other	21.3%

$N = 218$

Source: Religion in Urban America Program (Livezey et al. 1994).

Table 3.5

Housing, Social Welfare, and Economic Activities of Chicago Area Congregations

Do you offer services to people in need of:		Is your church active on the following public issue? (Housing)		
		N	Yes	No
Employment	Yes	107	22.5%	72.2%
	No		77.5%	27.8%
Shelter	Yes	213	40.7%	69.8%
	No		59.3%	30.2%
Food	Yes	213	69.3%	88.9%
	No		30.7%	11.1%
Immigration Problems	Yes	213	26.0%	54.0%
	No		74.0%	46.0%
Other	Yes	212	19.3%	41.9%
	No		80.7%	58.1%

Source: Religion in Urban America Program (Livezey et al. 1994).
Note: One degree of freedom

in housing are less likely to collaborate with business (45 percent) and more likely to collaborate with other religious organizations (87.3 percent), community organizations (82.5 percent), and social service agencies (76.2 percent). The Chicago religious congregation survey also highlights collaboration patterns linked to the nature of the congregations' involvement in various social welfare

Table 3.6

Chicago Area Congregations' Involvement in Housing and Other Public Issues

Is your church active on the following public issues:		Is your church active in housing?		
		N	Yes	No
Land use/zoning	Yes	83	45.5%	4.2%
	No		54.5%	95.8%
Job training and/or	Yes	213	58.7%	12.7%
placement	No		41.3%	87.3%
Neighborhood anticrime	Yes	213	81.0%	31.3%
issues	No		19.0%	68.7%
Issues affecting the elderly	Yes	134	63.3%	27.9%
	No		36.7%	72.1%
Other	Yes	211	31.7%	16.9%
	No		68.3%	83.1%

Source: Religion in Urban America Program (Livezey et al. 1994).
Note: One degree of freedom

Figure 3.6   **Chicago Area Congregations' Involvement in Social Welfare and Economic Issues**

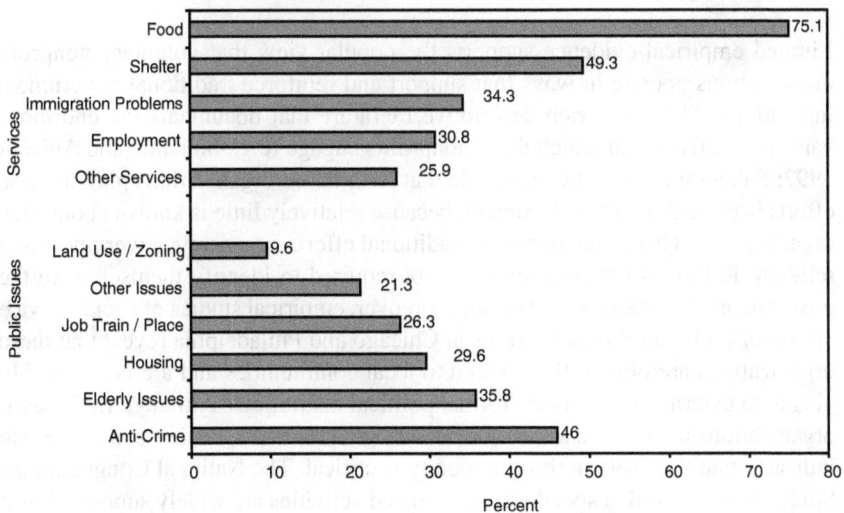

Source: Religion in Urban America Program (Livezey et al. 1994).

Table 3.7

Differential Collaboration by Chicago Area Religious Congregations Engaged in Housing

Collaborators		Is your church active in housing?		
		N	No	Yes
Government	Yes	85	33.3%	21.9%
	No		66.7%	78.1%
Business	Yes	84	45.5%	11.0%
	No		54.5%	89.0%
Community organizations	Yes	211	82.5%	52.7%
	No		17.5%	47.3%
Social service organizations	Yes	213	76.2%	52.7%
	No		23.8%	47.3%
Other religious institutions	Yes	213	87.3%	61.3%
	No		12.7%	38.7%
Other	Yes	206	20.6%	8.4%
	No		79.4%	91.6%

Source: Religion in Urban America Program (Livezey et al. 1994).
Note: One degree of freedom

and economic issues, with few congregations indicating a tendency to collaborate with government or business (Table 3.8).

Faith-Based Organizations as an Alternative to Government

Limited empirical evidence supports the popular view that voluntary nonprofit organizations operate in ways that support and reinforce traditional government institutions. There is a rich descriptive literature that documents the enormous variety of activities in which these nonprofits engage (e.g., Salamon and Anheier 1997; Salamon 2001). The exact role that faith-based organizations play in these efforts is quite difficult to document, because relatively little is known about such organizations. This is due in part to traditional efforts to separate government and religion. Religious congregations are not required to identify themselves to the government, and many do not do so. Moreover, empirical studies of social service efforts of faith-based organizations in Chicago and Philadelphia reveal that these organizations are often tightly bound to local communities and are not as highly visible to external actors as are formal political institutions. Although faith-based organizations may not be as recognizable as government agencies, some research indicates that their role in the community is critical. The National Congregations Study makes clear that social services-related activities are widely supported by a variety of religious organizations. The case material from Philadelphia and Chicago suggests that these activities are not only tied to support of public policy, but often involve direct support from and cooperation with public institutions.

Table 3.8

Collaboration by Chicago Area Religious Congregations Involved in Public Issues

Collaborator		Housing	Employment	Shelter	Food	Land use/ zoning	Job training/ placement
Public issue							
Government	Yes						
	No		**		***		
Business	Yes	***					
	No	***	***		**	***	***
Community organizations	Yes	***	***	***	***	**	***
	No						
Social service organizations	Yes	***	***	***	***		***
	No						
Other religious institutions	Yes	***					
	No		**	***	***		**
Other	Yes	**					
	No						

Source: Religion in Urban America Program (Livezey et al. 1994).
Note: Chi-Square test of independence significance, one degree of freedom.
***Significant at .01, **significant at .05

Figure 3.7   **Collaborators for Chicago Area Religious Congregations**

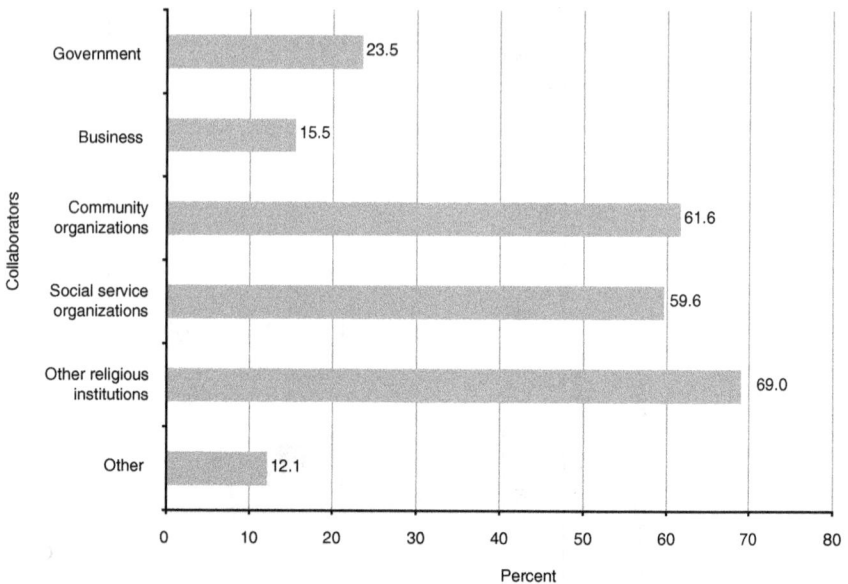

Source: Religion in Urban America Program (Livezey et al. 1994).

The Role of Nongovernmental Organizations in Michigan

National and state surveys pointing to high levels of citizen alienation from government institutions suggest both a need and an opportunity for nongovernmental agencies to be active in providing social services. Data obtained from the Institute for Public Policy and Social Research at Michigan State University through the quarterly State of the State Survey provide a dynamic picture of public opinion about nongovernmental social service providers. The data show that public attitudes are more complex than one might expect.

Figure 3.8 reports both the percentage of the population that strongly agrees and the sum of those individuals who somewhat and strongly agree with the statement that the "need for charitable organizations is greater now than five years ago." The data reported in Figure 3.8 were collected over seven surveys administered between 1995 and 2009 and show broad agreement with the notion that the need for charitable organizations is increasing. On average, 87 percent of Michigan residents agreed that the need for charitable organizations was increasing, with levels of agreement varying from a low of 82 percent in 1999 to a high of 95 percent in 2009.[7] Approximately 45 percent of survey respondents indicated a strong degree of agreement with the claim over time, suggesting an ongoing public perception that charitable organizations need to step in and provide services.

The question of how the public perceives charitable capacity was explored in

Figure 3.8   **Is the Need for Charitable Organizations Greater Now Than Five Years Ago**

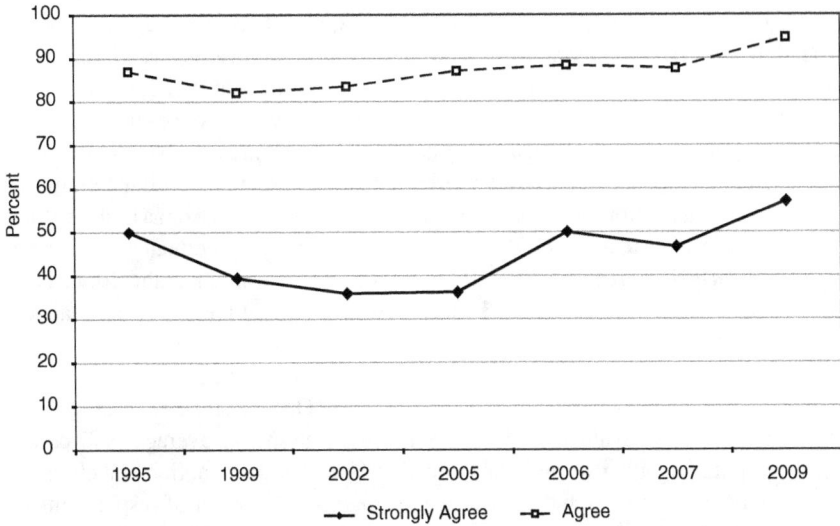

Source: IPPSR (2009).

Figure 3.9   **Are Charitable Organizations More Effective Than They Were Five Years Ago**

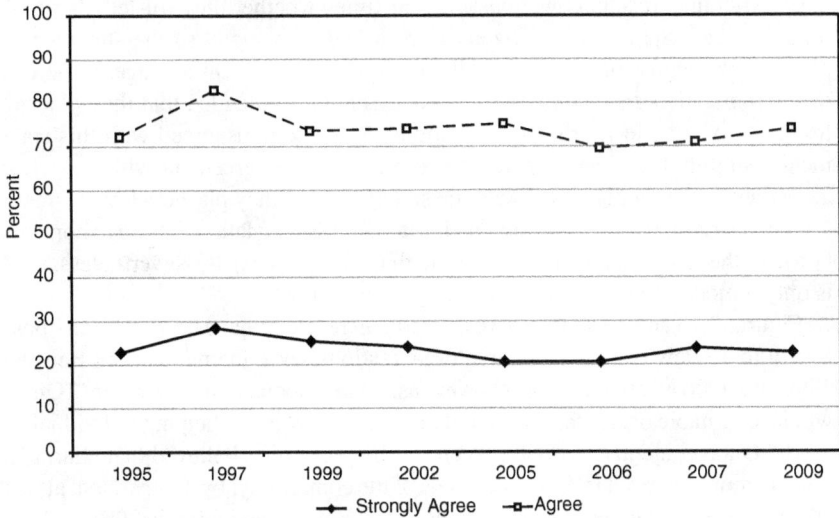

Source: IPPSR (2009).

another question that was asked eight times between 1995 and 2009. Figure 3.9 reports citizen response to the question of whether charitable organizations had become more effective over the previous five years. Between 1995 and 2009, an average of 74 percent of all respondents indicated at least some agreement with the view that charitable organizations were becoming more effective. Significantly fewer citizens expressed strong agreement with this view. On average just less than 24 percent expressed strong agreement. As with perceived need for charitable organizations, attitudes toward organizational effectiveness are quite stable over time. The percentage of the population expressing some agreement with the claim that charitable organizations were becoming more effective ranges from a high of almost 83 percent in 1997 to a low of 70 percent in 2006. Strong agreement ranged from a high of nearly 28 percent in 1997 to a low of 21 percent in 2005 and 2006. These data clearly show that citizens are more optimistic about the increasing capacity of charitable organizations relative to that of governmental institutions.

Figure 3.10 measures a third aspect of public attitudes toward charitable organizations by asking whether they are honest and ethical. Once again, there is evidence of a generally positive evaluation of charitable organizations. An average of 77 percent of the population either strongly or somewhat agreed with the notion that charitable organizations are honest and ethical. An average of 23 percent of respondents expressed strong agreement with the statement. Overall, this pattern of response is relatively consistent over time. However, there does appear to be a modest increase in support of the view that charitable organizations are honest and ethical.

Figures 3.11 and 3.12 directly address the issue of whether the public trusts charitable organizations. Somewhat surprisingly, public trust is lower than one would expect based on the earlier State of the State indicators. Between 1999 and 2006, Michigan residents were asked four times whether they trusted charitable organizations. Specifically, citizens were asked to respond to the statement "I place a low degree of trust in charitable organizations." On average 45 percent of the population gave some level of endorsement to the idea that they placed a low level of trust in charitable institutions; 55 percent disagreed with this statement.[8] Slightly less than 12 percent expressed strong agreement with that view; 23 percent strongly disagreed with the statement that they placed a low degree of trust in charitable organizations. The limited number of data points and short time between them makes it difficult to argue that any trend exists. Nevertheless, there is only a modest change in citizen response over time.

Figures 3.13 and 3.14 indicate that Michigan residents have been generally positive in their view of how charitable organizations serve the population. Between 1999 and 2006 Michigan residents were asked to respond to the statement "On the whole, charitable organizations do not do a very good job in helping individuals in need." On average just over 30 percent of the population believed that charitable organizations were not meeting the needs of the community; by comparison, almost 70 percent disagreed with the statement. Interestingly, beginning in 2002, citizens were less likely to believe that charitable organizations were not doing a very

Figure 3.10   **Are Charitable Organizations Honest and Ethical?**

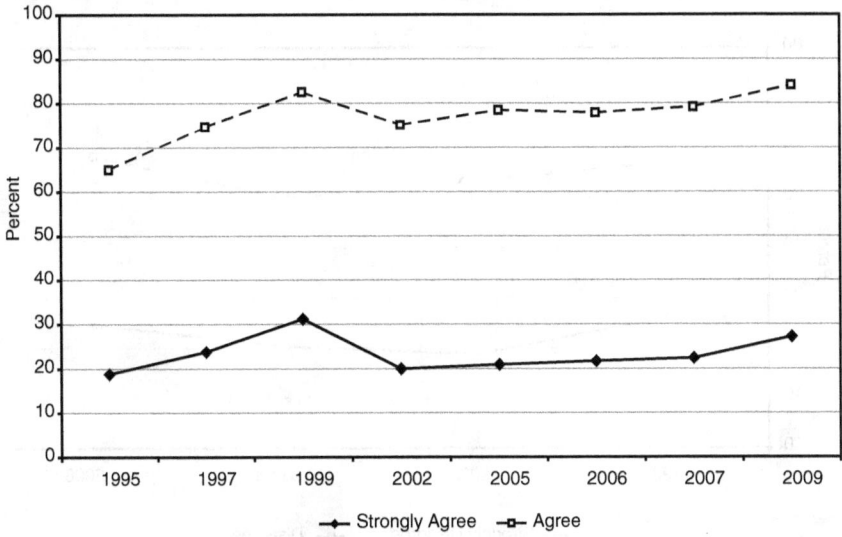

Source: IPPSR (2009).

Figure 3.11   **Individuals Place Low Levels of Trust in Michigan Charitable Organizations, Agree**

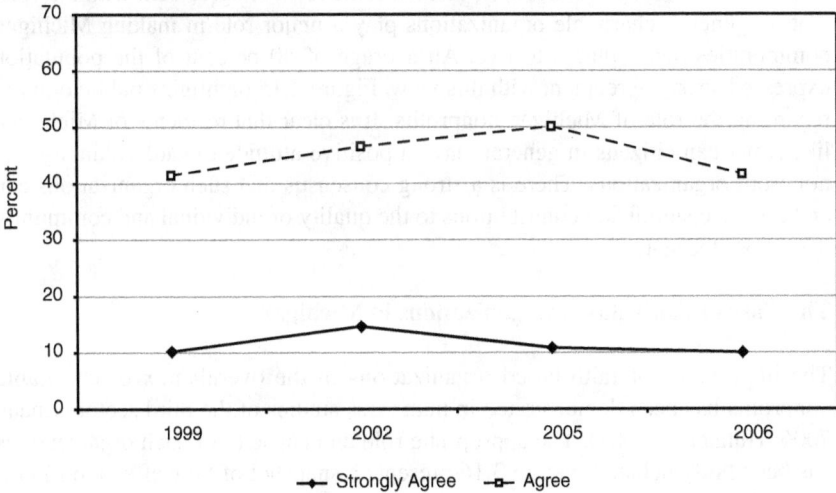

Source: IPPSR (2009).

Figure 3.12   **Individuals Place Low Levels of Trust in Michigan Charitable Organizations, Disagree**

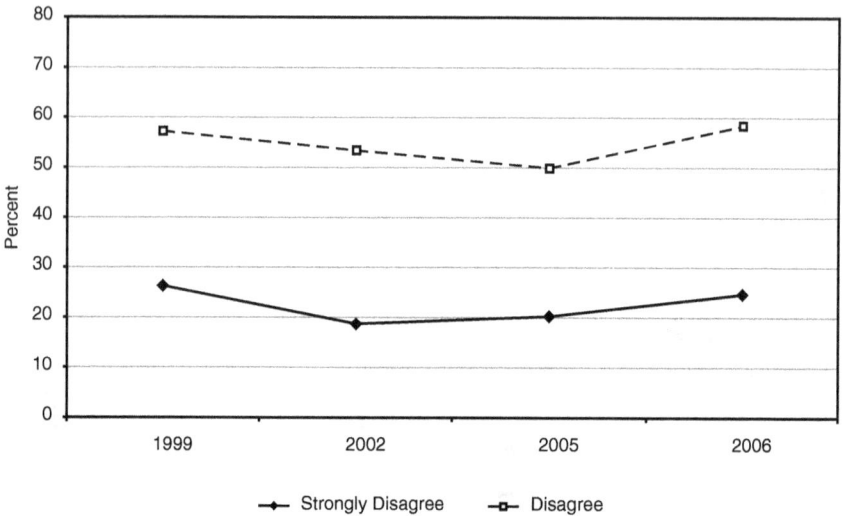

Source: IPPSR (2009).

good job of helping individuals in need. That would suggest a general sentiment toward believing that there was indeed a role for charitable organizations to play in serving the population and that these organizations were successful in carrying out that role. Thus it is not surprising that between 1999 and 2006, an average of 87 percent of Michigan residents indicated some level of agreement with the view that, in general, charitable organizations play a major role in making Michigan communities better places to live. An average of 40 percent of the population expressed strong agreement with this view. Figure 3.15 highlights public opinion regarding the role of Michigan nonprofits. It is clear that residents of Michigan, like American citizens in general, have a positive attitude toward voluntary and nonprofit organizations. There is a strong consensus that such organizations can and do make significant contributions to the quality of individual and community life across the state.

The Case of Faith-Based Organizations in Michigan

The importance of faith-based organizations in the overall mix of charitable nonprofits has been demonstrated in numerous studies of the third sector (Cnaan 2006; Hula et al. 2007). The appropriate role and capacity of such organizations has been hotly debated. Figure 3.16 presents a snapshot of how effective Michigan residents perceived religious congregations to be in providing social welfare services. It is clear from Figure 3.16 that there has been broad agreement that

Figure 3.13   **Charitable Organizations Could Do a Better Job of Helping People in Need, Agree**

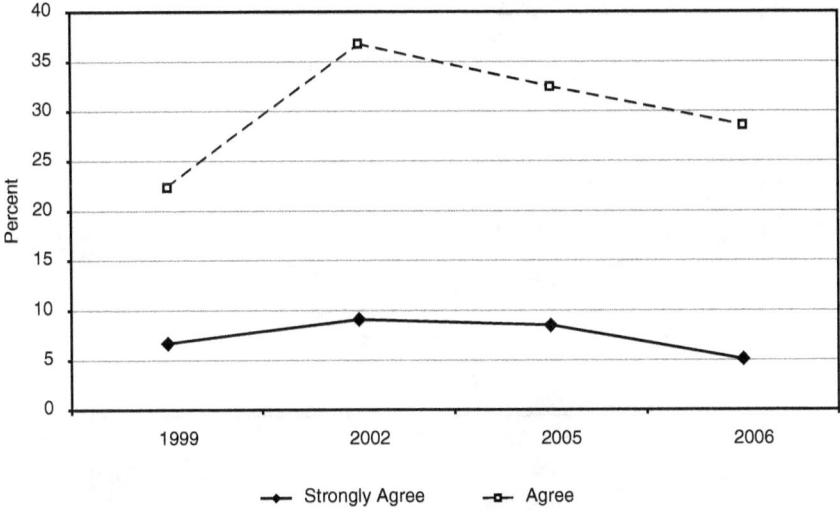

Strongly Agree   Agree

Source: IPPSR (2009).

Figure 3.14   **Charitable Organizations Could Do a Better Job of Helping People in Need, Disagree**

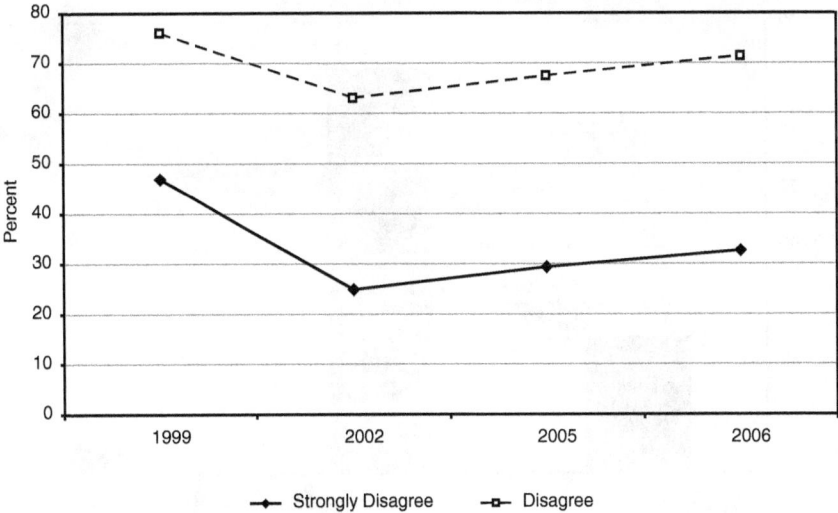

Strongly Disagree   Disagree

Source: IPPSR (2009).

Figure 3.15   **Michigan Communities Are Better Because of the Work of Charitable Organizations**

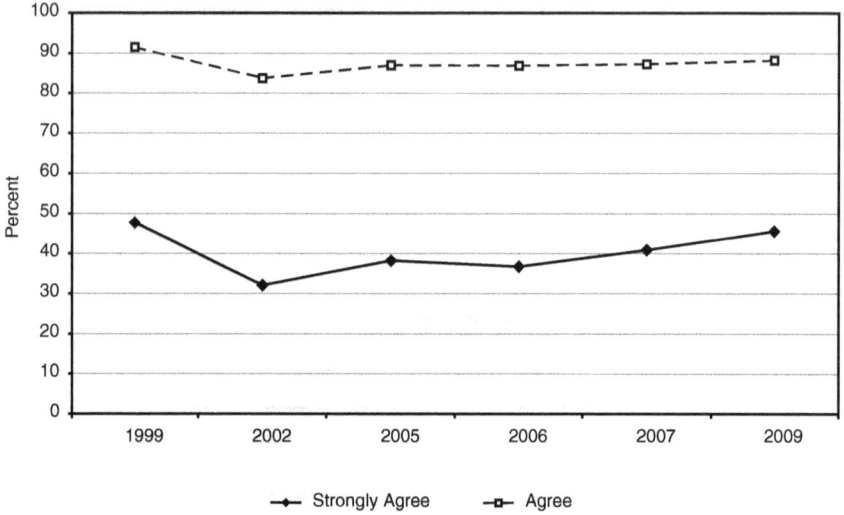

Source: IPPSR (2009).

Figure 3.16   **How Effective Do You Believe Local Religious Congregations Are at Serving the Needs of the Poor?**

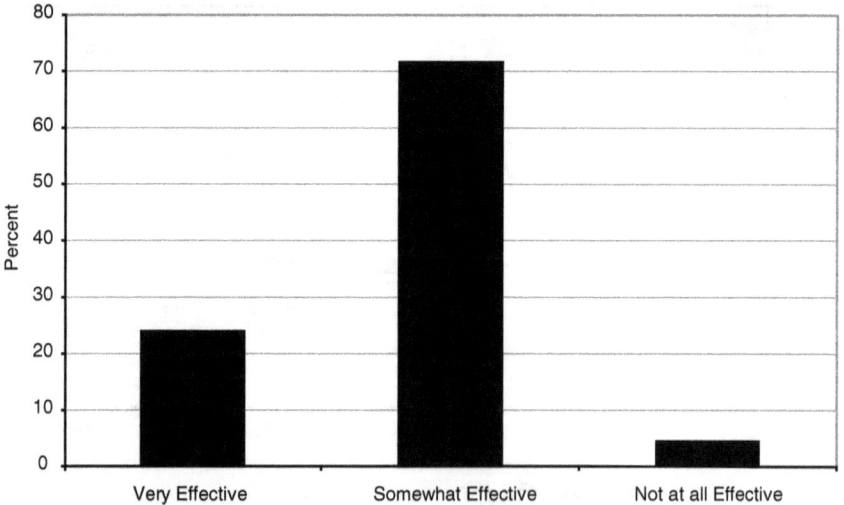

Source: IPPSR (2009).

religious congregations are effective. In 2001, state residents were asked whether they thought that religious congregations were effective in serving the needs of the poor. Over 95 percent of Michigan residents saw congregations as either very effective or somewhat effective. Twenty-four percent of the population reported that congregations are very effective.

Because different questions were asked, it is, unfortunately, not possible to directly compare public attitudes toward religious organizations and secular non-profit charitable organizations. It does seem reasonable to argue, however, that the data reviewed here support the general conclusion that charitable organizations of all types enjoy strong public goodwill. What is not as clear, however, is whether that goodwill translates into support for greater public sector funding of these institutions. In the same 2001 State of the State Survey that revealed over 95 percent agreement with the notion that religious congregations were at least somewhat effective in providing social services, 59 percent of the same residents were in favor of increasing public funding to religious congregations to expand their social service programs.

Summary

There can be little doubt that nonprofit voluntary organizations play an important role in the network of organizations that produce and distribute publicly funded goods and services in the United States. Moreover, there is a good deal of evidence that there is public support for this arrangement. Nongovernmental organizations have long been seen in American culture as desirable alternatives to more formal public institutions. Widespread suspicion of public institutions has long been characteristic of American political culture, and recent public opinion data suggest that such mistrust may be increasing. In contrast, the public continues to see nongovernmental voluntary organizations as effective and deserving of public support.

The status of faith-based organizations in the overall social welfare is, of course, more complex. This is due in part to the fact that a good deal of faith-based activity is largely hidden from public view. As Cnaan (2006) and his associates have noted, faith-based organizations sometimes provide a wide range of social services without any government support at all. Such activities tend not to be highly visible beyond a rather narrow target audience. Efforts like the National Congregations Study, however, strongly suggest that faith-based organizations not only serve as private social service agencies but are quite active in the provision of publicly financed goods and services. The key to understanding the impact of such efforts is to identify where such engagement occurs, what organizations are active in the process, and what public goods are actually being provided. The other part of the puzzle is to assess such efforts in light of companion services provided by secular nonprofits and the interactions of both types of nonprofits with each other and with government. This broader context forms the focus of the new data analysis presented in the rest of this book.

Notes

1. These data include respondents who claimed they trusted government "most of the time" and those reporting that they trusted government "some of the time."

2. At the time of the 1994 survey, Bill Clinton (D) was president of the United States, with a Democratic majority in both the House and Senate. From 1995 to 2000, Clinton faced a Republican-controlled Congress. George W. Bush was president during the 2002, 2005, and 2008 surveys. While the Senate was evenly split, Republicans held an advantage in the House of representatives in 2001 and 2002; Republicans controlled Congress in 2005 and Democrats in 2008. At the time of the 2009 survey, Barack Obama (D) was paired with a Democratic Congress. This suggests that public sentiment toward the federal government was not necessarily tied to one party being in majority control. At the state level, John Engler (R) was governor of Michigan from 1994 to 2004; Jennifer Granholm (D) was the governor of Michigan when the 2005–2009 surveys were conducted. The Republican party had control of the Michigan legislature in 1995–1996 and 2005–2006. Control of the House and Senate was split in 2002–2003 and 2008–2009. Both Engler and Granholm saw shifts in the control of the state legislature under their tenure, one of which gave full party control to Republicans under the Engler administration. Even so, public sentiment was less tied to party control and more to an overall sense of what was and wasn't accomplished by elected officials.

3. The data from the 1998 and 2006–2007 National Congregations Study were downloaded from the Association of Religion Data Archives, www.thearda.com, and were collected by Mark Chaves (Chaves 1998; Chaves and Anderson 2008).

4. The data from the 1996 survey were downloaded from the Association of Religion Data Archives, www.thearda.com, and were collected by Lowell W. Livezey, Elfriede Wedam, and Larry L. Greenfield (Livezey et al. 1996). Religious congregations and government organizations are excluded from the sample.

5. In 1996, 24.5 percent of the service delivery organizations responding to the Chicago Area social service provider survey indicated that policy advocacy was also an important programmatic and service role that they played.

6. The data from the 1994 survey were downloaded from the Association of Religion Data Archives, www.thearda.com, and were collected by Lowell W. Livezey, Elfriede Wedam, Paul D. Numrich, David D. Daniels, Larry G. Murphy, Matthew J. Price, Peter R. D'Agostino, Janise Hurtig, and William Peterman (Livezey et al. 1994).

7. For the purposes of the Michigan State of the State Surveys, charitable organizations are defined as those organizations that are involved in giving, donating, providing, caring for others, or helping others in general (IPPSR1997).

8. Negative perceptions based on the aftermath of Hurricane Katrina (21.5 percent), perceptions of mishandling/mismanagement of funds (21 percent) and being ineffective at helping those in need (12.1 percent), and a general lack of trust (20.2 percent) are the most commonly cited reasons that people were less willing to trust charitable organizations.

References

Blackwood, Amy, Kennard T. Wing, and Thomas H. Pollak. 2008. *The Nonprofit Sector in Brief*. Washington, DC: Urban Institute.

Chaves, Mark. 1998. *National Congregations Study: Data File and Codebook*. Tucson: University of Arizona, Department of Sociology. http://www.thearda.com.

Chaves, Mark, and Shawna Anderson. 2008. *National Congregations Study: Cumulative Data File and Codebook*. Durham, NC: Duke University, Department of Sociology. http://www.thearda.com.

Chaves, Mark, Shawna Anderson, and Jason Byassee. 2009. *America's Congregations at the Beginning of the 21st Century.* National Congregations Study. www.soc.duke.edu/natcong/Docs/NCSII_report_final.pdf.

Cnaan, Ram A. 2006. *The Other Philadelphia Story: How Local Congregations Support Quality of Life in Urban America.* Philadelphia: University of Pennsylvania Press.

de Toqueville, Alexis. 1969. *Democracy in America.* NY: Harper and Row. (Orig. pub. 1835).

Gormley, William T. 1991. *Privatization and Its Alternatives.* La Follette Public Policy Series. Madison: University of Wisconsin Press.

Hanke, Steve H., and Academy of Political Science (U.S.). 1987. *Prospects for Privatization.* New York: Academy of Political Science.

Hula, Richard C. 1988. *Market-Based Public Policy.* London: Macmillian.

Hula, Richard C., Cynthia Jackson-Elmoore, and Laura A. Reese. 2007. Mixing God's Work and the Public Business: A Framework for the Analysis of Faith-Based Service Delivery. *Review of Policy Research* 24(1): 67–89.

Institute for Public Policy and Social Research. 1997. *State of the State Survey* 10 (Winter). East Lansing: Michigan State University. www.ippsr.msu.edu/SOSS.

———. 2009. Longitudinal State of the State Survey Data File, 1994–2005. *SOSS* 1–48. www.ippsr.msu.edu/SOSS.

IPPSR. *See* Institute for Public Policy and Social Research.

Jackson, Cynthia Y. 1994. Production and Financing Choices for Municipal Services: Contracting and Franchising. Ph.D. dissertation, University of Southern California, Los Angeles.

Livezey, Lowell W., Elfriede Wedam, and Larry L. Greenfield. 1996. *Survey of Religious, Social Service and Community Organizations in Metropolitan Chicago.* www.thearda.com.

Livezey, Lowell W., Elfriede Wedam, Paul D. Numrich, David D. Daniels, Larry G. Murphy, Matthew J. Price, Peter R. D'Agostino, Janise Hurtig, and William Peterman. 1994. *Survey of Congregations in Metropolitan Chicago.* www.thearda.com.

Osborne, David, and Ted Gaebler. 1992. *Reinventing Government: How the Entrepreneurial Spirit Is Transforming the Public Sector.* Reading, MA: Addison-Wesley.

Roper Center. 2008. *Public Opinion Archives: Confidence in Institutions.* Surveys by the Gallup Organization. www.ropercenter.uconn.edu.

Salamon, Lester M. 2001. Scope and Structure: The Anatomy of America's Nonprofit Sector. In *The Nature of the Nonprofit Sector,* ed. J. Steven Ott, 23–39. Boulder, CO: Westview Press.

Salamon, Lester M., and H.K. Anheier. 1997. *Defining the Nonprofit Sector: A Cross-National Analysis.* New York: St. Martin's Press.

Savas, Emanuel S. 2000. *Privatization and Public-Private Partnerships.* New York: Chatham House.

4

Mapping the Civil Society

Methods and Data

Faith-based organizations (FBOs) define only one element of an enormously complex network of actors and institutions within the civic society. Understanding the public policy role of FBOs is further complicated by a relative absence of empirical research or even accessible descriptive data. In an effort to limit this complexity, the research design underlying this work focuses on one state: Michigan. There are several advantages to a single-state approach. Examination of faith-based service provision within a single state controls for state legislation in housing, community development, and public funding. A single-state focus also allows for in-depth understanding of the methods and outcomes of faith-based service provision. The use of one state admittedly reduces the potential generalizability of findings. However, the state of Michigan presents a relatively representative case on a number of important of economic, demographic, and political dimensions.

While often characterized as a classic Rust Belt state, there are many areas of Michigan that remain rural, or where the primary source of income is tied to tourism and agriculture, or both. Michigan, the eighth most populous state, also has a high percentage of minorities and ethnic groups concentrated in distinct geographical regions. There are areas of the state that are distinctly more liberal, whereas others are conservative in both political and lifestyle preferences. Many blue-collar communities in Michigan experienced in-migration from the South beginning in the early twentieth century and, at the start of the twenty-first century, remained distinctly working class. Other areas in the state have seen a suburban explosion of middle-class and upper-middle-class wealth. Thus, Michigan embodies a microcosm sufficiently heterogeneous in client groups and service nonprofits to provide a good sense of changing modes of public service provision. As one of the earliest U.S. states hit by the global recession of the early twenty-first century, it also illustrates the role of nonprofits in a time of increasing challenges to state and local public service provision.

Overall Research Strategy

A nested research design was employed using data from surveys, face-to-face interviews, network analysis, and archival analysis (Bennett 2002; Coppedge 2002). The benefits of nested research designs are that they combine data sets amenable to statistical analysis with in-depth examinations that can address factors and forces not visible in aggregate data. The nested approach also increases the validity of measurement instruments and enhances the ability to make causal connections (Lieberman 2002). In short, combining qualitative and quantitative methods provides the depth and complexity revealed by individual cases and the power of broader statistical patterns. Such a design is essential to the study of faith-based service provision for several reasons:

- There is little extant quantitative research on the topic. While the national studies by Chaves (1999, 2004) provide critical information on faith-based community development activities, the questions are too general to elicit the detailed information necessary to understand the changing nature of government funding of faith-based service provision and comparisons between faith-based and secular nonprofits are not possible.
- Many existing case studies provide limited and nongeneralizable snapshots of the activities of just a few, often atypically large and well-resourced, FBOs. This research design provides generalizable data, amenable to statistical analysis, but also includes the qualitative analysis necessary to present a more complete sense of innovations in faith-based service provision and the nature of relationships between government and faith-based organizations.
- Triangulation of data collection and analysis methods provides for more accurate results, allows for comparisons and validation across methods, and accesses and presents information in multiple ways (Denzin 1984; Flick 1998; Stake 2000). Just as some information is better measured by open versus forced-choice questions, the use of network analysis and interviews provides a different view of the world than survey responses.

The rest of the chapter focuses on two key elements of the research design: the data collection process and analysis strategies. Additional methodological details are provided in Appendix A.

Data Sources

Both quantitative and qualitative data are employed in this analysis. Quantitative data from several preexisting surveys are used to set the context for the analysis conducted in this study. The major sources of new quantitative data include three separate surveys, one of which was designed and administered directly by the research team and two of which were provided by an organizational partner for the study. The surveys are:

1. *Michigan CDC Accomplishments Survey* (2003 CEDAM Survey). The Community Economic Development Association of Michigan (CEDAM) provided raw data from a general mail survey sent to all members of the

organization. CEDAM is a nonprofit that served as an organizational partner for part of the research.[1]

2. *Community Economic Development Association of Michigan Industry Survey* (2007 CEDAM Survey).[2] CEDAM provided raw data from a second general mail survey sent to all members of the organization. The questions on the second survey varied in some cases from the original survey conducted four years prior.

3. *Nonprofit Housing Provider Survey*. This mail survey sent to a broad population of housing providers included extensive questions related to housing provision, focusing on differences between faith-based and secular organizations. This survey was constructed by the authors and distributed in 2007 and 2008. While including a number of questions from the first CEDAM survey for comparability, the Nonprofit Housing Provider Survey was more extensive and detailed and was sent to a larger population.

Substantive Focus of Key Surveys

Michigan CDC Accomplishments Survey 2003 CEDAM Survey

Questions for this pilot survey were written by CEDAM administrators and were primarily designed to improve member services (the complete 2003 CEDAM survey is provided in Appendix A1). CEDAM staff conducted the survey via telephone and mail between Fall 2003 through Spring 2004. The survey collected baseline data on housing production, commercial development, open-space and green-space development, and community facilities development. Data were also collected on the services associated with housing, community building, and economic development provided by CDCs, as well as technical assistance, and capacity-building needs, and general demographics. Respondents included both faith-based and secular CDCs[3]; thus it was possible to isolate housing and community development activities as well as service activities associated with the development activities for each type of nonprofit and compare them.

CEDAM Industry Survey 2007 CEDAM Survey

In August 2007 CEDAM staff conducted a second membership survey via telephone, mail, and the Web using Survey Monkey.[4] Questions were written by CEDAM staff and were primarily designed to assess the impact of CDCs in Michigan's neighborhoods and communities (the complete 2007 survey is provided in Appendix A2). Similar to the earlier survey, this survey collected data on Michigan CDC operations, housing production, commercial development, open- and green-space development, and community facilities development. Data were also collected on the services associated with housing, community building, asset building, social services, and economic development provided by CDCs. The survey included questions about the funding environment, policy environment, and other factors influencing the ability to provide products and services.

Nonprofit Housing Provider Survey

The authors conducted a mail survey of nonprofit (secular and faith-based) service providers in the housing and community development arena in Michigan, between Fall 2007 through Spring 2008 (Nonprofit Housing Provider Survey 2007–2008). The purpose of the survey was to ascertain levels and nature of activity, organizational goals, overall impact of policy efforts of the organization, nature of clients, service provision modalities, degree and nature of collaboration in the service delivery network, funding sources and arrangements, and other organizational structural attributes. Questions for the survey were drawn from other surveys employed in several published studies (Chaves 1998; Reese and Shields 1999, 2002; Reese 2000, 2004; Chaves and Tsitsos 2001; Reese et al. 2002; Chaves 2004; CEDAM 2004; Owens and Smith 2005). Questions were added and some revisions made to adapt previously tested surveys to the purposes of this study. Question formats included open-ended and forced-choice questions. Questions focusing on collaboration and service partners were formatted so that subsequent network analysis could be applied. The final survey, reviewed by the Michigan State University Institutional Review Board (IRB), focused on the following issues:

- Extent of religious affiliation;
- Nature of religious affiliation (for FBOs);
- Internal capacity (e.g., staff, volunteers, budget);
- Organizational structure of housing activities;
- Number and type of housing activities;
- Funding sources;
- Nature of clients served (e.g., neighborhood or citywide, age, race);
- Perceived success of activities;
- Participation in collaboration with faith-based, secular, and/or public organizations;
- Other electoral or political activities of service providers;
- Extent of cooperation with citizen or community-based groups; and
- Attitudes about, and experiences with, public funding.

The complete survey is contained in Appendix A3.

Target Populations, Response Rates, and Representativeness

The population for the 2003 and 2007 CEDAM surveys was composed of members of CEDAM and the Michigan Training and Technical Assistance Collaborative (MITTAC). The statewide nonprofit housing survey conducted by the authors was sent to the population of nonprofit housing providers in the state. Since there was no preexisting list of housing service providers in the state (and this is probably the case in most states), significant effort was devoted to creating a list that represented, as closely as possible, the population of nonprofit housing providers. Appendix A4 provides greater detail on the survey populations. Response rates were as follows:

- *2003 CEDAM Survey:* A total of 176 surveys were distributed, with a 51 percent response rate. Because the survey was conducted by CEDAM prior to any involvement by the authors, attempts to enhance response rate were not controlled.
- *2007 CEDAM Survey:* A total of 185 surveys were distributed, with a 44 percent response rate. The CEDAM staff made numerous attempts to get responses from all of the organization's membership and eventually made the decision to "balance the interest of time against the interest of 'perfect' data" (CEDAM 2008, 9).
- *Nonprofit Housing Provider Survey:* After extensive efforts to attain the highest response rate possible, 99 out of 386 organizations responded to the survey, a 26 percent response rate. While not exemplary, this is an adequate response rate and certainly within the range of rates for other mail surveys administered to nonprofit organizations since the late 1990s (Babbie 1990; Hager et al. 2003). The most likely response bias would be for the most active housing service providers to be represented.[5]

Representativeness of survey respondents appears quite sound on a number of attributes including geographic location, urban, suburban, and rural organizations, and population size of the city where the nonprofits are located.

2003 CEDAM Survey: The regional distribution of respondents matched that of the membership base throughout the state (Table 4.1, Maps 4.1 and 4.2).

2007 CEDAM Survey: The survey represented organizations from over 30 cities and approximately 30 counties across Michigan (CEDAM 2008), serving urban, suburban, and rural populations (Map 4.3, Figure 4.1). The regional distribution of the respondents matched that of the membership base throughout the state relatively closely, with some underrepresentation of the southwest and central regions and overrepresentation of the Detroit area (Table 4.2).

Nonprofit Housing Provider Survey: Survey respondents were located in all regions and urban areas of the state (see Map 4.4) and covered 35 counties. It is useful to clarify again that this was a population survey rather than a sample; no sampling frame was used and sampling statistics are not calculable. The respondents were compared to the population where possible and found to be quite representative. Data available for comparison primarily related to geographic attributes and included: city of location, city population, county of location, and zip code of location. Other attributes desirable for comparison such as faith-based versus

Table 4.1

Regional Distribution of Survey Respondents and CEDAM/MITTAC Membership

Michigan Region	Respondents	Population
Upper Peninsula	6%	3%
Northern Lower/Thumb	6%	5%
Southwest	15%	15%
Central	10%	13%
Southeast	23%	20%
Historical Michigan (Detroit)	40%	44%
N	90	176

Table 4.2

Regional Distribution of 2007 CEDAM Survey Respondents and CEDAM/MITTAC Membership

Michigan Region	Respondents	Population
Upper Peninsula	9%	3%
Northern Lower/Thumb	7%	5%
Southwest	18%	15%
Central	18%	13%
Southeast	16%	20%
Historical Michigan (Detroit)	32%	44%
N	82	182

secular nature, size, activities, and so on were impossible to obtain since such data were not available for nonrespondents. Overall, responding organizations were located in communities that were much the same size as those of the population of organizations. There does not appear to be any systematic bias in location of respondents (see Table 4.3). Although responding organizations were located in cities with slightly lower population sizes, the difference is not significant.

The respondent and population organizations did not differ by county of location by more than two cases for 51 of Michigan's 83 counties (see Table 4.4). There are 22 counties not represented in the data set; however, they had fewer than two organizations within the population. Representation of counties in the data set differs by more than 3 percent for only three counties: Ingham (4.6 percent more in the population), Kent (5.2 percent more among respondents), and Wayne (3.1 percent more in the population).[6]

Finally, there were 175 total zip codes in the population; 105 of these are not represented among respondents. Most of the missing zip codes had very few organizations in them, however. The largest missing zip code had fourteen organizations in it. The most underrepresented zip codes are as follows:

Map 4.1 **CEDAM Regions**

Source: Community and Economic Development Association of Michigan (2004, p. 21).

1. **Upper Peninsula** counties: Alger, Baraga, Chippewa, Delta, Dickinson, Gogebic, Houghton, Iron, Keweenaw, Luce, Ontonagon, Mackinac, Marquette, Menominee, Schoolcraft

2. **Northern Michigan** counties: Alcona, Alpena, Antrim, Arenac, Benzie, Charlevoix, Cheboygan, Crawford, Clare, Emmet, Gladwin, Grand Traverse, Huron, Iosco, Kalkaska, Lake, Leelanau, Manistee, Mason, Mecosta, Missaukee, Montmorency, Ogemaw, Osceola, Oscoda, Otsego, Presque Isle, Roscommon, Sanilac, Tuscola, Wexford

3. **Southwest Michigan** counties: Allegan, Barry, Berrien, Branch, Calhoun, Cass, Kalamazoo, Kent, Muskegon, Newaygo, Oceana, Ottawa, St. Joseph, Van Buren

4. **Central Michigan** counties: Bay, Clinton, Eaton, Gratiot, Hillsdale, Ingham, Ionia, Isabella, Jackson, Midland, Montcalm, Saginaw, Shiawassee

5. **Southeast Michigan** counties: Genesee, Lapeer, Lenawee, Livingston, Macomb, Monroe, Oakland, St. Clair, Washtenaw, Wayne [excluding Detroit]

6. **Historical Michigan:** This region includes Detroit, Hamtramck, and Highland Park.

Map 4.2   Location of CDC Members Responding to the 2003 CEDAM Survey

Source: Community and Economic Development Association of Michigan (2004, p. 12).

- 48723 (Caro): missing fourteen organizations;
- 48912 (Lansing): missing eight organizations;
- 48203 (Highland Park): missing six organizations.

Respondents overrepresent several zip codes; there are only three where the respondents and population differ by 2 percent or more. All of these are areas of central cities where public housing needs are greatest and hence there are the most providers:

- 48201 (Detroit): difference = 2.1 percent;
- 49503: (Grand Rapids): difference = 2.1 percent;
- 48503: (Flint): difference = 2.0 percent.

Map 4.3   **Location of CEDAM Members Responding to the 2007 Survey**

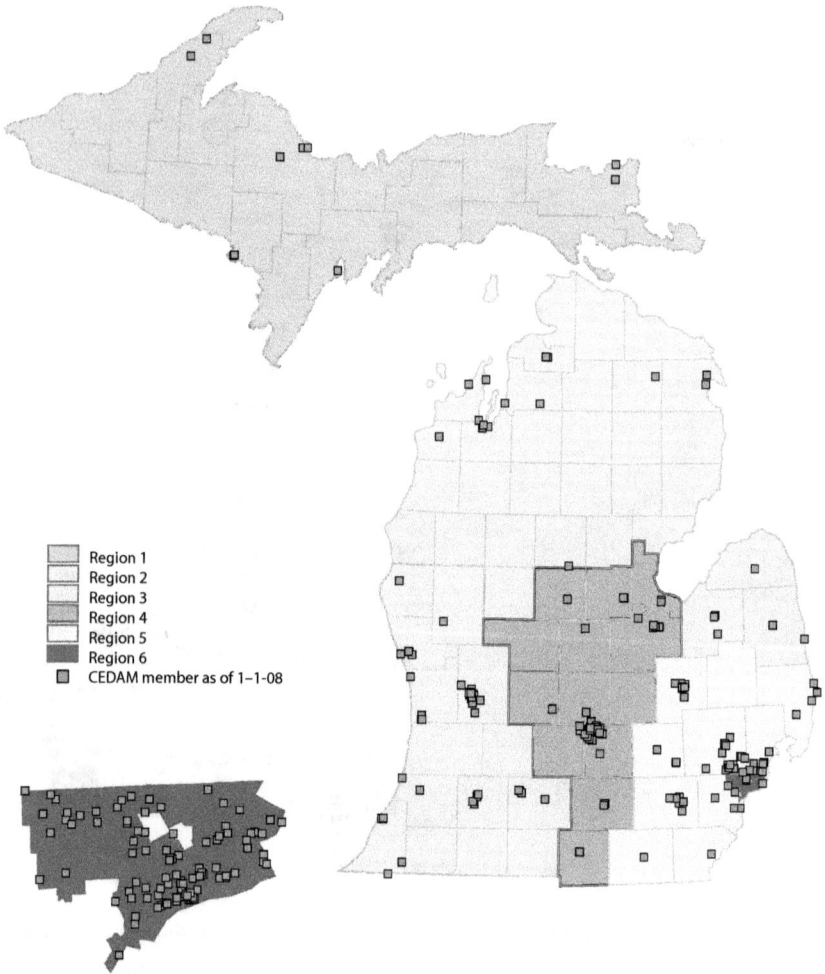

Region 1
Region 2
Region 3
Region 4
Region 5
Region 6
☐ CEDAM member as of 1–1-08

Source: Community and Economic Development Association of Michigan (2008, p. 55).

Qualitative Analysis

In addition to the quantitative data obtained from the surveys discussed above, qualitative data from a number of sources were employed in this research. These included a set of open-ended questions in each of the surveys, mission statements published by faith-based organizations, and a variety of public documents. In addition to these sources, face-to-face interviews were conducted in three housing provider networks to attain greater detail on each housing system (target regions are

Figure 4.1   **Communities Served by Members of the CEDAM/MITTAC**

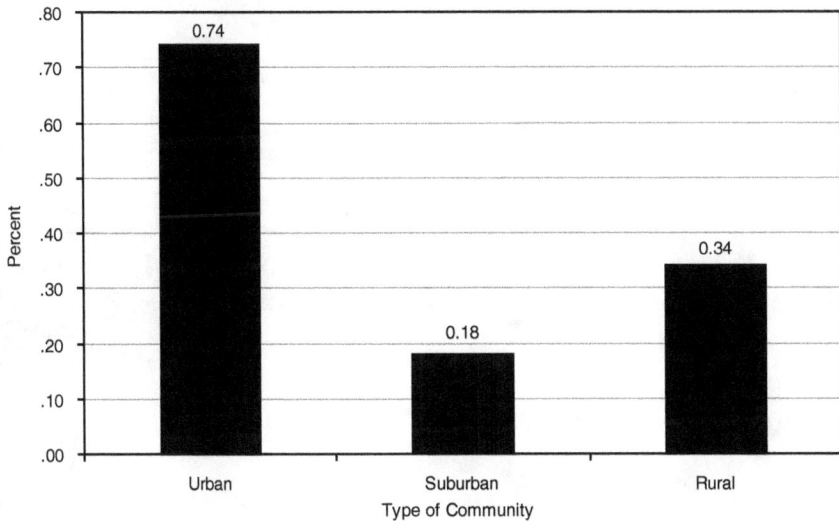

described in the next section). Appendix A5 specifies the individuals interviewed (by professional role) in each of the regions. Interview questions are provided in Appendix A6 and generally focused on the following topics or themes:

- General state housing policy and funding mechanisms
- Local organizations involved in housing
- Assessment of organizational capacities, abilities, and effectiveness
- Secular versus faith-based housing activity and contribution
- Extent of cooperation and competition between housing providers
- Involvement of nonprofit providers over time
- Connections between housing provision and political or policy activism
- Connections between housing provision and other community activities.

Network Analysis

Network analysis was employed for data analysis purposes but was also used to select regions of the state for face-to-face interviews. Social network analysis allows for exploration of ties, connections, and attachments among groups and focuses on the social context and behavior of relationships between actors (Scott 1991; Durland and Fredericks 2005). Network analysis measures underlying relationships and transactions, shows subsets of actors within a network that have ties to other networks, describes how centralized or decentralized a network is,

Map 4.4   **Respondents to Nonprofit Housing Provider Survey**

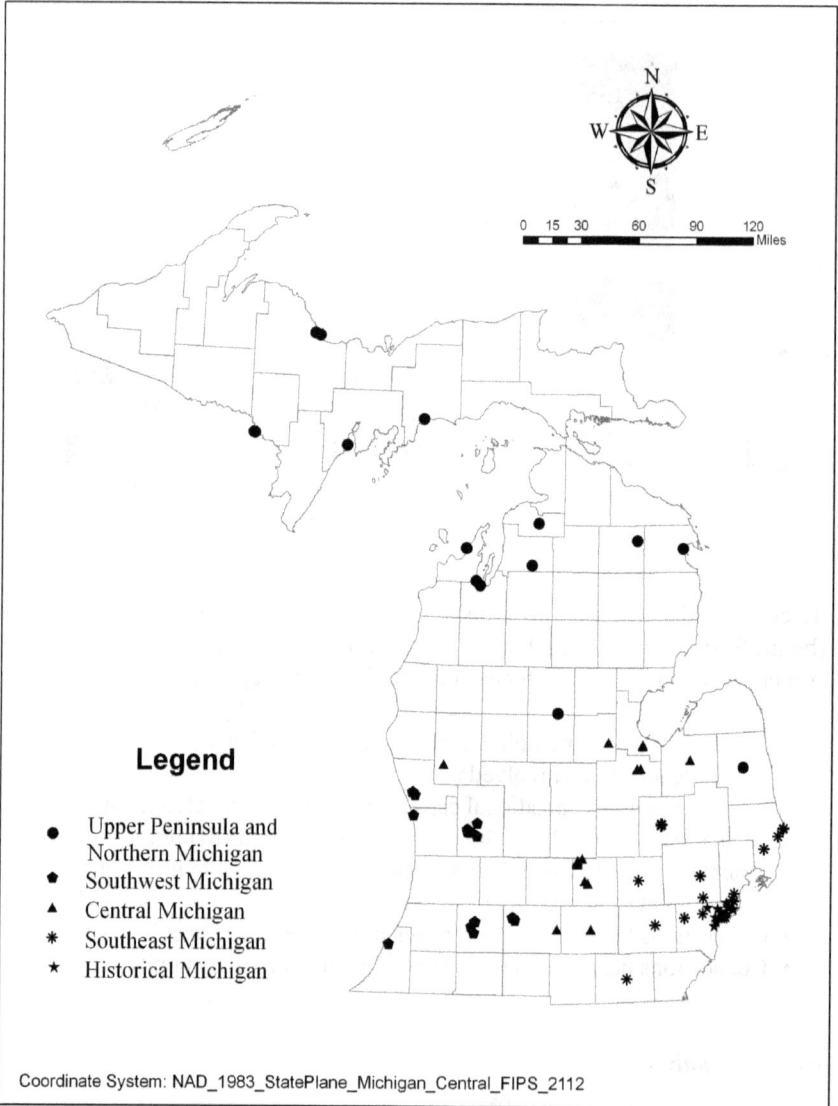

Coordinate System: NAD_1983_StatePlane_Michigan_Central_FIPS_2112

Created by Minting Ye.

identifies reciprocity among groups, and portrays the total connections or ties among actors (in this case service providers). This is done statistically through the use of algorithms and the examination of structural elements such as dyads or cliques (Jablin and Putnam 2001; Durland and Fredericks 2005; Hanneman and Riddle 2005). The program UCINET, version 6.166,was used to analyze the

Table 4.3

Population of Municipalities (Nonprofit Housing Provider Survey)

	Minimum	Maximum	Mean	Median
Respondents	2,267	951,270	265,146	77,145
Population	1,055	951,270	343,476	119,128

Mean difference: 78,330
Median difference: 41,983
$t = 1.70$ critical $t = 1.96$

Table 4.4

Responding Organizations by County Differing by Two or More Cases
(Nonprofit Housing Provider Survey)

County	Respondent %	Population %	Difference
Ingham	5.6	10.2	4.6
Kent	10.1	4.9	5.2
Oakland	3.4	5.7	2.3
Saginaw	3.4	1.5	1.9
Tuscola	1.1	3.8	2.7
Washtenaw	1.1	2.4	1.3
Wayne	25.8	28.9	3.1
Calhoun	3.4	0.9	2.5
Dickinson	2.2	0.7	1.5
Grand Traverse	2.2	0.9	1.3

survey questions explicitly included for this purpose (Borgatti 2002; Borgatti et al. 2002).

Social network analysis provides a way to model relationships and determine how those relationships structure intense and complex interactions among multiple actors (Scott 2000). There are two primary network analysis techniques: centrality and structural equivalence analysis. The former maps power positions among actors in a network including the number of ties an actor has to others (degree centrality), distance from one actor to others in the network (closeness centrality), and the extent to which an actor is positioned between other actors (betweenness and centrality). The latter examines whether actors within a particular group have the same ties to the same other actors (Hanneman 2001; Ren 2007). While the focus is on the structure of relationships, it is also important to maintain perspective on the discrete contributions and roles of individuals and organizations, and similarly, to understand the underlying value systems that facilitate, nurture, and solidify social relations (Emirbayer and Goodwin 1994). Therefore, it is often useful to combine social network analysis with other methodologies to ensure a fuller understanding of the nature of interactions and impacts of various actors. Network analysis is one component of this multi-method study, which, among other things, examines the attitudes, actions, and impacts of organizational leaders engaged in affordable housing provision.

A data set of partnerships among organizations and institutions involved in affordable housing was created based on responses to questions on the Nonprofit Housing Provider Survey that asked organization respondents to identify their collaborators on housing-related activities. Visual representations of these data were then created using the NetDraw program available in UCINET Version 6.166 (Borgatti et al. 2002; Borgatti 2002). Findings indicated that most of the partnerships occurred at the local or metropolitan regional scale, except for partnerships with state and federal housing bureaucracies. As will be described more fully later, because of the number of cases and complexity of ties, network analysis was most easily interpretable when conducted separately for different regions of the state. Specifically five regional networks were analyzed: Northern Michigan (upper and upper lower peninsula), Southwestern Michigan, Southeastern Michigan, Mid-Michigan, and the city of Detroit. The latter was broken out from the rest of Southeastern Michigan because the density of the Detroit network made interpretation difficult.

Three of the regional networks appeared theoretically interesting: the Detroit network, the Southwest Region (with the core being the Grand Rapids metropolitan area), and the Northern Michigan region. These three networks were the focus of subsequent face-to-face interviews. The Detroit network was chosen because of the high representation of faith-based nonprofits. The centrality of faith-based organizations appears to coincide with a lesser role for government within the network. Further, there are only limited ties between faith-based and public sector actors: the city of Detroit itself appears particularly isolated. In comparison, the Grand Rapids area network illustrates closer ties between faith-based and governmental actors. Indeed, several primary core organizations (or governing nonprofits) are visible, whereas the Detroit network is more fragmented. Finally, the Northern Michigan network provides a view of service provision in a more rural context. Here faith-based organizations appear less important with secular nonprofits having a more primary role. As in Detroit, public sector actors are not well represented in the network. In short, three separate models are represented by the case networks:

- Strong faith presence with moderate local government (Detroit network);
- Strong secular presence with weak local government (Northern network);
- Partnerships between a core of nonprofit and public actors (Grand Rapids network).

Analytical Techniques

Data from surveys and interviews were analyzed using a variety of methods. Because the mailed surveys included both open and closed question formats, statistical as well as network (as previously discussed) and content analysis were conducted.

In addition to survey responses, the websites of all responding organizations were examined and their mission statements content analyzed to assess and compare overall purposes and emphases.

The quantitative analysis of survey data presented later in the book includes basic descriptive statistics, factor analysis for the purpose of data reduction and the identification of underlying concepts within the data, and various correlational techniques: crosstabs, difference in means tests, bivariate correlations, and regression analysis. Factor analysis frequently underlies much of the subsequent analyses. Factor analysis "is an exploratory multivariate technique used to assess the dimensionality of a set of variables," for example "to assess whether a number of scales have a single dimension underlying them" (Green and Salkind 2003, 295). It is a data reduction technique that reduces a large number of potentially overlapping variables or measures into a smaller number of factors. Factor analysis can be used for "exploration" to identify any underlying dimensions in a set of data, or for "confirmation" to test for the presence of theoretically identified factors. A primary use of factor analysis is for classification or description where "interdependent variables" are grouped into "descriptive categories . . . with similar characteristics or behavior" (Rummel 2002, 6). In the case of the research here, survey questions that measure similar behaviors or attitudes can be grouped together to form conceptually unique factors; thus factor analysis is used to "define dimensions underlying existing measurement instruments," that is, the CEDAM and MSU survey questions (Green and Salkind 2003, 297). Factor analysis involves two stages: (1) extracting factors from a correlation matrix using principal components analysis to account for the largest amount of variability among the variables included in the survey and (2) rotating factors to create solutions with different numbers of factors to settle on the one that is most interpretable. Thus, while the unrotated factors successively define general patterns within the data, rotated factors "delineate the distinct clusters of relationships, if such exist" (Rummel 2002, 23). Varimax rotation is used throughout to create uncorrelated factors (orthogonal). This means that the factor loadings, but not necessarily the resulting indices, are uncorrelated (Rummel 2002) and are more clearly interpretable than if oblique rotation were employed (Green and Salkind 2003). Final factor solutions are based on four criteria:

- a priori expectations about the factors based on previous research or theory;
- absolute values of the eigenvalues;
- relative values of eigenvalues; and
- relative interpretability of rotated solutions (Green and Salkind 2003, 298).

Responses to open-ended questions were recorded verbatim and analyzed using QSR NVivo 8 software. Mission statements were analyzed in the same manner. The data analysis sections that follow incorporate the findings of the content analysis in narrative fashion and also indicate where qualitative information derived from the analysis in QSR NVivo 8 and network analysis were used to create new variables and entered back into the SPSS 17 database.

Figure 4.2   **Managing and Analyzing Qualitative Data**

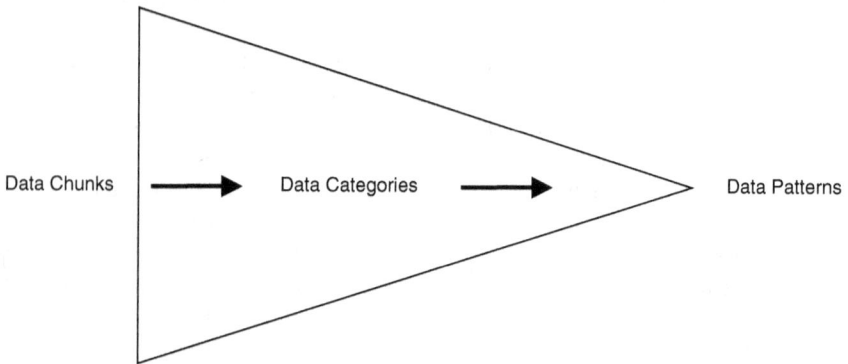

The qualitative data in the study were managed through a four-step iterative process:

1. Open-ended survey questions were read and memoed to develop familiarity with the data and identify main themes. Memoing provided an opportunity to record initial insights and questions that emerged immediately after reviewing the data.[7]
2. The survey data were then examined to develop detailed and comprehensive descriptions of the context in which organizations conducted their activities, key stakeholders, collaborators, and networks.
3. The third step of the data management process was data classification. This included categorizing, coding, and grouping the data into thematic units.
4. The final step involved identifying data patterns—in other words, interpreting and synthesizing the organized data into general conclusions.

This process was repeated for all of the qualitative data including open-ended survey questions, interview notes, and organizational records. In the case of interview notes and organizational records, step two also involved developing detailed descriptions of the setting, participants, activities, and knowledge and awareness of political engagement and impact. Thus the broad framework for analyzing the qualitative data can be summarized as a process of going from a large amount of data chunks (or pieces of data) to data categories and finally a winnowing down to data patterns (Figure 4.2).

The overall analytic strategy outlined here allows for consideration of multiple hypotheses and provides a robust investigation of research questions (Lijphart 1971; Yin 1994; Marshall and Rossman 1999). The quantitative and qualitative data are examined to determine whether they provide convergent analysis or contradictory findings in need of reconciliation. The combination of methods provides a stronger overall analysis than would single analytic techniques (Creswell et al. 2003) and ensures that all elements of the theoretical models presented in Chapter 1 are fully and robustly tested. The following analysis chapters provide data, interpretations, and conclusions based on these mixed methodological approaches. Multiple waves of surveys along with the contextual information drawn from the interviews and content analysis provide an in-depth assessment of the service and, ultimately, political roles of nonprofits, particularly those that are faith-based, in civil society.

Notes

1. CEDAM is a voluntary association of CDCs (community development corporations), individuals, and other organizations focused on promoting and expanding community-based housing and economic development in Michigan. CEDAM activities include building the capacity of CDCs and other community development partners; generating public and private resources for CDCs; providing a forum for member input in public policy debates; and bringing local, regional, and national organizations together to foster community-based economic development (CEDAM 2004).

2. Throughout this book, the Michigan CDC Accomplishments Survey is referred to as the 2003 CEDAM Survey and the CEDAM Industry Survey is referred to as the 2007 CEDAM Survey.

3. The survey did not contain a question indicating whether an organization was faith-based, a drawback of both CEDAM surveys (the statewide survey conducted by the authors did explicitly question respondents about faith nature). Common sense suggests that the faith orientation of an organization cannot be determined by name alone. Though it may be less apparent, a simple examination of organizational mission statements is also fallible since an organization may not be explicit about its religious intent and purpose. Empirical findings demonstrate this as well (Ebaugh et al. 2003). This research employs self-identification measures to determine whether an organization is faith based or secular. Accordingly, responding organizations were contacted by the research team via telephone and e-mail to identify the extent and nature of their religious or secular status. Among the 90 organizations, 29 identified themselves in the follow-up phone call as faith-based, 51 as secular, and 11 organizations could not be reached to verify their status.

4. The primary delivery method for this survey was by mail. However, instructions on the survey directed members to CEDAM's website to access the survey via the Web using Survey Monkey. Members also had the opportunity to schedule a phone appointment to complete the survey with a member of the CEDAM staff. Any member that did not complete and return the survey by the designated deadline was then called to schedule a phone appointment to complete it (CEDAM 2007).

5. An advance recruitment letter explaining the project and inviting participation in the study was mailed one month before surveys were distributed in October of 2007. After the survey was mailed, postcard reminders were sent, followed by a re-mailing of the survey to nonrespondents. About two months after the survey was initiated, all nonresponding organizations were contacted by phone. In some cases the organizations were no longer in existence and they were removed from the population list. Any organization that no longer had its survey was

sent another. Six months from the time of the original survey mailing, all CEDAM members (the core of the population list) were sent a reminder letter encouraging them to respond to the survey, from the director of CEDAM (on CEDAM letterhead), along with yet another survey. In short, every reasonable effort was made to increase response rates.

6. This overrepresentation is probably due to the use of the membership list from the Community Development Advocates of Detroit (CDAD). That organizations within Detroit zip codes specifically are only overrepresented by 2 percent, however, suggests that the use of this list has not significantly caused Detroit nonprofits to be overrepresented and most probably accurately reflects the greater involvement of particularly faith-based nonprofits in service provision in Detroit (Reese 2004).

7. Memoing occurred right after each interview so that immediate reactions could be noted. If additional insights, questions, and reactions emerged after reading the interview notes, these notes were also memoed.

References

Babbie, Eric R. 1990. *Survey Research Methods.* Belmont, CA: Wadsworth.

Bennett, Andrew. 2002. Where the Model Frequently Meets the Road: Combining Statistical, Formal, and Case Study Methods. Paper presented at the annual meeting of the American Political Science Association.

Borgatti, Steve P. 2002. *NetDraw: Graph Visualization Software.* Harvard, MA: Analytic Technologies.

Borgatti, Steve P., Martin G. Everett, and Linton C. Freeman. 2002. *UCINET for Windows: Software for Social Network Analysis* (Version 6.166). Harvard, MA: Analytic Technologies.

CEDAM. *See* Community Economic Development Association of Michigan.

Chaves, Mark. 1998. *National Congregations Study: Data File and Codebook.* Tucson: University of Arizona, Department of Sociology.

———. 1999. *Congregations' Social Service Activities.* (Policy brief). Washington, DC: Urban Institute.

———. 2004. *Congregations in America.* Cambridge, MA: Harvard University Press.

Chaves, Mark, and William Tsitsos. 2001. Congregations and Social Services: What They Do, How They Do It, and with Whom. *Nonprofit and Voluntary Sector Quarterly* 30(4): 660–683.

Community Economic Development Association of Michigan (CEDAM). 2004. *Standing Strong: Rebuilding Neighborhoods and Revitalizing Communities: 2004 CED Accomplishments.* Lansing, MI: CEDAM.

———. 2008. *CDC Industry Report: Initial Findings.* Detroit: CEDAM.

Coppedge, Michael. 2002. Using Nested Inference to Explain Democratic Deterioration in Venezuela. Paper presented at the annual meeting of the American Political Science Association.

Creswell, John W., Vicki L. Plano Clark, Michelle L. Gutmann, and William E. Hanson. 2003. Advanced Mixed Methods Research Designs. In *Handbook of Mixed Methods in Social and Behavioral Research,* ed. A. Tashakkori and C. Teddlie, 209–240. Thousand Oaks, CA: Sage.

Denzin, Norman K. 1984. *The Research Act.* Englewood Cliffs, NJ: Prentice Hall.

Durland, Maryann M., and Kimberly A. Fredericks. 2005. *Social Network Analysis in Program Evaluation: New Directions for Evaluation.* Vol. 107. San Francisco, CA: Jossey-Bass.

Ebaugh, Helen Rose, Paula F. Pipes, Janet Saltzman Chafetz, and Martha Daniels. 2003. Where's the Religion? Distinguishing Faith-Based from Secular Social Service Agencies. *Journal for the Scientific Study of Religion* 42(3): 411–426.

Emirbayer, Mustafa, and Jeff Goodwin. 1994. Network Analysis, Culture, and the Problem of Agency. *The American Journal of Sociology* 99(6): 1411–1454.

Flick, Uwe. 1998. *An Introduction to Qualitative Research: Theory, Method and Applications.* London: Sage.

Green, Samuel B., and Neil J. Salkind. 2003. *Using SPSS for Windows and Macintosh.* 3d ed. Upper Saddle River, NJ: Prentice Hall.

Hager, Mark A., Sarah Wilson, Thomas H. Pollak, and Patrick Michael Rooney. 2003. Response Rates for Mail Surveys of Nonprofit Organizations: A Review and Empirical Test. *Nonprofit and Voluntary Sector Quarterly* 32(2): 252–267.

Hanneman, Robert A. 2001. *Introduction to Social Network Methods.* faculty.ucr.edu/~hanneman/networks/nettext.pdf.

Hanneman, Robert A., and Mark Riddle. 2005. *Introduction to Social Network Methods.* Riverside: University of California.

Jablin, Fredric M., and Linda Putnam. 2001. *The New Handbook of Organizational Communication: Advances in Theory, Research, and Methods.* Thousand Oaks, CA: Sage.

Lieberman, E.S. 2002. Seeing Both the Forest and the Trees: Nested Analysis in Cross-National Research. Paper presented at the annual meeting of the American Political Science Association, Boston.

Lijphart, Arend. 1971. Comparative Politics and the Comparative Method. *American Political Science Review* 65 (September):682–693.

Marshall, Catherine, and Gretchen B. Rossman. 1999. *Designing Qualitative Research.* 3d ed. Thousand Oaks, CA: Sage.

Owens, Michael L., and R. Drew Smith. 2005. Congregations in Low-Income Neighborhoods and the Implications for Social Welfare Policy Research. *Nonprofit and Voluntary Sector Quarterly* 34(3): 316–339.

Reese, Laura A. 2000. Should the Government Regulate Prophets? Methodological Problems with Research on Faith-Based Economic Development. *Economic Development Quarterly* 14(4): 376–383.

———. 2004. A Matter of Faith: Urban Congregations and Economic Development. *Economic Development Quarterly* 18(1): 50–66.

Reese, Laura A., Raymond A. Rosenfeld, and David Fasenfest. 2002. The State of Local Economic Development Policy. In *The 2002 Municipal Year Book,* 10–17. Washington, DC: International City/County management Association.

Reese, Laura A., and Gary Shields. 1999. Economic Development Activities of Urban Religious Institutions. *International Journal of Economic Development* 2:165–199.

———. 2002. Faith-Based Economic Development. In *Public Policies for Distressed Communities Revisited,* ed. F.S. Redburn and T.F. Buss, 113–125. New York: Lexington Books.

Ren, Xuefei. 2007. Building Globalization: Transnational Architectural Production in Urban China. Ph.D. dissertation, University of Chicago.

Rummel, Rudolph J. 2002. Understanding Factor Analysis. Based on Rummel, R.J., 1970, *Applied Factor Analysis.* www.hawaii.edu/powerkills/UFA.HTM.

Scott, John. 1991. *Social Network Analysis: A Handbook.* Thousand Oaks, CA: Sage.

———. 2000. *Social Network Analysis: A Handbook.* 2d ed. Thousand Oaks, CA: Sage.

Stake, Robert E. 2000. Case Studies. In *Handbook of Qualitative Research* (2d ed.), ed. Norman K. Denzin and Y.S. Lincoln. Thousand Oaks, CA: Sage.

Yin, Robert K. 1994. *Case Study Research: Design and Methods.* 2d ed. Thousand Oaks, CA: Sage.

Part II

A Question of Capacity:

The Debate on the Role and Effectiveness of the Nonprofit Sector

5

Federal Programs and the
Michigan Housing Network

What organizations like the Michigan State Housing Development Authority can do is provide the resources through the distribution networks that we have. The secret is not in a government check being issued out to a developer to build a house, or giving it to a city to give to a developer to pave a street. It's investing those resources through the delivery system, which is for-profits, the nonprofits [secular], and the faith based. This is all part of the collaborative that creates the new neighborhood and the place that the next generation is going to come to.

—Michigan state housing official

The low- and moderate-income housing market in Michigan is comprised of a complex network of government agencies and nonprofit and for-profit organizations. Describing this system is difficult for a number of reasons. Although the overall number of relevant actors is large, many organizations are very small. Often local providers work on a very narrow scale with a well-defined target population or a minimal resource base. Further complexity is introduced by the fact that funding support for organizations interested in providing low- and moderate-income housing is often cobbled together from a great many sources. Thus, funding patterns can appear to be chaotic and sometimes unstable. One fact is certain: there is no well-established census of housing providers in the state. Indeed, there is significant dispute over what organizations would properly be included in such a census. The goal of this chapter is to provide a sketch of the low-income housing market and the role that faith-based organizations play in it.

Federal Actors

It is impossible to understand the state's low- and moderate-income housing market without reference to federal programs and policy. There can be no serious dispute that the number of individuals and households impacted by federal programs simply overwhelms any purely state, local, or private effort. In 2008, it was estimated that 4.3 million American households participated in a federal housing program.[1] This included just under 1 million households in the traditional public housing market, 1.4 million households in subsidized privately owned multifamily units, and 1.9 million households participating in the Housing Choice Voucher Program (U.S. Department of Housing and Urban Development, 2008).

Although federal programs dwarf all other efforts, the role of state and local organizations (both public and private) is absolutely critical in any effort to understand actual policy outcomes. The reason is simple: the federal government produces very little housing. In fact, federal actors have only modest administrative and oversight authority over how federal dollars are spent. Rather than designing and implementing programs, federal agencies rely on a collection of state and local, private and public agencies. A regional official of the federal Department of Housing and Urban Development (HUD) stated this quite clearly:

> I like to explain by way of saying that HUD now is really not in the retail business; we're in the wholesale business. By that I mean the dollars in our programs will flow through other entities. For example, under Community Planning and Development, block grants, home funds, and funds for people with AIDS, dollars for people who are homeless will flow through an organization. We will not go directly to the recipients. Now, having said that, our biggest partner [in Michigan], is the state of Michigan, primarily MSHDA. They basically are the conduit for block grants to go to other than entitlement cities. They are the conduit, for the Section 8 statewide program, where they have an agent in each county and the same thing for Community Planning Development and Home Funds. The major portion of the dollars that they use to build in these smaller cities will flow through MSHDA. [2]

The bulk of federal housing dollars are administered by the Department of Housing and Urban Development. Other programs scattered across the federal government have an important impact on local housing, however. For example, rural communities receive housing assistance from several programs located in the United States Department of Agriculture. Since specific programs have different impacts and engage different organizations at the state and local level, it is useful to provide a brief sense of at least some of the major federal programs operating in the state of Michigan.

Public Housing

Public housing is perhaps the best-known federally supported program promoting low- and moderate-income housing.[3] The program was established in 1937 as part of the New Deal, and committed the federal government to fund the construction of moderate-income housing directly. However, responsibility for the location, construction, maintenance, and administration of the resulting housing stock was delegated to local public housing authorities. State and local governments created these independent agencies specifically for this purpose. In 2009, there were 3,200 active local public housing authorities in the United States operating 1,194,311 units of housing. The state of Michigan had approximately 23,763 units of public housing (U.S. Department of Housing and Urban Development 2009b).

Public housing was not created to serve very low-income or minority citizens. It had in fact two quite different goals. The first was to provide housing to the "submerged middle-class," people who were temporarily unemployed, or employed at low wages, during the Great Depression (Stoloff 2004). Public housing was also promoted as an economic stimulus to create jobs in the building trades. In its early years, public housing largely served a white working-class constituency in relatively low-density developments (Bratt 1989). It is thus clear that the early public housing program was perceived quite differently than its current incarnation. The essential character of the program began to change in the 1940s and 1950s (Hula 1991). The Housing Act of 1949 implemented explicit priorities for very low-income people, income limits, and maximum rents.[4] These income limits penalized the upwardly mobile and had the effect of forcing moderate-income families out of public housing. In the same period local authorities came to embrace high-rise development as a model. Generally these designs were justified on the basis of reduced overall cost. Of particular importance was the reduction in land needed for development. Other changes in the physical design of housing were also being implemented. Limits on quality were often explicitly incorporated into public housing. Such limitations were justified by arguing that if public housing is less desirable than that available in the private sector, there will be a guaranteed incentive for public housing residents to seek higher quality housing elsewhere. While the impact of such decisions on resident motivations is debatable, it is clear that such decisions hastened the physical deterioration of the public housing stock.

Public housing programs have never been popular with residents or the broader citizen constituency. Many people have raised ideological objections, regarding the program as an unwarranted intrusion into the private housing market. The popular perception that the program is a failure has been reinforced by media reports of crime and social disorganization within the "projects."[5] Increasing rents and reduction of services simultaneously led to widespread tenant dissatisfaction. The system faced a number of rent strikes in the 1960s, with residents demanding reductions in rental rates. In response, the Brooke Amendment was incorporated into the 1969 Housing Act to limit rent to no more than 25 percent of income (raised to 30 percent in 1981). These reductions served to further hamper the capacity of public housing administrators to address critical maintenance needs, and almost certainly accelerated the physical decline of public housing stock.

There has been no significant federal expenditure for the construction of new public housing since 1981. Limited funding has been targeted to local authorities for rehabilitation of existing units. Funded rehabilitation efforts often include the destruction of existing obsolete or deteriorated structures and replacing them with less dense developments with higher quality units. While such renovations improve the quality of public units they often have the unintended consequence of reducing the total number of units available to low-income households.[6]

It is interesting to note that the public has distorted images of public housing. For example, contrary to popular perception, a significant proportion of public housing is now targeted for seniors. More than half (52 percent) of all public housing residents are elderly or have disabilities. About 40 percent of public housing residents remain in units less than three years (Stoloff 2004). While the thought of public

housing in the United States conjures up visions of enormous high-rise developments, only 27 percent of current units are located in such buildings. Thirty-two
percent of units are garden apartments and 25 percent are single-family homes or
townhouses. Since the 1970s, almost all of the housing built for families has been
scattered-site development with fifty or fewer units.[7]

Given the governing structure of the public housing program, it is not surprising
that neither faith-based nor secular nonprofit organizations have played a major role
in it. There is, however, an interesting footnote in the history of public housing in
which some engagement between faith-based organizations, local authorities, and
HUD did occur. In the 1980s the Reagan administration was searching for a long-
term solution to perceived failures of the program. One experiment that received
a good deal of public attention was having tenants manage, or perhaps even own,
public housing projects. In a number of jurisdictions tenant organizations sought
to accept this challenge. Often these organizations had strong faith components.
Ultimately, however, the concept of tenant-based management was abandoned by
HUD (Hula 1991).

Housing Choice Vouchers

A major source of discontent with public housing was the ideological view that
government simply had no role to play in the housing market. Others argued that
while such efforts were legitimate, government policy should be crafted in a way
that engaged the capacity and creativity of the private sector. As early as the 1949
Housing Act, efforts were made to replace public housing with alternative strategies
that relied on more market and market-like programs to promote the production of
low- and moderate-income housing. By the early twenty-first century, that view
dominated federal housing policy. Section 8 of the 1974 Housing Act provided
funds to pay a landlord the difference between 30 percent of household income
and a public housing authority (PHA)–determined payment standard—about 80 to
100 percent of the fair market rent (FMR) (Kingsley 1991). The Section 8 program
initially had three subprograms: New Construction, Substantial Rehabilitation, and
Existing Housing Certificate programs. The Moderate Rehabilitation Program was
added in 1978, the Voucher Program in 1983, and the Project-based Certificate
Program in 1991. The number of units a local housing authority can subsidize
under its Section 8 programs is determined by Congressional funding. Since its
inception, some Section 8 programs have been phased out and new ones created,
although Congress has always renewed existing subsidies.

Housing Choice Vouchers are not distributed to states on the basis of a formula.
Rather, funding levels are based on the total number of units that local authorities
have requested since the program was established in 1974.[8] Local PHAs commonly
allocate and monitor these funds.[9] The local unit issues a voucher to an income-
qualified household. The household then identifies a unit to rent. If the unit meets
Section 8 standards, the administering agency then pays the landlord an amount

equal to the difference between actual rent and 30 percent of adjusted income. The rent must be comparable to that of other units in the area, as determined by the administrating unit (U.S. Department of Housing and Urban Development 2009b). Figure 5.1 presents the national distribution of federally subsidized housing units. Of the almost 3 million subsidized units in the United States in 2009, 65 percent were based on a tenant voucher program. Thirty-three percent were traditional public housing. The remaining 2 percent of public housing units were handled by a variety of smaller subsidy programs.[10] Figure 5.2 shows that in distribution Michigan was very similar to the national profile, although it was even more dependent on vouchers. In Michigan approximately 70 percent of almost 70,000 federally subsidized units were based on tenant vouchers. Only 28 percent of these units were made up of traditional public housing. Approximately 2 percent were based on other, smaller subsidy programs.

Targeted Housing Support for the Low-Income Elderly and Disabled

HUD has two smaller programs that are of particular interest to this research in that they often are implemented through faith-based organizations. The Section 811 program is targeted for the disabled and Section 202 to the elderly. The programs operate in similar ways by providing funds to nonprofit organizations to develop rental housing with available supportive services. Funds are also provided to cover the costs of developing housing and need not be repaid as long as the housing is available for at least 40 years for occupancy by very low-income seniors (under Section 202) or very low-income people with disabilities (under Section 811). Rent support funds are also available to nonprofit groups to cover the difference between the residents' contributions toward rent and the cost of operating the project.

In 2009, Section 202 was the largest direct housing construction federal grant program in operation (Bright 2009). Since 1959, when the program was initiated, Section 202 has supported the construction of approximately 6,200 projects with a total of 250,000 residential units (Bright 2009). The Section 811 program has supported the construction of more than 30,000 units since its inception. A separate tenant-based rental assistance component assists 14,000 households with disabilities living in private rental market properties.

Low-Income Housing Tax Credit

The Low-Income Housing Tax Credit (LIHTC) was authorized under the Tax Reform Act of 1986 as a means to promote private investment in low- and moderate-income housing. The LIHTC offers substantial federal tax credits to investors (both non- and for-profit) providing equity financing for rental housing. Credits may be given for new construction, rehabilitation, or the acquisition of rehabilitated housing. The amount of the credit is based on the

Figure 5.1   **Federal Program Support for Subsidized Housing in the United States**

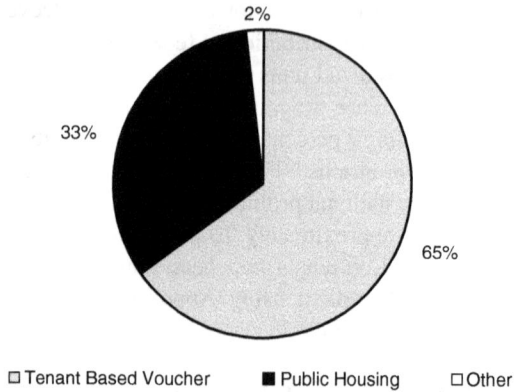

2%

33%

65%

☐ Tenant Based Voucher   ■ Public Housing   ☐ Other

Source: U.S. Department of Housing and Urban Development (2009b).

Figure 5.2   **Federal Program Support for Subsidized Housing in Michigan**

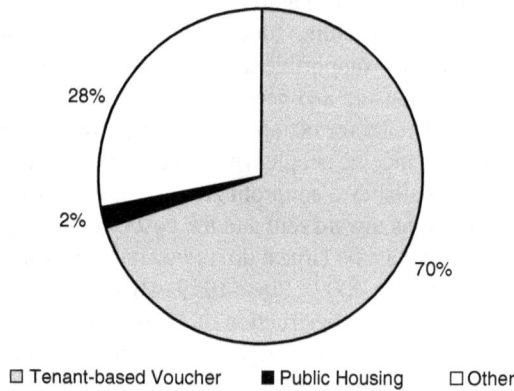

28%

2%

70%

☐ Tenant-based Voucher   ■ Public Housing   ☐ Other

Source: U.S. Department of Housing and Urban Development (2009b).

- Amount of credits awarded to the project in the project competition;
- Actual cost of the project;
- Tax credit rate announced by the IRS; and
- Percentage of the project's units rented to low-income tenants.

The LIHTC has become the primary vehicle for federal support of the development of new and rehabilitated affordable rental housing (Oakley 2008). Figure 5.3 shows the annual production of low- and moderate-income housing that LIHTC has produced since 1995. Abt Associates (2006) estimates that the tax credit program produced over 1.5 million units between 1987 and 2003. Indeed, the American Bankers Association argues that LIHTC "stands as the only significant federal support for expanding the stock" (American Bankers Association 2004, 12).[11] Although LIHTC projects are required to meet a minimum of federal regulation and standards, a great deal of discretion is left to the state agencies that implement the program. Each allocating state agency develops a Qualified Allocation Plan that relates the use of credits to housing needs and priorities and administers the competition among developers that awards credits. Figure 5.4 illustrates the importance of the LIHTC in Michigan, showing both the total number of units and the number of low-income units produced under the program between 1987and 2006.

Other Programs

Many federal programs not centered in HUD are also active in Michigan. Several programs of the U.S. Department of Agriculture target the nation's small town and rural housing needs. These include a single-family housing program that promotes home ownership as well as home repair and renovation. In 2008 the USDA provided a total of $733 million for rural development in Michigan (U.S. Department of Agriculture 2009). This included $430 million for single-family housing programs. The USDA also administered a smaller program providing approximately $7,000,000 in assistance to rental housing in the state (ibid.).

Federal Experience with Faith-Based Organizations

As has been noted, a number of federal programs utilize nonprofit organizations in the construction and maintenance of subsidized housing. Sometimes this federal-nonprofit link is direct, as in the case of housing for the elderly and disabled. More often the link is indirect, since state authorities make the allocation decisions. A regional HUD officer noted that faith-based organizations have long been active in such programs:

> The 202 program is designed for the elderly, 62 and above. We will provide, under a grant if they're successful, because it's competitive—the dollars for building the structure. We will also give them [the developers] an operating subsidy, just like we do for public housing, because those tenants basically will pay 30 percent of their adjusted income. Because of income limits, the dollars they would pay for their rent was [sic] not enough to make the development work. So, that's one program that several faith-based organizations have used over the years. The Catholics have used it, the Presbyterians, the Lutherans and we've had some smaller ones lately. . . . I think there's a small faith-based organization that has one 202. The 811 program is the same concept, but designed for the disabled population. That can be either physical or mental.

Figure 5.3   **Annual Production of LIHTC Units**

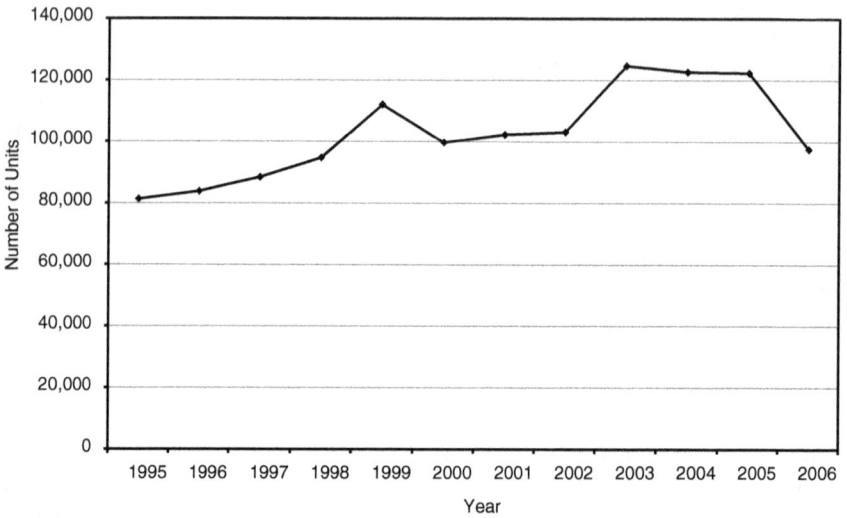

Source: Climaco et al. (2009).

Figure 5.4   **Annual Production of LIHTC Units in Michigan**

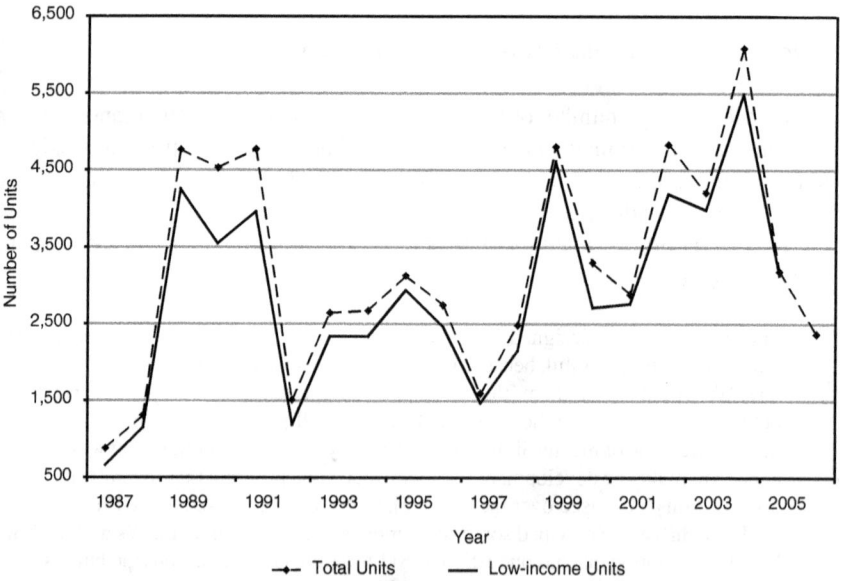

Source: U.S. Department of Housing and Urban Development (2009a).

Another HUD representative made this point even more emphatically with respect to Section 202 housing:

> [I]t was always targeted to nonprofits and it is an area where some of these mega faith-based nonprofits, Catholic Charities and Lutheran Social Services, have had, I don't want to say a lock on it, but almost a lock on it.

For the most part HUD officials interviewed seemed genuinely supportive of efforts of faith-based organizations to initiate housing programs. Nevertheless, there was a strong sense that not all such organizations are equal, and that it is important to partner with the correct organization. It is hardly surprising that the most commonly cited desirable attribute was sufficient capacity. Faith-based organizations were seen to vary widely in the ability to perform up to a necessary standard. A regional HUD official observed:

> I would say from my experience working with larger faith-based organizations like the Lutheran Social Services that they have tremendous capacity. It is because they are stable, they are institutionalized, they have a corporate structure, so maybe it is more of the comfort level of one bureaucracy dealing with another, because they are bureaucracies certainly too. They have a corporate structure, if you are working with a subsidiary or a branch—they have a fallback structure to lean on. They are not just making up rules as they go along. They are part of a larger corporation. It can be more businesslike in that regard.

Organizations also show important differences in their willingness to compromise what they see as core values to meet requirements for federal dollars. Another HUD official noted:

> The Salvation Army has an interesting history with HUD and the federal government. For many, many, many years they adamantly refused to participate in federal programs because of the restrictions that federal agencies would place on them in terms of any kind of new service and being overtly proselytizing and so on. But at some point in their history, it must have been, I think around the '80s, maybe early '90s, their head corporation to the extent it exists, told each of their branch subsidiaries that they could make their own ethical judgments about whether to accept or apply for federal funding. At that point you have Salvation Army organizations doing business with government, with HUD, but not so much as an umbrella; it is each individual subsidiary.

At least historically, organizations like the Salvation Army could not be enticed to accept federal funds, because of fear that such funding would undermine the fundamental religious character of the organization. But, as the quote demonstrates, this may be changing for many faith-based organizations, a trend clearly demonstrated in the data analyses to come.

Michigan Actors

State authorities play an important role in the network of organizations engaged in low- and moderate-income housing. Like the federal government, however, state agencies seldom actually produce housing. Instead they serve as a source of funding and oversight, leaving the production of housing to much smaller public and private organizations. Faith-based organizations comprise a large portion of these producers.

The Michigan State Housing Development Authority

The Michigan State Housing Development Authority (MSHDA) was created in 1966 as an independent agency to promote affordable housing across the state. Unlike many states, Michigan has no central state authority charged with housing development, but a decentralized agency, MSHDA, without direct ties to standard government authority. Overall policy and programs of the authority are determined not by the governor or the state legislature but by a board comprised of eight members, five of whom are appointed by the governor and must be confirmed by the state senate, and three of whom are key state officials—the treasurer and the directors of the Michigan Department of Labor and Economic Growth and the Michigan Department of Human Services. Thus the organization has a good deal of autonomy in the design and implementation of its mission. When asked how much influence state authorities had over MSHDA programs and priorities, one MSHDA official explained:

> It's not structured in that regard. We are pretty much our own policy-making body. Now, obviously you mirror the commitment and the priorities of the administration, whoever's administration it may happen to be. But we're given a mission. How we fulfill it and the policies that we employ and the like, that's our responsibility.

Primary funding for MSHDA does not come from state general funds; working funds mainly come from two other sources. First, the agency serves as a major distributor of federal dollars targeted to housing efforts in the state. This includes significant federal money for Low-Income Housing Tax Credits, as well as an allocation of housing vouchers. In addition, MSHDA is empowered to sell tax-exempt bonds and use the proceeds to provide loans to developers to finance the construction of low-income housing and subsidies in the form of loans and mortgage credit certificates to individuals who buy houses.

In its early years, MSHDA was a small organization that focused almost exclusively on the direct financing of moderate-income housing construction. The organization expanded from fewer than twenty employees to over two hundred. As the staff expanded, so did the mission.[12] By 2009, MSHDA was active in a number of substantive areas including community development, housing vouchers, rental development, and homelessness. Increasingly, MSHDA has attempted to link neighborhood and community development to the issue of low- and moderate-income housing. An MSHDA official describes the strategy this way:

> So, the idea is to use our resources to strategically invest in projects that will either stabilize neighborhoods or make them more affordable. In either case, the effort is to

create more income diversity, to create more vibrancy through more home ownership and single-family housing, more stability, less transience, and to generally—especially in the case of a neighborhood that needs revitalizing like Baker-Donora—to change the market perception of that neighborhood. So if somebody comes in, they say, "Wow, this would be an OK place to live," as opposed to "Get me out of here," and "I want to build a house in a township." So, we're basically looking at strategically important neighborhoods and communities, or good projects of opportunity that can help improve the quality of life for folks in our housing and other neighbors as a result of our investments.

In 2009, MSHDA had a variety of projects under way to improve access to affordable housing, provide incentives for urban revitalization, and increase the number of green communities in the state. MSHDA has the authority to refinance mortgages for those families and individuals having financial difficulty and qualifying for the organization's low-interest loans. In addition, the authority has been given the ability to provide assistance to state and local governments in obtaining foreclosed properties for redevelopment. MSHDA also has a series of partners in Southeast Michigan working to revitalize the region. Partners include developers, faith-based organizations, and local governments that work toward the mission of MSHDA. MSHDA has also partnered with the Michigan Land Bank Fast Track Authority (MLBFTA) and the Great Lakes Capital Fund (GLCF) to achieve additional development of affordable housing. In 2006, MSHDA expanded its economic and community development work in the Detroit area by creating a Southeast Michigan development division.

MSHDA plays a dominant role in the state's low- and moderate-income market. The agency reported the following outcomes for 2008 (Michigan State Housing Development Authority 2009):

- Single-family Mortgage Loan Programs: Financed 2,640 single-family homes with a value of $264,181,644.
- Multifamily Lending Program: Committed $57,375,959 in loans to support financing of 14 developments containing a total of 1,170 housing units. Another $82,567,595 in loans was committed and pending to 10 additional developments to create 1,368 units.
- Low-income Housing Tax Credits: Allocated $21.1 million in federal Low-income Housing Tax Credits to 38 developers. The credits will build more than 2,100 units of affordable rental housing for low- to moderate-income families, the elderly, people with disabilities, and those at risk of homelessness.
- The Housing Choice Voucher Program: Allocated federal Housing Choice Vouchers to 23,031 very low-income families.

As evidenced by the outcomes above, MSHDA is a key source of funding and support for a number of organizations active in providing low- and moderate-income housing. One MSHDA official explained it this way:

[MSHDA is] a financial institution with a social contract. We make money by making loans and mortgages, and investing in real estate developments that provide housing to very specific targeted audiences. Housing is produced by those developers, and those builders, and those agencies or for-profit and nonprofits, who apply for our funding.

The leadership in MSHDA sees facilitating the capacity of other organizations as one of its major roles. An MSHDA official described the organization as follows:

We help people build houses. MSHDA doesn't build anything. We help people build. We're a financial institution, not a bank, but a financial institution. We make it possible for people [to get homes] in the way of loans and mortgages and capital to do those things that will produce those products and those communities that are a part of policy commitments of this state, to produce and provide. But it's private industry, nonprofit groups, collaborative groups, who are building today what tomorrow is calling for.

MSHDA officials also see nonprofits as important partners in efforts to promote low- and moderate-income housing. A number of MSHDA officials made this clear, for example:

There's a critical role for the nonprofit organization. First of all, it has a degree of flexibility that for-profit organizations or tax-funded organizations do not have. Secondly, they can specialize their mission. As a nonprofit organization, they have much more flexibility. They can react to change, they can force change. I think most nonprofits also carry what I would consider a message of conscience. They represent something. These are believers. These are people who believe. I've been in a position where I have said privately to myself, "God, save me from dedicated believers!" But in the long run, that's the passion you need for any kind of policy to ever be successful.

Nonprofits are usually an extension of some set of core values. They really truly are. I think the nonprofit community probably impacts the moral compass of society more than anything, I really believe that. I've seen it up close, and particularly in the work that we're engaged in.

There can be no doubt that MSHDA is committed to working with a variety of nonprofit organizations. Like their federal colleagues, however, that commitment is constrained by a view that many nonprofits lack the administrative capacity to oversee certain MSHDA programs. For example, nonprofits have generally been unsuccessful in efforts to administer home vouchers.[13] One senior staff member at MSHDA noted her initial surprise at this fact:

[W]e have this rent subsidy program, and how we deliver across the state is through contracted housing agents. That's what we call them. They're either limited liability corporations, someone who owns their own business, a nonprofit, or a local unit of government. Primarily where we've had the most success is LLC's, limited liability corporations.

I thought there are a lot of nonprofits out there that we have found that are really good at delivering housing, because they have service dollars, they're working with the same population, and they potentially would be great agents. But what they have to do in the voucher program is so much different from the services side. It's because it's HUD's largest program. So they monitor and audit it all the time, and it's a program where you have to dot your i's and cross your t's and get things in on time. It isn't so much the services side as somebody who can deal with regulations, deal with paperwork, get things in, get people contracted, whatever. And so it's a different kind of personality.

Overall, there is a strong consensus at MSHDA that its faith-based and secular nonprofit partners are effective and are doing good work. Unfortunately, there is also a strong sense that this effort is largely being overwhelmed by the state's dire economic conditions. Housing officials across the state were asked whether strengthening the capacity of nonprofit partners was a priority in improving the production of low- and moderate-income housing. The response was generally negative, largely because other needs were so great:

> We can talk about the situation in Michigan without really talking about the national housing problem, because we were there first. Now all these states are screaming. I go to these national meetings, and everybody's going, "Oh, we're running a deficit! Oh, we're running a deficit!" It's like, "Hey, cry me a river." I mean, when we were there two years ago, and I was paying my own way to come to these meetings, you guys said, "Oh, that's too bad." I said, "Well, we're glad to have you join us, because that's the only way we're going to get any help."

Community Economic Development Association of Michigan

The Community Economic Development Association of Michigan (CEDAM) was incorporated in 1998 as a nonprofit collaboration of organizations interested in promoting the redevelopment and renewal of Michigan communities. CEDAM has the specific goal of promoting economic and neighborhood development by providing member training and promoting collaborative efforts among members. Although CEDAM's initial membership was almost entirely composed of the state's community development corporations, current membership has expanded beyond this base and now includes government agencies, housing development organizations, financial institutions, and individuals. As shown in Figure 5.5, CEDAM has come to represent a significant portion of the hundreds of organizations active in community development and housing in Michigan.

In 2007, CEDAM membership was comprised of 50 percent community development corporations, 30 percent individuals, and 20 percent "others" (Community Economic Development Association of Michigan 2008). A CEDAM staff member describes the organization's membership as follows:

> About half of our membership is those nonprofits that exist to either build housing or support the community or offer social services programming. The other 200-ish members are groups that are supportive of our mission—individuals, perhaps other

Figure 5.5   **CEDAM Membership, 1999–2007**

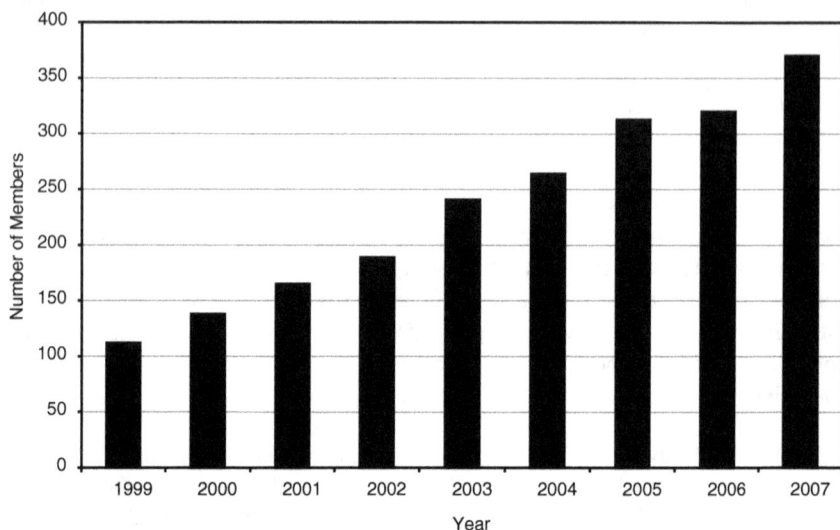

nonprofits that sort of work for our members, groups like the ones we share this building with. Then we have some for-profit developers that do partner with us. We have
banks that are members, some other financial organizations. Generally, those are the
kind of [people] that fill out those other six board slots. Places like LISC, or the Federal
Home Loan Bank.

A board elected from the membership governs the organization. CEDAM also
has a relatively small paid staff to run day-to-day operations, monitor policy, and
fundraise through grant writing and other avenues. Although CEDAM is a membership organization, dues provide only a small fraction of its operating budget.
A large portion of the operating funds for CEDAM comes from public sources,
particularly grants from MSHDA.

CEDAM has impacted housing and community development efforts in Michigan
in a variety of ways. Training of Michigan community development corporations is
a priority for CEDAM and is done through partnerships with HUD, the Michigan
Housing Trust Fund (MHTF), and MSHDA. The organization offers members a
series of training courses in real estate and community development and works
with faith-based organizations on these matters. CEDAM also provides some direct
services to members such as reduced cost insurance.

CEDAM collaborates with other organizations on specific programs. For example, CEDAM is a partner in the Michigan Asset Building Policy Project, which
attempts to help individuals advance their careers and get out of poverty through
education, job training, and improvement in personal finance skills. CEDAM works
with the Michigan Community Reinvestment Coalition to provide better access
to credit in communities with low to moderate incomes. In addition, the organiza-

tion holds an affordable housing conference each year in conjunction with other groups. CEDAM partners with Habitat for Humanity and a number of community development corporations to implement Vision 2020, which targets areas of very poor housing for renewal.[14]

Perhaps CEDAM's most important role is that of policy advocate for organizations working in community revitalization and housing. Indeed, as one CEDAM official notes, the advocacy role was a primary motivation in the creation of the organization:

> I mentioned we were formed in 1998. A group of people came together and represented community development corporations from across the state with the question—why aren't we better connected? Why aren't we better represented in Lansing? Who is our group? They came together realizing that there is this need to organize, to have a group that was doing advocacy work—both with the legislature, but also with the state departments. Who is that group that was telling the story?
>
> Our mission over the past 10 years has been one of predominantly advocacy. We see our goal as on one hand telling the story, making sure that we're getting information about the work that our members do out there, so that people know the good work that they're doing. That translates into the legislature, it translates into state departments, and we work quite closely with MSHDA. But, there are a number of other departments like MEDC [Michigan Economic Development Corporation], that don't necessarily have a familiarity with nonprofits, and with the great work that they were doing with such, such little resources.

CEDAM actively tracks legislation at all levels of government. The organization has close ties to members of the state legislature, and is seen by many as an effective lobbying organization. They also encourage their members to be active at the state level. A CEDAM official describes the process of engaging members:

> Because one thing we realize is that, our members might do things locally, they might invite an elected official to a ribbon-cutting. The more advanced ones might have really good relationships, but most of them are just unfamiliar with the legislative process. These are people with community advocacy at their heart, social services at their heart, wanting to improve their community. But they may not be politically astute. So we brought about 60 of our members, we trained them on the legislative process, on lobbying. Then we sent them up to meet with their legislators. I think it worked out really well. We got a lot of great comments from our members, "I didn't know what was going on," "I didn't know how to do this," "thank you for showing me how easy it is, really." So we probably had made contact with about 30 legislative offices that day with 60 members, and we considered it a real success.

Organizational Overview

As was noted in Chapter 4, ninety-nine organizations responded to the statewide housing provider survey conducted by the authors. These data form the core of the analysis to be presented in this volume. Sixty-four of the respondents identified themselves as secular organizations. Just over one-third of the respondents (35) claimed to be faith-based. The faith-based sample can be divided by the role faith plays in the organization. Figure 5.6 shows that the role of religion varies a good deal across organizations active in the low-income housing market. The least common examples of faith-based organizations involved in housing in this study are congregations and collaboratives of congregations.[15] Only about 9 percent of faith-based nonprofits studied fall into these categories. Organizations that see their work as based on religious principles (49 percent) or acknowledge collaboration with religious organizations (43 percent) are more typical.

These data suggest that the motivation driving many nonprofit organizations to be involved in the production of low-income housing is more strongly related to fundamental principles than opportunities to proselytize. A leader of a faith-based organization put it this way:

> This is a Christian ministry; we make no bones about that. Yet on the other hand we have absolutely no specific performance or engagement requirements. We let the resident know who we are and why we are, and we do offer opportunities for religious activity. But he or she, the resident, is in no way, shape, or form expected to participate, required to participate.

This understanding is reinforced by a number of comments from those active in faith-based organizations. Similarly, several representatives of faith-based organizations stressed the importance of providing services to a broad constituency not defined by race, ethnicity, or religious preference, for example:

> We believe very much in an important passage in the New Testament in 2 Corinthians Chapter 5, where we read that we've been reconciled to God through Christ, the old is gone, the new has come. Therefore, be His ambassadors.[16] A couple of lines later it says don't receive the grace of God in vain.[17] A lot of times Christians interpret that as meaning simply, a spiritual matter. You know, is your heart right with God? We say, that we believe in Christ's lordship over all of the universe. That reconciliation applies to everything and the fact that the old is gone and the new has come. That means broken economic relationships between the landlord and tenant have been reconciled. That means crummy house designs and broken aesthetic relationships have been made new. Everything about the human experience with one another and with one's environment has been, if you accept it, has been restored and transformed.
>   We are building for people whom God loves and it doesn't matter if they are poor or if they are Latino or if they are single moms or they are former drug addicts, we are building for people whom God loves. So we build them right.

Other officials stressed the importance of recognizing and being responsive to various religious doctrines and beliefs.

> When we are talking with churches and faith-based organizations you want to be sensitive to that particular denomination's language; when you say this word, this is what it means and over here, this is what it means. Then you want to be sensitive to

Figure 5.6   **The Role of Religion in Low-Income Housing Nonprofits**

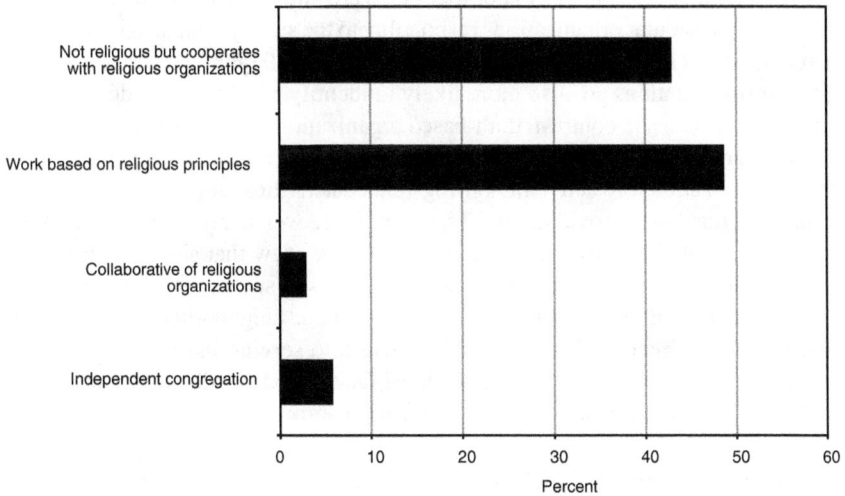

those things. But we really try to focus on what is our common mission, you know together as faith-based people. I mean I go to the Jewish synagogue once a year and talk to the fifth graders about why we work together and they've raised a little money for Habitat and we give it to a house with a family that I can show them a picture of and they are happy about it. We are all in this together. So, as the faith community becomes more open, its concerns about favoring certain religions or lifestyles become less and less of an issue.

It is important to emphasize that while many of these faith-based housing organizations are open to serving a broad community, some tension does exist between the internal faith dimension of the organization and the need for external links to the community. One organization director described the internal debate around an effort to develop a mission and value statement as follows:

We talk a lot about it, especially as we develop some value statements. And there was one statement that we got stuck on where we were trying to say we value the faith, the beliefs of others, of other faith traditions. And our group could not come to consensus on that, because they could accept it, but they couldn't value it.

Of course, some faith-based organizations do focus exclusively on members of their own faith community. Such organizations are much less likely to engage in the general community, and more likely to eschew cooperation and avoid public funding.[18] Yet the number of housing faith-based organizations in the survey serving primarily their own members is quite small, at 16 percent.

Figure 5.7 provides an overview of the substantive focus of the organizations responding to the survey. Approximately 45 percent of the organizations indicated that housing is their primary focus. Interestingly, secular organizations are much more likely to identify housing as a major focus than are faith-based organizations. Some 55 percent of secular organizations responding to the survey indicated housing was a major focus. This compares to less than 40 percent of all faith-based organizations. Secular organizations are also more likely to identify neighborhood development as a primary focus. In contrast, faith-based organizations are more likely to identify economic development and social services as major foci. Note, however, that all of these organizations are active in housing-related activities ranging from neighborhood development to providing social services. Moreover, many organizations reject a "housing" label because they have embraced the view that simply focusing on shelter is not likely to address the underlying issues of specific families in need or generate conditions necessary for long-term, sustained neighborhood development. They are more interested in a holistic approach to serving individuals, families, and communities. A representative of a local faith-based housing nonprofit clearly articulated the motivations behind this holistic approach:

> [I]f we were a machine, you'd open up the little door in the back of the machine [and] you'd see three gears: real estate development, finance, residential construction, and housing empowerment and education services [*sic*]. There are fine finance bankers and investors around town and there are good construction companies. But there is nobody that wraps those two things, wraps finance and construction together with services that ensures that the house will be a place of success for its occupant. Or said the other way around, that the family will, in fact, not only achieve housing success, but go on to broader life accomplishment.
>
> We are a builder because we want to be in full control of the quality, the timetable, and the budget. But, we are the educator and the empowerment organization because we want people to grow and to achieve. We want them to be able to be engaged in the whole array of civic opportunity.

Figure 5.8 illustrates specific housing activities reported by organizations in more detail. It shows that there are consistent patterns across faith-based and secular nonprofits in housing activities. Both groups are most likely to focus on rental property; home-ownership and other educational programs are also common. Some differences between faith-based and secular organizations can also be seen, however. Perhaps most interesting is the fact that faith-based organizations seem to be much more engaged in efforts to promote the construction of new housing.

Chapter 6 explores in greater detail the organizational characteristics of secular and faith-based housing providers. As one might expect, these organizations show a good deal of variation in size, overall budget, level of professionalism, and substantive focus. Even a cursory review suggests some interesting patterns, however. First, it seems clear that both secular and faith-based housing providers tend to be quite small relative to what might be perceived as their potential "markets." For example, one observer summarized the output of a local chapter of Habitat for Humanity in this way:

We build 20 to 25 houses a year, which is a pretty high number. Most Habitat affiliates build three houses a year or less. We have almost 30 employees. That breaks into the construction department which includes our volunteer coordinator and some assistants that we use in there; there are probably six or eight in that department. In 2008 I think we worked with over 4,000 volunteers and we have some volunteers that work with us every week. They are what we call our weekday regulars and they are great to have because it is hard to get groups out in the middle of the week. Saturdays are just crazy.

Certainly the construction of 20 to 25 houses is not a minor accomplishment. Nevertheless, 25 units of low- and moderate-income housing are unlikely to have a measurable impact on the state's (or even a city's) low-income population. Consider, for example, that federal funding provides almost 70,000 units in the state. To understand the impact of these organizations, it is necessary to examine the full range of interactions among them. Of particular importance are the cooperative links that exist between organizations. Some of the linkages occur between state and local organizations. The importance of the Michigan State Housing Development Authority has already been mentioned. Other state organizations also play important coordinating roles. For example, one Habitat for Humanity representative noted that the state unit of Habitat for Humanity serves as a broker with MSHDA for local chapters:

Michigan Habitat has been instrumental in really getting us into MSHDA. MSHDA does not accept applications from Habitat, Muskegon Habitat, Grand Rapids Habitat. They don't want to have to sort through who can really use the money and who can't. So they give Michigan Habitat the task of doing that. We get well over $1 million every year from MSHDA to distribute to Habitat affiliates.

Collaboration and cooperation also exist among local units. For example, according to a representative of a local faith-based organization in the Grand Rapids area, the Permanent Housing Coordinating Council works to coordinate activities of 20 to 25 organizations.

It meets once a quarter. Next Monday's meeting, it is about 20 maybe 24, 25 different agencies that are represented. Some of them are producing housing in quantity like we do. Some of them only do certain kinds of repair, some of them just do finance. We have a very high level of communication and collaboration with one another. The other very large organization in town is something called the Dwelling Place. We are about ready to do a major collaboration of about a $17 million joint venture on an existing development that is in deep, deep doodoo. We are going to buy it and we are going to basically gut it and put it right.

The same FBO representative noted that coordination extends even to the matter of personnel: "We even have a couple of unwritten rules about raiding each other's staffs. We never recruit from one another."

A second feature of these housing organizations is a relative degree of specialization. For example, a number of commentators noted that the large "established"

Figure 5.7   **Substantive Focus of Organizations Responding to Housing Provider Survey**

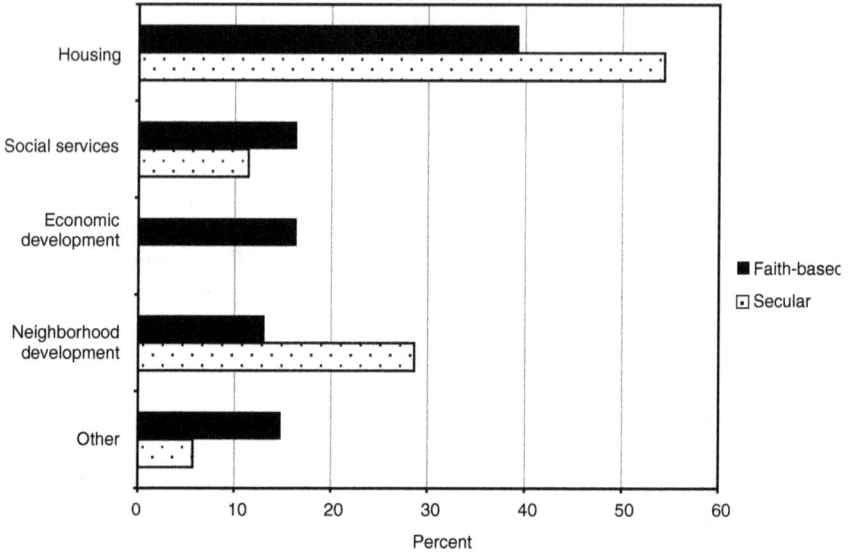

Figure 5.8   **Housing Activities Reported on Housing Provider Survey**

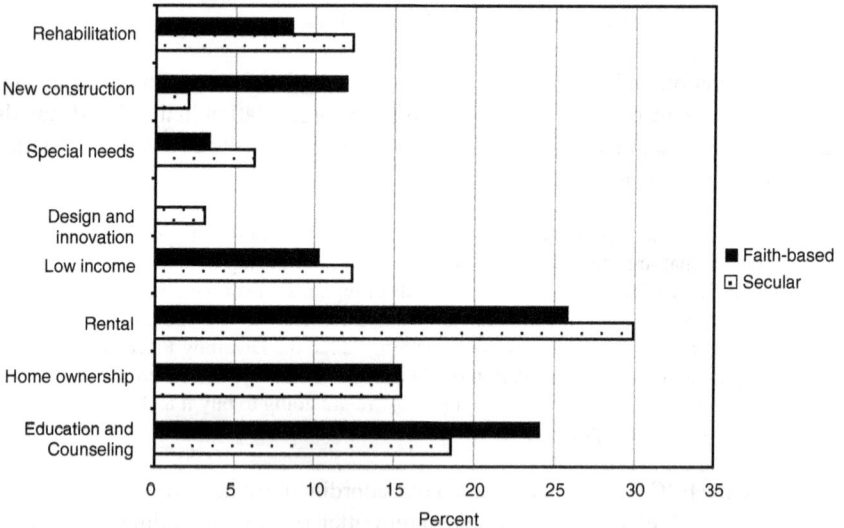

Note: Figure 5.8 was constructed by aggregating open-ended responses to the following question: "Please list and describe the two most important housing activities your organization is engaged in."

faith-based organizations such as Catholic Charities and Lutheran Social Services have a virtual monopoly on HUD-financed housing for the elderly and disabled. Other organizations tend to focus on creating rental housing and ownership opportunities for low-income households. Finally, a number of organizations place a high priority on temporary shelter and providing services to the homeless.

One of the most important questions about our sample of faith-based organizations is, of course, the role of faith in the organization. Obviously, all organizations that accept public funding are required by law to provide services without regard to religious affiliation. Nevertheless, as has been noted, working in the interface between the sacred and secular world can lead to internal stress. One leader in Habitat for Humanity recalled the tensions generated in the national organization over the appropriate role of its Christian roots:

> Christian ministry means you welcome all people and you work with all people that want help and some standard housing. So that's been the model which I've worked under here and it is pretty much the direction, the way that the international organization has gone as well. Unfortunately, it wasn't always that way. For example, our founder, Millard Fuller, who passed away a couple weeks ago, was a powerful leader and great entrepreneur. But his vision of what Christian ministry meant was quite Southern, in terms of more of an evangelical fundamental type of approach. Even though he welcomed all people, if you had an event let's say where you were working with a Jewish synagogue and you decided you wanted to be sensitive to those people, he would get really upset if you would take down a sign that said you are a Christian organization.

Ultimately the debate over the appropriate role of religious ideology in Habitat for Humanity led to removal of Millard Fuller as the national director of the organization. Even organizations that seem comfortable with servicing a nondenominational clientele may face internal and external pressures on the issue of faith. A Habitat for Humanity representative recalled an example of how the organization held its ground in the face of external pressure.

> We make it vividly clear that this whole business about participation, it is not a requirement, but we make it just as clear that people do know who we are and why we are. *We do have a requirement that about three-quarters of the positions in the organization be occupied by people who can affirm and hold a statement of identity, which is in effect a faith statement* [emphasis added]. One time, one governmental unit decided to take issue with us about that, [indicating that] it was discrimination. We were able to demonstrate a) the legality of the position and b) the inclusiveness of our practice. They basically went away and we never heard another issue.

Concluding Thoughts

This chapter has documented a complex network of government agencies and nonprofit and for-profit organizations that make up the Michigan low- and moderate-income housing sector. Based on even this cursory analysis it is clear that faith-based nonprofits play an important role in efforts to expand housing opportunities to Michigan citizens. It is equally clear, however, that if one is to assess the existing impact (and perhaps estimate future potential) of such efforts, it is essential that faith-based nonprofits be understood within the context of this broader housing system. The housing provision system has a long history of federal legislation, state housing policy, and implementing organizations at, primarily, the state and local levels. Nonprofit organizations, be they secular or faith based, are critically dependent on the financial and administrative resources of public agencies. In the absence of fundamental restructuring, it would seem to make little sense to speak of the potential of such organizations independent of public resources (see the discussion of funding in Chapter 6). As will be described in more detail later, beyond resources, the implementation of housing creation, maintenance, and associated support services also involves a complex set of relationships among nonprofits and between nonprofits and other public and private sector actors.

Finally, the qualitative evidence provided in this chapter also points to a good deal of complexity in what it means to be a faith-based organization. The largest and most active faith-based housing providers do not, in general, appear to be tightly connected to religious congregations. Instead, the role of faith in faith-based organizations engaged in housing in Michigan is to define a social mission. To be sure, that mission can and does take a number of forms. This variety will be a key question in the chapters to follow.

Notes

The quotes in this chapter come from personal interviews conducted in 2009 with representatives of the Michigan State Housing Development Authority, the Department of Housing and Urban Development, the Community and Economic Development Association of Michigan, and various faith-based organizations engaged in the housing arena in Michigan.

1. Note that this does not include what is generally considered to be the largest federal housing subsidy program: tax rules that permit the deduction of interest charges from one's federal income tax. These off-budget expenditures are excluded from the present discussion since they primarily benefit middle- and upper-income households.

2. Entitlement cities for the Community Development Block Grant Program (CDBG) include: principal cities of Metropolitan Statistical Areas (MSAs), other metropolitan cities with populations of at least 50,000, and qualified urban counties with populations of at least 200,000. These jurisdictions automatically receive CDBG funds on the basis of an established formula. Nonentitlement cities are eligible to apply for funding on a project-by-project basis. MSHDA is the Michigan State Housing Development Authority.

3. For a brief but informative overview of the public housing program see Stoloff (2004) and Bratt (1989).

4. Interestingly, the 1949 Housing Act created a number of market-based incentives to support housing for middle-class families. The result was the encouragement of large-scale migration of white citizens to the suburbs.

5. Race also plays a role in the public's view of public housing. From the 1960s, public housing was seen as a "minority group" program.

6. Since 1991, these redevelopment efforts have been organized through a HUD grant program, Hope VI. As of 2005, Hope VI had distributed $5.8 billion through 446 block grants to local authorities. The largest individual grant was $50 million.

7. The percentage of families receiving other forms of subsidized housing is much higher. The Center on Budget and Policy Priorities (2009) reports that 54 percent of all housing vouchers are targeted for low-income families. Nineteen percent of vouchers are allocated to the disabled and 17 percent to the elderly.

8. During the 1970s and 1980s, HUD offered housing authorities the opportunity to apply both to renew their existing Section 8 vouchers and also to obtain new increments of vouchers. Some housing authorities were more proactive in requesting new increments, while others requested few or none (Corporation for Supportive Housing 2009).

9. Not all of the voucher funding is allocated through local PHAs. In Michigan, for example, MSHDA has responsibility for allocating some of these funds.

10. "Other" programs include project-based certificates, project-based vouchers, combined project vouchers and certificates, homeownership vouchers, Section 8 Moderate Rehabilitation, and Section 8 Moderate Rehabilitation-Single Room Occupancy.

11. The demand for LIHTC was significantly reduced by the strong recession of 2008–2009.

12. The expansion or redefinition of organizational goals has not always been linear or without controversy. Indeed, a recent effort to shift the organization's priorities almost exclusively to homelessness led to a good deal of internal conflict and ultimately the removal of an executive director.

13. There are some exceptions to the observations. For example, a handful of faith-based organizations include the management of housing vouchers in their portfolio of activities.

14. Vision 2020 is a coalition of nonprofit and for-profit organizations that seek to "develop local comprehensive revitalization plans that focus resources on locally identified (*geographic*) target areas to eliminate substandard housing and the conditions which cause it by 2020" (Vision 2020, 2007).

15. It should be noted that congregations and the larger, better known, faith-associated organizations like Catholic Social Services, Lutheran Social Services, and the Salvation Army were not the focus of this study. Rather the intent was to examine other types of faith-based organizations engaged in housing.

16. This is a reference to two verses: "Therefore if any man be in Christ, he is a new creature: old things are passed away; behold, all things are become new" (2 Corinthians 5:17, New International Version [NIV]); and "Now then we are ambassadors for Christ, as though God did beseech you by us: we pray you in Christ's stead, be ye reconciled to God" (2 Corinthians 5:20, NIV).

17. This is a reference to: "As God's fellow workers we urge you not to receive God's grace in vain" (2 Corinthians 6:1, NIV).

18. Several sources cite the Salvation Army as an example of a faith-based organization that engages in social services as a means to proselytize, rather than providing service as an end in itself.

References

Abt Associates. 2006. *Are States Using the Low-Income Tax Credit to Enable Families with Children to Live in Low Poverty and Racially Integrated Neighborhoods?* Prepared for Poverty and Race Action Council and the National Fair Housing Alliance. Cambridge, MA: Abt.

American Bankers Association. 2004. *Housing Policy for the 21st Century American Bankers.* Washington, DC: American Bankers Association, America's Community Bankers, Mortgage Bankers Association, National Association of Home Builders, National Association of Realtors.

Bratt, Rachel G. 1989. *Rebuilding a Low-Income Housing Policy.* Philadelphia: Temple University Press.

Bright, Kim. 2009. Section 202 Supportive Housing for the Elderly. www.aarp.org/research/housing-mobility/accessibility/fs65r_housing.html.

Center on Budget and Policy Priorities. 2009. Policy Basics: The Housing Choice Voucher Program. www.cbpp.org.

Climaco, Carissa, Meryl Finkel, Bulbul Kaul, Ken Lam, and Chris Rodger. 2009. Updating the Low-Income Housing Tax Credit (LIHTC) Database: Projects Placed in Service Through 2006. http://www.huduser.org/Datasets/lihtc/report9506.pdf.

Community Economic Development Association of Michigan. 2008. CDC Industry Report: Initial Findings. Detroit, Community and Economic Development Association of Michigan. Lansing, MI: CEDAM.

Corporation for Supportive Housing. 2009. Guide to Financing Supportive Housing: Department of Housing and Urban Development—Housing Choice Voucher Program (Section 8). http://www.csh.org.

Hula, Richard C. 1991. Alternative Management Strategies in Public Housing. In *Privatization and Its Alternatives,* ed. W.T. Gormley, 134–162. Madison: University of Wisconsin Press.

Kingsley, G. Thomas. 1991. Housing Vouchers and America's Changing Housing Problems. In *Privatization and Its Alternatives,* ed. W.T. Gormley, 115–133. Madison: University of Wisconsin Press.

Michigan State Housing Development Authority. 2009. *2007–2008 Annual Report.* Lansing: Michigan State Housing Development Authority.

Oakley, Deidre. 2008. Locational Patterns of Low-Income Housing Tax Credit Developments: A Sociospatial Analysis of Four Metropolitan Areas. *Urban Affairs Review* 43(5): 599–628.

Stoloff, Jennifer. 2004. A Brief History of Public Housing. Paper presented at the Annual Meeting of the American Sociological Association, San Francisco. www.allacademic.com/meta/p108852_index.htm.

U.S. Department of Agriculture. 2009. *Michigan 2008 Progress Report.* Washington, DC. http://www.rurdev.usda.gov/mi/annual%20report08%201%20page.pdf.

U.S. Department of Housing and Urban Development. 2008. Researching HUD's Housing Programs. *Research Works* 5(6): 5–7.

———. 2009a. LIHTC Database Access. http://lihtc.huduser.org/.

———. 2009b. Resident Characteristics Report (RCR). www.hud.gov/offices/pih/systems/pic/50058/rcr/.

Vision 2020. 2007. Vision 2020: A Challenge for Michigan's Neighborhoods and Communities. www.vision2020michigan.org.

6

Structure and Capacity of Housing Nonprofits

[C]ommunities are basically looking to nonprofits to help them. So then the question becomes, do the nonprofits have the capacity to be of any serious assistance and that varies from one nonprofit to the next.

—HUD official

Research previously discussed suggests a number of factors that may affect the extent and nature of a nonprofit organization's housing and other community service activities: age, size, financial status, and staffing (Lincoln and Mamiya 1990; Hall 1992; La Barbera 1992; Chang et al. 1994; Devita et al. 1999; Reese and Shields 2000; Chaves and Tsitsos 2001).[1] A perennial question about the increasing service role of nonprofits is whether they have the capacity to operate as a viable alternative to public provision. This chapter explores the capacity of housing nonprofits in Michigan and makes explicit comparisons between faith-based and secular organizations. It sheds light on the efficacy of expanding the use of nonprofits for housing service provision and identifies specific areas where capacity building appears to be needed to more fully realize the potential service roles of nonprofits.

Organizational Capacity

Capacity can be examined along several dimensions, including structure (e.g., human and financial capital), programs, networks, and politics (see Table 6.1). Structural capacity is often the first marker of capacity and one indicator of the potential for success in achieving organizational goals. Federal and state housing officials are quick to note that there are both potentialities and challenges associated with the capacity of nonprofit organizations. One HUD representative noted

There are some [nonprofit organizations] that are stable, have been around since 1959 doing things that are HUD and housing oriented and others are relatively new, they may sometimes have money, sometimes they don't and I guess it will be a challenge.

A state housing official noted:

Table 6.1

Types of Capacity

Type of Capacity	Purpose	Activity
Structural		
Organizational	Managerial support, staff training, and internal structure	Human resources training
Financial	Operational support and fundraising assistance	Seeking grants, loans, and contracts
Programmatic	Partnerships with for- and nonprofit agencies, increased representation of the community on the board of directors[a]	Building and maintaining housing, economic development, and service delivery
Networking	Partnerships to manage specific programs, community building	Building networks with businesses, nonprofits, government agencies, and philanthropic groups
Political	Acknowledgment by city government, public relations, and policy reform	Constituent advocacy and mobilization

Source: Glickman and Servon (1998, 2003) and Nye and Glickman (2000).

[a]Silverman (2009) argues that obtaining community representation on the boards of community-based housing organizations, as well as community participation with the activities of these organizations, can sometimes be inhibited by three key factors: rules (or lack of) for board composition, competition over boundaries, and the position/stance of the organization's executive director. A visual depiction of potential barriers to increasing representation of the community on an organization's board of directors is presented in Appendix B (Figure B1).

> I will say that as a general rule no matter if you had church beginnings or you didn't, if you don't think like a business and run like a business, then you don't build the capacity that you need to have to do this hard work. . . . [However] I am finding pretty high-capacity nonprofits meaning that their executive directors and staff are very well trained and very experienced.

These observations are not limited to secular nonprofits. As a representative of the Michigan State Housing Development Authority (MSHDA) noted, there are "a lot of good high-capacity groups that got their beginnings from their church." It seems that for many government officials, the key issue is whether an organization has the ability to provide housing services. Another MSHDA official quickly pointed out that

> there [are] dozens, if not hundreds, of faith-based organizations we've been working with, and we always have. I think to us in the day-to-day operation of our programs, I would have to say that whether a group is faith-based or not is not really a factor, either positive or negative. What is a factor is capacity. Can they keep track of money? Can they get housing units done? Can they use our resources efficiently? As long as they aren't cramming some doctrine down somebody's throat, we don't care whether they're faith-based or not.

Given its importance, structural capacity is the focus of the discussion in this chapter. Issues related to programmatic, network, and political capacity and activities are addressed in detail in Chapters 7 through 11; even so, it is useful to take an overarching look here at these other dimensions of capacity.

In order to increase programmatic, networking, and political capacity, an organization should be efficient at producing housing (Nye and Glickman 2000). Many individuals and organizations active in housing development would argue that part of being efficient is being smart, and simultaneously being cognizant of the age-old quantity-versus-quality debate. As one director of a faith-based housing organization noted:

> [W]e need to understand the huge, huge, huge, huge power of design in the effectiveness of community development. And by that I mean, if we aren't creative and responsible in the shaping of the spaces where we want people to live then it is not going to be effective, it is not going to be long lasting. There are housing organizations that say, "Give me a million dollars and I will build you ten $100,000 houses and 10 families will be warm and dry." But there will be another organization that says, "Give me a million dollars and I will build eight high-quality houses, eight families will be warm and dry, and because I have been careful with the design, all the people who pass by, all the people who live next door, all the people with whom those residents interact will get a different idea, will have a different experience about affordable housing and about [the] affordable housing's occupant." So, do you want 10 houses and 10 families warm and dry? Or do you want eight houses and warm and dry families with a whole community understanding and supporting? We [the housing-development community, in general] too often go for the quantity, way too often.

Slowly building relationships with government institutions over time is another way to increase programmatic, networking, and political capacity (Nye and Glickman 2000). Government and nonprofit organization officials alike stress the importance of networking and working together to achieve programmatic goals and to advance their collective agendas. An official from MSHDA highlighted this point, noting that it is about

> looking to partners in state corners. It's a willingness to say, "We can't do this all by ourselves." I mean, who is it we collaborate with? Who do we partner with? And you have partners out there saying, "If we change the way we [do] business . . . using [our organization] as a public service delivery system, we'll have all we need."

Maintaining flexibility is also an important component of capacity, particularly with respect to collaborations and partnerships, as it facilitates the organization's responsiveness and resilience (Glickman and Servon 1998, 2003). The centrality of organizational flexibility is exemplified in the experiences of a highly regarded faith-based housing organization in Michigan that refined its activities to address an emerging and systemic housing-related issue.

> We provide the home-ownership counselor training for the whole state of Michigan. MSHDA hires us to train people who are getting MSHDA certified. We wrote the cur-

riculum. We know home-ownership education like the back of our hand. We are good. But we are not doing it now. Huge amounts of our energy, 80 percent or better, has gone to foreclosure intervention.

In Michigan, there is also some evidence that specific sets of organizations have been recognized as possessing the necessary political capacity to shape what occurs in the housing arena. A representative of the state housing authority noted:

> [T]he Anti-Homeless Coalition across the state is a really eclectic mix of faith-based groups, social groups, political groups. We've got for-profit developers, nonprofit developers, all working in it. Now they don't see that as a challenge, they see it as part of the objective. . . . [They] think they're a part of the conscience, OK? That coalition is an awful lot of what the late Phil Hart was to the United States Senate. Phil Hart was the conscience of the United States Senate. This coalition is actually the conscience and the moral compass of what we're [MHSDA] doing. Because if we do it right, to the audiences that we exist to serve, and we do so with both those who make no profits and those who do make a profit, and they're both very critical pieces of the economy, we will have accomplished the goal: Housing First.[2]

One might argue that each succeeding dimension of capacity relies on the existence of a strong base. In other words, it is unlikely that an organization will have a great deal of political capacity if it does not have an appropriate level of structural, programmatic, and networking capacity (see Figure 6.1). The remainder of this chapter examines the structural capacity of nonprofit organizations address- ing housing issues in Michigan.

Structural Capacity

Previous research suggests significant variability in the staffing and resources of nonprofit organizations. For example, community development corporations (CDCs) have been found to range in staff size from as few as ten to well over 1,100, making it difficult to compare capacity across organizations (National Alliance of Community Economic Development Associations 2007). In 1990, the median staff size of CDCs nationally was seven paid employees (Walker 1993). A 2005 national survey of CDCs shows a stable pattern of staff size: median size of seven full-time staff, three part-time staff, and five volunteers (National Congress for Community Economic Development 2005). Similar staff sizes have been observed for other types of faith-based and secular human service agencies (Clerkin and Grønbjerg 2007). Research on housing nonprofits in Texas, however, suggests higher staffing levels, with a mean of forty paid staff (Ebaugh et al. 2003).

In general, it appears that faith-based organizations (FBOs) rely more heavily on volunteers than secular organizations do, perhaps because they have a lower proportion of their budget covered by public funding (Hodgkinson and Weitzman 1993; Cnaan 1997; Printz Platnick 1998; Chaves 2002; Monsma 2002; Twombly 2002; Ebaugh et al. 2003, 2006). Indeed, nonprofit organizations that receive more

Figure 6.1 **Dimensions of Organizational Capacity**

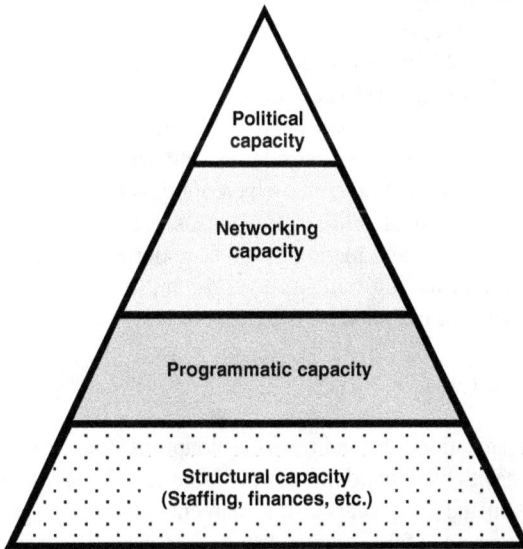

Political
capacity

Networking
capacity

Programmatic capacity

Structural capacity
(Staffing, finances, etc.)

government funding tend to rely more heavily on paid staff for critical organizational functions and less on volunteers (Salamon 1987a, 1987b; VanTil 1988; Smith and Lipsky 1993). Faith-based and secular organizations depend on a variety of funding sources including the government, banks, foundations, individuals, and a range of other secular agencies and religious organizations (Walker 1993). While FBOs tend to rely heavily on religious sources of funding, secular agencies tend to rely more heavily on secular sources and the government for funding (Burt et al. 1999; Ebaugh et al. 2003). It is not clear, however, that less government funding translates into smaller budgets overall for FBOs (Hula et al. 2008). This section next presents a discussion of the structural capacity of nonprofits as indicated in the 2003 and 2007 Community Economic Development Association of Michigan (CEDAM) membership surveys (the Michigan CDC Accomplishments Survey [2003] and the CEDAM Industry Survey 2007). Comparisons are then made with nonprofit capacity as indicated by the statewide service provider survey conducted by the authors.

2003 and 2007 CEDAM Surveys

Overall capacities among CEDAM members over time appear stable although direct comparisons are not possible due to differences in the metrics of response options to the two waves of surveys (ordinal versus interval measures, for example). Wide variability in staff size is visible among CEDAM organizations with full-time employees, ranging from none to 123 in 2003 and from one to 499 in 2007 (Table 6.2). The average full-time staff size for the 2003 survey is seven employees; the average staff size of organizations responding to the 2007 survey is much larger, at almost thirty-nine employees. Numbers of volunteers appear a bit smaller for the CEDAM organizations in 2003 (averaging seven) but in 2007 they appear to be much more in line with what is typically expected based on previous studies (average of twenty-three). Age of organizations is similar with most years of operation ranging around twenty for the 2003 respondents and thirteen for the 2007 respondents.

The budget pattern also appears similar among organizations responding to the two surveys.[3] Many CEDAM members have modest budgets of $500,000 or less or between $500,000 and $1 million. Responses to both surveys have a bimodal element: the largest numbers having budgets under $500,000, but a reasonable number of nonprofits having budgets over $4 million. Information on specific budget sources was not included on the CEDAM surveys.

Nonprofit Housing Provider Survey

The profile of organizations responding to the Nonprofit Housing Provider Survey appears to be in line with other national studies (Table 6.3). Most responding nonprofits are between eleven and thirty years old; 14 percent are quite new and 12 percent are over fifty. This represents a fairly normal distribution of ages. Staff sizes are quite modest: the plurality, 39 percent, has between one and five full-time employees. Fifteen percent have over one hundred paid staff, however, indicating that staff sizes may be U-shaped, with a number of relatively small and then some quite large organizations, roughly corresponding to the budget bimodality found in the CEDAM surveys. This again suggests the difficulty in generalizing about nonprofit staff capacities.

The distribution of part-time and volunteer staff is more uniform. Fifty-one percent have between one and five part-time staff and 35 percent have between one and five volunteer staff. Relatively large percentages have no part-timers (23 percent) or volunteers (26 percent). Again, there are some very large organizations (3 percent) that have more than one hundred part-time staff (6 percent have more than one hundred volunteers). Overall, reliance on volunteers is quite modest among housing nonprofits in the state.

Budget size among respondents to the Nonprofit Housing Provider Survey is also U-shaped, with most organizations having modest budgets, but then a relatively large number (30 percent) having budgets of over $4 million. Forty-four percent of housing nonprofits have budgets of $500,000 or less annually (these represent total budgets from all sources). As a group, housing nonprofits rely heavily on public funding: 53 percent use it to a large extent, 20 percent to a moderate extent (Table 6.4). At the other extreme, 65 percent do not receive funding from religious organizations. After government funding, the most common source of nonprofit revenues is foundations (25 percent use foundation support to a large or moderate extent). Thirty-nine percent have no support from corporations, 36 percent have no revenue from banks, and 33 percent have no donation income. But as will be shown later, source of revenue varies considerably by the nature of the nonprofit.[4]

Table 6.2

CEDAM Survey Organization Traits 2003 and 2007

Characteristic	Min		Max		Average	
	2003	2007	2003	2007	2003	2007
Number full-time employees	0	1	123	499	6.72	38.47
Number part-time employees	0	1	72	300	2.92	28.52
Number volunteers	0	2	3	63	0.07	23.24
Age	5	3	50	64	20.08	13.45
Budget	$0	$15,000	$16,116,393	$50,000,000	$1,770,268[a]	$3,879,093

Budget category	%	
	2003	2007
$0–$500,000	49	43
$500,001–$1,000,000	14	11
$1,000,001–$1,500,000	5	7
$1,500,001–$2,000,000	5	3
$2,000,001–$2,500,000	3	5
$2,500,001–$3,500,000	4	1
$3,500,001–$4,000,000	4	1
Over $4,000,000	15	24

$N = 90$ in 2003; $N = 75$ in 2007

[a] Values for an outlying, very well-funded organization (budget = $68,000,000) have been removed.

Table 6.3

Nonprofit Housing Provider Survey: Organizational Resource Traits

Characteristic	N	%
Age of organization		
0–10 years	14	14
11–20 years	23	33
21–30 years	21	21
31–40 years	9	9
41–50 years	10	10
Over 50 years	12	12
Number of full-time staff		
None	8	9
1–5	33	39
6–10	8	9
11–25	9	11
26–50	8	9
51–99	6	7
100 or more	13	15
Number of part-time staff		
None	16	23
1–5	36	51
6–10	7	10
11–25	3	4
26–50	0	0
51–99	7	10
100 or more	2	3
Number of volunteers per week		
None	19	26
1–5	25	35
6–10	7	10
11–25	8	11
26–50	5	7
51–99	4	6
100 or more	4	6
Organization's budget (from all sources)		
$0–$100,000	17	18
$100,001–$250,000	15	16
$250,001–$500,000	9	10
$500,001–$1 million	6	6
$1,000,001–$1.5 million	8	8
$1,500,001–$2 million	7	7
$2,000,001–$2.5 million	2	2
$2,500,001–$3 million	2	2
$3,000,001–$3.5 million	0	0
$3,500,001–$4 million	1	1
$4,000,001 and above	28	30

$N = 99$

Table 6.4

Budget Sources for Nonprofits in the Housing Provider Survey

% Budget source	Reliance on source (%)			
	Large extent	Moderate extent	Some extent	None
Religious organization	0	3	32	65
Donations	3	7	57	33
Foundations	6	19	50	26
Corporations	1	6	54	39
Government	53	20	17	10
Banks	5	8	51	36

Faith-Based and Secular Differences

While it is interesting to note the structural capacities of nonprofit housing providers generally, the main focus here is to explore the differences between faith-based and secular nonprofits. This section explores capacity differences between the two types of organizations that may impact service viability as well as the extent and nature of services provided. Results from the CEDAM sample will be discussed first, followed by data obtained from the more comprehensive Nonprofit Housing Provider Survey. Overall, the findings are very similar.

CEDAM Surveys

Table 6.5 compares secular and faith-based housing nonprofits by years in operation, total employees, and annual budget for CEDAM organizations according to the 2003 survey. The 2007 survey did not include most of these variables; and for those that were included in both surveys, the form of the responses was not comparable (ordinal in one survey, interval in another, for example). Therefore, this discussion is limited to the 2003 survey.

Although there appears to be a great deal of variation in the basic structural indicators presented in Table 6.5, faith-based or secular status explains little of the observed variation. The central tendency data are somewhat misleading, however, in that they include a large faith-based nonprofit, which results in a set of average scores that give the impression that the "average" faith-based nonprofit is significantly larger than it actually is. The values presented in parentheses for annual budget and total employees are the recalculated means with the single large organization dropped from analysis. The recalculated means suggest that FBOs are somewhat smaller and have fewer employees than their secular counterparts. But these differences are of smaller magnitude than differences within each category of organization, and do not rise to the level of statistical significance. Interestingly, for this group of respondents, secular organizations rely on volunteers more than on

Table 6.5

Profile of Organizations in 2003 CEDAM Sample

	Organization type	N	Mean	Std. deviation	Std. error mean	t-test significance
Year founded	Secular	48	1986	12	1.7	.45
	Faith-based	27	1988	8	1.6	
Number of years in business	Secular	48	21	12	1.7	.45
	Faith-based	27	19	8	1.6	
501(c)3 Status[a]	Secular	51	1	.000	.000	.33
	Faith-based	29	1	.18	.03	
Annual budget	Secular	42	$2,323,652	$3,434,243	$529,915	.51
	Faith-based	26	$3,728,840 [$1,157,993]	$13,217,195	$2,592,105	
Total employees[s]	Secular	46	14.5	40	5.9	.53
	Faith-based	27	24.56 [6]	95	18.3	
Total number of full-time employees	Secular	42	8.76	21	3.2	.29
	Faith-based	24	4.08	5.4	1.1	
Total number of volunteers	Secular	42	.12	.55	.085	.51
	Faith-based	24	.04	.2	.042	
Total number of part-time employees[a]	Secular	42	4.4	15	2.4	.15
	Faith-based	24	.92	1.1	.22	
Total number of employees with benefits	Secular	37	4.9	10.9	1.8	.49
	Faith-based	22	3.2	4.0	.8	
Total number of employees without benefits	Secular	37	5.9	22	3.7	.42
	Faith-based	21	.95	1	.24	
Ratio of volunteers to employed workers	Secular	41	.0140	.07	.01	.01***
	Faith-based	23	.0017	.01	.001	

[a]t-test computed with group variance not assumed to be equal across groups. Otherwise equal variance assumed. Assumption used based on result of Levene's Test for Equality of Variances.

***Significant at the 0.01 level.

[ ] recalculated values after dropping one very large faith-based nonprofit.

paid staff, as well as more than FBOs do. This runs counter to evidence presented in the studies cited earlier and in data from the Nonprofit Housing Provider Survey conducted by the authors.

For the five traits that were included on both CEDAM surveys (year founded, budget, full- and part-time employees, and volunteers), there are again no significant differences between the 2007 survey (not in the table) and the 2003 survey. Nevertheless, faith-based organizations responding to the 2007 CEDAM survey have more full- and part-time employees than their secular counterparts. Although not statistically different, FBOs have a mean of fifty-five full-time employees as compared to thirty-three full-time employees in secular organizations and a mean of thirty-six as compared to twenty-five part-time employees (FBOs and secular, respectively) in 2007, bringing the results more in line with those in the literature and the housing provider survey conducted by the authors. Budgets are larger for faith-based organizations again in the 2007 survey ($6,635,030 versus $2,944,043 for secular), yet the difference is not statistically significant.

Nonprofit Housing Provider Survey

Table 6.6 illustrates differences between sacred and secular nonprofits on general capacities as found in the Nonprofit Housing Provider Survey. There is no significant difference in the age of faith-based and secular housing providers; the average age for both is 25 years. There is also very little difference in staffing. FBOs have slightly more volunteers but the difference is only significant at the .10 level (shown because the variability in the number of cases across cells suppresses the chi-square somewhat). There is also no significant difference in overall budget size. While FBOs appear to serve more clients, the difference is also not significant. In short, basic capacities of faith-based and secular nonprofits in the housing arena are essentially identical.

It is in the sources of funding that the organizations are significantly different, an area of potential policy importance. The Nonprofit Housing Provider Survey shows that FBOs are significantly more likely to get revenue from corporations, individual donations, and religious bodies than are their secular counterparts. Conversely, secular nonprofits are significantly more likely to have government funding. It appears then that FBOs make up for their lower levels of government funding through a more diversified set of funders. Only foundation and bank funding are indistinguishable between the two types of organizations. Tables 6.7 and 6.8 provide more detailed breakdowns of the overall percentages of budget from each source. Secular nonprofits get very little funding from religious organizations, while half of the FBOs get from 1 to 25 percent of their budgets from religious sources. Overall, government funding is essential to the operation of all nonprofits; FBOs, however, get more money from a wider variety of organizations across the board.

More interesting, perhaps, are the results from several survey questions exploring why nonprofits were not receiving public funding. Respondents indicating an

Table 6.6

Faith-Based and Secular Capacity Comparisons, Nonprofit Housing Provider Survey

Characteristic	Type of organization			Chi square
	Faith-based	Secular	All orgs	
Average age of organization	24	26	25	45.59
Mean number of staff positions				
Full-time paid	6.10	11–24	11–24	1.02
Part-time paid	1–5	6.10	1–5	4.69
Volunteer	6.10	1–5	6.10	12.18*
Funding sources (any amount of funding, in %)				
Government	83	93	90	9.85**
Banks/financial institutions	73	58	64	3.32
Corporations	73	54	61	9.01**
Foundations	82	70	75	1.95
Individual donations/offerings	82	58	67	7.71**
Religious bodies	59	21	35	15.00***
Average operating budget ($)	$1,500,001–$2,000,000	$1,000,000–$1,500,000	$1,500,001–$2,000,000	9.89
Percent of budget				
Development activities	24	27	26	12.55
Housing projects, programs, services	54	55	55	27.57
Management and related expenses	19	14	16	24.86
Other	22	22	22	17.35
Clients served	250–499	100–249	100–249	9.04

***Significant at .01, **significant at .05, *significant at .10.

Table 6.7

Sources and Percentage of Funding by Organizational Type (Broad Categories), Nonprofit Housing Provider Survey

	Percent of funding							
	None		1–25%		26–59%		60–100%	
Funding source[e]	Faith-based	Secular	Faith-based	Secular	Faith-based	Secular	Faith-based	Secular
Government	17	7	17	16	31	13	34	64***
Secular organizations[a]	72	118	186	137	30	34	12	11
Religious organizations	41	79	50	21	9	0	0	0***

Notes: Row percentages do not total to 100 because of missing data. Individual donations and offerings are not reflected in these data.
[a]The secular organizations category includes banks/financial institutions, corporations, and foundations; thus percentages add up to 300.
***Significant at 0.01 level, Chi-Square test of independence.

Table 6.8

Sources and Percentage of Funding by Organizational Type (Specific Categories) Nonprofit Housing Provider Survey

	Percent of funding							
	None		1–25%		26–59		60–100%	
Funding source	Faith-based	Secular	Faith-based	Secular	Faith-based	Secular	Faith-based	Secular
Government	17	7	17	16	31	13	34	64***
Banks/financial institutions	27	42	64	44	6	9	3	6
Corporations	27	46	70	44	0	9	3	0***
Foundations	18	30	52	49	24	16	6	5
Individual donations/offerings	18	42	65	53	12	4	6	2***
Religious bodies	41	79	50	21	9	0	0	0***

Note: Row percentages do not total to 100 because of missing data.
***Significant at 0.01 level, Chi-Square test of independence significance.

absence of government funding were asked why that was the case (Table 6.9). Although the number responding was small (particularly for secular organizations), the data shed light on potential barriers to public funding that will be discussed in more detail later in the chapter. Nonprofits not receiving government funding are most likely to indicate that it is because they have applied for funding but have failed to get it or that funding is not available for their particular activities. This suggests that most nonprofits would like to receive public funding if they could get it. The only difference between faith-based and secular nonprofits (significant at the .10 level) relates to the issue of strings or red tape associated with public financing. FBOs are more likely to avoid government funding because they see the strings attached as undesirable or onerous. Concerns among some faith-based advocates reported in the literature, that public funding will change the missions of FBOs, do not appear to be shared by the faith-based survey respondents here.

Barriers to Capacity

Some of the more commonly noted barriers to nonprofit housing development include financing and organizational capacity issues such as technical assistance, training, and general operating support (Vidal 1992; Walker 1993; Schwartz et al. 1996). Scholars and practitioners agree that building organizational capacity and providing sufficient and timely technical assistance to nonprofit organizations are vital to their continued success and ability to provide services in a systematic and sustained manner. Although organizations may have the skill sets and resources to provide technical assistance, nonprofit organizations that perceive that requesting assistance will negatively impact future funding options may be reluctant to seek assistance from the government (Mitchell et al. 2002). In the housing arena, some CDCs have been reluctant to admit capacity problems out of a fear that such an admission would negatively impact funding (Bratt and Rohe 2005).

Barriers to Success

Questions about barriers to success and the need for technical assistance were asked only on the 2003 CEDAM survey, since the primary goal of that effort was to define existing and future programmatic and training needs. As a result, the following discussion is solely based on data from that survey.

Contrary to what some of the literature suggests, CEDAM organizations were quite willing to identify barriers or obstacles to their involvement in the housing arena, perhaps because they were comfortable doing so to their own advocacy organization. Seventy-nine of 90 organizations (88 percent) reported at least one barrier to expanding the scope and capacity of their organization. Fifty of ninety organizations (56 percent) pointed to specific barriers within the local planning process, and thirty-two of ninety (36 percent) identified barriers to obtaining needed training and technical assistance. Figure 6.2 demonstrates that there is a strong

Table 6.9

Reasons for Not Having Public Funding (in percent), Nonprofit Housing Provider Survey

Why not take public funding	Strongly agree		Agree		Neutral		Disagree		Strongly disagree	
	Faith-based	Secular	Faith-based	Secular	Faith-based	Secular	Faith-based	Secular	Faith-based	Secular
Not eligible	0	17	0	17	20	17	20	0	60	50
Policy against	0	0	0	0	33	17	17	0	50	83
Applied but failed	43	17	0	17	0	17	43	0	14	50
Funding not available for activities	20	17	20	17	20	17	20	0	20	50
Do not need	0	0	17	0	17	17	17	0	50	83
Too many strings*	43	0	14	0	0	67	29	17	14	17
Changes mission	0	0	0	0	40	17	40	17	20	67

*Significantly different at the .10 level, Chi-Square test of independence significance.

Figure 6.2   **Impediments to Achieving Organizational Mission**

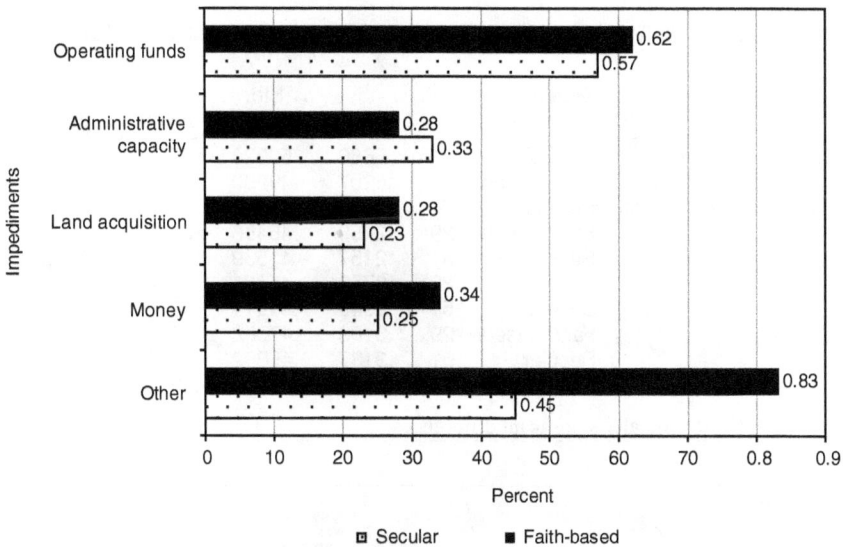

Note: No statistically significant differences in impediments for faith-based or secular organizations.

agreement between secular and nonprofit providers as to major impediments to growth and expanded organizational capacity. Indeed, data in Table 6.10 clearly indicate that there are no significant differences between types of nonprofits in the barriers they perceive to achieving their organizational missions. While it is hardly surprising that there is a significant consensus that the major impediment faced is a lack of operating funds, there is also a remarkable coherence across organizational types in perception of additional problems. Faith-based and secular organizations perceive the same barriers to growth in housing production: operating funds, administrative capacity, land acquisition, and resources to fund projects. Indeed, behind operating funds, the other factors are seen as barriers with about the same frequency among sacred and secular respondents. Again, this is consistent with the literature highlighting the challenges that organizations face in providing affordable housing (see for example Table 2.5 as compiled from Schwartz et al. [1996]).

There are, however, interesting differences in how organizations perceive barriers to obtaining needed technical support (Table 6.11). Lack of knowledge, time, staff capacity, and funding are all cited as barriers to obtaining technical assistance. FBOs are much more likely to identify funding as a major barrier to obtaining technical assistance. Interestingly, they are much less likely to identify staff capacity as a problem. Funding is the only factor that has some degree of statistical significance. None of the other differences reach statistical significance.

A similar pattern emerges with respect to perceived barriers to organization and

Table 6.10

Impediments to Achieving Organizational Mission, 2003 CEDAM Survey

	Organization type	N	Mean	Std. deviation	Std. error mean	t-test significance
Operating funds	Secular	51	.5686	.50020	.07004	.654
	Faith-based	29	.6207	.49380	.09170	
Administrative capacity	Secular	51	.3333	.47610	.06667	.599
	Faith-based	29	.2759	.45486	.08447	
Land acquisition	Secular	51	.2157	.41539	.05817	.549
	Faith-based	29	.2759	.45486	.08447	
Money	Secular	51	.2549	.44014	.06163	.599
	Faith-based	29	.3103	.47082	.08743	
Other	Secular	51	.3137	.46862	.06562	.557
	Faith-based	29	.3793	.49380	.09170	

Note: No statistically significant differences.

Table 6.11

Barriers to Receiving Needed Technical Assistance, 2003 CEDAM Survey

	Organization type	N	Mean	Std. deviation	t-test significance
Funding[a]	Secular	51	.1373	.34754	.090*
	Faith-based	29	.3103	.47082	
Lack of knowledge	Secular	51	.0588	.23764	.859
	Faith-based	29	.0690	.25788	
Lack of time[a]	Secular	51	.0588	.23764	.505
	Faith-based	29	.1034	.30993	
Staff capacity	Secular	51	.0784	.27152	.125
	Faith-based	29	.0000	.00000	
Other	Secular	51	.1569	.36729	.858
	Faith-based	29	.1724	.38443	

[a]Indicates *t*-test computed with group variance not assumed to be equal across groups. Otherwise equal variance assumed. Assumption used based on result of Levene's Test for Equality of Variances.
    *Significant at the 0.10 level.

project planning (Table 6.12). Overall, nonprofits are most likely to perceive bureaucratic politics and the availability and nature of land for housing to be the biggest barriers to success in housing development.[5] FBOs are more sensitive to perceived political and bureaucratic barriers than are secular organizations. Secular nonprofits, on the other hand, see more problems with local regulations, such as city ordinances. Finally, FBOs are somewhat more concerned with funding issues. Only with regard to barriers presented by local ordinances are the organizations significantly different.

Table 6.12

Perceived Barriers to Project Planning Process, 2003 CEDAM Survey

	Organization type	N	Mean	Std. deviation	t-test significance
Zoning[a]	Secular	51	.0588	.23764	.286
	Faith-based	29	.1379	.35093	
Lot size, availability, cost[a]	Secular	51	.1569	.36729	.860
	Faith-based	29	.1724	.38443	
Bureaucracy/politics	Secular	51	.1569	.36729	.010*
	Faith-based	29	.4138	.50123	
Citizens/NIMBY[a]	Secular	51	.0784	.27152	.718
	Faith-based	29	.1034	.30993	
Ordinance problems[a]	Secular	51	.0784	.27152	.044**
	Faith-based	29	.0000	.00000	
Financial	Secular	51	.0588	.23764	.188
	Faith-based	29	.0000	.00000	
Other	Secular	51	.0980	.30033	.663
	Faith-based	29	.0690	.25788	

[a]Indicates t-test computed with group variance not assumed to be equal across groups. Otherwise equal variance assumed. Assumption used based on result of Levene's Test for Equality of Variances.
**Significant at the 0.05 level, *Significant at the 0.10 level

Technical Assistance and Training Needs

The 2003 CEDAM survey asked housing nonprofits to identify needed areas of technical assistance and training. These questions included housing concerns and also mentioned topics in community planning, commercial development, and commercial strip development. Overall, in the area of housing, nonprofits are most likely to indicate a need for technical assistance with the use of tax credits, conducting market studies, and neighborhood planning (Table 6.13).

Secular and faith-based housing nonprofits gave similar preference to nineteen of twenty possible areas of technical assistance. Technical assistance in the area of tax credits was the single exception to this pattern for housing-related services. Here FBOs expressed a need for more technical assistance than did their secular counterparts. FBOs also expressed a need for more technical assistance for neighborhood planning and market studies. Figure 6.3 highlights some of the key technical assistance needs identified by the organizations. Recognizing the need to provide technical assistance and training to housing nonprofits, particularly FBOs, officials from MSHDA noted that the organization worked with the Governor's Office of Faith-Based Initiatives to develop "two or three kinds of large training events, and then various regional training events."

Despite some differences in self-identified technical assistance needs, spending devoted to technical assistance and training is not significantly different between

Table 6.13

Technical Assistance Needs Identified by Organizations, 2003 CEDAM Survey

	Organization type	N	Mean	Std. deviation	Std. error mean	t-test significance
Housing						
Management	Secular	51	.1765	.38501	.05391	
	Faith-based	29	.2414	.43549	.08087	.492
Tax credits	Secular	51	.1373	.34754	.04867	
	Faith-based	29	.3103	.47082	.08743	.090*
Real estate management	Secular	51	.0000	.00000	.00000	
	Faith-based	29	.0345	.18570	.03448	.326
Housing support	Secular	51	.0784	.27152	.03802	
	Faith-based	29	.1034	.30993	.05755	.708
Other	Secular	51	.3137	.54736	.07665	
	Faith-based	29	.1724	.38443	.07139	.288
Community planning						
Market studies[a]	Secular	51	.0000	.00000	.00000	
	Faith-based	29	.1034	.30993	.05755	.083*
Neighborhood planning[a]	Secular	51	.0980	.30033	.04205	
	Faith-based	29	.2759	.45486	.08447	.066*
Strategic planning	Secular	51	.0588	.23764	.03328	
	Faith-based	29	.0345	.18570	.03448	.613
Other	Secular	51	.1176	.32540	.04556	
	Faith-based	29	.0690	.25788	.04789	.464
Commercial development						
Financing[a]	Secular	51	.0980	.30033	.04205	
	Faith-based	29	.2069	.41225	.07655	.219
Procedural-operational[a]	Secular	51	.0980	.30033	.04205	
	Faith-based	29	.2069	.41225	.07655	.219
Staff development[a]	Secular	51	.0980	.30033	.04205	
	Faith-based	29	.2069	.41225	.07655	.219

Other[a]	Secular	51	.0980	.30033	.04205	.219
	Faith-based	29	.2069	.41225	.07655	
Commercial strip development						
Design assistance[a]	Secular	51	.0392	.19604	.02745	.159
	Faith-based	29	.0000	.00000	.00000	
Staff development[a]	Secular	51	.0196	.14003	.01961	.454
	Faith-based	29	.0000	.00000	.00000	
Business development[a]	Secular	51	.0392	.19604	.02745	.159
	Faith-based	29	.0000	.00000	.00000	
Other[a]	Secular	51	.0392	.19604	.02745	.159
	Faith-based	29	.0000	.00000	.00000	

[a]Indicates t-test computed with group variance not assumed to be equal across groups. Otherwise equal variance assumed. Assumption used based on result of Levene's Test for Equality of Variances.

* Significant at the 0.10 level.

Figure 6.3 **Technical Assistance Needs**

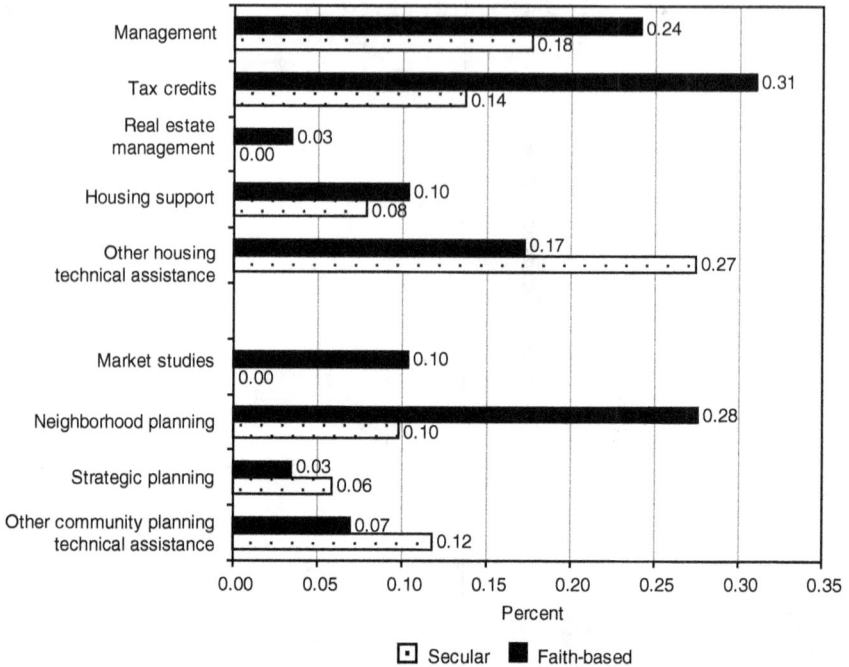

Management — 0.24 / 0.18
Tax credits — 0.31 / 0.14
Real estate management — 0.03 / 0.00
Housing support — 0.10 / 0.08
Other housing technical assistance — 0.17 / 0.27
Market studies — 0.10 / 0.00
Neighborhood planning — 0.28 / 0.10
Strategic planning — 0.03 / 0.06
Other community planning technical assistance — 0.07 / 0.12

Percent

□· Secular   ■ Faith-based

the two types of organizations. The only significant difference in technical assistance capacity is that FBOs received significantly more of their legal services at reduced rates, perhaps allowing them to devote the same amount of resources to other organizational actives as secular nonprofits (Table 6.14).

Figure 6.4 reports responses to questions about "problems" in obtaining financial support for projects. Approximately 20 percent to 22 percent of all nonprofit housing organizations see private foundations, corporations, and federal agencies as sources of problems in financing projects. Yet, there again seems to be no systematic difference between secular organizations and FBOs in expressing such concerns. Dissatisfaction with state agencies is a bit lower for FBOs, with 14 percent of FBOs and 28 percent of secular organizations expressing concern. Major differences appear with respect to city and county agencies; FBOs are much more likely to perceive them as serious barriers to potential project financing. It is unclear whether these perceptions are the result of prior negative experiences or a general mistrust of government agencies.

Based on these data several conclusions can be posited about differences in barriers and technical assistance needs between faith-based and secular nonprofits:

• Monetary resources are a greater barrier to FBOs than their secular counterparts in housing production and service provision.

Table 6.14

Technical Assistance Characteristics of Secular and FBOs, 2003 CEDAM Survey

	Organization type	N	Mean	Std. deviation	Std. error mean	t-test significance
Technical assistance budget[a]	Secular	40	9456	16610	2626	.30
	Faith-based	21	24810	65576	14310	
Training budget	Secular	30	20095.00	55732.830	10175	.72
	Faith-based	20	10395.00	26525.390	5931	
Total number of reported activities	Secular	51	7.6078	3.68824	.51646	.12
	Faith-based	29	6.2759	3.61442	.67118	
Percentage of legal services paid at market rate	Secular	34	.51	.450	.077	.040**
	Faith-based	21	.25	.420	.092	
Percentage of legal services paid at reduced rate	Secular	31	.43	.426	.076	.535
	Faith-based	20	.35	.414	.093	
Percentage of legal services provided free	Secular	29	.43	.405	.075	.162
	Faith-based	25	.59	.435	.087	
Annual legal budget[a]	Secular	40	4528.18	6707	1060.402	.19
	Faith-based	22	11173.55	22241	4741.975	

[a]t-test computed with group variance not assumed to be equal across groups. Otherwise equal variance assumed. Assumption used based on result of Levene's Test for Equality of Variances.
**Significant at .05 level.

Figure 6.4   **Impediments to Financing Projects in the Housing Arena**

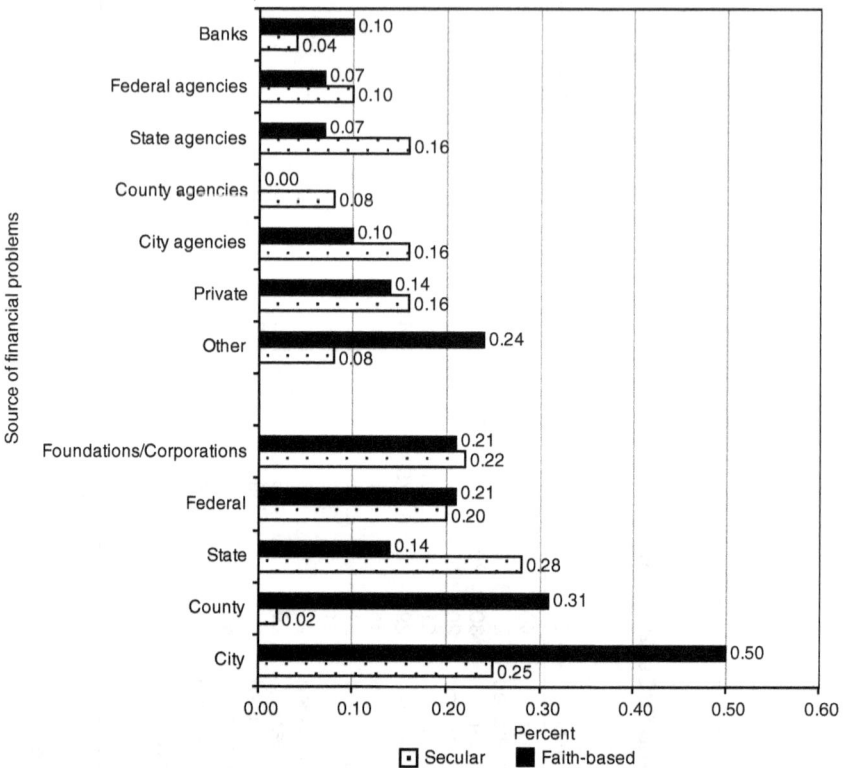

- FBOs need more technical assistance on tax credit housing, neighborhood planning, and market studies than do secular housing providers.
- FBOs are less likely than secular housing providers to identify staff capacity as a problem.
- FBOs are more sensitive to perceived political and bureaucratic barriers in the housing arena than are secular organizations.
- FBOs are much more likely than secular housing organizations to perceive city and county agencies as serious barriers to potential project financing.

An obvious question at this point is whether the differences noted above are due to the faith-based or secular nature of the nonprofits or simply an artifact of size and budget differences. Barriers and training needs were also explored in relationship to these factors. Overall, nonprofits with resource constraints (meaning smaller budget and staff size) find land acquisition, administrative staff capacity, and local ordinances to be particular barriers to success. They also need more training or technical assistance in housing support, commercial strip financing, tax credits, real estate management, and commercial management development.[6] With only two exceptions for specific categories of budget and staff size, the relationships between type of organization (faith-based or secular) and the technical assistance needs and barriers noted earlier disappear when controls are added.[7] This suggests that most barriers and resulting technical assistance needs are the result of staffing and budgetary deficiencies rather than the faith-based versus secular nature of the organization per se. Barriers caused by bureaucracy and local politics seem particularly problematic for FBOs, however, since FBOs with low to moderate budgets and small staff sizes still noted significantly greater concerns about these issues. Although there were no significant differences between faith-based and secular nonprofits on staff or budget, it is possible that variation in the nature of funding source creates barriers for some FBOs. Specifically, it is possible that their lack of public funding and reliance on other sources limits resources for training and capacities to address local political processes.

Discussion and Summary

The findings here have important policy implications for the service-provision role of nonprofits, public funding of that role, and the differences (or lack thereof) between faith-based and secular nonprofit providers. On basic capacities such as staff, experience, and budget, faith-based and secular nonprofits are essentially identical. Yet, while many organizations are quite experienced and a number have very large budgets, there are also a number of nonprofits with overall budgets of less than $500,000 and whose staff sizes are quite small; generally around the national average of seven. Volunteers do not appear to offset the small staff sizes. Faith-based nonprofits, in particular, see staffing levels as a barrier to achieving their organizational mission. In both the statewide and 2003 CEDAM surveys, staff size, budget, and time in operation are significantly and positively correlated at the .01 level although the analysis of barriers and technical assistance deficits suggests that budget constraints are more problematic. While this is not surprising, it is worthwhile to note that it creates consistent cleavages among nonprofits in their capacity to act as a service alternative or even enhancement to public provision. A relatively small group of nonprofits benefit in terms of large budgets and staff capacity and clearly have the wherewithal to provide services if they choose to do so. Many more nonprofits, both faith based and secular, are limited with respect to all types of resources. A survey of Detroit-area nonprofits conducted in the summer and fall of 2008 suggests that staff and revenue are declining in the wake of the generalized economic distress in the area (Community Development Advocates of Detroit, 2008). In 2008, 46 percent of CDCs in Detroit reported a decrease in staff compared to two years earlier, 60 percent indicated a reduction in revenue, and 52 percent a reduction in overall budget. Concomitantly, 39 percent indicated they have reduced projects over the same time period. Assistance with operating support was the most consistent barrier noted throughout the Community Development Advocates of Detroit (CDAD) survey. This continues to suggest a limited and perhaps declining resource base among nonprofits at the same time that public need is likely to be increasing.

The most important difference between the two types of nonprofits appears to be in their funding sources. While both faith-based and secular nonprofits get the bulk of their funding from public sources, secular organizations are significantly more likely to be publicly funded. Probably as a result, FBOs draw resources from a wider variety of sources including, not surprisingly, religious ones. Given that overall budgets are quite similar, this may actually be of benefit to faith-based nonprofits, since it appears that they are better positioned to withstand cutbacks in public funding potentially engendered by weak economic times. They may be more vulnerable to the tightening of credit in the banking industry, however. If public funding of nonprofit service provision were to increase and all other funding held constant, FBOs would be likely to benefit most.

On the other hand, faith-based nonprofits appear to face a slightly different set of barriers and challenges to capacity and have somewhat different technical assistance needs. Generally, it appears that FBOs have greater difficulty navigating relationships with the public sector and its attendant rules and regulations. When FBOs do not seek out public funding it is most likely because of the red tape associated with such funding. FBOs are more likely to see local and county agencies as getting in the way of their housing efforts and they appear to need greater assistance with several state housing programs including tax credits and the required housing market studies. Navigating community planning processes, including zoning and land availability, also appear more problematic for faith-based nonprofits. Thus, despite having equal capacities and potentially greater revenue-raising opportunities, faith-based nonprofits may be more limited in the housing they can provide simply because they are less experienced at or have more difficulty with interacting with government at all levels.

Obviously, most of these issues are quite amenable to technical assistance and training. Tax credits can be explained and assistance with market studies provided. Analysis in subsequent chapters more explicitly examining the interactions between FBOs and political actors and processes will shed light on the extent to which these barriers can be overcome or represent more essential limits on the capacity of faith-based actors to have a more extensive role in service provision. This analysis also begs the question of whether capacity (as indicated by such features as staffing and budgets) actually makes a significant difference in service output or any other activities of nonprofits. While it seems self-evident that capacity matters in the nature and extent of services provided, how much it matters, in what ways, and which aspects of capacity matter most will be addressed in subsequent chapters.

Notes

The quotes in this chapter come from personal interviews conducted in 2009 with representatives of the Michigan State Housing Development Authority, the Department of Housing and Urban Development and faith-based organizations engaged in the housing arena in Michigan.

1. The research also indicates that denomination, theology, pastoral characteristics, pastoral initiative, extent of political activities, and being located in a census tract with low educational attainment affect the community service activities of faith-based organizations.

2. Although this particular comment reflects on efforts to address homelessness, it is emblematic of the political potential of nonprofit housing providers.

3. It is important to remember that there is overlap in the populations and respondents of the three surveys, although the housing provider survey conducted by the authors for this project contains a broader and more comprehensive population list.

4. Perceptions of the quality of housing produced by nonprofit organizations can also increase the amount of funding available to organizations with higher performance ratings (Silverman 2008).

5. Housing developers are often frustrated by their interactions with government bureaucracies as well as by the quality of services. However, Van Ryzin and Freeman (1997) note that for-profit companies report greater dissatisfaction than nonprofits.

6. Chi-square and significance levels for significant differences related to budget and staff are as follows:

	Chi-square	Sig
Budget		
Land acquisition barrier	16.27	.05
Technical housing assistance, housing support	15.61	.05
Commercial strip development, financing	21.99	.05
Lack of time for training is barrier	15.67	.05
Technical assistance planning for tax credits	14.69	.07
Tech. asst. for commercial dev. tax credits	21.21	.05
Local ordinance barrier	14.47	.07
Staff		
Administrative capacity barrier	8.75	.07
Technical asst. commercial strip staff dev.	9.70	.05
Technical asst. planning for real estate mgt.	14.99	.05
Technical asst. commercial management dev.	9.70	.05

7. Significant relationships between type of organization and barriers caused by bureaucracy remain for organizations with budgets between $1,500,001 and $2,000,000. Significant relationships between type of organization and barriers caused by bureaucracy remain for organizations with staff sizes between zero and five.

References

Bratt, Rachel G., and William M. Rohe. 2005. Challenges and Dilemmas Facing Community Development Corporations in the United States. *Community Development Journal* 42(1): 63–78.

Burt, Martha R., Laudan Y. Aron, Toby Douglas, Jesse Valente, Edgar Lee, and Britta Iwen. 1999. *Homelessness: Programs and the People They Serve—Summary Report. Findings of the National Survey of Homeless Assistance Providers and Clients.* Washington, DC: Urban Institute.

Chang, Patricia M.Y., David R. Williams, Ezra E.H. Griffith, and John Young. 1994. Church-Agency Relationships in the Black Community. *Nonprofit and Voluntary Sector Quarterly* 23(2): 91–105

Chaves, Mark. 2002. Religious Organizations: Data Resources and Research Opportunities. *American Behavioral Scientist* 45(10): 1523–1549.

Chaves, Mark, and William Tsitsos. 2001. Congregations and Social Services: What They Do, How They Do It, and With Whom. *Nonprofit and Voluntary Sector Quarterly* 30(4): 660–683.

Clerkin, Richard M., and Kirsten A. Grønbjerg. 2007. The Capacities and Challenges of Faith-Based Human Service Organizations. *Public Administration Review* 67(1): 115–126.

Cnaan, Ram A. 1997. *Social and Community Involvement of Religious Congregations Housed in Historic Religious Properties: Findings from a Six-City Study.* Final Report to Partners for Sacred Places. Philadelphia: University of Pennsylvania.

Community Development Advocates of Detroit (CDAD). 2008. CDC Industry Report: Initial Findings. Detroit: CDAD.

Devita, Carol J., Tobi J. Printz Platnick, and Eric C. Twombly. 1999. *Findings from the Survey of Community Services of Faith-Based Organizations in New Jersey.* Washington, DC: Center for Nonprofits and Philanthropy, Urban Institute.

Ebaugh, Helen Rose, Paula Pipes, Janet Saltzman Chafetz, and M. Daniels. 2003. Where's the Religion? Distinguishing Faith-Based from Secular Social Service Agencies. *Journal for the Scientific Study of Religion* 42(3): 411–426.

Ebaugh, Helen Rose, Paula Pipes, and Janet Saltzman Chafetz. 2006. Where's the Faith in Faith-Based Organizations? Measures and Correlates of Religiosity in Faith-Based Social Service Coalitions. *Social Forces* 84(4): 2259–2272.

Glickman, Norman J., and Lisa J. Servon. 1998. More Than Bricks and Sticks: Five Components of Community Development Corporation Capacity. *Housing Policy Debate* 9(3): 497–539.

———. 2003. By the Numbers: Measuring Community Development Corporation Capacity. *Journal of Planning Education and Research* 22:240–256.

Hall, Peter Dobkin. 1992. *Inventing the Nonprofit Sector.* Baltimore: Johns Hopkins University Press.

Hodgkinson, Virginia A., and Murray S. Weitzman. 1993. *From Belief to Commitment: The Community Service Activities and Finances of Religious Congregations in the United States.* Washington, DC: Independent Sector.

Hula, Richard C., Cynthia Jackson-Elmoore, and Laura A. Reese. 2008. The Emerging Role of Faith-Based Organizations in the Low-Income Housing Market. In *Innovations in Effective Compassion: Compendium of Research Papers Presented at the Faith-Based and Community Initiatives Conference on Research, Outcomes, and Evaluation,* ed. Pamela Joshi, Stephanie Hawkins, Jeffrey Novey, and RTI International, 103–146. Washington, DC: U.S. Department of Health and Human Services, Office of the Assistant Secretary for Planning and Evaluation, The Center for Faith-Based and Community Initiatives.

La Barbera, Pricilla A. 1992. Enterprise in Religious-Based Organizations. *Nonprofit and Voluntary Sector Quarterly* 21:51–67.

Lincoln, C. Eric, and Lawrence H. Mamiya. 1990. *The Black Church in the African American Experience.* Durham, NC: Duke University Press.

Mitchell, Roger E., Paul Florin, and John F. Stevenson. 2002. Supporting Community-Based Prevention and Health Promotion Initiatives: Developing Effective Technical Assistance Systems. *Health Education and Behavior* 29(5): 620–639.

Monsma, Stephen V. 2002. Faith-Based Organizations as Partners with Government in Providing Welfare to Work Services. Paper presented at the annual meeting of the American Political Science Association, Boston.

National Alliance of Community Economic Development Associations (NACEDA). 2007. *Community Development Fact Sheet.* Arlington, VA: NACEDA.

National Congress for Community Economic Development (NCCED). 2005. *Reaching New Heights: Trends and Achievements of Community-Based Development Organizations, 5th National Community Development Census.* Washington, DC: NCCED.

Nye, Nancy, and Norman J. Glickman. 2000. Working Together: Building Capacity for Community Development. *Housing Policy Debate* 11(1): 163–198.

Printz Platnick, T.J. 1998. Faith-Based Service Providers in the Nation's Capitol: Can They Do More? Public Policy Brief, Charting Civil Society, no. 2, April. (No. 2). Washington, DC: Urban Institute.

Reese, Laura A., and Gary Shields. 2000. Faith-Based Economic Development. *Policy Studies Review* 17(2/3): 84–103.

Salamon, Lester M. 1987a. Of Market Failure, Government Failure, and Third-Party Government: Toward a Theory of Government-Nonprofit Relations in the Modern Welfare State. *Journal of Voluntary Action Research* 16(1–2): 29–49.

———. 1987b. Partners in Public Service: The Scope and Theory of Government-Nonprofit Relations. In *The Nonprofit Sector: A Research Handbook,* ed. Walter W. Powell, 99–117. New Haven, CT: Yale University Press.

Schwartz, Alex, Rachel G. Bratt, Avis C. Vidal, and Langley C. Keyes. 1996. Nonprofit Housing Organizations and Institutional Support: The Management Challenge. *Journal of Urban Affairs* 18(4): 389–407.

Silverman, Robert Mark. 2008. The Influence of Nonprofit Networks on Local Affordable Housing Funding: Findings from a National Survey of Local Public Administrators. *Urban Affairs Review* 44(1): 126–141.

———. 2009. Sandwiched between Patronage and Bureaucracy: The Plight of Citizen Participation in Community-based Housing Organizations in the U.S. *Urban Studies* 46(1): 3–25.

Smith, Steven Rathgeb, and Michael Lipsky. 1993. *Nonprofits for Hire: The Welfare State in the Age of Contracting.* Cambridge, MA: Harvard University Press.

Twombly, Eric M. 2002. Religious versus Secular Human Service Organizations: Implications for Public Policy. *Social Science Quarterly* 83(4): 947–961.

Van Ryzin, Gregg G., and Wayne E. Freeman. 1997. Viewing Organizations as Customers of Government Services: Data from Maryland's Housing Development Programs. *Public Productivity and Management Review* 20(4): 419–431.

VanTil, Jon. 1988. *Mapping the Third Sector: Voluntarism in a Changing Social Economy.* New York: Foundation Center.

Vidal, Avis C. 1992. *Rebuilding Communities: A National Study of Urban Community Development Corporations.* New York: New School for Social Research, Community Development Research Center.

Walker, Christopher. 1993. Nonprofit Housing Development: Status, Trends, Prospects. *Housing Policy Debate* 4(3): 339–414.

Part III

Empirical Findings on the
Role and Effectiveness of the
Nonprofit Sector in Michigan

7

Housing Provision

Context by Sectors and Trends Over Time

We're a state that has by varying guesstimates three-and-a-half to five-and-a-half years of inventory of vacant housing stock. You don't address the housing needs and the community development needs by building more stock. . . . What you do is create the kinds of cities that the kind of populations you're trying to attract are looking for. And that gets you to this whole sense of place, where you have good housing, you have affordable housing, you have a mix and balance of housing attracting the kind of populations you want, because that's where they can work, that's where they can live, that's where they can play.

—Michigan State Housing Development Authority official

Walker (1993) highlighted several dimensions of nonprofit production of housing, including the level of development, type of unit developed, and institutional relationships that facilitate housing development.[1] This chapter provides an overview of nonprofit housing provision and an explicit comparison of the housing provision activities of faith-based and secular organizations in Michigan, including consideration of other traits that might impact the types and extent of housing and housing-related services provided. It begins with a discussion of the findings of the 2003 and 2007 Community Economic Development Association of Michigan (CEDAM) surveys and continues with analysis of the Nonprofit Housing Provider Survey and interviews conducted by the authors in 2007 and 2009, respectively.

CEDAM Surveys: Trends over Time

CEDAM 2003

In the 2003 survey CEDAM members were asked to identify which of forty-three specific activities they were active in. The activities fall into four main categories: housing (16 examples), business development (9 examples), social services (14 examples), and other (4 examples). Figure 7.1 highlights the range of specifically housing-related activities in which these nonprofit organizations engage. Overall, construction and renovation of homes for ownership are the most common housing activities (67 percent). Construction and renovation of single-family homes is similarly widespread (66 percent). Over half of the organizations provide or renovate rental housing (59 percent). Given the focus on single-family homes, scattered-site

Figure 7.1   **Housing Activities of CEDAM Members, 2003 Survey**

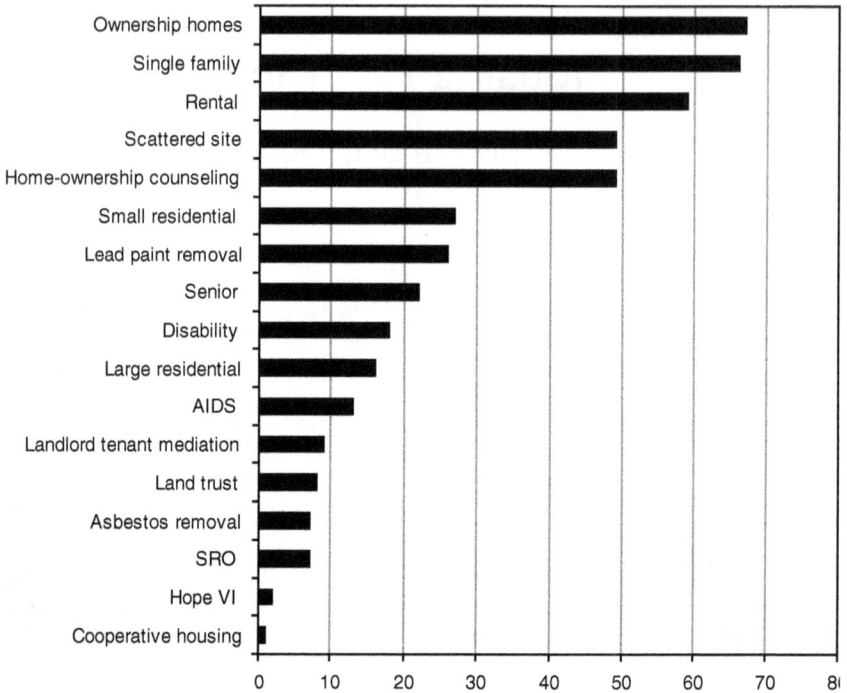

housing (49 percent) is more common than large residential developments or cooperative housing. Almost 49 percent of the organizations provide home-ownership services including credit counseling, training in maintenance and upkeep, and assistance in obtaining financing. Housing for seniors is common (22 percent) as are programs for the removal of lead paint (26 percent). Very few nonprofits are engaged in large residential developments (16 percent), landlord-tenant mediation (9 percent), or cooperative housing (1 percent).

Overall, faith-based and secular nonprofits do not provide substantially different amounts of housing services. Table 7.1 compares faith-based organizations (FBOs) and secular organizations with respect to the number of functionally distinct activities they report. There is little apparent difference between faith-based and secular nonprofit housing organizations in this regard. There are some differences in the number of housing units reported and projected, however. The data reported in Table 7.2 present small but interesting differences between FBOs and secular organizations. In all cases, FBOs show somewhat greater levels of housing output (i.e., projects, units, and future units). This difference is greatest for future projects. The implication is that if these projections turn out to be accurate, then there may be a gap between faith-based and secular housing unit production in the future, with

Table 7.1

Activities of CEDAM Secular and Faith-Based Housing Nonprofits 2003

	Organization type	N	Mean	Std. deviation	Std. error mean	t-test significance
Total number of reported activities	Secular	51	7.3	4.0	.56	
						.717
	Faith-based	29	6.9	4.1	.76	
Total number of reported housing activities	Secular	51	3.4	3.1	.43	
						.631
	Faith-based	29	3.3	2.8	.52	
Total number of reported nonhousing activities	Secular	51	3.4	3.1	.43	
						.912
	Faith-based	29	3.3	2.8	.52	

Note: The differences are measured by computing a *t*-test between the mean number of organizations within each type reporting activity in that area.

the former providing more housing and related services. A comparison of faith-based and secular nonprofits in the provision of specific types of housing activities reveals that for only one activity, condominiums for lease or ownership, does the difference in provision near statistical significance (see Appendix B, Table B1). For all other types of housing activities there are no significant differences among the two types of nonprofit organizations.

CEDAM 2007

Questions on the 2003 and 2007 CEDAM surveys are not completely comparable and more activities are included on the latter survey. As indicated in Figure 7.2, the most common housing activities of CEDAM members in the 2007 survey are home-buying training and home repair programs (52 percent each). Home-ownership training and single-family housing provision are also very common (50 percent each). These activities are closely followed by foreclosure prevention programs (new to the survey at 44 percent), multifamily rental housing (40 percent), lead paint abatement programs (35 percent), and individual development accounts (30 percent). As in 2003 the least common housing activities are cooperative housing provision (no nonprofits are doing this), land trusts (2 percent), asbestos removal (7 percent), AIDS housing (7 percent), and single-room occupancy (SRO) housing (7 percent).

There are two activities for which differences between secular and faith-based nonprofits are significant at the .10 level: FBOs are more active in foreclosure prevention and counseling and secular nonprofits are more active in land trusts, although this is not an area of focus for either type of organization (see Appendix B, Table B2). Other areas of relatively larger differences include single-family owner-

Table 7.2

Housing Output[a] from CEDAM Secular and Faith-Based Housing Nonprofits 2003

	Organization type	N	Mean	Std. deviation	t-test significance
Total number of existing housing projects	Secular	41	2.2	1.4	
	Faith-based	19	2.8	1.2	.11
Total number of units in existing projects	Secular	51	57	89	
	Faith-based	29	63	84	.77
Total number of units in future (i.e., planned) projects	Secular	51	34	62	
	Faith-based	29	63	87	.09*

[a]Output represents housing projects, units in existing projects, and projected units in future projects.
*Significant at the 0.10 level. Significance levels at 0.10 are reported due to the relatively small number of respondents. It is possible that the study is underpowered to detect true relationships, if any exist. A larger number of respondents may have revealed greater differences.

Figure 7.2   **Housing Activities of CEDAM Members, 2007 Survey**

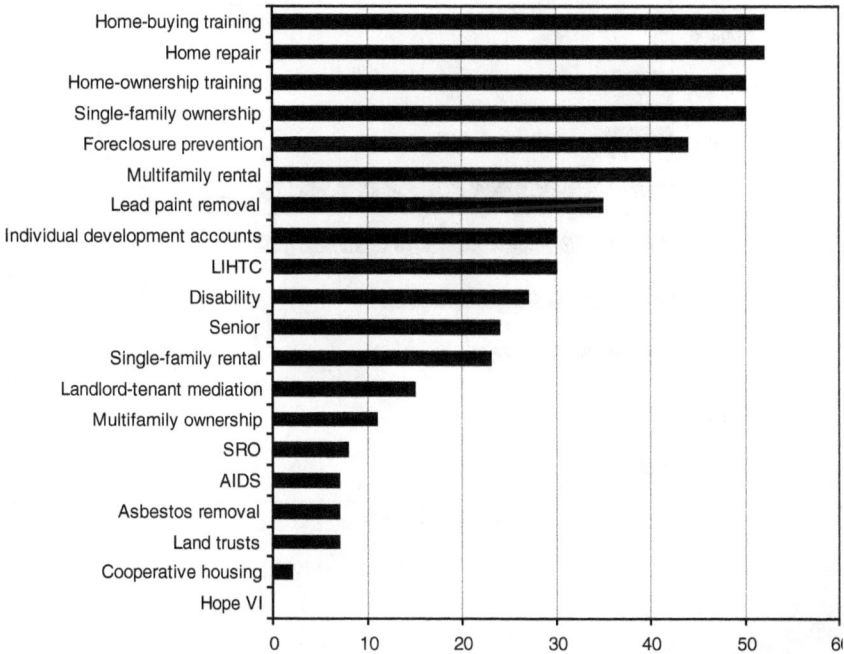

ship housing, individual development accounts (IDAs), and multifamily ownership housing (FBOs are more active in all cases). Indeed, FBOs are more active in 12 of the 20 areas although some of the differences are minuscule.

Changes in Activity 2003–2007

The lists of activities in the two CEDAM surveys are quite dissimilar, making it difficult to use them to compare changes over time in the housing services provided by nonprofits. Figure 7.3 shows change for those activities included on both surveys with the same wording. It is possible, however, that apparent reductions in activity are simply an artifact of organizations being able to respond to a greater variety of activities on the 2007 survey. It appears that activity in the areas of lead paint remediation and senior and disability housing has increased over time. HOPE VI participation and AIDS housing have decreased, as has building homes for owner-ship, although this question is divided into two parts on the 2007 survey (single- and multi-family housing) which may account for the difference. Home-ownership counseling, land trusts, and SRO housing remained largely unchanged.

Secular nonprofits increased their activity over time in the areas of lead paint remediation and disability housing (Figure 7.4). They decreased activity levels for home-ownership counseling, AIDS housing, senior housing, HOPE VI participa-

Figure 7.3   **Change in Activity, 2003–2007: All Nonprofits**

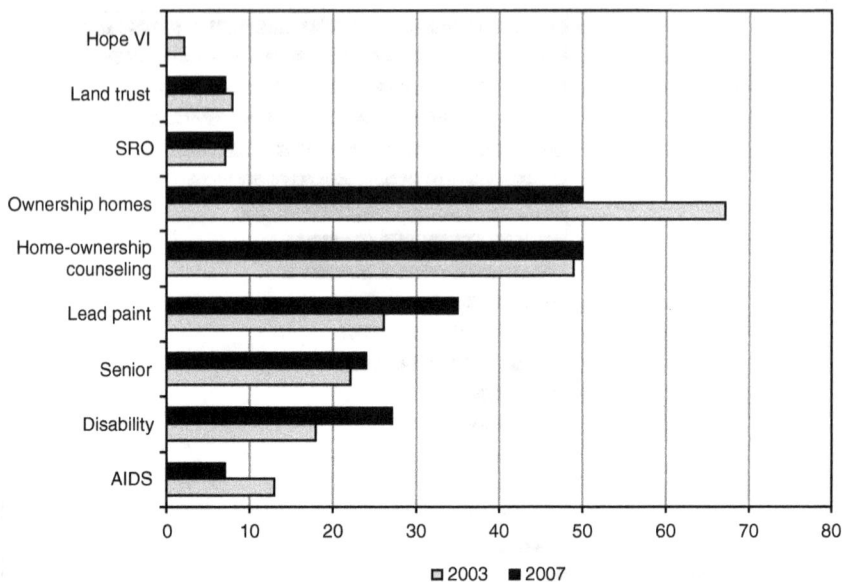

Source: 2003 and 2007 CEDAM surveys.

Figure 7.4   **Change in Activity, 2003–2007: Secular**

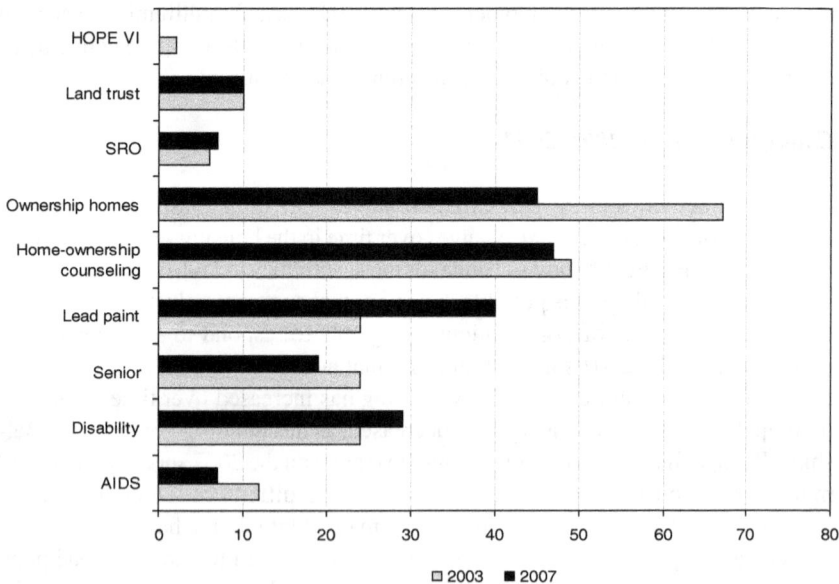

Source: 2003 and 2007 CEDAM surveys.

Figure 7.5   **Change in Activity, 2003–2007: Faith-Based**

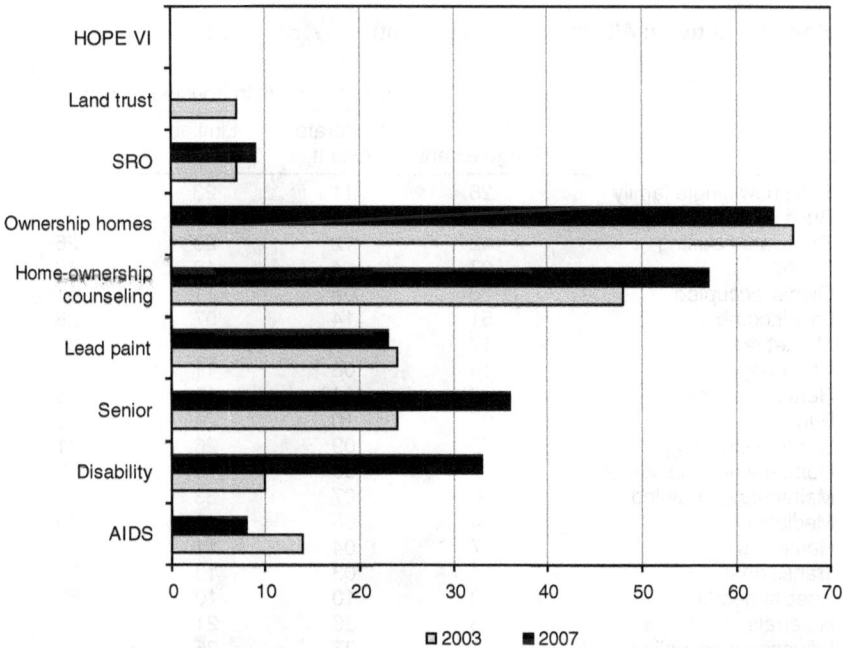

☐ 2003   ■ 2007

Source: 2003 and 2007 CEDAM surveys.

tion, and homes for ownership, although the latter could be the result of question wording. Land trust and SRO activities are roughly stable. FBOs are more likely to have increased or remained stable in their service activities (Figure 7.5). Greater activity is evident for SRO housing, home-ownership counseling, senior housing, and disability housing. HOPE VI activity, homes for ownership, and lead paint remediation remained about the same. Only AIDS housing and land trusts decreased among FBOs. These findings again suggest that there may be an increase in the proportion of housing and housing services provided by faith-based nonprofits that appear to be slightly more stable or even expansive in their service activities. While Michigan's economy may forestall increases in the short term, there appears to be promise in the long run regarding faith-based housing service provision.

Nonprofit Housing Provider Survey

Overall Housing Activity

There is reasonably wide variation in the extent of activity among nonprofits in specific types of housing activities (Table 7.3). The greatest numbers of nonprofits are very active in low-income housing and assistance, housing renovation, owner-

Table 7.3

Housing Activity: All Nonprofit (in percent)

	Extent of involvement in housing activity			
	Large extent	Moderate extent	Limited extent	None
Build new single family	26	11	23	41
Build new multifamily	21	14	19	47
Renovate housing	42	12	20	26
Rental	27	14	16	43
Owner-occupied	30	08	11	51
Low-income	51	14	07	28
Market rate	17	07	14	62
Utility payments	13	08	11	69
Rental assistance	20	14	10	56
Furniture	05	10	24	61
Credit counseling	25	09	26	41
Home-ownership counseling	30	09	16	45
Maintenance training	16	07	33	44
Mediation	04	08	19	69
Homeless	17	04	11	68
Transitional	14	03	13	70
Special needs	23	10	10	57
Referrals	23	36	21	20
Influence local policy	15	27	35	23
Influence state policy	09	26	34	32
Other	10	17	03	70

occupied housing, and home-ownership counseling. Moderate activity is most common in the areas of housing referrals and influencing state and local housing policy. Over 60 percent of the nonprofits indicate that they have no activity in many areas: market-rate housing, utility payment assistance, furniture assistance, mediation, homeless sheltering, and transitional housing. Thus, it seems clear from the survey (and is borne out in interviews) that there is a high level of specialization among nonprofits in the types of housing services they provide. Additionally, as will be shown later, the housing focus is related to the nature and purpose of collaborative activities as well as other determinants of housing activities.

Several nonprofits provided examples of their most important housing activities. For example, an FBO in the Detroit area focused on developing housing for the elderly, while FBOs in Grand Rapids and rural Northern Michigan focused on building new single-family homes, providing mortgage assistance, loan servicing, and home-ownership training. When reporting on home-ownership training, one Habitat for Humanity affiliate notes that "each family must attend training prior to closing on their home. This training includes maintenance, financial responsibility and budgeting, nutrition, basic parenting skills" (Nonprofit Housing Provider Survey 2007–2008). By comparison, secular nonprofits in Detroit comment on their activities in housing renovation, rental housing, rental assistance, and emergency (shelters) and transitional housing. The construction and renovation of multifamily housing is a priority activity for several secular nonprofits in Grand Rapids. In Tuscola County (the thumb area of Michigan) and rural Northern Michigan, secular nonprofits indicate that it is important for them to build homes for both rental and ownership, and to couple that activity with the provision of zero-interest loans and supportive services like home-ownership counseling and credit counseling. What becomes evident is that FBOs and secular nonprofits alike place a premium on combining brick-and-mortar projects with loan services and a range of supportive services and counseling to ensure the stability and sustainability of both the individuals and the communities that they serve. This suggests that wraparound or housing plus services (Granruth and Smith 2001) are a part of the approach to providing housing in Michigan. Even so, housing output remains an essential component in the mix of activities for nonprofit organizations.

Overall output of housing units also shows wide variation, depending on the type of unit produced or renovated (Table 7.4), while the total numbers of new and renovated units are quite similar (means of 151 and 111 respectively). Many more units of new multifamily, new rental, and new low-income housing are produced than new and renovated single-family, new owner-occupied, and new and renovated market-rate housing, for example. Not surprisingly, nonprofits focus on the housing needs of families, lower-income, and senior populations as opposed to market-rate housing. Single-family home production appears to focus more on rentals than on home ownership although, over time, the rentals may convert to owned homes. This is likely to be the case with rentals supported through the state's low-income tax credit, which only supports low-income rentals, and HOME programs, which only support low-income housing.

Not surprisingly, the mortgage credit crisis of 2009 took a significant toll on the capacity of all nonprofit organizations to produce new housing stock. There was a significant shift toward efforts to maintain existing housing through various education and anti-foreclosure efforts. These transformations were noted by the leader of one large nonprofit organization:

> And I sometimes compare staff as of two or three years ago or four, to obstetricians; for [the] most part delivering a baby is a good thing. Right, it is a happy part of medicine for the most part. In the last couple of years, the obstetrician staff down on the third floor has become the oncology staff. They have gone from the good news of labor and delivery to the bad news of chemotherapy, surgery, and unfortunately too many deaths from mortgage foreclosure. The 11 people in that department are all HUD and MSHDA [Michigan State Housing Development Authority] Certified Housing Counselors; for four of them their first language is Spanish. We provide the home-ownership counselor training for the whole state of Michigan. MSHDA hires us to train people who are getting MSHDA certified. We wrote the curriculum. We know home-ownership education like the back of our hand. We are good. But we are not doing it now. Huge amounts of our energy, 80 percent or better of the energy of that department . . . has gone to foreclosure prevention, or I would say, foreclosure intervention.[2]

Table 7.4

Housing Output: All Nonprofit

	Mean	
Type of housing	New	Renovated
Total[a]	151	111
Single family	31	60
Multifamily	121	58
Rental	100	53
Owner-occupied	4	37
Low income	94	63
Market rate	17	5
Senior	32	17
Special needs	10	5
Family	80	46

[a]The total is not the sum of the categories that follow, since the types of housing are not mutually exclusive.

Nonprofit Housing Provider Survey: Comparison of FBO and Secular Activity

The Nonprofit Housing Provider Survey included a larger variety of housing activities and was sent to a wider variety of housing providers than either of the CEDAM surveys. Based on this survey, additional differences between faith-based and secular providers are evident, suggesting that there are more similarities among CEDAM members than among housing nonprofits at large, or that providers differ more in more detailed aspects of housing provision (Table 7.5), or both. FBOs report significantly more activity in the areas of new single-family, owner-occupied, and special needs housing. They also provide more maintenance training and home-ownership counseling services and are more likely to engage in renovation. In short, where there are significant differences, faith-based nonprofits are indicating higher levels of service. Secular nonprofits provide more rental assistance, although this difference is significant at only the .10 level. Thus, the 2003 CEDAM findings of higher current and projected housing production for FBOs appear to be borne out in the 2007 Nonprofit Housing Provider Survey. Although not significantly different in overall levels of housing activity, FBOs are almost twice as likely to indicate large increases in activity between 2003 and 2007, again suggesting that housing output may diverge in the future, with faith-based organizations taking on a relatively greater service load (Table 7.6).

Figure 7.6 shows the overall level of clients served from 2003 through 2007 by housing nonprofits in the state. While many organizations serve only modest numbers of clients (1–25), most meet the needs of at least 100 clients per year and a large portion serve over 1,000 clients. Again, although not significantly different,

Table 7.5

Housing Development Activities of Statewide Faith-Based and Secular Nonprofit Organizations

To what extent do you provide the following housing services?

	% Large		% Moderate		% Limited		% None	
	Faith-based	Secular	Faith-based	Secular	Faith-based	Secular	Faith-based	Secular
Build new single-family***	47	14	9	12	21	24	24	51
Build new multifamily	29	16	18	12	15	21	38	52
Renovate housing***	37	46	23	05	29	14	11	35
Rental	29	26	20	10	14	17	37	47
Owner-occupied**	32	29	15	03	18	07	35	60
Low-income	60	46	14	14	09	07	17	34
Market rate	11	21	09	05	23	09	57	66
Utility payments	06	17	06	09	12	10	77	64
Rental assistance*	09	27	24	09	09	10	59	54
Furniture	06	05	09	10	32	19	53	66
Credit counseling	27	24	12	07	35	20	27	49
Home-ownership counseling*	34	28	17	03	17	16	31	53
Maintenance training**	26	10	14	03	31	34	29	53
Mediation	03	05	09	07	18	20	71	69
Homeless	18	17	06	03	12	10	65	70
Transitional	18	12	06	02	09	15	67	71
Special needs**	24	21	18	05	18	05	39	68
Referrals	19	26	47	29	25	19	09	26
Influence local policy	12	17	24	29	46	29	18	25
Influence state policy	06	10	27	25	49	25	18	39
Other	00	13	00	21	00	04	100	63

***Difference between faith-based and secular significant at the .01 level, **.05 level, *.10 level.

Table 7.6

Change in Housing Activity, Secular and Faith-Based Nonprofit Organizations (in percent)

Involvement in housing activity past five years (2003–2008)	Faith-based	Secular
Large increase	41	26
Moderate increase	28	31
Same	22	35
Moderate decrease	06	04
Large decrease	03	06

Note: Not significant at the .05 level.

Figure 7.6 **Clients Served by Nonprofit Organizations, 2003–2007**

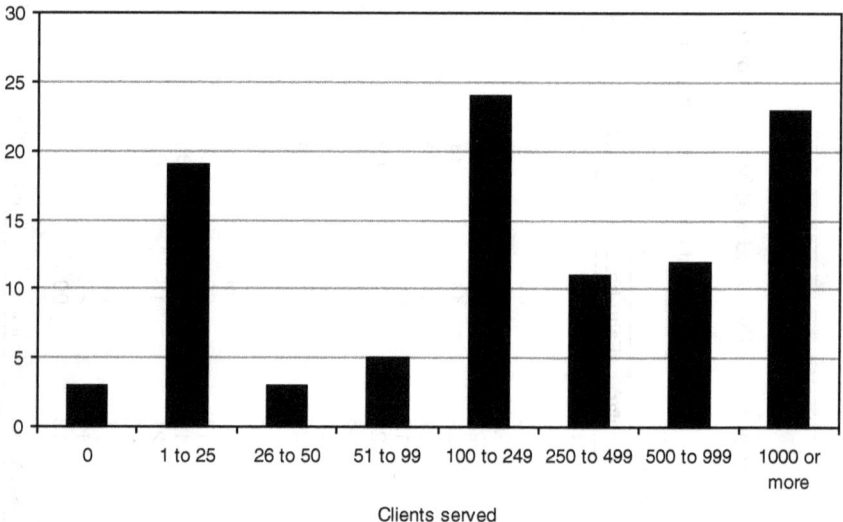

FBOs indicate service to a higher number of clients. Table 7.7 provides detail on the number of housing units produced by faith-based and secular nonprofits from 2003 through 2007. Secular organizations indicate provision of significantly more renovated units. They also indicate higher numbers of renovated owner-occupied and low-income units. Thus, while respondents from FBOs are likely to indicate higher levels of service activity, this does not appear to translate into more units of housing produced or renovated except possibly for new single-family homes. It is also possible that FBOs are emphasizing services related to unit production so that some of their output is not being represented here.

To facilitate further analysis via data reduction, the eighteen housing activities were entered into a factor analysis. Results in Table 7.8 indicate that there are four

Table 7.7

Housing Production of Statewide Faith-Based and Secular Nonprofit Organizations

Type of housing	New units (mean)		Renovated units (mean)	
	Faith-based	Secular	Faith-based	Secular
Total[a]	73	205	43	167**
Single-family	40	26	30	80
Multifamily	33	179	13	87
Rental	09	159	09	82
Owner-occupied	05	04	09	55 *
Low-income	16	145	10	98*
Market	17	18	00	08
Senior	46	24	06	25
Special needs	01	16	00	08
Family	10	122	07	72

[a]The total is not the sum of the categories that follow, since the types of housing are not mutually exclusive.
**Significantly different at the .05 level, * .10 level.

conceptually different types of housing service activities: housing support activities, home ownership and related services, building and renovating, and special needs housing.[3] Housing support activities focus on services, often related to emergency or temporary housing needs, as opposed to brick-and-mortar projects. Running homeless shelters, offering transitional housing, and referring clients to appropriate housing sources serve the needs of individuals looking for temporary housing. Mediation services and assistance with rents, utilities, and furniture support clients once they are in some type of housing. There are no significant differences between faith-based and secular organizations in the levels of housing support services (Table 7.9).

Support of home ownership appears to be a conceptually different focus from services related to housing and temporary sheltering. The focus of home-ownership activities includes construction of new single-family housing and services related to ownership including credit counseling, ownership counseling, and home-maintenance training. Faith-based nonprofits are significantly more likely to be providing ownership-related support and construction than are secular nonprofits (difference of means test significant at .01 level [Table 7.9]).

Another distinct focus of housing nonprofits is construction and renovation of housing (i.e., brick-and-mortar projects), clearly indicating that some nonprofits specialize in building housing while others focus on different types of housing assistance or support. The building and renovating factor includes renovation of existing housing of all types and building and renovating rental housing, ownership housing, low-income housing, and market-rate housing. With the exception of a focus on single-family homes, it appears that those nonprofits focusing on construc-

Table 7.8

Rotated Factor Matrix for Housing Activities

	Housing support services	Ownership housing and services	Build and renovate	Multifamily/ Special needs
Utility assistance	**.765**	−.004	.214	−.168
Rental assistance	**.843**	.019	.048	.143
Furniture assistance	**.837**	.098	−.036	.013
Mediation	**.729**	.120	−.028	.080
Homeless shelter	**.823**	.086	−.096	.295
Transitional housing	**.785**	.032	.064	.170
Referrals	**.594**	.481	.048	−.151
Build new single-family	−.209	**.731**	.092	.329
Credit counseling	.232	**.812**	.270	−.099
Ownership counseling	.072	**.868**	.260	−.119
Maintenance training	.190	**.845**	.013	.061
Renovates	.026	.415	**.734**	.019
Build/renovate rentals	.273	−.034	**.667**	.466
Build/renovate ownership	.008	.447	**.706**	−.101
Build/renovate low-income	.074	.395	**.518**	.502
Build/renovate market	−.082	−.005	**.752**	.138
Build new multifamily	.081	.023	.224	**.870**
Special needs housing	.539	−.129	−.064	**.610**
% of variance explained	26.10	19.30	14.36	10.89

tion do so without regard to the specific types or market. Secular and faith-based nonprofits are not significantly different in their propensity to focus on building and renovating activities (see Table 7.9).

It should be noted, however, that provision of multifamily housing is not included in the general building and renovating factor. Thus, the organizations focused on housing construction appear to specialize in single-family or small multifamily units that are not designed for home-ownership. A conceptually separate factor includes multifamily housing and special needs housing, which would incorporate complexes for the elderly and other individuals with special support needs. Faith-based nonprofits are again significantly more likely to focus on larger-scale, multifamily housing construction (difference of means test significant at .05 level [Table 7.9]) when compared to secular nonprofits.

To assess the extent of effort directed toward each housing activity, open-ended questions asked respondents to indicate and describe their first and second most important housing activity. The individual activities were coded and placed in the categories presented in Table 7.10. Clearly more specific activities were identified in the open-ended responses. Activities related to administration, planning, and general housing policy making are indeed components of nonprofit housing activity. Rehabilitation and new construction, however, are clearly the most important activities of nonprofits. While response numbers are too small for statistical analysis, FBOs are

Table 7.9

Difference in Housing Factors Means

	Faith-based mean	Secular mean	t score	Significance
Housing support services	−.007	.004	.049	.96
Ownership housing and services***	−.336	.195	2.50	.01
Build and renovate	−.153	.100	1.14	.26
Multifamily/Special needs**	−.282	.165	2.05	.04

Note: Lower score represents values that are higher on the index.
***Significantly different at the .01 level, **.05 level.

Table 7.10

Self-Described Most Important Housing Activity (in percent)

	Faith-based	Secular	Total
Rehabilitation	10	33	25
New construction	48	13	25
Rental	10	07	08
Home-ownership training/education	07	17	13
Emergency/transitional housing	14	06	08
Special needs housing	07	07	07
Admin/planning/policy	03	09	07
Cash assistance	00	07	05

more likely to mention new construction, rental housing, and emergency or transitional housing activities as being most important. Secular nonprofits mention rehabilitation, home-ownership training, policy, and cash assistance more frequently.

Responses to the question about the second most important housing activity are similar (Table 7.11), although rehabilitation and new construction activities are almost identical between sacred and secular nonprofits. FBOs are much more likely to be engaging in home-ownership training services as their second most important activity, and cash assistance services of secular nonprofits increase.

The Venn diagram below (Figure 7.7) presents a slightly different sense of the nature of nonprofit housing activities by showing the most typical complexes of services. Most nonprofits do not provide a single service but focus on several housing-related activities or service components. The organizations selected for the figure are those that are active in building and renovating housing. The greatest number (twenty) of these nonprofits is active in all other areas of housing as well: associated services, multifamily housing, and owner housing services and development. Fewer organizations active in building and renovation also engage in only housing support services (two) or only multifamily housing (four). The more

Table 7.11

Self-Described Second Most Important Housing Activity (in percent)

	Faith-based	Secular	Total
Rehabilitation	22	25	24
New construction	13	12	13
Rental	09	08	08
Home-ownership training/education	35	18	24
Emergency/transitional housing	00	02	01
Special needs housing	04	06	06
Admin/planning/policy	09	08	08
Cash assistance	04	16	13
Other	04	04	04

Figure 7.7   **Other Housing Activities for Organizations Actively Engaged in Building and Renovation**

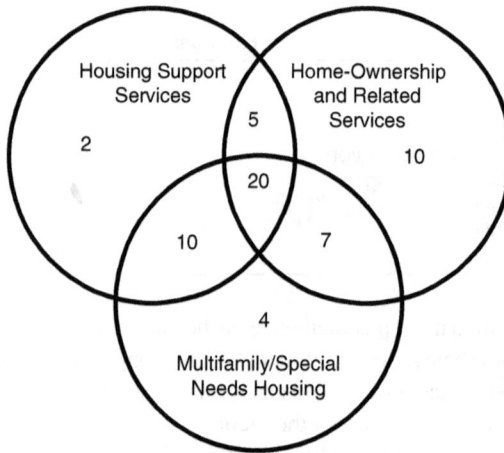

common combination of other activities for organizations active in building and renovation are to provide associated services and multifamily housing (ten), just home ownership services (ten), or home ownership services and multifamily housing (seven). In short, nonprofits active in building and renovating tend to provide other types of housing services across the board, but if there are limits, housing support services are less frequently the focus.

Correlates of Housing Activities

The literature has explored a number of determinants of faith-based social service and economic development activities (discussed in Chapter 2). Many of these explanatory variables were included in the Nonprofit Housing Provider Survey conducted by the authors and were used to examine the correlates of specific housing activities. The four dimensions identified by factor analysis (see Table 7.9) were used as dependent variables for this analysis: associated housing services, ownership services, build and renovate housing, and multifamily or special needs housing.

The nonprofits that are most likely to be providing associated housing services are those that are also providing home ownership services and building multifamily (special needs) or congregate housing, as suggested in the Venn diagram just discussed (see Figure 7.7 and the correlation matrix in Appendix B, Table B3). They have more full- and part-time staff, more volunteers, and larger budgets. While it might logically be expected that larger staff and more resources would lead to significantly more service activity across the board, this is not the case, as will be discussed later. Resources do not appear to be correlated with ownership services, for example. More involvement in associated housing services is correlated with larger funding components from religious organizations, individual donations, and the government. Nonprofits serving low-income clients are more likely to provide associated housing services, not surprisingly, considering that such activities relate to emergency housing and support for housing. Organizations providing more associated housing services are also more likely to have increased their general housing activity over time.

Since patterns of collaboration are a central focus of this study (see Chapters 9 and 10), correlations between collaboration patterns and services are particularly interesting. Nonprofits providing more associated housing services are more likely to be collaborating with social service and mental health agencies, state government, religious and ethnic organizations, schools, and hospitals. As will be seen, collaboration patterns differ by housing service type. Organizations collaborating on the following activities are more likely to be providing associated housing services: housing provision, providing and receiving services, receiving funds from other organizations, making and receiving referrals, and giving and receiving policy advice. They are significantly more likely to use collaboration for pooling resources, avoiding redundancies, and receiving referrals (see Appendix B, Table B3).

To determine which correlates are the best predictors of nonprofit housing activities, multiple regressions were run with the four housing service areas as the dependent variable: associated housing services, ownership services, build and renovate housing, and multifamily housing. There is a high level of multicollinearity among the several resource indicators (e.g. full- and part-time staff, volunteers, and budget); therefore these variables were combined into a single resource indicator for the purpose of multiple regression using factor analysis.[4] Because so many collaborators and reasons for collaboration are correlated with several of the activity areas, multicollinearity was again a concern. To address this, factor analyses were run on types of collaborators (Table 7.12) and reasons for collaboration (Table 7.13). The types of collaborators basically broke into two conceptually different groups: governmental and nongovernmental actors. Governmental or public sector collaborators include social service and mental health agencies as well as state and local government organizations. Nongovernmental or private collaborators include religious and ethnic organizations and advocacy and private organizations. Schools and hospitals also load on this factor. Hospitals are generally private but may include public or quasi-public bodies. Schools are generally public but appear to be more conceptually similar to the other nongovernmental organizations than the social service agencies in the other factor.

Consistent with the literature (Gray 1989; Winer and Ray 1997; Chaskin et al. 2001), there appear to be four major purposes for collaboration: to provide services, to build organizational or network assets, to engage in political or policy activity, and to develop or support neighborhoods (Table 7.13).[5] Service collaboration includes conducting activities related to the provision of services, obtaining the resources necessary to provide service, and making sure that clients are directed to the proper organizations for gaining service. Organizational development or network maintenance activities include: attempts to avoid redundancies in services and resources, bridge building across organizations, some referrals, and advocacy. Also loading on this factor are collaborative efforts to develop new programming. There is another set of collaborations clearly more focused on the policy arena. Providing and receiving policy advice and influencing state and local policy load on a single factor. Finally, collaboration for the purpose of neighborhood development and improvement represents a conceptually separate set of activities. For each dimension identified in Table 7.12 and 7.13, a second set of factor analyses was computed using only those variables loading highly on the identified dimensions. Factor scores from these analyses serve as indicators of independent variables in the regression, in those instances when individual variables are highly intercorrelated; otherwise the individual variable is used.

In general, one might expect the type of housing activities that an organization engages in to be related to organizational characteristics (including staffing, age, budget, and faith-status), funding sources, population served and location, as well as types of collaborators and reasons for collaboration (Table 7.14).[6] Thus, providing a particular complex of housing services can be explained as follows:

Housing Activity = F (Organizational Characteristics, Funding Sources, Population Served, Location, Collaboration)

$$Y = \alpha + \beta_1 OC_{1i} + \beta_2 FS_{2i} + \beta_3 PS_{3i} + \beta_4 L_{4i} + \beta_5 C_{5i} + \varepsilon_i$$

Where: Housing Activity is modeled as four separate dependent variables (associated housing services, ownership services, build and renovate, and multifamily housing); and
Collaboration includes both the type of collaborator and reason for collaborating.

In short, the relative influence of any one of these components understandably varies with the type of housing activity. Therefore, the regression models ultimately

Table 7.12

Rotated Factor Matrix for Collaborators

	Governmental actors	Nongovernmental actors
Social service organizations	.66	.45
Mental health organizations	.59	.35
Local government organizations	.83	−.02
State government organizations	.80	.10
Religious organizations	.06	.75
Ethnic organizations	.11	.74
Schools	.16	.72
Hospitals	.31	.65
Advocacy organizations	.41	.51
Private organizations	.13	.66

presented vary for each of the four dependent variables, measured as housing activity in the following areas: associated housing services, ownership services, build and renovate, and multifamily housing.[7] A fifth dependent variable measuring reported change in housing activity is also included in the analysis.

Associated Housing Services

Table 7.15 provides the results of the regression analysis with associated housing services as the dependent variable. As is the case for all these multiple regression analyses, only those independent variables significantly correlated to the dependent housing activity index in bivariate analysis are included (see Appendix B, Table B3). Nonprofits providing higher levels of associated housing services are those that have more resources overall to provide service, have more funding from donations, and have higher levels of collaboration specifically for service provision. They are also more likely to serve low-income individuals and collaborate with governmental actors. Overall, the variables in the model account for 50 percent of the variation in the extent of activity in associated housing services. Collaboration for providing service and having government collaborators are the best predictors of associated housing services.

Home-ownership Services

Nonprofits most likely to be active in home-ownership services are those that also provide more associated housing services and engage in building and renovation. They are those that are faith-based. Organizations with more donation income focus more heavily on ownership services than do those that primarily serve families and low-income clients. These nonprofits are more likely to be collaborating with state government, religious organizations, and the private sector. Their

Table 7.13

Rotated Factor Matrix for Reasons for Collaboration

Collaborate to:	Collaborate for services	Collaborate for organization/network building	Collaborate for policy input	Collaborate for neighborhood development
Provide housing	**.55**	.00	.01	.25
Provide other services	**.72**	.24	.05	.28
Receive housing service	**.76**	.13	.15	.03
Receive other service	**.80**	.18	.12	.00
Provide funds	**.59**	.12	.18	-.06
Receive funds	**.35**	.13	.09	.33
Refer clients	**.66**	.35	.30	-.02
Provide service to referrals	**.64**	.44	.01	.06
Pool resources	**.64**	.07	.23	.39
Avoid redundancy	.12	**.77**	.15	.07
Bridge building	.26	**.77**	.04	.11
Receive referrals	.14	**.60**	.01	-.14
Advocacy	.25	**.77**	.25	.01
Offer new programs	.13	**.70**	.37	.24
Provide policy advice	**.60**	-.01	**.67**	.14
Receive policy advice	**.55**	.09	**.71**	.13
Influence local policy	**.50**	.08	**.74**	.11
Influence state policy	.08	.28	**.81**	.04
Influence national policy	-.04	.39	**.78**	.11
Neighborhood development	.36	-.03	.02	**.77**
Improve neighborhood conditions	-.19	.32	.33	**.69**

Table 7.14

Key Variables

Variable	Measure
Organizational characteristics	• Staffing resources (part- or full-time, volunteers) • Age of organization • Budget • Faith-status

Funding source	• Donations
	• Religious funding
	• Governmental funding
	• Private (secular) funding
	  – Foundations
	  – Corporations
	  – Banks

Population served	• Own members • Senior citizens • Inner-city residents • Citywide clients • Residents of specific neighborhoods • Specific racial groups • Families • Low-income clients • Religious affiliation
Region/location	• Northern MI • Central MI • Southwest MI • Southeast MI • City of Detroit

Type of collaborators	• Governmental collaborators
	  – Social service organizations
	  – Mental health organizations
	  – Local government organizations
	  – State government organizations
	• Nongovernmental collaborators
	  – Religious organizations
	  – Ethnic organizations
	  – Schools
	  – Hospitals
	  – Advocacy organizations
	  – Private organizations

(continued)

collaborative activities are most likely to focus on making referrals to other organizations, enhancing neighborhood development, and pooling resources. Multiple regression analysis[8] (Table 7.16) indicates that of these correlates, serving poor families[9] is the only variable that remains significantly correlated with ownership services, although collaborating for neighborhood development is very close to significance. The variables only account for 29 percent of the variation in home-ownership services.

Table 7.14 *(continued)*

Variable	Measure

Reason for collaboration	• Collaborate for service
	  – Provide housing
	  – Provide other services
	  – Receive housing service
	  – Receive other service
	  – Provide funds
	  – Receive funds
	  – Refer clients
	  – Provide service to referrals
	  – Pool resources
	• Collaborate for organization/network building
	  – Avoid redundancy
	  – Bridge building
	  – Receive referrals
	  – Advocacy
	  – Offer new programs
	• Collaborate for policy
	  – Provide policy advice
	  – Receive policy advice
	  – Influence local policy
	  – Influence state policy
	  – Influence national policy
	• Collaborate for neighborhood development
	  – Neighborhood development
	  – Improve neighborhood conditions

Building and Renovation

Nonprofits that engage in more building and renovation activities also provide more ownership services and multifamily and special needs housing. They have more full-time staff, larger budgets, and are older. They are significantly more likely to be serving seniors, families, and low-income clients. The only types of organizations they appear to collaborate with are neighborhood based. When collaborating, nonprofits engaging in more building and renovating are more likely to do so to provide housing, to enhance neighborhood development, and to receive funds. In multiple regression analysis, only providing services to poor families remained significantly correlated (Table 7.17). Together the variables in the regression account for 26 percent of the variation in building and renovation activity.

Building Multifamily and Special Needs Housing

Construction of multifamily and special needs housing is correlated with the provision of associated housing services as well as building and renovating activity.

Table 7.15

Regression Analysis, Associated Housing Services

	b	S.E.	Beta	Significance
Organizational characteristics				
Resources	.43	.11	.36	.00***
Funding source				
Donations	.27	.12	.19	.03**
Religious funding	.14	.17	.08	.40
Governmental funding	.08	.08	.09	.32
Population served				
Low-income clients	.02	.13	.02	.85
Type of collaborator				
Governmental collaborators	.33	.10	.32	.00***
Nongovernmental collaborators	−.19	.11	−.19	.07
Reason for collaboration				
Collaborate for service	.34	.12	.33	.00***
Collaborate for policy	−.18	.11	−.17	.10
Constant	−1.54	.64		.02
Multiple R^2 = .50				
N = 96				

$***p < 0.01, **p < 0.05$

Table 7.16

Regression Analysis, Home-ownership Services

	b	S.E.	Beta	Significance
Organizational characteristics				
Faith-based	.15	.21	.08	.48
Funding source				
Donations	.25	.14	.18	.09
Population served				
Citywide clients	.12	.09	.13	.17
Poor family clients	.32	.11	.33	.01**
Type of collaborator				
State collaborators	.04	.12	.04	.74
Religious collaborators	−.04	.18	−.03	.80
Private collaborators	.16	.16	.11	.32
Reason for collaboration				
Collaborate for neighborhood dev	.20	.10	.21	.06
Collaborate to pool resources	−.08	.13	−.07	.56
Collaborate to refer clients	.08	.11	.08	.50
Constant	−1.67	.82		.05
Multiple R^2 = .29				
N = 98				

$**p < 0.05$

Table 7.17

Regression Analysis, Building and Renovation

	b	S.E.	Beta	Significance
Organizational characteristics				
Age of organization	.01	.01	.11	.30
Resources	.14	.13	.12	.29
Population served				
Serves seniors	.16	.10	.16	.13
Serves poor families	.21	.10	.22	.03**
Type of collaborator				
Neighborhood association collaborator	.14	.10	.14	.17
Reason for collaboration				
Collaborate for housing provision	.04	.10	.04	.69
Collaborate to receive funding	.09	.09	.10	.32
Collaborate for neighborhood dev	.11	.10	.11	.31
Constant	−1.04	.37		.01
Multiple R^2 = .26				
N = 96				

**p < 0.05

Table 7.18

Regression Analysis, Multifamily and Special Needs Housing

	b	S.E.	Beta	Significance
Organizational characteristics				
Resources	.26	.11	.22	.02***
Faith-based	.26	.19	.13	.17
Location				
Central region	−.22	.23	−.09	.33
Type of collaborator				
Mental health org. collaborators	.21	.10	.23	.05**
Hospital collaborators	.05	.13	.04	.73
Advocacy orgs collaborators	.04	.12	.04	.73
Reason for collaboration				
Collaborate to receive funds	.11	.09	.12	.33
Housing increase	.07	.09	.08	.41
Constant	−.92	.54		.08
Multiple R^2 = .28				
N = 98				

***p <0.01, **p < 0.05

The more active nonprofits are faith based and have more full- and part-time staff and larger budgets; they are also more likely to be located in the central part of the state. They are more likely to have increased housing activity over the past five years. Nonprofits more active in multifamily and special needs housing are more likely to collaborate with mental health organizations, hospitals, and advocacy groups. Their collaboration tends to involve the receipt of funding from such groups, presumably to support special needs housing in particular. In multiple regression analysis, only the amount of resources and collaboration with mental health organizations remained significantly correlated with multifamily and special needs housing (Table 7.18). All of the variables account for 28 percent of the variation in the dependent variable.

Change in Housing Activity

The types of organizations most likely to have increased activities in housing between 2003 and 2007 are those with greater resources: full-time staff and larger budgets. They receive more of their funding from religious organizations. Nonprofits indicating increases in housing activity also provide more associated housing services and multifamily and special needs housing. They are more likely to be serving seniors, to work in collaboration with mental health agencies, hospitals, and advocacy groups, and to be located in the City of Detroit. In multiple regression analysis, no variables remained significantly correlated to increases in housing activity; resource levels came the closest. Not surprisingly, these variables only account for 15 percent of the variation in increase in housing activity (Table 7.19).

Satisfaction with Housing Activities

A final issue related to the provision of housing and housing services is some sense of the quality of outcomes. The Nonprofit Housing Provider Survey asked respondents to indicate their level of satisfaction with the amount and quality of housing produced by their organization and the overall goal attainment of their organizations. While the CEDAM surveys did not deal with this issue specifically, they asked respondents (in open-ended questions) to highlight at least one of their activities in community development. It is not unreasonable to assume that organizations would describe activities of which they were most proud. Findings on satisfaction with housing output from the CEDAM and the Nonprofit Housing Provider surveys are discussed next.

CEDAM

As part of the 2007 survey conducted by the Community and Economic Development Association of Michigan, nonprofit organizations engaged in housing were asked to highlight at least one story about their work in community development that might be worthy of additional study. Twenty-nine of the eighty-two responding organizations (35 percent) shared stories of accomplishments, partnerships, or both. Five examples from around the state are noted below. The Coalition on Temporary Shelter (COTS) in Detroit reported the success of the Housing First model, noting "Families are excited about obtaining nice housing. Landlords are happy to find

Table 7.19

Regression Analysis, Change in Housing Activity

	b	S.E.	Beta	Significance
Organizational characteristics				
Resources	.23	.14	.17	.09
Population served				
Serves seniors	.12	.11	.11	.29
Location				
Detroit region	.31	.24	.13	.20
Type of collaborator				
Mental health org. collaborators	.05	.12	.06	.71
Hospital collaborators	.17	.15	.13	.28
Advocacy orgs collaborators	.10	.14	.07	.51
Constant	1.09	.53		.04
Multiple R^2 = .15				
N = 98				

paying tenants."[10] Northeast Michigan Affordable Housing in Alpena reported on their participation in the Vision 2020 to rehabilitate housing for low-income individuals and families.[11] Kalamazoo Neighborhood Housing Services took pride in its recognition by the Michigan State Housing Development Authority for "building, rehabilitating and most importantly—selling—homes to Low- to Moderate-income people." In addition, Dwelling Place of Grand Rapids reported completing the first "HUD Mark to Market Restructuring combining LIHTC" in Michigan.[12] Finally, Circle of Love community development corporation in Saginaw noted, "We empower our clients with the necessary tools to realize their American dream of homeownership, whether newly constructed homes or existing. Individuals coming out of prison w/ no hope of obtaining anything, let alone a home—they have been successful through our program—Praise God! Dreams do come true."

Michigan nonprofits were not simply building and rehabilitating housing, they were staying current with technology and paying attention to growing environmental and health concerns in communities. Habitat for Humanity of Kent County was excited to have an affordable home certified by the Leadership in Energy and Environmental Design (LEED) system, noting, "All houses in our future will be LEED certified for the benefit of the homeowner's affordability, health and sustainability." Similarly, the Genesis Non-profit Housing Corporation in Grand Rapids reported "building the first nonprofit residential development under the LEED-H criteria and gaining LEED silver rating" and creating the "first Michigan affordable housing development to obtain funding from the Michigan Green Build Initiative." When reflecting upon innovations undertaken by its organization, the Greater Eastside Community Association noted that it was the "first (and still only) organization in Flint to build Energy Efficient." As noted earlier, nonprofit housing organizations do much more than simply brick-and-mortar projects, and many engage in nonhousing activities. The Washtenaw Affordable Housing Corporation reported that it holds "regular resident meetings at our multifamily sites to do community organizing. From those community organizing efforts, the residents at one multifamily site organized a summer camp for youth."

Nonprofit organizations engaged in housing in Michigan were also asked to discuss their innovation in community development and to note strategies that the organizations employed. Twenty-one of the eighty-two responding organizations (26 percent) provided examples of innovations they had undertaken. Organizations reported engaging in capacity-building activities, making use of technological advancements, and implementing a number of mixed-use development projects. The Economic Opportunity Committee of St. Clair County reported combined activities in housing and job training:

> EOC through a variety of partnerships created the first ever privately funded community renaissance zone. Through this partnership we re-focused all housing and revitalization efforts of all partners to one 12 block area significantly changing the appearance and stability of the neighborhood. In addition to the partnership we created the community house, a two unit rental home where families were moved in and provided services to assist them to pay off debt, clean up credit become mortgage ready. At completion, they then purchased one of the newly renovated or constructed homes in the neighborhood. As one family moved out another was moved in. A partnership with the St. Clair County Regional Educational Service Agency (RESA) trained unemployed workers between the ages of 17 and 30 in the construction trade.

Several organizations were also proud of the various partnerships they had developed with for-profit organizations and other nonprofit housing providers.

Nonprofit Housing Provider Survey

Overall, respondents to the Nonprofit Housing Provider Survey tend to be very positive about the outcomes of their efforts, particularly regarding housing quality (Figure 7.8). Over 80 percent of respondents indicated that they were satisfied with the quality of housing provided by their organization and over 76 percent were satisfied with the organization's overall goal attainment. Respondents were slightly less happy with the quantity of housing provided, although almost 63 percent indicated satisfaction on this point. Respondents from faith-based nonprofits are consistently more satisfied with their organization's outputs than are those from secular nonprofits, although these differences are not statistically significant (Table 7.20).[13]

The nature of the nonprofit is not a good predictor of respondent satisfaction with organizational outcomes. For purposes of correlation analysis, the three satisfaction questions were combined into a single satisfaction index. This index is comprised of factor scores generated by a factor analysis of the three indicators (Table 7.21). Correlation

Figure 7.8   **Satisfaction with Organization's Accomplishments**

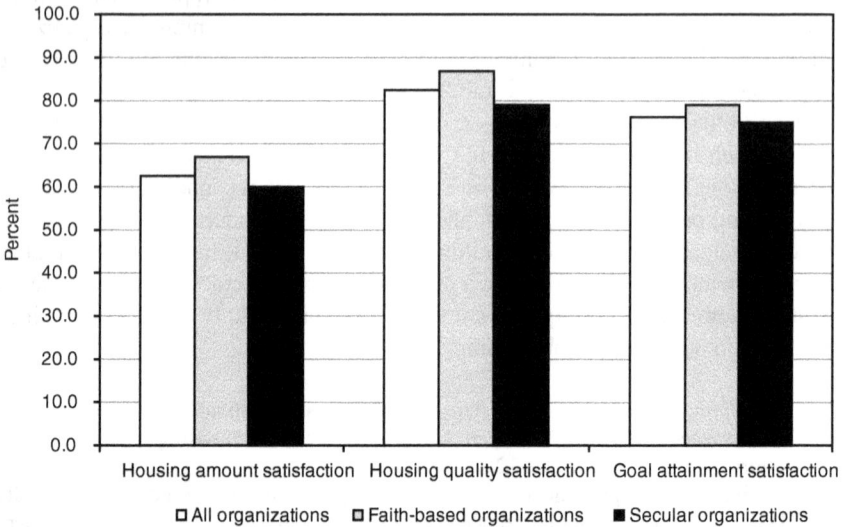

Table 7.20

Difference in Means Satisfaction Questions

	Faith-based mean	Secular mean	*t* score	Significance
Satisfaction with amount of housing	2.33	2.47	.59	.56
Satisfaction with quality of housing	1.56	1.70	.73	.47
Satisfaction with goal attainment	2.15	2.07	−.39	.70

Note: Lower score represents values that are higher on the index.
***Significantly different at the .01 level, **.05 level.

analysis indicates that very few variables are actually related to outcome satisfaction (see Appendix B, Table B4). Variables that appear to increase outcome satisfaction include more activity in building and renovation, collaboration with mental health agencies, larger full-time staffs, and larger budgets. In short, respondents from organizations that produce more housing appear to be more satisfied with the quantity, quality, and goal attainment of their organizations. Respondents also appear more satisfied with their organization's housing outcomes if it receives less funding from foundations. Having more full-time employees and larger budgets—allowing nonprofits to produce more housing—also are positively correlated with respondent satisfaction with outcomes. Since responses to the three satisfaction questions may logically have more to do with

Table 7.21

Outcome Satisfaction Factor

	Factor loading
Satisfaction with amount of housing	.88
Satisfaction with quality of housing	.84
Satisfaction with goal attainment	.79

the attitudes of the respondent than the organization per se, correlations were also run with several personal traits of the respondents: education, years with organization, race, and gender. None of these variables were significantly correlated with satisfaction.

Discussion and Conclusions

Several points about the housing activities of faith-based and secular nonprofits are worth reemphasizing. These are posed below and relate both to general patterns of housing activities and to the primacy of collaboration, particularly with faith-based organizations, in the service activities of nonprofits.

- There is significant specialization in the housing activities of nonprofit organizations. Some, particularly those better financed, focus on building and renovating, or multifamily or special needs housing. Others, presumably those that are smaller and less well financed, focus on home-ownership services. Although not involving bricks and mortar, associated housing services still require financial resources to pay for furniture, utilities, and rent, demanding a resource-rich nonprofit.
- Among those most active in building and renovating housing, engaging in other housing activities, particularly multifamily and associated housing services, is common.
- Resources matter in determining what nonprofits specialize in, particularly for construction and associated services. Budget appears to be more critical than staff.
- Collaboration and the nature of collaborators are important in nonprofit provision of housing and housing services across the board.
- Most nonprofits are satisfied with the quantity and quality of their housing outcomes. Those that have more staff and larger budgets, and hence build more housing, are more likely to be satisfied with their outcomes.
- Being a faith-based organization (in rare cases) or having faith-related collaborators or funders (in many cases) is significantly correlated to housing activity for four of the five housing activity measures.
- Because of the very few differences found between faith-based and secular housing activity, it appears that patterns of collaboration among faith organi-

zations are more important than the faith or secular nature of any individual organization.

• Neighborhood collaborators or collaborations that support neighborhood development are also important to two of the four activities: building and renovation and home-ownership services. This suggests that many aspects of housing are intricately tied to the larger neighborhood environment.

• None of the independent variables performed particularly well in multiple regression. There are probably several reasons for this. First, the relatively small number of cases means that regressions are not as robust as would be ideal. Second, even with the use of index variables, there was a good deal of multicollinearity among the independent variables. This can be seen in the relatively high R^2 values given the very few variables remaining significantly correlated in multiple regression analysis. Because of these issues, the correlation analysis (presented in Appendix B) probably provides the better sense of relationships in the data.

Overall, it is clear that collaborative activities and networks are central to the housing provision activities of nonprofits across the board; the specific importance of collaboration is discussed in more detail in Chapters 9 and 10. In short, who you work with may well be more important than who you are in regard to service provision.

Notes

The quotes in this chapter come from personal interviews conducted in 2009 with representatives of the Michigan State Housing Development Authority and faith-based organizations engaged in the housing arena in Michigan; as well as written responses to the 2007 CEDAM survey.

1. See Table 2.3 for an overview of examples of how nonprofit organizations are involved in housing production.

2. A portion of this quote was used to make the point about the importance of flexibility as a measure of organizational capacity in Chapter 6.

3. To estimate levels of activity for housing support activities, home ownership and related services, building and renovating, and special needs housing, an additional factor analysis was computed for each set of activity indicators that loaded highly on each dimension. Factor scores computed from these separate analyses were used as indicators for levels of activity on each dimension.

4. Factor results are as follows:

Variable	Loading
Full-time staff	.92
Part-time staff	.85
Volunteers	.66
Budget	.89

5. These broad reasons for collaboration map onto several of the types of organizational capacity highlighted by Glickman and colleagues (e.g., Glickman and Servon 1998, 2003; Nye and Glickman 2000) as discussed in Chapter 6 (see Table 6.1). For example, one might surmise that organizations that collaborate to provide services or develop and support

neighborhoods are increasing their programmatic organizational capacity. The ability to build organizational and network assets is linked to an organization's networking capacity, which can be enhanced through efforts to branch out and partner with others. Similarly, an organization draws on its political capacity and that of others when it collaborates to engage in political or policy activities.

6. Interview data demonstrate that each of the four dependent variables (associated housing services, ownership services, build and renovate, and multifamily housing) is a distinct service provision/engagement choice for organizations and, as such, should be treated as a distinct dependent variable. As indicated in Appendix B (Table B3), these four housing service areas are highly interrelated. Thus, although the four activity areas are correlated, factor analysis indicates that they represent four distinct underlying concepts.

7. There is a high degree of multicollinearity between the set of sixteen independent variables that demonstrate correlations with the four dependent variables. In addition, the correlation analysis suggests that not all variables influence each of the dependent variables, further indicating the appropriateness of estimating distinct regression models for each of the four dependent variables.

8. Individual collaboration variables were used in the regression analysis, rather than the collaboration indexes, in those instances where there is only one collaborator out of an index or one purpose for collaboration out of an index in the bivariate correlations. This is the case for the models for home-ownership services (Table 7.16), building and renovation (Table 7.17), building multifamily and special needs housing (Table 7.18), and changes in housing activity (Table 7.19).

9. Serving families and serving low-income clients are significantly correlated with each other and were combined into a single index using factor analysis. Factor results are as follows:

Variable	Loading
Serves families	.82
Serves low-income	.82

10. The Housing First model focuses on placing homeless individuals or families immediately in their own homes, typically apartments, rather than transitioning them through emergency shelters and temporary housing.

11. One of the goals of Vision 2020 is to work in partnership with nonprofit organizations and the government to eliminate substandard housing. In 2007, there were thirteen Michigan counties (out of 83) actively engaged in Vision 2020, and another fourteen that were interested (Vision 2020, 2007).

12. The Mark-to-Market (M2M) program was authorized by the Multifamily Assisted Housing Reform and Affordability Act of 1997 (MAHRA), to address the rising costs of rent subsidies in HUD's Section 8 multifamily housing program and preserve affordable rental housing.

13. In Figure 7.8, the five-point satisfaction scale (very satisfied, satisfied, neutral, dissatisfied, very dissatisfied) has been collapsed so that just the percentage satisfied is shown. The mean scores in Table 7.20 include the full five-point scale. In this case the mean goal satisfaction of secular nonprofits is higher than that of FBOs, but again the difference is not significant.

References

Chaskin, Robert J., Prudence Brown, S. Venkatesh, and Avis Vidal. 2001. *Building Community Capacity.* New York: Aldine De Gruyter.

Glickman, Norman J., and Lisa J. Servon. 1998. More than Bricks and Sticks: Five Components of Community Development Corporation Capacity. *Housing Policy Debate* 9(3): 497–539.

———. 2003. By the Numbers: Measuring Community Development Corporation Capacity. *Journal of Planning Education and Research* 22:240–256.

Granruth, Laura B., and Carla H. Smith. 2001. *Low-Income Housing and Services Programs: Towards a New Perspective.* Washington, DC: National Low-income Housing Coalition.

Gray, Barbara. 1989. *Collaborating: Finding Common Ground for Multiparty Problems.* San Francisco: Jossey-Bass.

Nye, Nancy, and Norman J. Glickman. 2000. Working Together: Building Capacity for Community Development. *Housing Policy Debate* 11(1): 163–198.

Vision 2020. 2007. *Vision 2020: A Challenge for Michigan's Neighborhoods and Communities.* www.vision2020michigan.org.

Walker, Christopher. 1993. Nonprofit Housing Development: Status, Trends, Prospects. *Housing Policy Debate* 4(3): 339–414.

Winer, Michael, and Karen Ray. 1997. *Collaboration Handbook: Creating, Sustaining, and Enjoying the Journey.* St. Paul, MN: Amherst H. Wilder Foundation.

8

Scope and Extent of
Broader Community
Involvement and Trends Over Time

[W]e also sponsor an awful lot of activity that doesn't build a house, but it helps create
a community in which that house is located, which is going to make it an attractive
house. We partner with a number of nonprofit organizations, and through our sponsor-
ships and through our investment in their activities it permits them to deliver those
other elements that are needed.

—Michigan State Housing Development Authority Official

The role of nonprofits in providing housing to low- and moderate-income households is the central focus of this study. Nevertheless, these organizations also engage
in a number of other community-based social service and economic development
activities. A key implication of the theory presented in Chapter 1 is that the housing
and other social service activities of nonprofits are tied to broader policy-related
activities that increase political power for nonprofits in local and state decision making. To examine these issues, an explicit consideration of community involvement
beyond the housing arena is necessary. This chapter explores the broader community
involvement of nonprofit organizations using the two surveys by CEDAM and the
Nonprofit Housing Provider Survey, conducted by the authors.

CEDAM Surveys: Trends over Time

CEDAM 2003

Surveys were conducted of CEDAM members in 2003 and 2007, primarily to
identify areas of training needs and other membership services that could be provided by CEDAM. Questions on the two waves of surveys are not identical, but
comparisons over time are made when possible. As noted previously, in the 2003
survey CEDAM members were asked to identify which of forty-three specific activities were areas in which they were active. These included housing (16 examples),
social services (14 examples), business development (9 examples), and other (4
examples). Housing activities were explicitly explored in Chapter 7. Community
development activities beyond housing are examined in this chapter. Because of the

tight connections between housing and community or neighborhood development, a full consideration of nonprofit activity in housing must include analysis of these broader community-building activities. The following discussion focuses on social service, business development, and other neighborhood activities.

Figure 8.1 indicates overall levels of service provision among CEDAM members in 2003. The activities span social services, health services, youth development, and community organizing. Youth (20 percent) and day care (14 percent) services are clearly the most common across all organizations. Twelve percent of nonprofits provide crime prevention services or programs, 8 percent offer cultural programs, and 6 percent offer summer camps. Fewer nonprofits engage in teen pregnancy counseling (2 percent) or voter registration drives (3 percent). There are no significant differences among faith-based and secular nonprofits in the types of social service programs offered (Table 8.1). Arts programming comes closest to statistical significance at .10, with faith-based nonprofits being more likely to offer such services. With the exception of crime prevention and cultural programs, FBOs are slightly more likely to offer most types of social services.

These nonprofits also undertake economic development activities. For example, commercial development activities are offered by 22 percent of the nonprofits, again illustrating the close ties between housing and community development (Figure 8.2). Other relatively common activities are brownfield redevelopment (14 percent), business district creation (16 percent), and development of microenterprises (12 percent). Less common are small business loans (7 percent) and business incubators (6 percent). Moreover, very few nonprofits are engaged in industrial development (3 percent). There are some significant differences between faith-based and secular nonprofits in the provision of business development services. Faith-based organizations (FBOs) are more likely to operate for-profit businesses and are more involved in the formation and operation of business districts or main street development projects. Secular nonprofits are significantly more likely to develop microenterprises (Table 8.2).

There are several other activities common among nonprofits that did not fit neatly into the social service or economic development categories (Figure 8.3). These include energy conservation programs (13 percent), mixed-use development projects (19 percent), and community reinvestment activities (16 percent). As with social services, there are no significant differences between FBOs and secular nonprofits in the provision of these services (Table 8.3).

CEDAM 2007

The 2007 CEDAM survey offers a relatively similar picture of nonprofit community involvement across the state, although new activities were added to the survey after 2003 (Figure 8.4). Community organizing, which was not on the earlier survey, is the most common social service activity, with 50 percent of nonprofits engaging in this. The next most common activities are youth programs (35 percent), home-

Figure 8.1   **Overall Social Service Activities, 2003**

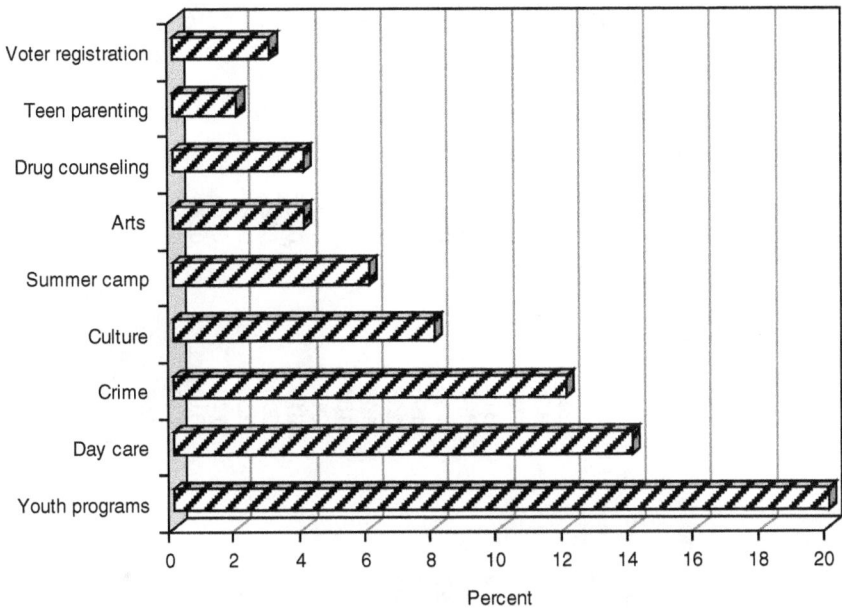

Figure 8.2   **Overall Business Development Services, 2003**

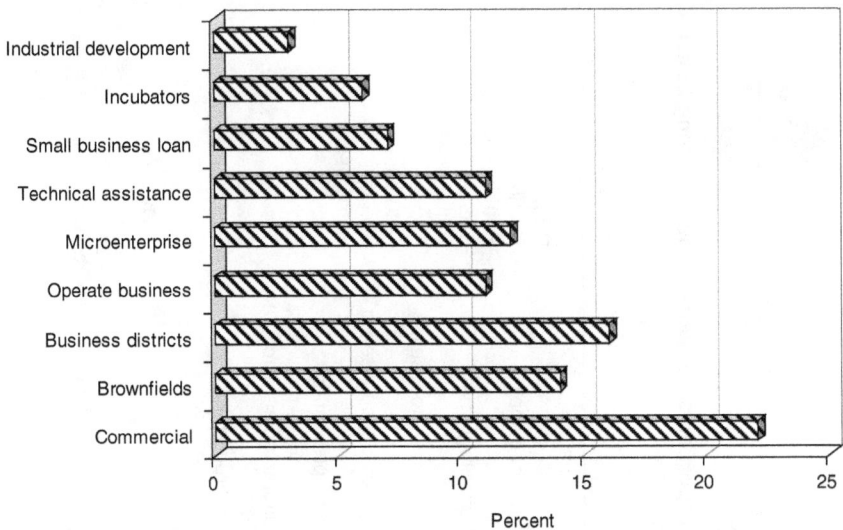

Table 8.1

Proportion of Organizations Reporting Specific Social Service Provided, by Organization Type, CEDAM 2003

	Organization type	N	Proportion responding yes	Std. deviation	Std. error mean	t-test significance
Day Care	Secular	51	.16	.367	.051	.858
	Faith-based	29	.17	.384	.071	
Summer camp[a]	Secular	51	.04	.196	.027	.320
	Faith-based	29	.10	.310	.058	
Youth programs	Secular	51	.20	.401	.056	.418
	Faith-based	29	.28	.455	.084	
Drug abuse counseling	Secular	51	.04	.196	.027	.563
	Faith-based	29	.07	.258	.048	
Teen parent counseling	Secular	51	.02	.140	.020	.709
	Faith-based	29	.03	.186	.034	
Crime prevention	Secular	51	.14	.348	.049	.665
	Faith-based	29	.10	.310	.058	
Cultural programs/centers	Secular	51	.10	.300	.042	.663
	Faith-based	29	.07	.258	.048	
Arts program	Secular	51	.02	.140	.020	.101
	Faith-based	29	.10	.310	.058	
Voter registration	Secular	51	.02	.140	.020	.687
	Faith-based	29	.03	.186	.034	

[a]Indicates t-test computed with group variance not assumed to be equal across groups. Otherwise equal variance assumed. Assumption used based on result of Levene's Test for Equality of Variances.

Table 8.2

Proportion of Organizations Reporting Specific Business Development Services, by Organization Type, 2003

	Organization type	N	Proportion responding yes	Std. deviation	Std. error mean	t-test significance
Commercial development	Secular	51	.24	.428	.060	.773
	Faith-based	29	.21	.412	.077	
Industrial development	Secular	51	.02	.140	.020	.687
	Faith-based	29	.03	.186	.034	
Incubator development	Secular	51	.04	.196	.027	.916
	Faith-based	29	.03	.186	.034	
Operate a business[a]	Secular	51	.04	.196	.027	.090*
	Faith-based	29	.17	.384	.071	
Brownfield redevelopment	Secular	51	.14	.348	.049	.677
	Faith-based	29	.17	.384	.071	
Small business loan program	Secular	51	.08	.272	.038	.441
	Faith-based	29	.03	.186	.034	
Small business technical assistance	Secular	51	.12	.325	.046	.492
	Faith-based	29	.07	.258	.048	
Microenterprise development[a]	Secular	51	.18	.385	.054	.029**
	Faith-based	29	.03	.186	.034	
Business district/Main street development	Secular	51	.22	.415	.058	.055*
	Faith-based	29	.07	.258	.048	

[a]Indicates t-test computed with group variance not assumed to be equal across groups. Otherwise equal variance assumed. Assumption used based on result of Levene's Test for Equality of Variances.
**Significant at the 0.05 level, *Significant at the 0.10 level.

Figure 8.3   **Overall Other Services, 2003**

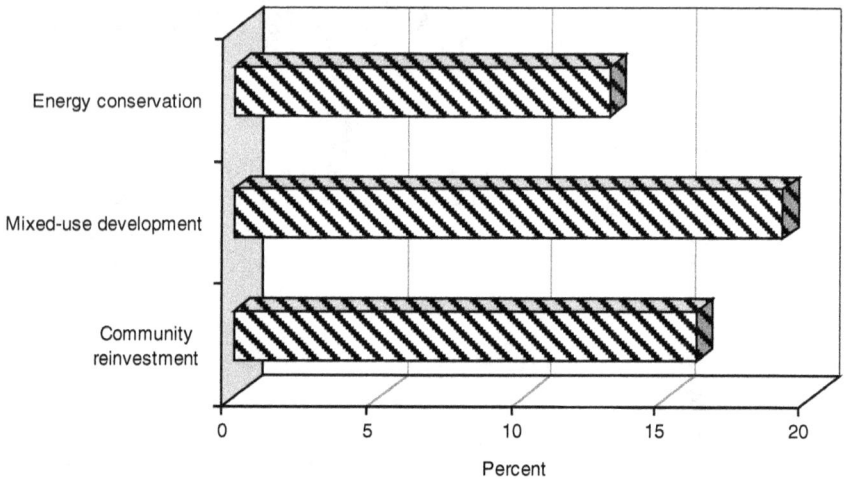

less services (34 percent), tax-preparation assistance (28 percent), and after-school programs (25 percent). The least common community service activities include prisoner reentry programs (7 percent), voter registration drives (8 percent), and teen pregnancy counseling services (11 percent). As in 2003, there are no differences between faith-based and secular nonprofits in the types of social service activities they engage in (Table 8.4). The largest differences are in the areas of crime prevention and teen parenting counseling (with secular organizations more active) and youth programs (with FBOs more active), but again, the differences are not significant.

The 2007 survey indicates some changes since 2003 in the most common business development services (Figure 8.5). Commercial development (30 percent), facade improvement programs (28 percent), main street and business district development (27 percent), and green space and park development (26 percent) are the most common activities. Business incubators (0 percent) and industrial development (3 percent) remain among the least common activities, however. There are no significant differences between faith-based and secular nonprofits in the types of economic development services provided although FBOs are more likely to operate businesses, the difference closest to being significant (Table 8.5). Although not reaching statistical significance, there are relatively large differences between faith-based and secular nonprofits in mixed-use development; faith-based nonprofits are more likely to engage in this activity. As in social services and business development, there are no significant differences between FBOs and secular nonprofits in their involvement with energy conservation, although secular organizations are more likely to undertake activities related to energy conservation (Table 8.6).

Table 8.3

Proportion of Organizations Reporting Other Services, by Organization Type, 2003

	Organization type	N	Proportion re-sponding yes	Std. deviation	Std. error mean	t-test significance
Mixed-use development	Secular	29	.14	.351	.065	.492
	Faith-based	51	.18	.385	.054	
Energy conservation	Secular	29	.24	.435	.081	.822
	Faith-based	51	.16	.367	.051	
Community reinvestment	Secular	29	.14	.351	.065	.658
	Faith-based	51	.18	.385	.054	

Table 8.4

Proportion of Organizations Reporting Specific Social Service Provided, by Organization Type, 2007

Organization type		N	Proportion responding yes	Std. deviation	Std. error mean	t-test significance
Day care	Secular	32	.16	.37	.07	.54
	Faith-based	12	.08	.29	.13	
Summer camp[a]	Secular	34	.12	.33	.06	.37
	Faith-based	12	.25	.45	.13	
Youth programs	Secular	34	.32	.48	.08	.50
	Faith-based	14	.43	.51	.14	
Drug abuse counseling	Secular	33	.12	.33	.06	.70
	Faith-based	12	.17	.39	.11	
Teen parent counseling	Secular	32	.09	.30	.05	.51
	Faith-based	12	.17	.39	.11	
Crime prevention[a]	Secular	35	.26	.44	.08	.13
	Faith-based	12	.08	.29	.08	
Cultural programs/Centers	Secular	32	.22	.42	.07	.93
	Faith-based	13	.23	.44	.12	
Voter registration[a]	Secular	29	.07	.26	.05	.78
	Faith-based	10	.10	.32	.10	

[a]Indicates t-test computed with group variance not assumed to be equal across groups. Otherwise equal variance assumed. Assumption used based on result of Levene's Test for Equality of Variances.

Table 8.5

Proportion of Organizations Reporting Specific Business Development Services, by Organization Type, 2007

	Organization type	N	Proportion responding yes	Std. deviation	Std. error mean	t-test significance
Commercial development	Secular	33	.30	.47	.08	.85
	Faith-based	11	.27	.47	.14	
Industrial development[a]	Secular	29	.00	.00	.00	.34
	Faith-based	10	.10	.32	.10	
Incubator development	Secular	30	.00	.00	.00	
	Faith-based	10	.00	.00	.00	
Operate a business[a]	Secular	29	.14	.35	.07	.14
	Faith-based	8	.38	.52	.18	
Brownfield redevelopment[a]	Secular	33	.12	.33	.06	.22
	Faith-based	13	.31	.48	.13	
Small business loan program	Secular	29	.17	.38	.07	.60
	Faith-based	10	.10	.32	.10	
Small business technical assistance	Secular	31	.26	.45	.08	.31
	Faith-based	10	.10	.32	.10	
Business district/Main street development	Secular	31	.29	.46	.08	.59
	Faith-based	10	.20	.42	.13	

[a]Indicates t-test computed with group variance not assumed to be equal across groups. Otherwise equal variance assumed. Assumption used based on result of Levene's Test for Equality of Variances.

Table 8.6

Proportion of Organizations Reporting Other Services, by Organization Type, 2007

	Organization type	N	Proportion responding yes	Std. deviation	Std. error mean	t-test significance
Mixed-use development	Secular	32	.03	.18	.03	.14
	Faith-based	13	.23	.44	.12	
Energy conservation	Secular	37	.27	.45	.07	.56
	Faith-based	11	.18	.41	.12	
Facade improvement	Secular	29	.31	.47	.09	.52
	Faith-based	10	.20	.42	.13	
Greenspace/Park development	Secular	34	.27	.45	.08	.82
	Faith-based	13	.23	.44	.12	
Urban agriculture/Food systems	Secular	33	.06	.24	.04	.40
	Faith-based	12	.00	.00	.00	
Green building[a]	Secular	33	.15	.36	.06	.30
	Faith-based	13	.31	.48	.13	
After-school programs	Secular	34	.21	.41	.07	.28
	Faith-based	14	.36	.50	.13	
Head Start	Secular	34	.21	.41	.07	.78
	Faith-based	12	.17	.39	.11	
School readiness	Secular	31	.13	.34	.06	.76
	Faith-based	12	.17	.39	.11	
Literacy programs	Secular	33	.24	.44	.08	.60
	Faith-based	12	.17	.39	.11	
Tax preparation assistance	Secular	34	.29	.46	.08	.68
	Faith-based	9	.22	.44	.15	

Food bank or Community nutrition[a]	Secular	35	.11	.32	.06	.11
	Faith-based	14	.36	.50	.13	
Homeless services	Secular	37	.32	.48	.09	.70
	Faith-based	13	.39	.51	.14	
Job counseling/Job training	Secular	35	.20	.41	.07	.54
	Faith-based	12	.17	.39	.11	
Prisoner reentry[a]	Secular	33	.09	.29	.05	.08*
	Faith-based	12	.00	.00	.00	
Community organizing	Secular	36	.47	.51	.08	.56
	Faith-based	16	.56	.51	.13	

[a]Equal variance assumed based on result of Levene's Test for Equality of Variances.
*Significant at the 0.10 level.

Figure 8.4   **Overall Social Service Activities, 2007**

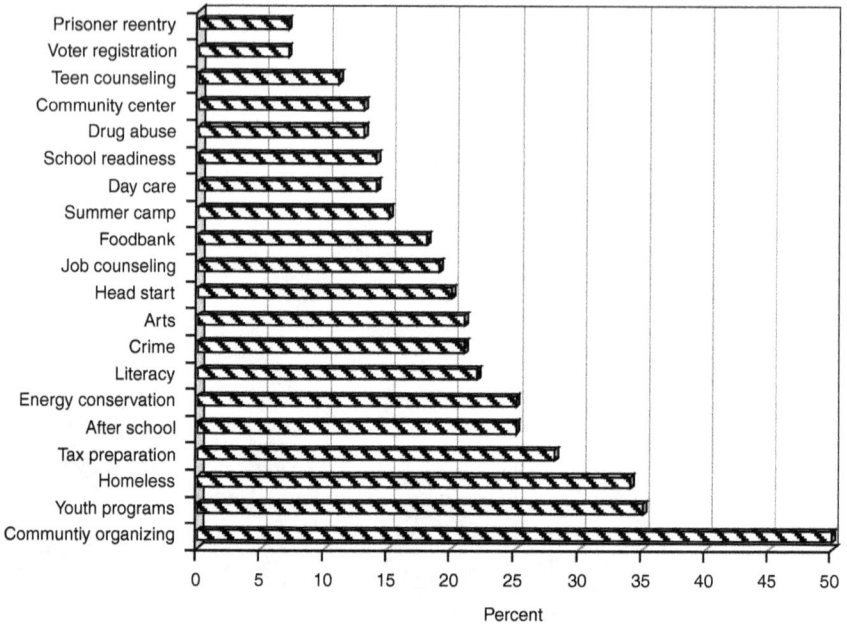

Figure 8.5   **Overall Business Development Services, 2007**

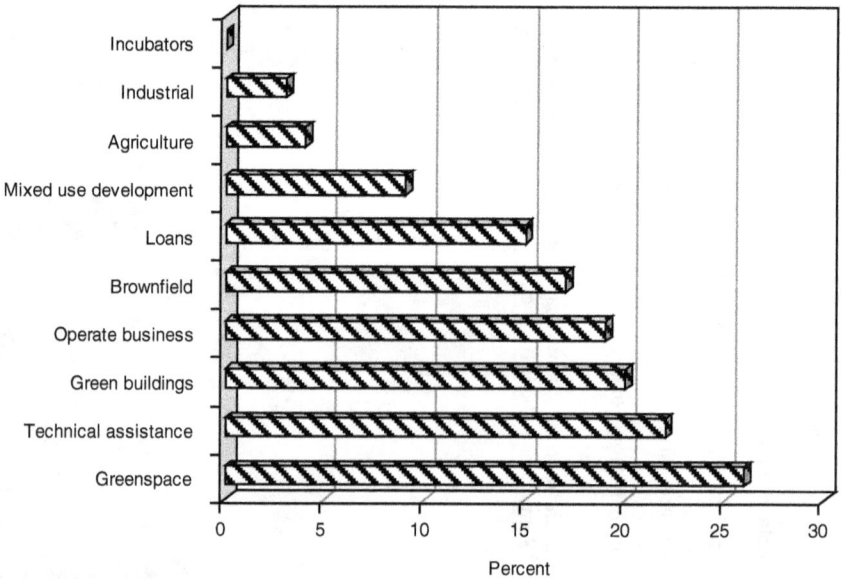

Changes in Activity 2003–2007

The proportion of nonprofits involved in social services overall increased between 2003 and 2007. Of the eight activities included on both surveys, the number of organizations involved increased for seven and remained the same for just one: day care (Figure 8.6). Figures 8.7 and 8.8 show changes over time in social services among secular and faith-based nonprofits, respectively. Comparing these two figures, it appears that the overall increases in social services are the result of activity increases among secular organizations. Indeed, FBOs decreased their social service activities in the areas of day care and crime prevention programs, although increases are evident for the other types of social services.

Figure 8.9 presents changes in economic development activities over time. Here activity increased in four areas: brownfield development, operation of businesses, small business loans, and technical assistance to small businesses. Small business incubators decreased to no activity and industrial development remained stable (and low). Activity in mixed-use development declined while energy conservation training increased over time (Figure 8.10). The decreased activity in the former, however, is completely due to reductions among secular nonprofits. Patterns of change in economic development for faith-based and secular nonprofits are quite different from those in social services (Figures 8.11 and 8.12). In the case of economic development, secular nonprofits had decreased activity for mixed-use development, brownfields, industrial development, and incubators. Faith-based nonprofits, on the other hand, show increased activity in all areas except incubators between 2003 and 2007.

The number of nonprofits active across all community service areas increased for twelve activities, decreased for two, and remained stable for two others. It appears that FBOs may have reduced some of their social service offerings, while increasing economic development efforts. It should be noted, however, that the 2007 survey was conducted before the very significant national economic downturn occurred, which is likely to have stressed the resources of nonprofits. Because the CEDAM surveys only asked whether responding organizations did or did not engage in a particular activity, the analysis does not assess effort, resources devoted to, or extent of services produced—only whether nonprofits were engaging in a particular activity. The Nonprofit Housing Provider Survey conducted by the authors provides a more comprehensive sense of activity levels, as described in the following section.

Nonprofit Housing Provider Survey

Activities and Levels of Effort

The Nonprofit Housing Provider Survey provides a slightly different assessment of the broader community activities of nonprofits in Michigan. Overall, nonprofits

Figure 8.6   **Comparison of 2003 and 2007 Social Services**

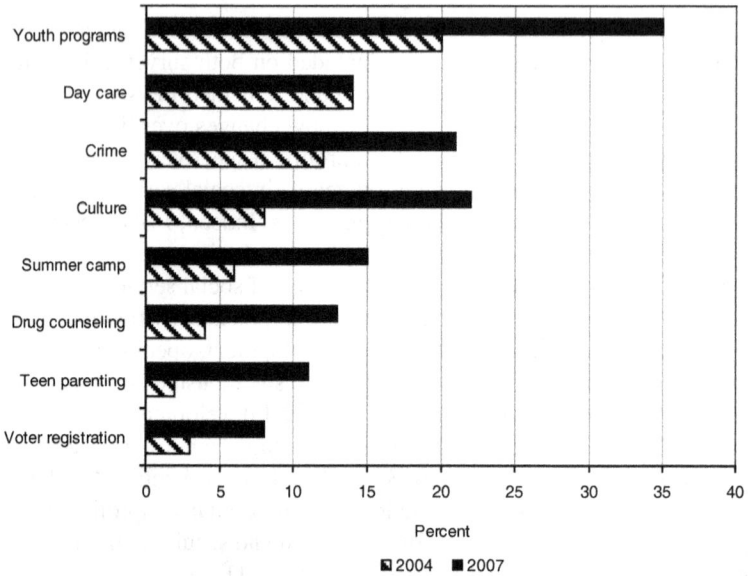

Note: The questions related to culture and the arts are not identical in the two surveys. In 2003, there were two questions, one on cultural programs/centers and one on the arts. In 2007, there was a single question asking about cultural/arts programs. For comparison purposes the 2003 question asking about cultural programs was the one used.

Figure 8.7   **Secular Social Services, 2003–2007**

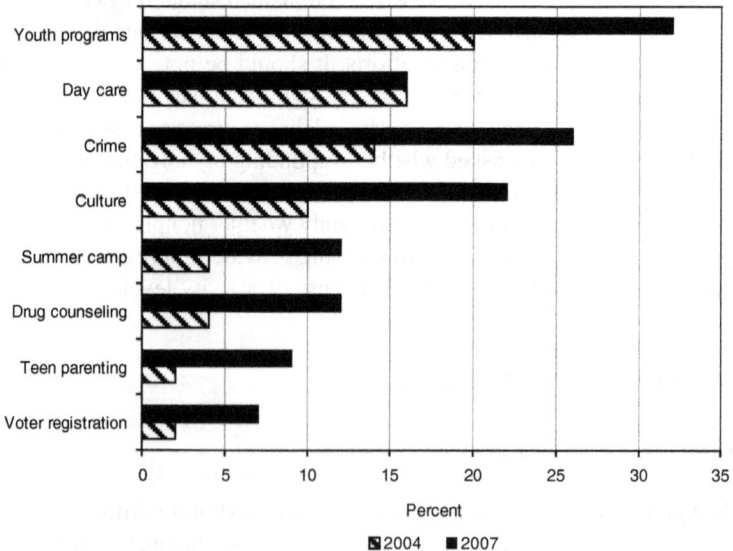

Figure 8.8   **Faith-Based Social Services, 2003–2007**

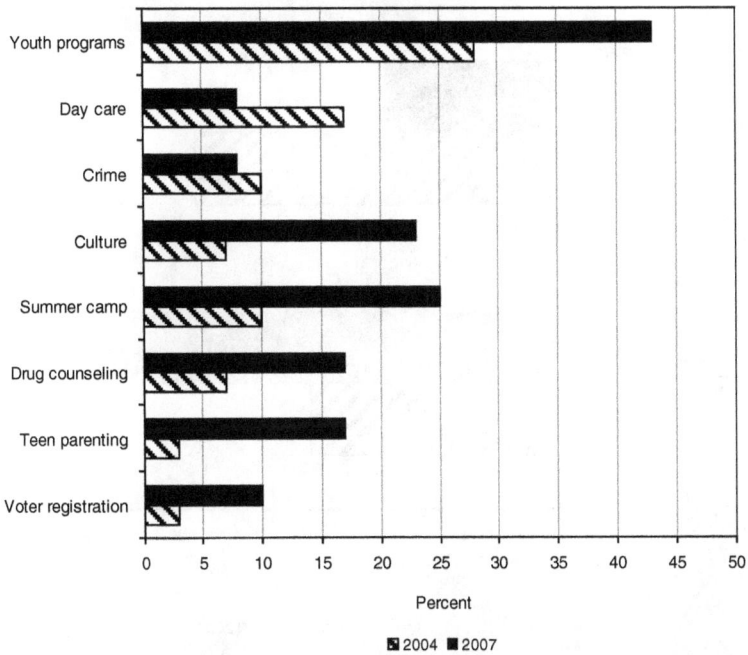

Percent

■ 2004 ■ 2007

Figure 8.9   **Comparison of 2003 and 2007 Economic Development**

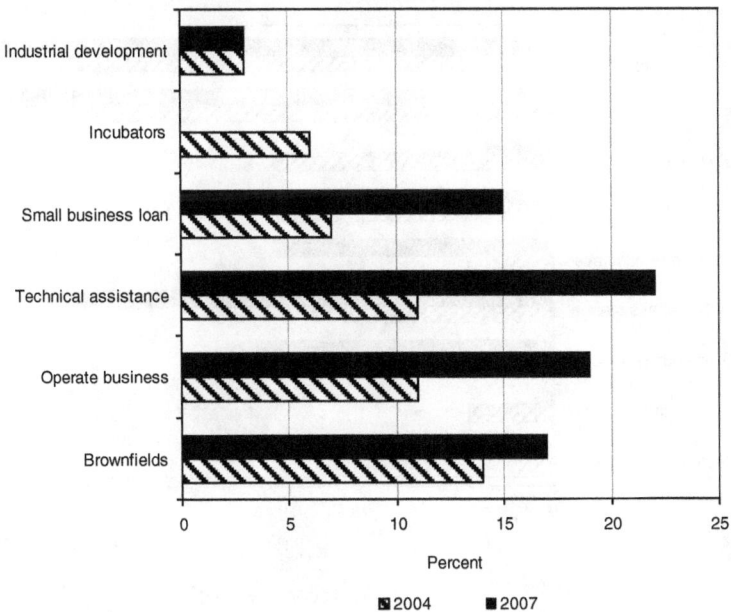

Percent

■ 2004   ■ 2007

Figure 8.10   **Comparison of 2003 and 2007 Other Services**

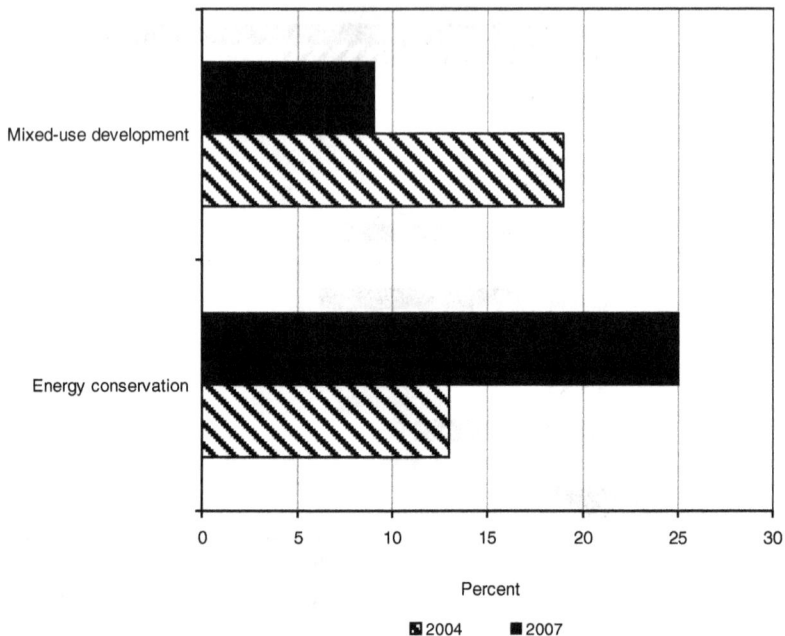

Figure 8.11   **Secular Economic Development, 2003–2007**

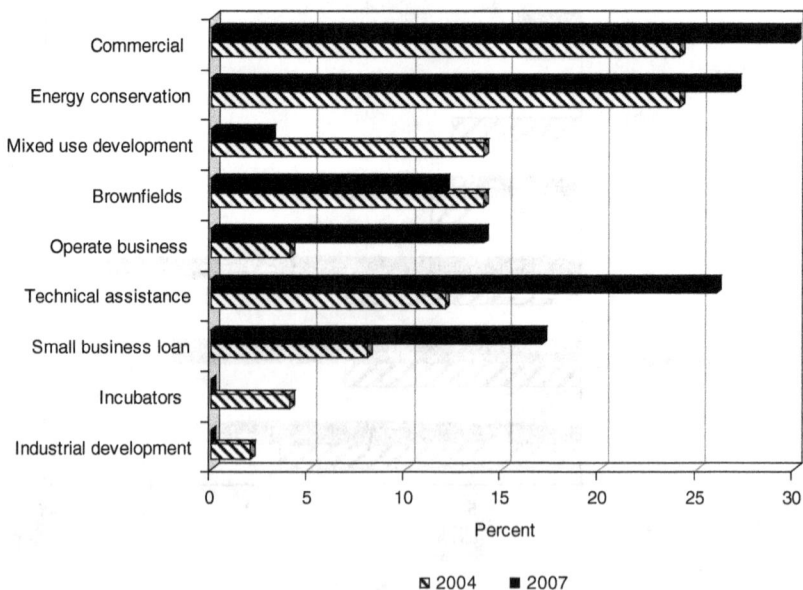

Figure 8.12   **Faith-Based Economic Development, 2003–2007**

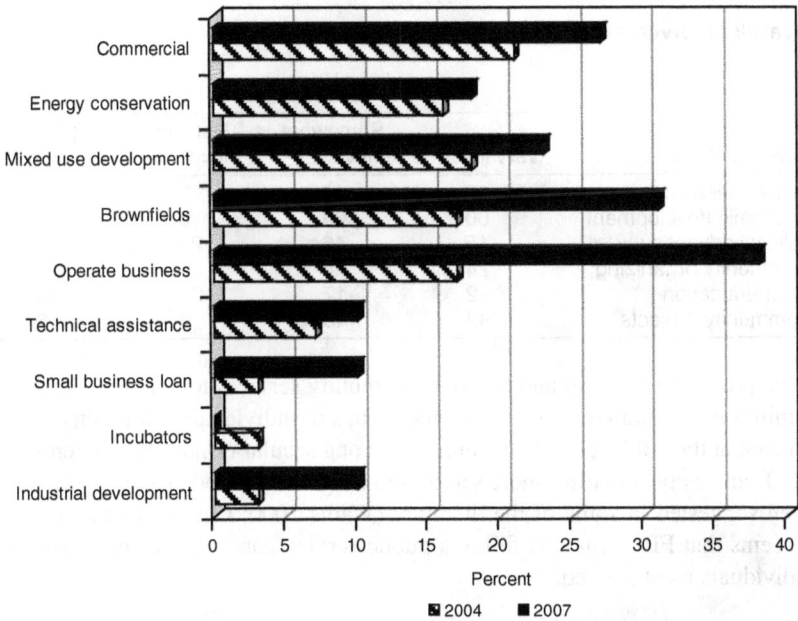

are most likely to be involved in economic development, community projects, and service delivery (Table 8.7). Faith-based nonprofits are significantly more likely to indicate that they are involved in the delivery of services (Table 8.8).

Table 8.9 provides more detailed data on twenty-six community activities across an array of service areas, while Figure 8.13 provides a visual presentation of the number of organizations indicating they were always or often involved in each service activity. Clearly, the provision of direct assistance to individuals and families is the most common activity. This is followed by education, assisting other organizations or agencies, and working with public bodies on service provision. Emergency assistance and loans are also common. Few of these nonprofits are regularly engaged in political activities, service to immigrants, or environmental justice activities. Beyond the significant difference in the extent of involvement in the delivery of services, faith-based and secular organizations are not significantly different in the frequency with which they provide any individual service, as indicated in Table 8.10.

Types of Clients Served

While the differences in service provision between secular and faith-based nonprofits are quite modest, it appears that the two types of organizations are serving slightly different client groups (Table 8.11). Specifically, FBOs are more likely

Table 8.7

Overall Involvement in Activities (in percent)

| | Extent of involvement | | | |
Type of activity	Very involved	Somewhat involved	Not very involved	Not involved at all
Deliver services	63	18	6	13
Economic development	60	29	8	2
Political advocacy	15	46	22	17
Community organizing	24	34	29	13
Voter education	2	17	22	59
Community projects	42	43	9	6

to be providing housing and broader community services to inner-city residents, families with children, and low-income groups or individuals. Although only significant at the .10 level and not common among secular or faith-based nonprofits, FBOs also appear to offer more services to religiously based groups. Thus, as has been suggested in some of the literature (Wallis 2000; Cnaan and Bodie 2001), it seems that FBOs may be filling a public service gap by providing services to individuals most in need.

Correlates of Nonhousing Activities

As with housing activities, the question of what types of organizations are providing what kinds of community services is a critical one. Because of the large number of nonhousing services included on the Nonprofit Housing Provider Survey, a factor analysis was conducted for the purposes of data reduction.[1] Results are presented in Table 8.12. Five conceptually different types of community services are present in the data: general social services, services focused on youth, economic development, social justice activities, and land development.[2] The social services factor includes various forms of direct assistance to clients and other agencies and organizations, including emergency assistance. It also includes several health-related services, such as physical health programs, mental health programs, and services to immigrants.

The youth services factor includes programming and services more directly focused on the needs of young people: general education services, recreation, substance abuse counseling, and assistance with work-skill development and job searches. Voter registration drives also load on this factor, since they include efforts to register first-time voters and younger adults. The economic development factor includes all of the small business development activities: loans to small businesses, technical assistance, small business incubators, and the development and support of business districts. The land development aspects of economic development appear conceptually different and load on a separate factor that includes brownfield and

Table 8.8

Overall Involvement in Activities by Organization Type (in percent)

Type of activity		Extent of involvement			
		Very involved	Somewhat involved	Not very involved	Not involved at all
Delivery of services**	Secular	56	20	7	18
	Faith-based	76	15	6	3
Community/economic development	Secular	62	30	7	2
	Faith-based	57	29	11	3
Policy advocacy	Secular	16	44	21	18
	Faith-based	12	50	24	15
Community organizing	Secular	23	26	34	16
	Faith-based	26	49	20	06
Voter education	Secular	2	15	23	61
	Faith-based	3	21	21	56
Community projects	Secular	44	34	12	10
	Faith-based	37	57	6	0

**Difference significant at the .05 level based on difference in means test.

Table 8.9

Frequency of Service Activity (in percent)

	Always	Often	Sometimes	Seldom	Never
Direct assistance	36	21	16	9	19
Assist other agencies	12	21	25	22	21
Physical health	10	13	23	17	37
Mental health	8	15	18	20	39
Education	20	28	24	12	17
Immigrant services	4	4	9	30	52
Recreation	4	10	22	20	44
Crime prevention	5	11	21	24	39
Emergency assistance	17	9	11	24	40
Substance abuse	9	9	10	19	54
Locate jobs	9	12	17	25	38
Work skills	7	13	18	23	40
Loan/give money	10	15	12	13	50
Business incubators	3	9	12	14	62
Technical assistance	4	7	14	10	65
Brownfields	4	8	19	17	52
Mixed-use	4	9	30	17	39
Business district	11	9	15	15	51
Community reinvestment	7	10	18	21	45
Social justice	9	10	20	19	44
Political activity	1	2	10	13	74
Voter registration	2	2	10	15	70
Work with public bodies	8	23	25	16	28
Work with private bodies	7	15	19	24	36
Environmental justice	2	7	16	23	52
Other	15	6	6	0	73

mixed-use development. Finally, four variables load together on what can conceptually be labeled a "social justice" factor. These variables are social justice–specific activities, participation in Community Reinvestment Act activities, explicitly political activity, and environmental justice activities. The five service factors serve as the dependent variables for the analysis that follows.

The Venn diagrams portrayed in Figures 8.14 and 8.15 highlight the nature of interactions among four of the five service factors: social services, economic development, youth services, and social justice.[3] The organizations included in Figure 8.14 are those that are actively involved in delivering social services, since organizations engaged in social services are likely to be a part of a larger network of organizations in a community. Most nonprofits (twelve) are also active in economic development, followed by youth services (nine) and the combination of youth services and social justice (nine). Eight organizations are active in the combination of economic development, youth services, and social justice activities and eight in the combination of youth services and economic development. There are five organizations that are active in the combination of economic development and

Table 8.10

Involvement in Specific Activities by Organization Type (in percent)

		How frequently does your organization engage in the following activities?				
	Type of activity	Always	Often	Sometimes	Seldom	Never
Direct assistance	Secular	34	20	15	07	24
	Faith-based	39	21	18	12	09
Assist other agencies	Secular	12	20	15	25	27
	Faith-based	12	21	42	15	09
Physical health	Secular	10	12	22	14	41
	Faith-based	09	16	25	22	28
Mental health	Secular	07	14	18	18	44
	Faith-based	09	16	19	25	31
Education	Secular	22	26	21	09	22
	Faith-based	15	30	30	18	06
Immigration services	Secular	05	03	10	22	59
	Faith-based	03	06	06	46	39
Recreation	Secular	03	12	20	17	48
	Faith-based	06	06	25	25	38
Crime prevention	Secular	05	07	20	22	46
	Faith-based	06	18	21	27	27
Emergency assistance	Secular	17	09	09	19	48
	Faith-based	16	09	16	34	25
Substance abuse	Secular	10	10	09	17	53
	Faith-based	06	06	12	21	55
Locate jobs	Secular	10	10	17	20	42
	Faith-based	06	15	18	32	29
Work skills	Secular	09	10	20	19	42
	Faith-based	03	19	13	31	34
Loan/Give money	Secular	09	17	15	10	49

(continued)

Table 8.10 (continued)

Type of activity	How frequently does your organization engage in the following activities?				
	Always	Often	Sometimes	Seldom	Never
Business incubators					
Faith-based	12	12	06	18	52
Secular	00	12	10	14	64
Technical assistance					
Faith-based	09	03	15	15	59
Secular	05	09	15	07	64
Brownfields					
Faith-based	03	03	12	15	67
Secular	05	07	17	17	54
Mixed-use					
Faith-based	03	09	24	18	47
Secular	03	09	29	17	41
Business district					
Faith-based	06	09	32	18	35
Secular	12	09	19	10	51
Community reinvestment					
Faith-based	09	09	09	24	50
Secular	09	09	14	19	50
Social justice					
Faith-based	03	12	24	24	36
Secular	05	10	14	25	46
Political activity					
Faith-based	15	09	30	06	39
Secular	02	02	10	09	78
Voter registration					
Faith-based	00	03	09	21	67
Secular	02	03	12	10	72
Public bodies[a]					
Faith-based	03	00	06	24	67
Secular	10	17	29	20	24
Private bodies[a]					
Faith-based	03	33	18	09	36
Secular	05	10	24	25	36
Environmental justice					
Faith-based	06	06	27	15	47
Secular	00	07	10	28	55
Other					
Secular	14	05	00	00	82
Faith-based	18	09	18	00	55

[a]Sits on boards of public or private organizations.

Figure 8.13   **Frequency of Service Delivery**

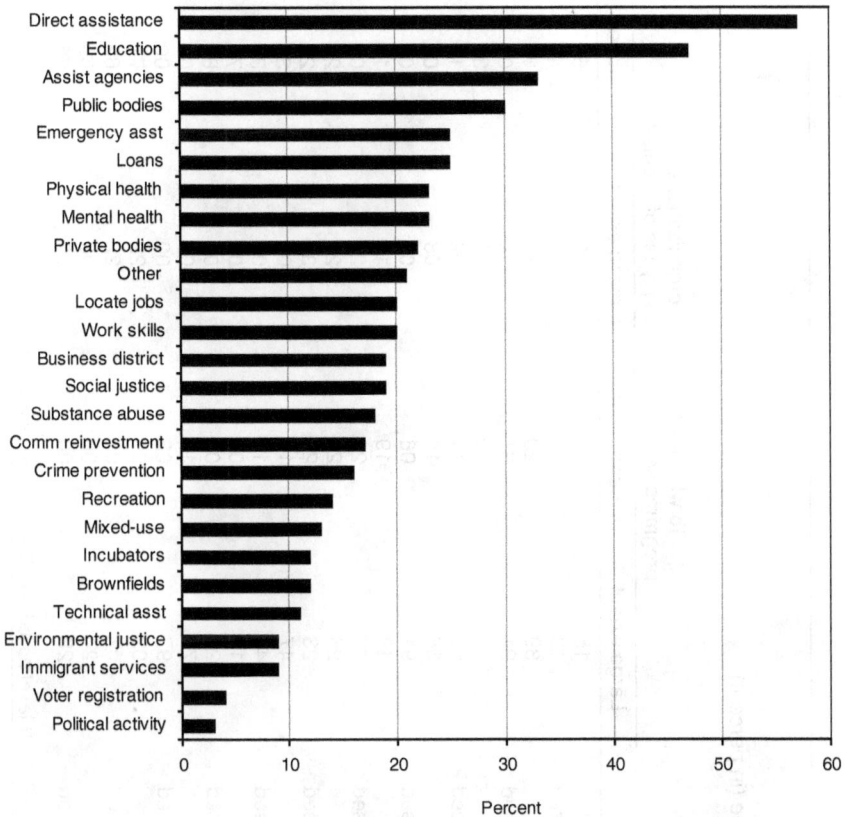

Percent

Note: This figure depicts the percentage of organizations that indicated that they were always or often engaged in these activities.

social justice. The fewest organizations are active in social justice activities alone (two). Nonprofits involved in social service delivery are also engaged in economic development, social justice activities, and youth services.

Figure 8.15 is based on those organizations that are active in housing construction and renovation. The greatest number of these organizations (twelve) also engage in a combination of economic development, social services, youth services, and social justice activities. The next most common combination of activities consists of economic development and social services (nine). Economic development, alone, is a common activity for seven of the organizations. None of the organizations report only providing youth services or engaging in social justice organizations. One organization reports that it does not engage in any of the noted nonhousing activities (not shown in the figure). Economic development is a key secondary activity for organizations involved in housing construction and renovation. This figure (8.15)

Table 8.11

Types of Clients Served by Organization Type (in percent)

Target clientele		To what extent do your organizations' programs serve the following types of clients?			
		Large extent	Moderate extent	Limited extent	None
Own members	Secular	15	07	20	57
	Faith-based	18	03	36	42
Senior citizens	Secular	39	20	31	10
	Faith-based	31	31	34	03
Inner-city residents**	Secular	47	12	09	33
	Faith-based	69	11	09	11
Families with children**	Secular	68	19	08	05
	Faith-based	91	06	03	00
Citywide clients	Secular	49	19	18	14
	Faith-based	47	24	21	09
Regional clients	Secular	26	20	26	28
	Faith-based	23	26	31	20
Specific neighborhood	Secular	47	16	02	35
	Faith-based	44	15	07	33
Specific racial/ethnic group	Secular	13	06	09	72
	Faith-based	28	04	04	64
Low-income individuals/families***	Secular	76	12	09	03
	Faith-based	97	03	00	00
Religious communities*	Secular	02	00	22	77
	Faith-based	07	07	22	63
Other	Secular	24	06	06	65
	Faith-based	29	00	06	65

***Difference significant at the .01 level, **.05 level, *.10 level based on difference in means test

Table 8.12

Factor Loadings: Nonhousing Activities

	Social Services	Youth Services	Economic Development Services	Social Justice	Land Development
Direct assistance	**.82**	.07	-.11	.04	-.09
Assist other agencies	**.81**	.26	-.06	.09	-.06
Physical health	**.63**	.38	-.13	.26	-.04
Mental health	**.64**	.38	-.19	.28	.04
Immigrant services	**.57**	.26	.24	.09	-.16
Emergency assistance	**.74**	.16	-.10	-.12	.16
Education	.44	**.40**	.21	.05	-.21
Recreation	.08	**.68**	.36	.15	-.06
Substance abuse	.36	**.70**	-.21	.06	.06
Locate jobs	.38	**.74**	.03	.14	-.16
Work skills	.36	**.74**	.05	.08	-.18
Voter registration	.21	**.71**	-.05	.32	.05
Loan money	.29	-.36	**.52**	.14	-.44
Incubators	-.06	.12	**.81**	.15	.20
Technical assistance	-.17	.11	**.85**	.17	.15
Business dev district	-.10	-.10	**.72**	.06	.47
CRA	-.02	.03	.19	**.66**	.15
Social justice	.25	.27	.02	**.80**	-.15
Political activity	.12	.32	.04	**.72**	.00
Environmental justice	-.01	.01	.17	**.60**	.28
Brownfield development	-.05	-.11	.18	.20	**.82**
Mixed-use development	.01	-.13	.34	.09	**.77**

Figure 8.14   **Other Nonhousing Activities of Organizations Delivering Social Services**

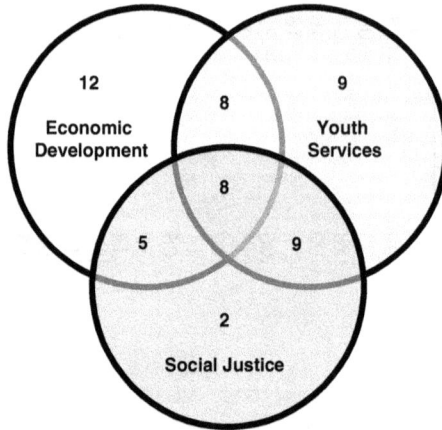

Note: Three nonprofits report no activity in any of these categories.

Figure 8.15   **Nonhousing Activities of Organizations Actively Involved in Housing Construction and Renovation**

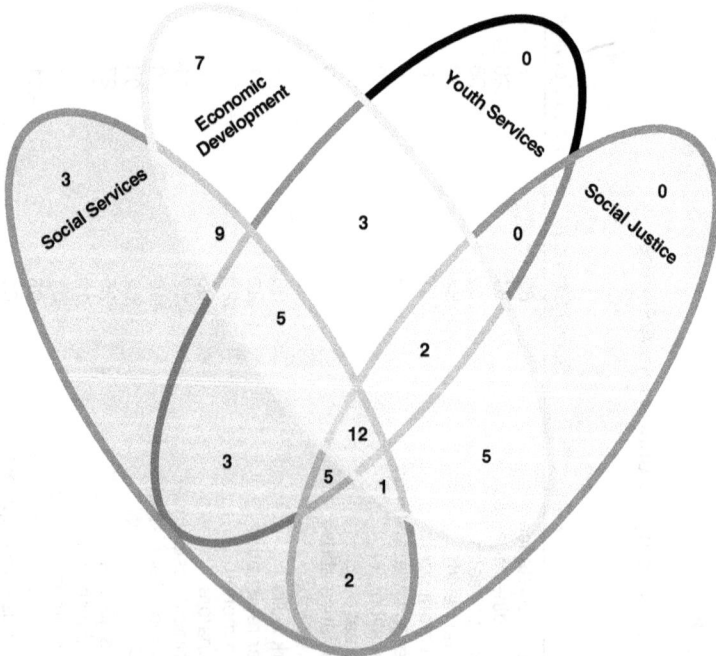

Note: Eight nonprofits report no activity in any of these categories.

depicts a more holistic approach to housing development, in which wraparound services are included in the organization's portfolio of activities.

Overall, these Venn diagrams suggest that nonprofits providing broader community services are likely to engage in a relatively complex mix of activities rather than focusing on just one or two. For nonprofits most actively engaged in providing housing, the most common combinations are to also provide social justice and economic development services or to deliver a mix of social and youth services.

The five service factors were used in correlation analysis with the structure and capacity variables and the housing activities as initially presented in the multivariate models in Chapter 7. Results of the correlation analysis are presented in Table 8.13. Social service provision is correlated with a number of variables. Nonprofits providing more social services also provide more youth services, social justice services, associated housing services, and multifamily and special needs housing. These organizations experienced an increased involvement in housing activity, have significantly more resources in terms of budget, staff, and volunteers, and have been in existence longer. They are more likely to be faith based and tend to receive greater portions of their funding from religious sources, donations, foundations, and the government. They tend to serve seniors and low-income individuals and collaborate with a variety of other social service actors: social service agencies, mental health agencies, religious organizations, ethnic organizations, schools, hospitals, advocacy groups, the private sector, and state (but not local) government. Their forms of collaboration cover the board: provision of social service is positively correlated with all but two of the twenty-two possible reasons for collaboration. The only things they are not collaborating on are neighborhood development and improving neighborhoods, which represent a greater economic-development focus.

Nonprofits providing more youth services have a different profile. These organizations are significantly more likely to be providing social services, social justice, and associated housing services. They have more full-time staff and larger budgets, but volunteers appear less important. Again, these are older nonprofits but are more likely to be serving a specific race and to be located in Southeast Michigan. They are significantly more likely to be collaborating with other social service agencies, mental health agencies, ethnic organizations, schools, and hospitals. They are collaborating on fewer activities, however. Collaborating—to provide services other than housing, to receive housing and other social services, to make and receive referrals, to pool resources, and to reduce redundancies—seems particularly important for nonprofits providing youth services. Nonprofits providing more youth services are also more likely to be engaged in collaboration for political activities: advocacy and influencing policy.

There are fewer correlates of providing economic development services. Nonprofits engaged in more economic development activity are more likely to be providing social justice and land development activities. Organizational resources

Table 8.13

Correlation Matrix of Service Indexes

	Social Services	Youth Services	Economic Development	Social Justice	Land Development
Types of community (nonhousing) activities					
Social services	1.00				
Youth services	.65***	1.00			
Economic development	−.17	.01	1.00		
Social justice	.25**	.42***	.30***	1.00	.21
Land development	−.17	−.12	.44***	.21	1.00
Types of housing services					
Associated services	.75***	.52***	−.18	.03	−.17
Ownership services	.13	−.03	.02	.01	−.02
Build and renovate	.19	−.10	.04	.16	.35***
Build multifamily, special needs	.40***	.11	−.11	.10	.20
Housing activity change	.32***	.19	.02	.19	.08
Organizational characteristics					
Faith-based+	6.06**	.84	.48	6.96***	1.41
Full-time staff	.68***	.33***	.04	.27**	−.03
Part-time staff	.52***	−.21	.04	.31**	.02
Volunteers	.32***	−.14	.04	.23	−.21
Budget	.58***	.28***	.03	.20	.02
Older age	.37***	.28**	.12	.26**	.08
Funding sources					
Religious funds	.33***	.16	−.04	.26**	−.20
Donations	.23**	.20	−.14	.07	−.42***
Foundation funds	.22*	.22	−.01	.21	−.15
Corporate funds	.15	.19	.08	.17	−.18
Govt funds	.26*	.17	−.03	.03	−.10
Bank funds	−.05	−.05	.19	.19	.12
Population served					
Own members	.10	.13	.41***	.26**	.15
Seniors	.27**	.08	.07	.13	.11
Inner-city	.06	.08	−.01	.30***	.04
Families	.13	−.05	−.10	.13	−.06
City-wide	.12	−.06	−.12	.08	−.09
Region	.13	.05	.07	.18	.07
Neighborhood	.04	.19	.19	.19	.21
Specific race	.17	.29*	.15	.31***	.18
Low-income	.34***	.12	−.36***	.17	−.26**
Religion	.18	.08	.16	.12	.05
Location					
Region+	6.56	13.87	9.42	7.14	10.24
North	2.99	1.74	.09	.20	2.38
Southwest	.80	.81	.13	.36	.46
Central	1.20	4.99	6.00**	1.97	1.28

Table 8.13 *(continued)*

	Social Services	Youth Services	Economic Develop- ment	Social Justice	Land Development
Southeast	2.31	6.55**	5.04	1.08	7.33
Detroit	.80	3.05	.35	6.11**	.59
Collaborates with					
Social service	.47***	.37***	−.09	.34***	−.10
Mental health	.69***	.47***	−.35***	.18	−.19
Local govt	.18	.07	−.04	.14	.02
State govt	.27**	.00	.10	.12	.06
Civic orgs	.19	.20	−.02	.05	−.29***
Neighborhoods	.04	.07	−.01	.20	.19
Religious	.41***	.20	−.02	.19	−.09
Ethnic	.47***	.32***	.03	.31***	.03
Schools	.50***	.37***	−.08	.24**	−.17
Hospitals	.55***	.42***	−.06	.25**	−.01
Advocacy	.29***	.18	.04	.53***	−.01
Private sector	.24**	.20	.09	.27**	−.09
Collaborates for					
Housing services	.33***	.14	−.21	.12	.01
Provide other service	.54***	.38***	−.10	.14	−.15
Receive housing ser- vices	.49***	.28*	−.08	.24**	.00
Receive other services	.57***	.35***	.06	.19	−.07
Provide funds	.29**	.10	.03	.18	.03
Receive funds	.42***	.13	−.37***	.07	−.02
Make referrals	.54***	.31***	−.07	.19	−.25**
Receive referrals	.61***	.31***	−.19	.08	−.25**
Neighborhood dev	.06	.03	.16	.21	.31***
Give policy advice	.27**	.18	.07	.28***	−.06
Receive advice	.34***	.21	.03	.36***	−.13
Influence policy	.32***	.29**	.07	.48***	−.08
Pool resources	.22**	.24**	.12	.31***	.17
Avoid redundancy	.41***	.23**	−.20	.23**	−.31***
Bridge building	.36***	.14	.02	.23**	−.13
Referrals	.45***	.20	−.17	.12	−.04
Advocacy	.51***	.23**	−.09	.36***	−.09
New programs	.42***	.20	−.15	.29***	−.12
Improve neighborhoods	.07	.02	.02	.18	.16
Promote religion	.25**	.14	.03	.36***	.09
Influence state policy	.30***	.02	−.05	.23**	−.12
Influence local policy	.33***	.15	−.16	.30***	−.21**

+Chi square statistic was used instead of a Pearson correlation because of the nominal nature of region and faith-based versus secular.

***Significant at the .01 level, **Significant at the .05 level.

do not seem particularly important. Nonprofits engaged in economic development are more likely to be serving their own members and less likely to be serving low-income individuals. They do not collaborate with mental health agencies and specifically do not collaborate to receive funding. They are more likely to be in the central region of the state.

Nonprofits providing more social justice services are more likely to be providing social services and youth services and to be engaged in economic development. They have more full- and part-time staff, but budget does not appear important, suggesting that effort rather than money is more critical to social justice pursuits. They are more likely to be faith based, receive a greater portion of their budgets from religious organizations, and serve their own members, inner-city residents, and groups of specific races. They also tend to be older organizations and located in the city of Detroit. They collaborate with a variety of other organizations in a manner more like the social service nonprofits: social service agencies, ethnic organizations, schools, hospitals, advocacy groups, and the private sector. Finally, they collaborate on a wide variety of activities including receiving housing services, giving and receiving policy advice, and influencing policy. They collaborate to pool resources, reduce redundancy, advocate, build bridging relationships with other organizations, establish new programs, promote religion, and attempt to influence state and local policy. Clearly, these organizations are more focused on the policy and political systems than nonprofits engaging in housing or other types of services, with the exception of social service providers.

Finally, nonprofits reporting more land development activity also are more engaged in economic development generally and in building and renovating housing. They are significantly less likely to receive funding from donations and are less likely to serve low-income individuals. They do not tend to collaborate with civic organizations, which suggests that they may be engaging in their land development activities without working through civic or neighborhood organizations. They are less likely to collaborate in order to make and receive referrals, avoid redundancies, or influence local policies and more likely to collaborate on neighborhood development. The primary differences between organizations focusing on land development and those focusing on economic development appear to revolve around the extent of social justice activities also conducted; those providing more economic development also engage in social justice activities while those focusing on land development build and renovate housing instead.

As in the case of housing activities, the types of community activities that an organization engages in are related to organizational characteristics, funding sources, the population served, the organization's location, and the types of and reasons for collaboration. The relative influence of any one of these factors will vary based on the service area and type of activity.

Community Activities = **F** (**O**rganizational Characteristics, **F**unding Sources, **P**opulation Served, **L**ocation, **C**ollaboration)

$$Y = \alpha + \beta_1 OC_i + \beta_2 FS_{5i} + \beta_3 PS_{5i} + \beta_4 L_i + \beta_5 C_i + \varepsilon_i$$

Where: Community activities are modeled as five separate dependent variables (social services, youth services, economic development, social justice, and land development); and
Collaboration includes both the type of collaborator and reason for collaborating.

To determine which correlates are the best predictors of the summary service activities indicators, multiple regressions were run, with the five service areas as the dependent variables. There is significant multicollinearity among collaborators and reasons for collaboration. Thus, as described in Chapter 7, index variables are used for these variables, resulting in two types of collaborators (governmental and nongovernmental) and four purposes of collaboration (to provide services, to engage in organization and network building, to participate in policy input, and for neighborhood development).[4] Using these factors for collaborators and purposes of collaboration, as well as the resource index already discussed, allows for a reduction in intercorrelations among the independent variables and simplifies the regression models considerably. Table 8.14 provides the results of the regression model for social service activity; in all cases, only those variables significantly correlated with the index of social service activity in correlation analysis are included in the multiple regression. The variables account for 56 percent of the variation in the extent of social service activities, although only four variables remain significantly correlated in multiple regression analysis: having more resources, being in existence longer, collaborating for the purposes of service provision, and having government collaborations. Collaborating with government actors is the most important variable contributing to the level of services provided.

The level of youth service activity is not as well explained by the variables in the model: only 21 percent of the variation is accounted for (Table 8.15) and none of the variables remain significantly correlated to youth services in multiple regression analysis. Economic development activities are better explained by the variables at hand; 35 percent of the variation in development is accounted for (Table 8.16). Clients appear important, with nonprofits engaging in more economic development tending to serve their own members and eschewing low-income clients. Avoiding collaboration with other organizations in order to receive funding and not collaborating with mental health organizations are also statistically significant. Serving membership is the best predictor of economic development activity. Because of this intensive inward focus, the nonprofits highest on the economic development index were identified. They tend to be county, city, or neighborhood-based housing nonprofits. Thus, it would appear that respondents may be interpreting "own members" to be the particular geographic service area.

Engaging in social justice activity remains related only to an organization's age in multiple regression analysis, with all variables accounting for 37 percent of the variance in social justice activities (Table 8.17). Collaborating with other organiza-

Table 8.14

Regression Social Services

	B	S.E.	Beta	Significance
Organizational characteristics				
Resources	.44	.11	.21	.03**
Faith-based	.05	.18	.03	.781
Older age	.01	.00	.01	.01**
Funding source				
Religious funding	−.04	.18	−.02	.84
Donations	−.15	.12	−.10	.23
Foundation funding	−.03	.10	−.03	.75
Government funding	−.07	.08	−.07	.40
Population served				
Serves seniors	−.02	.10	−.02	.88
Serves low-income	−.02	.13	−.01	.90
Type of collaborator				
Governmental collaborators	.24	.10	.24	.02**
Nongovernmental collaborators	.11	.11	.11	.30
Reason for collaboration				
Collaborate to provide service	.23	.11	.22	.05**
Collaborate for policy input	−.09	.11	−.09	.42
Collaborate for organizational development	.15	.10	.15	.16
Constant	−.44	.99		.66

Multiple R^2 = .56
N = 98

$**p < 0.05$

Table 8.15

Regression Youth Services

	B	S.E.	Beta	Significance
Organizational characteristics				
Resources	.05	.14	.04	.74
Older age	.01	.01	.18	.10
Population served				
Serves specific race	.16	.09	.17	.10
Type of collaborator				
Governmental collaborators	.18	.13	.18	.16
Nongovernmental collaborators	.10	.12	.10	.41
Reason for collaboration				
Collaborate for service provision	.15	.14	.15	.28
Collaborate for organizational development	.00	.13	.00	.98
Collaborate for policy input	−.04	.13	−.04	.75
Constant	−.29	.37		.43

Multiple R^2 = .21
N = 95

Table 8.16

Regression Economic Development

	B	S.E.	Beta	Significance
Location				
Central region	.34	.21	.14	.12
Population served				
Serve own members	.33	.08	.36	.00***
Serve low-income	−.24	.14	−.16	.09*
Collaborate with				
Mental health organizations	−.19	.09	−.20	.03**
Reason for collaboration				
Collaborate to receive funds	−.20	.08	−.21	.02**
Constant	.26	.37		.49
Multiple R^2 = .35				
N = 98				

***p< 0.01, **p < 0.05, *p < 0.10

tions for policy input and serving inner-city residents approach statistical significance. Finally, land development activity remains correlated with three variables in multiple regression analysis: less revenue from donations, more collaboration to rebuild neighborhoods, and less collaboration with civic organizations (Table 8.18). Thirty-seven percent of the variation in land development is accounted for by these variables.

Discussion

While this chapter has covered a number of complex relationships, it is possible to summarize the most important findings in a relatively parsimonious fashion. The most obvious conclusion is that there is very little difference between faith-based and secular nonprofits in Michigan in the types of broader service activities in which they engage. Certainly, there are fewer differences based on faith than there are for housing services. Collaborators and geography are the variables most consistently related to community service provision across the multiple regressions. The only case where religion is present in any regression analysis involves the importance of religious funding for social justice activities. Indeed, faith-based and secular nonprofits are significantly different at the .05 level only for microenterprise and business district development. At the .10 level, faith-based and secular nonprofits are different on only three additional activities: arts programming, the operation of for-profit businesses, and prisoner reentry programs.

General trends over time suggest that while faith-based nonprofits tend to provide more social services, the social service activities of secular nonprofits are increasing, while FBOs appear to be shifting somewhat to economic development

Table 8.17

Regression Social Justice

	B	S.E.	Beta	Significance
Organizational characteristics				
Resources	.01	.13	.01	.92
Faith-based	.02	.20	.01	.94
Older age	.01	.01	.20	.05**
Funding source				
Religious funding	.26	.19	.14	.18
Population served				
Serves own members	.09	.09	.09	.33
Serves inner-city residents	.13	.08	.17	.09*
Serves specific race	.12	.09	.13	.21
Location				
Detroit region	.18	.24	.08	.47
Collaborates with				
Social service organizations	.11	.13	.09	.42
Nongovernmental collaborators	.05	.13	.05	.71
Reason for collaboration				
Collaborate for policy input	.22	.12	.21	.07*
Collaborate for organizational development	.09	.11	.09	.44
Constant	−1.75	1.09		.11
Multiple R^2 = .37				
N = 98				

$**p < 0.05, *p < 0.10$

activities. Over time and across various surveys, it appears that the most common community service activities of nonprofits remain relatively consistent. In the area of social services, nonprofits tend to focus on youth and day care services, education, community organizing, direct assistance to the needy, and emergency assistance. The most common economic development activities are commercial development, brownfield redevelopment, business district creation, greenspace protection and enhancement, and facade improvement programs. It does appear clear that faith-based and secular nonprofits are significantly different in the types of clients served, with FBOs focusing on the groups and individuals most in need and most likely to fall through the public sector safety net: inner-city residents, families with children, and low-income individuals.

It appears that there are five conceptually distinct types of community activities beyond housing, each with a distinct profile of correlates. The provision of social services is dependent on resources, experience, and governmental collaborators, probably because so many of the component service activities involve populations with special and often complex needs: mental health patients, immigrants, and those needing emergency assistance, for example. Youth services are a separate area of specialization, tightly tied to the mental health professions and apparently serving youth

Table 8.18

Regression Land Development

	B	S.E.	Beta	Significance
Funding source				
Donations	−.47	.13	−.38	.00***
Population served				
Low-income	−.14	.16	−.09	.39
Collaborates with				
Civic organizations	−.23	.12	−.21	.03***
Reason for collaboration				
Collaborate to provide services	−.07	.10	−.07	.49
Collaborate for neighborhood development	.31	.09	.31	.00***
Collaborate to avoid redundancy	−.19	.13	−.15	.15
Collaborate to influence local policy	−.03	.08	−.04	.66
Constant	2.27	.54		.00
Multiple R^2 = .36				
N = 96				

***$p < 0.01$

from particular racial groups (based on correlation analysis). Economic development and land development activities are conceptually distinct, but both appear to involve organizations with few collaborative ties to other, particularly neighborhood-based, organizations. These development and land activities also appear to be geographically based, with services limited to the particular area of origin—counties or neighborhoods, for example. Social justice activities are interesting because they represent the only area with a distinct public policy focus and where religious support appears to be important.

Finally, there are several service complexes that appear to operate across the housing and community service areas. Organizations involved in associated housing services and in building and renovating housing also tend to provide more social services and youth services. Social justice activities are also prevalent within this service complex. Economic development and land development are part of a separate service complex that also includes social justice activities. Again, specialization among nonprofits is apparent but, once the analysis shifts beyond housing services, the faith nature of the nonprofit appears to become less important, even when collaborators are considered.

Chapters 9 and 10 focus specifically on the issue of collaboration. While patterns of faith-based versus secular collaborators appear particularly important for housing activities and perhaps less so for broader community services, the type and extent of collaboration was found to be almost consistently significant in correlation and regression analyses. Whom a nonprofit collaborates with and collaborates for appears to be critical to the nature and extent of service provision. As will be shown in Chapter 11, it is also a central factor in linking housing nonprofits into larger policy debates and, ultimately, the political system.

Notes

1. Many of these services have also been included on other surveys (Livezey et al. 1994, 1996; Chaves 1998).

2. Activity on each dimension is estimated by factor scores obtained from a second factor analysis limited to those factors loading highly on each dimension. There are several activities that loaded on more than one factor at .50 or stronger on the initial factor analysis. In these cases they were included in the factor where they had the highest loading. Three activities—crime prevention programs and working with public and private bodies—were excluded from the factor analysis because they failed to load on any factor. A five-factor solution is presented because it provided the most parsimonious factor solution and presented the most substantively logical allocation of underlying variables.

3. The land development service factor did not exhibit the same nature of interaction as did social services, youth services, economic development, and social justice.

4. Factor analysis for collaborators and purposes of collaboration is discussed in detail in Chapter 7. All factor analysis results are provided there.

References

Chaves, Mark. 1998. *National Congregations Study: Data File and Codebook.* Tucson: University of Arizona, Department of Sociology. www.thearda.com.

Cnaan, Ram A., and Stephanie C. Bodie. 2001. Philadelphia Census of Congregations and Their Involvement in Social Service Delivery. *Social Service Review* 74(4): 559–580.

Livezey, Lowell W., Elfriede Wedam, and Larry L. Greenfield. 1996. *Survey of Religious, Social Service and Community Organizations in Metropolitan Chicago.* www.thearda.com.

Livezey, Lowell W., Elfriede Wedam, Paul D. Numrich, David D. Daniels, Larry G. Murphy, Matthew J. Price, Peter R. D'Agostino, Janise Hurtig, and William Peterman. 1994. *Survey of Congregations in Metropolitan Chicago.* www.thearda.com.

Wallis, Jim. 2000. What's an FBO? In *What's God Got to Do with the American Experiment?* ed. E.J. Dionne Jr. and John J. DiIulio Jr. Washington, DC: Brookings Institution Press.

Part IV

Impacts and Implications

9

Collaborations and Partnerships
Networks for Housing Service Delivery

We want to partner with organizations who are community based so that once we leave the investment that we made is protected or nurtured. Because if we get the neighborhood to a tipping point, we want to work with organizations that can help organize the community, help to deal with some of the other neighborhood attributes that would make it a community of choice, such as community safety, community policing.
—Director of a faith-based housing organization

Collaboration and the composition of collaborators are important factors in the nonprofit provision of housing and housing-related services (see Chapter 7). Collaboration is consistently noted as a key influence on the nature and types of housing activity, even when other factors are irrelevant. More pertinently to this study, the faith nature of an organization's collaborators may be more important than whether a particular nonprofit is faith-based itself. The collaboration network appears to influence the type of housing services produced and the extent of focus on neighborhood development beyond housing, and it allows organizations from a variety of sectors to come together, creating potentially important policy or political resources.

Numerous entities participate in the planning and provision of affordable housing, including state and local governments, community development corporations, faith-based organizations, neighborhood associations, and other nonprofit and for-profit organizations. A key issue is how coordination and collaboration occur across and among this diverse set of stakeholders. Of particular interest are the types of partnerships that faith-based organizations form in order to provide housing and related services. Social network analysis is one mechanism for identifying the collaborations and alliances between actors and determining which actors serve in critical roles by working with and across a diverse set of stakeholders. Using social network analysis, it is possible to model complex social relationships and develop an understanding of how the conglomeration of relationships forms the structure of networked communities (Scott 2000). By highlighting the structure and nature of relationships, however, it is possible to neglect individual organizations and the various value systems in place that help to foster and solidify social relations (Emirbayer and Goodwin 1994). Therefore, social network analysis is one component of this multimethod study, which also examines the actions, attitudes, and motivations of organizations engaged in the housing arena. Collaboration and networks of service providers are particularly important for nonprofit organizations, both faith-based and secular. At the least, nonprofits must work with the public sector, often as the recipients of funding, but also as contractors. Because nonprofit resources are often limited, collaboration among service providers is essential as different organizations provide disparate aspects of service, refer clients to each other, and share resources and information. These service networks and the extent to which they cross lines between faith-based and secular organizations are the focus of the following analysis.

CEDAM Survey

Only the 2003 CEDAM survey explores collaborative relationships among nonprofits. The survey indicates that, overall, community development corporations and other housing nonprofits collaborate with federal, state, and local government agencies, as well as a variety of faith-based and secular nonprofits. This is consistent with observations by Keyes et al. (1996) that devolution forces local nonprofits to establish new collaborative relationships with other organizations in order to preserve and support housing activities, especially in light of declining federal, state, and private resources. In general, many of the nonprofit housing providers collaborate with the Department of Housing and Urban Development (HUD), the Michigan State Housing Development Authority (MSHDA), local housing commissions, the Local Initiative Support Corporation (LISC), Habitat for Humanity, and similar entities. Nonprofit housing providers are also willing to collaborate with some less commonly chosen organizations to ensure that they can deliver housing services or engage in housing development. Examples of such entities include the U.S. Department of Agriculture (USDA) and federal rural development agencies. Banks, foundations, colleges, and universities also emerge as partners for housing service provision or housing development in some instances. Many of the organizations responding to the 2003 CEDAM survey did not provide names of congregations, religious organizations, or neighborhood partners. For those that did, there is wide variety in the types of congregations, religious organizations, and neighborhood associations that act as partners for housing providers.

A key issue surrounding efforts to engage FBOs in the production and distribution of publicly financed goods and services is the long-term impact such engagement might have on cooperative arrangements among low-income housing providers. This is, of course, an extraordinarily difficult question to examine empirically. Table 9.1 summarizes the types of partners for the faith-based and secular nonprofits responding to the 2003 CEDAM survey. There are some interesting differences between FBOs and secular organizations. Though not rising to the level of statistical significance, 10 percent of FBOs report banks as partners, compared with 4 percent of secular organizations. In addition, FBOs are statistically more likely to partner with other, nontraditional partners (24 percent versus 8 percent). These partners are a diverse set of organizations ranging from neighborhood associations to low-income

Table 9.1

Categories of Project Partners by Organization Type

	Organization type	N	Percent organizations identifying partner type	Std. deviation	t-test of significance
Banks[a]	Secular	51	4	.20	
	Faith-based	29	10	.31	.32
Federal agencies	Secular	51	10	.30	
	Faith-based	29	7	.26	.66
State agencies[a]	Secular	51	16	.37	
	Faith-based	29	7	.26	.22
County agencies[a]	Secular	51	8	.27	
	Faith-based	29	0	.00	.04**
City agencies	Secular	51	16	.37	
	Faith-based	29	10	.31	.51
Individuals or private-sector partners	Secular	51	16	.37	
	Faith-based	29	14	.35	.82
Other partners[a]	Secular	51	08	.27	
	Faith-based	29	24	.44	.08*

Note: Based on partners identified over a series of existing and planned projects. Organizations are assigned a score of 1 for each type of partner, if they identify that type of partner in any reported project.

[a]Indicates t-test computed with group variance not assumed to be equal across groups. Otherwise equal variance assumed. Assumption used based on result of Levene's Test for Equality of Variances.

**Significant at the 0.05 level, *0.10 level.

housing developers (some faith based, some not). In contrast, secular organizations are statistically more likely to partner with public agencies. This pattern holds for federal, state, county, and city agencies. The difference between secular organizations and FBOs is particularly clear for state agencies (16 percent secular versus 7 percent FBO), county agencies (8 percent versus 0 percent), and city agencies (16 percent versus 10 percent). None of the survey questions address whether variation in project partners is due to organizational preferences or is somehow imposed by external constraints such as grant or funding requirements.

Nonprofit Housing Provider Survey

The 2007 survey of faith-based and secular housing providers conducted by the authors asked respondents to identify with whom they collaborate on housing and related activities. Examples of some of the activities on which these organizations collaborate include brick-and-mortar projects like building or renovating single-family homes and rental property, and support services like home-ownership

Table 9.2

Collaboration among Michigan Housing Providers on Housing Activities
(in percent)

Type of collaborator	Yes collaborate with . . .		
	All	Faith-based	Secular
Government collaborator	77	83	73
Nonprofit collaborator	61	69	56
Religious collaborator***	37	74	17
Neighborhood collaborator***	40	63	28
Other collaborator	28	29	28

***Significantly different at the .01 level for faith-based and secular organizations.

counseling and training, emergency assistance including temporary housing, and financial assistance to renters and home owners. Table 9.2 highlights collaboration specifically for housing activities by type of organization. In comparison to secular organizations, FBOs are significantly more likely to collaborate with other religious organizations and neighborhood associations. When it comes to housing-related activities, collaboration with the government and secular nonprofits is common for both secular and faith-based housing providers in Michigan.

Michigan nonprofits report collaborating to build and renovate single and multi-family housing for the purposes of home ownership and rental, as well as to provide financial and counseling services and emergency housing assistance. As one might expect, housing nonprofits collaborate with city governments as well as state and federal housing agencies (e.g., MSHDA, HUD). There is also a more eclectic group of governmental collaborators for housing in Michigan. For example, an organization dedicated to providing senior housing collaborates with a local library and an area hospital. Others that focus on providing low-income housing for families collaborate with governmental environmental agencies, a regional educational service agency, and the state prison. A number of nonprofit organizations come forth as collaborators for housing and related services, including some of the more familiar secular (United Way and Red Cross) and faith-based (Salvation Army and Focus Hope) organizations, as well as one less well-documented FBO, Thrivent for Lutherans, which is committed to providing financial and related services.[1] Those organizations collaborating with congregations indicate that they work with too many congregations to name; one nonprofit indicates that the number of their congregational partners ranges from 50 to 100 in any given year. Neighborhood-based organizations are seen as viable partners because they provide facilities for counseling and training programs, serve as a cohesive community asset, donate land for housing, and can be enlisted to help purchase run-down homes to clean up neighborhoods. Two examples of such organizations are the Dickinson County Neighborhood Partnership in rural Northern Michigan and the Roosevelt Park

Neighborhood Association in Grand Rapids. Some of the common collaborators in the "other" category are foundations, financial institutions, and private firms; similarly, volunteers and donors are identified as important collaborators. This last set of collaborators probably corresponds to a desire to access human and financial capital.

Collaborator Types

Housing nonprofits are engaged in an array of activities and collaborate with other organizations to fulfill all of their goals. The discussion that follows highlights the extent to which these nonprofits collaborate with particular types of organizations in general, which may well involve activities and services beyond housing. On average, regardless of the task undertaken, nonprofits in the housing arena tend to engage in a great deal of collaboration with social service organizations and local and state governments (Table 9.3). Yet very few of these nonprofits collaborate with religious organizations, advocacy organizations, or civic organizations. There is also limited collaboration with mental health organizations, schools, and hospitals. Of all of the various options, housing nonprofits are least likely to collaborate with ethnic organizations. They are just as likely to collaborate with neighborhood associations as they are to have limited interaction with them.[2] A few variations emerge when faith status is taken into consideration (Table 9.4). For example, although overall collaboration is limited, faith-based organizations are significantly more likely than secular organizations to partner with ethnic organizations. Not surprisingly, faith-based organizations are also more likely to collaborate with other religious organizations. These trends for broader collaboration (that is, on both housing and nonhousing activities) essentially mirror those for collaboration exclusively for housing-related service delivery (see Table 9.2).

Table 9.5 presents correlations between the various organizational collaborators; all statistically significant correlations are noted in bold. The purpose is to illustrate complexes of collaboration. There are statistically significant correlations between collaboration of housing service providers with social service organizations and with all of the other types of organizations, except for neighborhood associations and state government. Basically, service providers are trying to ensure that they have access to the resources necessary to serve their client base. Significant correlations also exist for collaborating with religious organizations, and collaborating with private sector organizations and other nonprofits, excluding civic organizations. These relationships suggest a broad base of support is enlisted to achieve organizational goals. The organizations that collaborate with ethnic organizations also tend to collaborate with advocacy organizations, neighborhood associations, private organizations, schools, hospitals, and mental health organizations. This might suggest that one goal of this type of population-specific organization is to meet the needs of an individual or family in a comprehensive manner.

The nature of collaboration with government entities varies. There are significant

Table 9.3

Overall Extent of Collaboration with Other Organizations (in percent)

	Degree of collaboration	
Organization type	Moderate/ Large extent	Limited extent to none
Social service complex		
Social service organizations	81.4	18.7
Religious organizations	29.5	70.5
Ethnic organizations	10.2	89.8
Mental health agencies	36.0	64.1
Schools	31.0	69.0
Hospitals	21.6	78.4
Policy complex		
Local government	89.9	10.1
State government	80.9	19.1
Advocacy organizations[a]	23.0	77.0
Civic organizations[b]	28.7	71.2
Neighborhood associations	52.3	47.7
Other		
Private sector organizations	50.6	49.4
Other organizations	37.5	62.5

[a]Includes lobbying groups.
[b]Examples include historical societies, Jr. League, Lions club, Rotary club, Kiwanis.

correlations between collaborating with local government and collaborating with state government, neighborhood associations, civic organizations, and hospitals. Collaboration with state government is also significantly correlated with collaborating with advocacy and private organizations, schools, and hospitals. The connections between government agencies, schools, and hospitals seem fairly straightforward. Similarly, neighborhood associations and civic organizations are likely to have more traction at the local level to address their specific issues and concerns. Private sector organizations and advocacy organizations may find it necessary to partner with the state to achieve broader or regional goals or to address more intractable problems and issues. That advocacy organizations have more ties at the state level is not surprising and probably reflects their lobbying activities.

Housing provider organizations that collaborate with advocacy groups also tend to collaborate with social service, mental health, religious, ethnic, and other nonprofit organizations, state government, schools, hospitals, and private sector organizations. In short, there is a great deal of correlation between collaboration with advocacy organizations and other entities. This suggests that many service-oriented organizations rely on others with a specific advocacy mission to carry their messages to the policy arena. Organizations that collaborate with civic groups also collaborate with schools, hospitals, and the private sector. This suggests relation-

Table 9.4

Faith-Based and Secular Collaboration with Other Organizations

Organization type		Degree of collaboration Moderate/ Large extent (%)	Mean[a]	t[b]	Significance
Social service complex					
Social service organizations	Secular	78	1.81		
	Faith-based	88	1.66	−.82	.42
Religious organizations	Secular	11	3.21		
	Faith-based	63	2.22	−5.73	.00***
Ethnic organizations	Secular	05	3.50		
	Faith-based	19	3.00	−3.15	.00***
Mental health agencies	Secular	34	2.80		
	Faith-based	39	2.58	−.96	.34
Schools	Secular	25	2.98		
	Faith-based	42	2.68	−1.41	.16
Hospitals	Secular	18	3.11		
	Faith-based	28	2.91	−1.09	.28
Policy complex					
Local government	Secular	89	1.46		
	Faith-based	91	1.61	.91	.37
State government	Secular	80	1.70		
	Faith-based	82	1.85	.80	.43
Advocacy organizations	Secular	20	3.07		
	Faith-based	28	2.91	−.86	.39
Civic organizations	Secular	30	2.88		
	Faith-based	26	2.94	.35	.73
Neighborhood associations	Secular	52	2.45		
	Faith-based	53	2.25	−.89	.38
Other					
Private sector	Secular	50	2.63		
	Faith-based	52	2.25	−.54	.59
Other organizations	Secular	29	3.29		
	Faith-based	50	2.60	−1.24[c]	.24

[a]A lower mean indicates more collaboration, mean values range from 3.32 for ethnic organizations to 1.52 for local governments.

[b]A negative value indicates faith-based organizations collaborate more than secular organizations.

[c]Equal variances are not assumed.

***Significant at .01

ships with those components of a community focused on human capital and overall community development.

Interestingly, housing service provider organizations that collaborate with civic organizations are unlikely to collaborate with neighborhood associations. Instead, they are much more likely to collaborate with religious, ethnic, and other

Table 9.5

Bivariate Correlations for Collaborating Organizations

	Social service	Religious	Ethnic	Mental health	Schools	Hospitals	Local gov't	State gov't	Advocacy	Civic	Neighbor-hood	Private	Other
Social service	1.00												
Religious	.38***	1.00											
Ethnic	.37***	.60***	1.00										
Mental health	.56***	.25**	.36***	1.00									
Schools	.41***	.51***	.39***	.51***	1.00								
Hospitals	.39***	.40***	.51***	.55***	.52***	1.00							
Local gov't	.42***	.15	.15	.24**	.16	.23**	1.00						
State gov't	.43	.20	.17	.26**	.22**	.27**	.60***	1.00					
Advocacy	.51***	.24**	.43***	.43***	.30***	.33***	.20	.30***	1.00				
Civic	.28***	.11	-.02	.25**	.27**	.25**	.23**	.17	.04	1.00			
Neighborhood	.17	.29***	.31***	.01	.16	.14	.36***	.12	.20	-.22**	1.00		
Private	.37***	.37***	.32**	.14	.47***	.38***	.10	.28***	.50***	.28***	.13	1.00	
Other	.52**	.43**	.33	.18	.23	.20	-.13	-.04	.61***	-.04	.45**	.72***	1.00
Total significant collaborations	10	9	8	9	9	10	6	6	9	7	5	9	5

Note: Collaboration measured on a four point scale ranging from "large extent" to "not at all."
***Significant at .01, **significant at .05.

nonprofit organizations and local government. These relationships make sense for neighborhood associations, indicating that there is a bond between community-focused organizations that links them to the decision-making structure within a city to achieve their common goals. There are no significant correlations between organizations that collaborate with the private sector and mental health organizations, local government, and neighborhood associations. The other collaborative relationships with the private sector suggest that, like government, the private sector is an important partner for nonprofit efforts in local communities. Similarly, religious organizations, having significant collaboration correlations for all groups except civic organizations and state and local government, are central collaborators for other community organizations.

It is also interesting to note collaborations for each type of organization—both for those groups most networked as well as those least connected (see Table 9.5). Social service organizations and hospitals are most integrated with other organizations, meaning that they have the highest number of significant correlations with other organizations and thus appear to be central in nonprofit collaboration. These organizations are followed by a large complex of groups including religious, mental health, school, advocacy, and private sector organizations. State and local government and neighborhood associations are the least well connected, suggesting that they may not be willing to collaborate or have less need to do so. This is probably not problematic in the case of neighborhood organizations, but the more limited collaborations between the public sector and nonprofits may be a cause for concern. When the focus is shifted specifically to FBOs, in addition to neighborhood associations and the public sector, civic and religious organizations are also less connected. The public sector, advocacy organizations, civic organizations, and neighborhood associations are the least connected when it comes to collaborating with secular organizations (see Table 9.6). Contrary to what might be expected, religious organizations appear to be have fewer network connections with FBOs (three network relationships) and to be more networked when it comes to collaborating with secular organizations (nine network relationships).

Secular versus Faith-Based Collaboration

Other interesting distinctions arise when the correlations of collaborating organizations are explicitly examined by faith status. Table 9.6 summarizes differences between FBOs and secular organizations. Secular organizations that collaborate with religious organizations also tend to collaborate with social service and mental health organizations, hospitals, neighborhood associations, and the local government (see Appendix B, Table B5 for additional details). Secular organizations that collaborate with ethnic associations also collaborate with schools and neighborhood associations. There are statistically significant correlations for secular organizations between collaboration with schools and collaboration with state government. Secular organizations that collaborate with civic organizations also tend to collaborate

Table 9.6

Statistically Significant Differences in Correlations for Organizations Collaborating with Faith-Based and Secular Organizations Engaged in the MI Housing Arena (all are positive correlations)

	Social service	Religious	Ethnic	Mental health	Schools	Hospitals	Local gov't	State gov't	Advocacy	Civic	Neighborhood	Private	Other
Social service	—												
Religious	Secular	—											
Ethnic	Both	Both	—										
Mental health	Both	Secular	FBO	—									
Schools	Both	Both	Secular	Both	—								
Hospitals	Both	Secular	Both	Both	Both	—							
Local gov't	Both	Secular					—						
State gov't	Both	Both	FBO	Both	Secular	FBO	Both	—					
Advocacy	Both	Both	FBO	Both	FBO	FBO	FBO	FBO	—				
Civic	FBO		Secular		Secular	Both	Secular			—			
Neighborhood	Both	Secular	Both	FBO	Both	Both	Both				—		
Private	Both	Both	Both		Both	Both	Secular	Both	FBO	FBO	FBO	—	
Other	Secular		Secular		FBO	FBO	Both	Secular	Secular	FBO	FBO	Both	—

Notes: Secular denotes a significant correlation only for secular organizations; FBO denotes a significant correlation for faith-based organizations only. Both indicate that the noted correlations are significant for secular nonprofit organizations and FBOs. These notations are based on 0.01 and 0.05 significance levels (see Appendix B, Tables B5 and B6).

with schools and the local government. Finally, there are statistically significant correlations for secular organizations collaborating with private organizations and the state government.

By comparison, patterns of collaboration for FBOs are highly correlated (see Appendix B, Table B6). For example, there is a significant correlation between collaborating with social service and with civic organizations. The same holds true for collaborations with mental health organizations and ethnic associations, as well as collaborations with hospitals, the state government, and other entities. FBOs that collaborate with advocacy organizations tend to collaborate with state and local governments, ethnic associations, schools, and hospitals. Similarly, FBOs report statistically significant correlations between collaborating with private organizations and with mental health organizations, civic organizations, and neighborhood associations. There is also a statistically significant correlation between FBOs collaborating with neighborhood associations and with other organizations.

Some of the correlations that emerge for the combined set of organizations do not manifest in the separate analysis of secular organizations and FBOs. The correlation between collaborating with mental health organizations and state and local organizations, while significant for the entire set of organizations, does not hold for FBOs or secular organizations analyzed separately. The correlation between collaborating with hospitals and local government is also only significant for the full complement of organizations. Likewise, the negative correlation for collaborating with civic organizations and neighborhood organizations is unique to the combined set of organizations; this correlation is not significant for either secular organizations or FBOs. There are also some correlations that only emerge for specific types of nonprofits. There is a significant correlation between secular organizations collaborating with religious organizations and the local government. There are significant correlations for FBOs collaborating with advocacy organizations and the local government, as well as with neighborhood associations and private organizations. Both secular and faith-based nonprofits demonstrate a significant correlation for collaborating with social service organizations and the state government. Like the other organization-specific correlations, however, these relationships do not rise to the level of significance for the full complement of organizations in the study (compare Table 9.5 to Table 9.6).

The patterns among collaborators can be summarized as follows:

- Social service agencies and hospitals are most likely to be noted as collaborators.
- Neighborhood associations are least embedded in a network of collaborators.
- Mental health agencies, schools, and hospitals form a consistent set of collaborators.
- Organizations collaborating with mental health agencies, schools, and hospitals also commonly collaborate with religious and ethnic organizations.

- Secular and faith-based nonprofits appear to have somewhat different patterns of collaboration.
- For secular nonprofits, social service agencies have the greatest variety of collaborations.
- For FBOs, social service agencies, private organizations, and advocacy organizations are most frequently noted as collaborating with other organizations.
- Overall, it appears that a broader and more complex set of collaborations surround faith-based nonprofits.

Change in Collaboration Over Time

The organizations responding to the Nonprofit Housing Provider Survey also note that their collaboration with social service organizations (68 percent) and state and local governments (64 percent and 67 percent, respectively) increased between 2003 and 2007. Their patterns of collaboration are essentially the same with all other types of organizations (Table 9.7). Although, in general, the frequency of collaboration is fairly stable, faith-based organizations are more likely than secular organizations to have increased their level of collaboration with other religious organizations during this same five-year period. This might suggest an increasingly insular tendency that may not be optimal for service capacity and provision (Table 9.8); the previous analysis and discussion, however, demonstrates that the level of interconnectedness that religious organizations have is greater when they are partnering with secular organizations than with other faith-based organizations. So it may well be that the faith community is working to enhance interorganizational partnerships for the purposes of achieving their desired outcomes in the arena of housing.

Network Analysis

In addition to categorizing collaborators by type, sector, and religious status (e.g., government, secular, faith-based), the Nonprofit Housing Provider Survey also requested that respondents identify their partners by name. Thus it is possible to map the nature of housing provider networks throughout the state. The resulting partnerships and collaborations among organizations engaged in the provision of affordable housing are displayed in Figures 9.1 through 9.4. The findings indicate that with the exception of targeted partnerships with state and federal agencies, most of the collaboration for the delivery of housing services occurs at the local or regional level. Because of the generally localized pattern of interorganizational partnerships and the complexity of the statewide network, the following discussion compares different regions within Michigan to highlight variations in the role of faith-based organizations in housing networks. Specifically, housing partnership networks in Wayne County and the City of Detroit (Figure 9.1), the Grand Rapids region (Figure 9.2), and rural Northern Michigan (Figure 9.3) are drawn from the survey responses of organizations within each region and also across the state.

Table 9.7

Extent of Change in the Degree of Collaboration with Other Organizations
(in percent)

Organization type	Change in degree of collaboration		
	Increased greatly/ somewhat	Remained the same	Decreased greatly/somewhat
Social service complex			
Social service organizations	68.2	30.6	1.2
Religious organizations	19.1	76.2	4.8
Ethnic organizations	9.8	84.0	6.2
Mental health agencies	28.2	65.9	5.9
Schools	31.0	61.9	7.2
Hospitals	23.8	69.0	7.2
Policy complex			
Local government	67.0	29.4	3.5
State government	63.5	29.4	7.1
Advocacy organizations[a]	21.7	73.5	4.8
Civic organizations[b]	25.0	67.9	7.2
Neighborhood association	46.5	50.0	3.6
Other			
Private sector	33.7	61.4	4.8
Other organizations	18.1	68.2	13.6

[a]Includes lobbying groups.
[b]Examples include historical societies, Junior League, Lions club, Rotary club, Kiwanis.

Visual representations of the networks are created using the NetDraw program (available in UCINET Version 6.166), and results of the network analysis are analyzed using techniques available in UCINET (Borgatti 2002; Borgatti et al. 2002). Each shape or node represents an organization, the connecting lines indicate partnerships, and the arrows point to the organization(s) that are identified as a partner by the organization from which the line originates. These regions are chosen as a focus for several reasons. The Detroit and Grand Rapids metropolitan areas represent the largest metropolitan statistical areas in the state and the northern region represents a more rural area. More importantly, the three regions illustrate distinctly different types of housing service networks. The regional differences illuminated through network analysis were also acknowledged by a state housing official:

> Michigan is really kind of three states. We've got northern Michigan, which is probably something analogous to the state of Maine. We've got western Michigan which has always been more economically diverse and is certainly buffeted but less damaged by the recent economic conditions than eastern and southeast Michigan, which is in desperate economic straits.

Table 9.8

Faith-Based and Secular Change in Collaboration with Other Organizations

Organization type		Change in degree of collaboration (in %)			
		Increased	Same	Decreased	Significance[a]
Social service complex					
Social service organizations	Secular	64	36	00	
	Faith-based	76	21	03	.91
Religious organizations	Secular	13	82	05	
	Faith-based	31	66	03	.06[b]*
Ethnic organizations	Secular	09	86	05	
	Faith-based	12	81	08	.87
Mental health agencies	Secular	32	61	07	
	Faith-based	21	76	03	.91
Schools	Secular	27	66	07	
	Faith-based	39	54	07	.41
Hospitals	Secular	23	70	07	
	Faith-based	25	68	07	.74
Policy complex					
Local government	Secular	69	27	04	
	Faith-based	63	33	03	.35
State government	Secular	69	24	07	
	Faith-based	53	40	07	.41
Advocacy organizations	Secular	22	75	04	
	Faith-based	21	71	07	.88
Civic organizations	Secular	29	68	04	
	Faith-based	18	68	14	.11
Neighborhood associations	Secular	39	59	02	
	Faith-based	61	32	07	.18
Other					
Private sector	Secular	34	64	02	
	Faith-based	33	56	11	.38
Other organizations	Secular	14	71	14	
	Faith-based	25	63	13	.32

[a]Based on difference in means test.
[b]Equal variances not assumed.
*Significant at the .10 level.

Faith-based organizations are regular partners in activities related to affordable housing provision in the City of Detroit and Wayne County (Figure 9.1).[3] Interestingly, several faith-based organizations frequently name the City of Detroit as a partner; fewer identify the county (i.e., Wayne County), the State of Michigan, or the Michigan State Housing Development Authority (MSHDA), and none name the Department of Housing and Urban Development (HUD).[4] This suggests that faith-based organizations in the Detroit area are more likely to work with city government than with other public sector institutions. Further, none of the secular or faith-based nonprofit organizations emerge as central actors in the housing arena.[5]

Figure 9.1   Detroit/Wayne County Housing Network

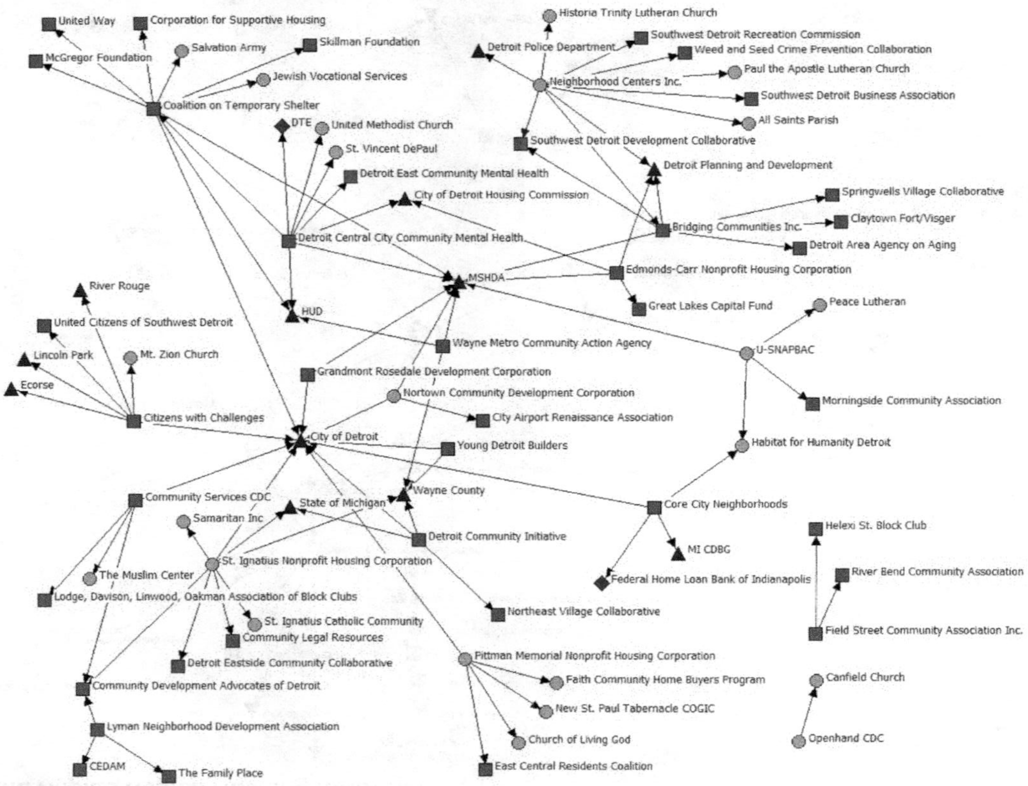

United Way
McGregor Foundation
Corporation for Supportive Housing
Salvation Army
Skillman Foundation
Jewish Vocational Services
Coalition on Temporary Shelter
United Methodist Church
DTE
St. Vincent DePaul
Historic Trinity Lutheran Church
Southwest Detroit Recreation Commission
Weed and Seed Crime Prevention Collaboration
Detroit Police Department
Neighborhood Centers Inc.
Paul the Apostle Lutheran Church
Southwest Detroit Business Association
All Saints Parish
Detroit Planning and Development
Springwells Village Collaborative
Claytown Fort/Visger
Detroit Area Agency on Aging
Peace Lutheran
Southwest Detroit Development Collaborative
Detroit East Community Mental Health
City of Detroit Housing Commission
Bridging Communities Inc.
Edmonds-Carr Nonprofit Housing Corporation
Great Lakes Capital Fund
U-SNAPBAC
Morningside Community Association
Detroit Central City Community Mental Health
MSHDA
Wayne Metro Community Action Agency
Nortown Community Development Corporation
City Airport Renaissance Association
Young Detroit Builders
Habitat for Humanity Detroit
HUD
Grandmont Rosedale Development Corporation
Wayne County
Detroit Community Initiative
Core City Neighborhoods
MI CDBG
Helen: St. Block Club
River Bend Community Association
Field Street Community Association Inc.
City of Detroit
State of Michigan
Northeast Village Collaborative
Federal Home Loan Bank of Indianapolis
Canfield Church
Openhand CDC
River Rouge
United Citizens of Southwest Detroit
Mt. Zion Church
Lincoln Park
Ecorse
Citizens with Challenges
Community Services CDC
Samaritan Inc
St. Ignatius Nonprofit Housing Corporation
St. Ignatius Catholic Community
Community Legal Resources
Pitman Memorial Nonprofit Housing Corporation
Faith Community Home Buyers Program
New: St. Paul Tabernacle COGIC
Church of Living God
East Central Residents Coalition
The Muslim Center
Lodge, Davison, Linwood, Oakman Association of Block Clubs
Detroit Eastside Community Collaborative
Community Development Advocates of Detroit
Lyman Neighborhood Development Association
CEDAM
The Family Place

▲ = government,   ■ = secular nonprofit,   ● = faith-based organization

238

Figure 9.2 **Grand Rapids Region Housing Network**

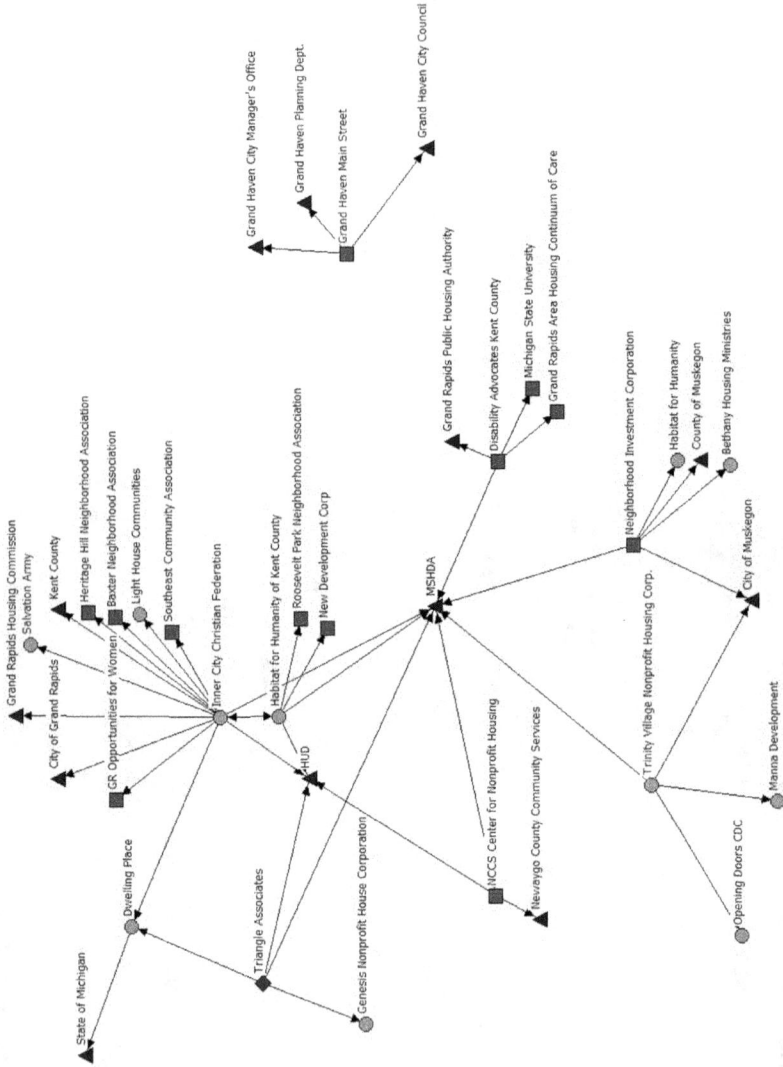

▲ = government, ■ = secular nonprofit, ● = faith-based organization

239

Figure 9.3 **Rural Northern Michigan Housing Network**

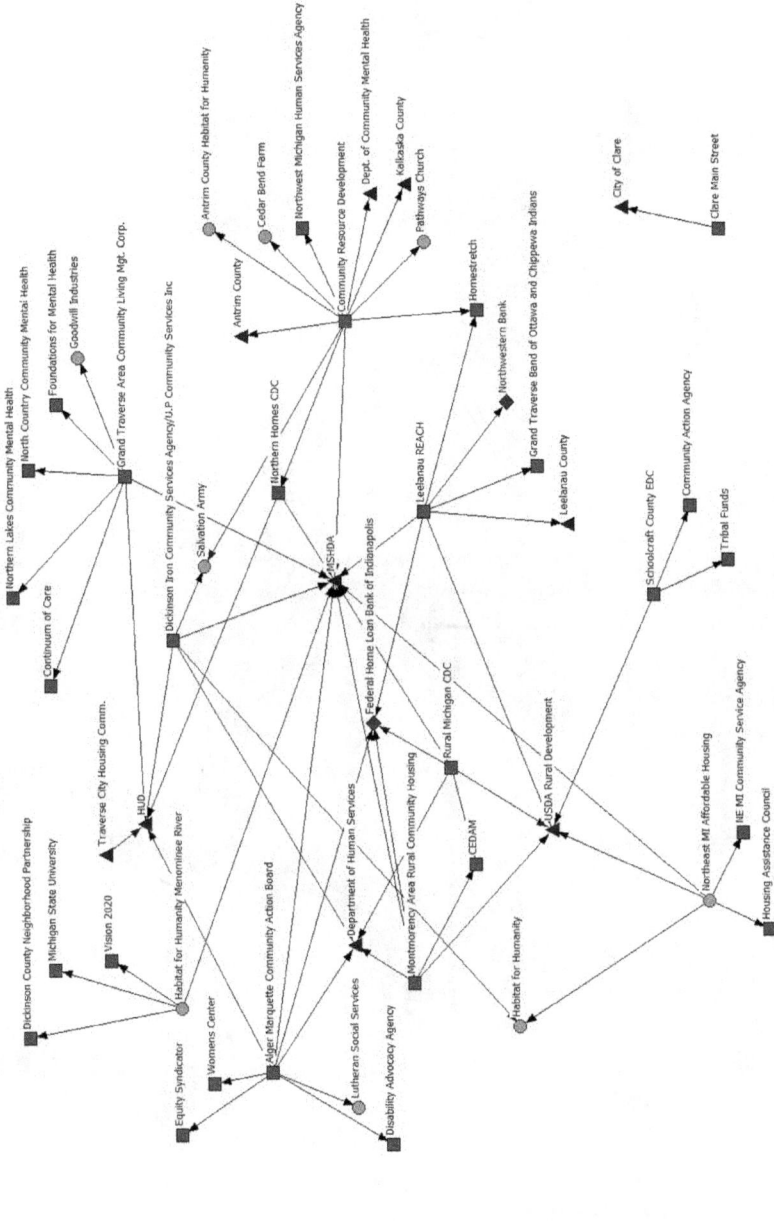

▲ = government, ■ = secular nonprofit, ● = faith-based organization

240

Figure 9.4 **State and Federal Agencies Housing Network**

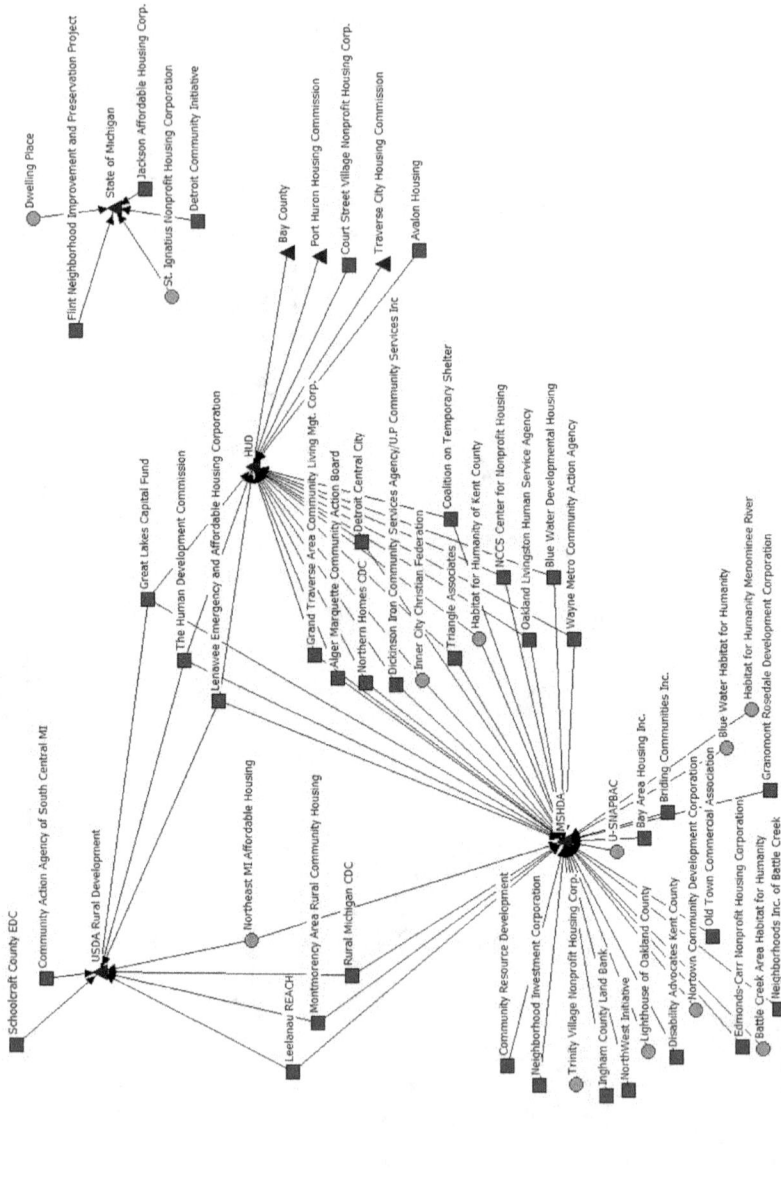

▲ = government, ■ = secular nonprofit, ● = faith-based organization

In other words, few organizations identify a specific set of nonprofits as key collaborators. This is interesting, given that there are twenty-three FBOs and thirty-nine secular nonprofit organizations identified as active in networks for housing in the Detroit area (Figure 9.1).[6] This suggests that there is a vast and sprawling network of nongovernmental organizations, each working with its own distinct set of partners. In short, the housing provision network in the Detroit region is quite fragmented—much more so than in the two regions to follow. A regional HUD official noted this fragmentation when asked whether there were nonprofits in the Detroit area that had an overall leadership role in the production of low-income housing :

> We were just having this discussion the other day with Senator Levin's office and one of the Detroit city council members. And we were going through the same exercise of who could be some really large umbrella nonprofit that would have a lot of respect across neighborhood lines. That people would acknowledge as having a lot of expertise. We were having a hard time coming up with them.

City and county governments are mentioned less frequently as housing partners in the Grand Rapids area, although MSHDA, the state housing agency, remains very important (Figure 9.2). There are also noticeably fewer faith-based organizations involved in housing partnerships in the Grand Rapids area. Even so, a few faith-based organizations stand out as key actors in the network. Habitat for Humanity of Kent County and the Inner City Christian Federation are mutual partners, and each one collaborates with a distinct set of secular nonprofits. Interview data confirm the importance of these two FBOs and indicate that a third nonprofit, Dwelling Place, also plays an important role in housing in the Grand Rapids area.[7]

Habitat for Humanity is a familiar entity.[8] It is an ecumenical Christian organization "dedicated to eliminating substandard housing and homelessness worldwide and to making adequate, affordable shelter a matter of conscience and action. Our ministry was founded on the conviction that every man, woman and child should have a simple, decent place to live in dignity and safety" (Habitat for Humanity International 2009). Similarly, the Inner City Christian Federation is a nonprofit housing corporation "whose leadership is motivated and programs shaped by, the belief that all people deserve safe, clean, affordable housing; our response to God's desire that we seek justice in our communities, our grateful response to the saving love of Jesus Christ, and our desire to have others see his love in action" (Inner City Christian Federation 2009). The mission of Dwelling Place is to improve "the lives of people by creating quality affordable housing, providing essential support services and serving as a catalyst for neighborhood revitalization" (Dwelling Place n.d.).

Further analysis of the network data confirms that these three organizations are well positioned to act as brokers between other organizations within the Grand Rapids network. "Betweenness centrality" measures how often a particular organization is on the shortest pathway between pairs of organizations in the network (Freeman 1979). Organizations with high betweenness centrality scores frequently act as a bridge between organizations that do not share a direct link. The three faith-based organizations highlighted here—Inner City Christian Federation, Habitat for Humanity, and Dwelling Place—are structurally positioned as brokers in the housing arena in Grand Rapids, meaning they serve as bridges between groups that are otherwise unconnected.[9] Each one has a betweenness score greater than all of the others in the network: Inner City Christian Federation has a score of 11, Dwelling Place, 3, Habitat for Humanity of Kent County, 2; each of the other organizations in the Grand Rapids network has a betweenness centrality score of 0.

There are eleven FBOs and twelve secular nonprofits identified as part of networks in the Grand Rapids area that provide housing and related services (see Figure 9.2).[10] Even though faith-based organizations in Grand Rapids appear to be less prevalent than they are in Detroit, several faith-based organizations have developed a broad set of partnerships that are primarily with other nonprofits rather than the government. The Grand Rapids–area network is less fragmented than the Detroit regional housing network. There are several distinct complexes of organizations with each association linked into central FBOs. Most of the organizations are tied to MSHDA. The City of Grand Rapids is much less connected than the City of Detroit; it was cited as a partner by only one organization—the Inner City Christian Federation. Overall, however, actors in Grand Rapids view the existing partnership between public and private actors as positive and productive. One executive of a prominent faith-based organization put it this way: "I hear from many, many observers that we have probably one of the very best, if not the best, example of effective horizontal public-private partnerships in the whole state."

The rural Northern Michigan network displays partnerships in a very different type of region. Faith-based organizations are somewhat less prevalent in this region. There are nine FBOs, most of which appear to work in isolation from each other, and twenty-seven secular organizations networked within this region for housing services (Figure 9.3).[11] The faith-based organizations typically work with MSHDA, the USDA Rural Development agency, and secular nonprofits. Ten nonprofits, only two of which are FBOs, identify MSHDA as one of their collaborators; four to five nonprofits also report working with HUD, USDA Rural Development, and/or the Department of Human Services. Since there is no major city in this region, it is not surprising that state and federal agencies play a larger partnership role here compared to more urbanized areas.

Several of the secular nonprofits in the region indicate that they work with a wide range of other organizations; nevertheless, these are all links emanating from the organization rather than ties to the organization. For example, Community Resource Development has eleven identified partnerships, including four FBOs, three secular nonprofits, and four state and county entities. The Alger-Marquette Community Action Board has eight links, with three state and federal entities, one FBO, three secular organizations, and the Federal Home Loan Bank of Indianapolis (FHLBI), a for-profit financial institution.[12] Similarly, the Grand Traverse Area Community Living Management Corporation has seven links, to MSHDA, HUD, and five other nonprofits, one of which is an FBO. Two FBOs, Salvation Army and Habitat for Humanity, have links to them from other organizations, indicating that they are viewed as partners by other organizations in the region. Similarly, two secular non-profits, Community Economic Development Association of Michigan (CEDAM) and HomeStretch, function as a key partner for other secular nonprofits.[13] This raises an important point about CEDAM: although it is located in mid-Michigan, its membership is genuinely statewide, giving it a significant role in housing and community development across Michigan.

Figures 9.1, 9.2, and 9.3 demonstrate that within each region, faith-based organizations partner with a diverse set of actors. Important differences emerge in each scenario, however. In Detroit, city government serves as a partner with several faith-based organizations. In the Grand Rapids area, faith-based organizations partner more readily with the state housing authority, secular nonprofits, and other FBOs, rather than with the local government. In rural Northern Michigan, there are fewer faith-based organizations engaged in housing; those present, however, partner with other organizations to provide housing and related services. Thus three distinct models are represented by these networks:

- Strong but fragmented faith presence with moderate local government involvement (Detroit network)
- Partnerships among a core of nonprofit and public actors (Grand Rapids network)
- Strong secular presence with weaker local government (Northern Michigan network)

The variable relationships with government entities across the state are also apparent from the network diagrams. To examine these distinctions further, in-degree centrality scores (Nieminen 1974; Freeman 1979) are calculated using UCINET Version 6.166 (Borgatti 2002; Borgatti et al. 2002). Centrality is a measure of organizational prominence or visibility within a network at a specific point in time. As such, it provides a snapshot of those organizations that are actively and extensively involved in relationships with other organizations within their network (Wasserman and Faust 1994; Hawe et al. 2004). Organizations with higher centrality scores have more extensive network relationships and are viewed as key actors; in essence, they are at the heart of the action. Likewise, organizations with low centrality scores work largely in isolation or are peripheral to the network. Of particular interest in this analysis is in-degree centrality that counts the number of linkages into a particular organization. It signals the extent to which an organization is connected to others and seen by other organizations as a key resource or influential player.

In-degree centrality scores are calculated for the public sector entities identified in the networks in order to examine their relationships with Michigan nonprofit organizations involved in housing. Table 9.9 reports normalized in-degree centrality scores for those governmental entities that are most central to the regional housing networks in Michigan. MSHDA is clearly central in the various regions; just as noteworthy, however, are the relative roles of local, state, and federal governments in each region. It is interesting to note the importance of the local public sector in Detroit, compared to the importance of the state in Grand Rapids, and of two federal agencies in rural northern Michigan. The analysis indicates that local government is most involved in housing in Detroit and hardly at all in rural northern Michigan; and conversely the federal government's role is greater in the rural area and in Grand Rapids, but quite limited in Detroit.

As noted earlier, for the state as a whole, the ability to work with federal and state agencies is central to the housing activities of nonprofit organizations across the various regions. The Michigan State Housing Development Authority has the most robust set of relationships with nonprofits, followed by numerous relationships between HUD and nonprofits throughout the state. Although these networks exist for both faith-based and secular organizations, more FBOs have relationships with MSHDA than with HUD. The USDA Rural Development and the State of Michigan are not as connected to nonprofit housing organizations in the state (see Figure 9.4, p. 240). Interestingly, more organizations report network linkages to the USDA Rural Development than to the State of Michigan.[14] It is not surprising that the Michigan State Housing Development Authority is involved with nonprofit organizations across Michigan. As one MSHDA official makes clear, that is in fact one of the purposes of this government entity, particularly the Office of Community Development, which focuses on "neighborhood revitalization projects and the role of housing as a piece of neighborhood revitalization." The same MSHDA official notes that in order to achieve their goal of sustainable housing and vibrant communities, the Office of Community Development:

> works with community-based nonprofits, and with local units of government to do programs for low-income home owners, home buyers, and for investor-owners who are renting and providing high quality housing to low-income tenants. . . . If we have a disinvested neighborhood, say in Lansing, we try to make sure that all units we do are in a single neighborhood, to change the perception of that neighborhood, change the market perception, change the way the market works in that neighborhood, to create sane, sustainable communities through our housing investments in cooperation with our nonprofit or local government partners.

Confirming the results that emerge from the social network analysis, interviews with key state officials validate that regional strategies are indeed important to pursue. For example, the Office of Community Development within MSHDA has ten field agents throughout the state assigned responsibility for specific counties (Appendix B, Map B1). The regional focus reflects MSHDA's efforts to take a comprehensive approach to working with nonprofits and local government officials, to meet an array of housing needs and stabilize the housing market. Within regions, neighborhoods and communities matter most, as one might expect. One MSHDA official notes that the Office of Community Development creates "affordable hous-

Table 9.9

Normalized In-Degree Centrality Scores of Public Sector Entities in the Regional Networks

Level of government	Detroit		Grand Rapids		Rural Northern MI	
			Regional network			
Federal	HUD	3.90	HUD	11.11	HUD	10.42
					USDA	10.42
State	MSHDA	10.39	MSHDA	19.44	MSHDA	20.83
Local	City of Detroit	12.99	City of Muskegon	5.56	City of Clare	2.08
	Wayne County	5.20	City of Grand Rapids	2.78	Leelanau County	2.08
			Kent County	2.78	Antrim County	2.08
					Kalkaska County	2.08

ing in a neighborhood, in a setting that's very desirable that otherwise would not be affordable for folks." But they do this in partnership with local organizations, typically community housing development organizations (CDHOs) (see Table 9.10 for examples).

Figure 9.4 and Table 9.11 highlight twelve FBOs and thirty-five secular housing nonprofits that have established working relationships with state and federal entities. State and federal agencies are connected to more secular nonprofits than FBOs and more of these connections occur at the state level, followed by state and federal partnerships. As might be expected, few nonprofits engaged in housing collaborate exclusively with the federal government; those that do are secular. Of the forty-seven organizations linked to state and federal networks, six FBOs and ten secular nonprofits appear to have established state-level networks and, on average, more regional network links than other organizations (Table 9.12).

MSHDA remains the government entity with the greatest number of ties to nonprofit housing providers in the state. They have established and preferred network linkages that allow them and their partner nonprofits to achieve mutual goals of providing housing and related services to Michigan communities. As one MSHDA official notes,

> there are specific nonprofits that we [MSHDA, Office of Community Development] have been dealing with year in, year out for a decade or more, because they get the job done and they are making substantial impacts on their neighborhoods over a period of years, and that's what it takes. . . . There is a core group of 40 to 50 nonprofits around the state that are our main constituency in this division, as well as most of the county governments, and probably a couple of dozen small city governments.[15]

The nature and extent of partnerships thus vary across the state in interesting ways:

- FBOs in the Detroit area are more likely to work with city government as compared to other public sector institutions.
- The housing provision network in the Detroit region is quite fragmented; there is a vast and sprawling network of nongovernmental organizations, each working with their own distinct set of partners.
- Three faith-based organizations in the Grand Rapids area—Inner City Christian Federation, Habitat for Humanity, and Dwelling Place—are structurally positioned as brokers in the housing arena in Grand Rapids. As such, they serve as bridges between groups that are otherwise unconnected.
- Faith-based housing organizations are less prevalent in rural Northern Michigan; those that are active are most likely to work with the state housing authority (MSHDA) as compared to any other type of organization.
- Because there is no major city in rural Northern Michigan, state and federal agencies play a larger role in housing than is typical for more urbanized areas.

Table 9.10

Representative Organizations That Partner with MSHDA

Location	Organization	Faith-based
Northern Michigan		
Traverse City	• Home Stretch	
Southwest Michigan		
Grand Rapids	• Dwelling Place	Yes
	• Inner City Christian Federation (ICCF)	Yes
	• Lighthouse Communities	Yes
Central Michigan		
Lansing	• Greater Lansing Housing Coalition[a]	
Southeast Michigan/ Wayne County		
Detroit	• U-SNAP-BAC	Yes
	• Bagley Housing Association[a]	
	• Northwest Detroit Neighborhood Development[a]	
Jackson	• Community Action Agency[a]	
Kalamazoo	• Neighborhood Housing Services[a]	

Source: Personal interview, 2009.

[a]Despite repeated attempts by the research team, these organizations did not respond to the nonprofit housing provider survey. Therefore there are no additional data available for systematic analysis as a part of this study. They are represented here because MSHDA official(s) identified them as a key partner in providing housing and related services to the citizens of Michigan.

- Local government is most involved in housing in Detroit and hardly at all in rural Northern Michigan; conversely the federal government's role is greater in the rural area and in Grand Rapids, but quite limited in Detroit.
- State and federal agencies are connected to more secular nonprofits than FBOs and more of these connections occur at the state level, followed by state and federal partnerships.

Concluding Thoughts

Overall, the analysis here shows that there is wide variety in the types of collaborators associated with nonprofit housing provision, ranging from banks to schools to units of government. While many aspects of collaborative networks are similar for secular and faith-based nonprofits, FBOs appear to have somewhat broader or more eclectic collaborators and have increased their collaboration over time. Among nonprofit collaborators, social service agencies and schools (including colleges and universities) appear particularly tightly tied to other organizations. In urban areas like Grand Rapids and Detroit, local organizations as well as state governments hold important positions in the housing provision network (local only in Detroit, state and local in Grand Rapids). In more rural areas of the state, federal actors become more prominent.

Table 9.11

State and Federal Collaborators for Michigan Nonprofit Housing Organizations

| | Locus of operation/Agency connection | | |
| | Organization Type | | |
Number of network connections[a]	FBO	Secular	Total
State			
State of MI only	2	3	5
MSHDA only	7	11	18
Subtotal: Only State Networks	9	14	23
State and Federal			
MSHDA and HUD	2	11	13
MSHDA and USDA	1	3	4
MSHDA, HUD and USDA	0	3	3
Subtotal: State and Federal Networks	3	17	20
Federal			
HUD only	0	2	2
USDA only	0	2	2
HUD and USDA	0	0	0
Subtotal: Only Federal Networks	0	4	4
Total	**12**	**35**	**47**

[a]The number of designated collaborators is based on those organizations identified in the Nonprofit Housing Provider Survey as collaborators or partners for specific responding organizations. As such, the numbers presented are expected to be undercounts of the actual collaborative relationships.

This chapter highlights two critical points. First, almost all nonprofits, secular and faith-based, collaborate with other organizations and the public sector to provide services. Moreover, these collaborative networks are diverse and complex but appear to vary by regions of the state. Thus, the question is not whether nonprofits collaborate to provide service but rather with whom, how much, and for what purposes. The last issue, purpose of collaboration, is addressed in Chapter 10.

Notes

We appreciate the insights and research assistance provided by Sarah Reckhow, who was a doctoral candidate at the University of California, Berkeley, at the time of the initiation of the project and interpretation of results for the social network analysis; she subsequently joined the political science faculty at Michigan State University. Dr. Reckhow conducted the social network analysis on behalf of the research team, providing the network diagrams (Figures 9.1 through 9.4) and calculating the centrality scores included in the discussion.

The unattributed quotes in this chapter come from personal interviews conducted in 2009 with representatives of the Michigan State Housing Development Authority, the Department of Housing and Urban Development, and a faith-based housing organization in Michigan.

1. Thrivent Financial for Lutherans is both a Fortune 500 financial services organization and a fraternal benefit society (not-for-profit membership organization). Its mission

Table 9.12

Organizations with the Most Ties to FBOs, Secular Organizations, Local, State, and Federal Government

| Organization | Type | Michigan | Number of collaborators[a] | | | | Name of government collaborator |
			Faith-based[b]	Secular	Government	Total	
Inner City Christian Federation (ICCF)	FBO	Grand Rapids	4	4	5	13	City of Grand Rapids (GR) GR Housing Commission Kent County MSHDA HUD
Community Resource Development, Inc.	Secular	Rural Northern	4	3	4	11	Antrim County Kalkaska County Dept of Comm. Mental Health MSHDA
Coalition on Temporary Shelter (COTS)	Secular	Detroit	2	5	3	10	City of Detroit MSHDA HUD
Neighborhood Centers, Inc.	FBO	Detroit	3	5	2	10	Detroit Planning Commission Detroit Police Department
St. Ignatius Nonprofit Housing Commission	FBO	Detroit	2	3	3	8	City of Detroit Wayne County State of Michigan
Detroit Central City Community Mental Health[b]	Secular	Detroit	2	2	3	7	Detroit Housing Commission MSHDA HUD
Alger Marquette Community Action Board[b]	Secular	Rural Northern	1	3	3	7	Department of Human Services MSHDA HUD
Grand Traverse Area Community Living Mgt Corp.	Secular	Rural Northern	1	4	2	7	MSHDA HUD
Bridging Communities, Inc.	Secular	Detroit	1	4	2	7	Detroit Planning Commission

(continued)

Table 9.12 (continued)

Organization	Type	Michigan	Number of collaborators[a]				Name of government collaborator
			Faith-based[b]	Secular	Government	Total	
Citizens With Challenges	Secular	Detroit	1	1	4	6	MSHDA City of Detroit River Rouge Ecorse Lincoln Park City of Detroit
Pittman Memorial Nonprofit Housing Corporation	FBO	Detroit	3	1	1	5	City of Detroit
Northeast Michigan Affordable Housing	FBO	Rural Northern	1	2	2	5	MSHDA USDA
Leelanau Reach[c]	Secular	Rural Northern	0	2	3	5	Leelanau County MSHDA USDA Rural Development
Dickinson Iron Community Services Agency	Secular	Rural Northern	2	0	3	5	Department of Human Services MSHDA HUD
Habitat for Humanity Kent County	FBO	Grand Rapids	1	2	2	5	MSHDA HUD
Neighborhood Investment Corporation	Secular	Grand Rapids	2	0	3	5	City of Muskegon Muskegon County MSHDA

Note: Provides an overview of all of the identified connections, irrespective of directionality; representing ties both into and from the organization.

[a] The number of designated collaborators is based on those organizations identified in the Nonprofit Housing Provider Survey as collaborators or partners for specific responding organizations. As such, the numbers presented are expected to be undercounts of the actual collaborative relationships.

[b] The number of faith-based collaborators is particularly susceptible to extreme undercounts since several organizations indicate that they collaborate with "a large number of congregations" or "too many congregations or religious organizations to name, [it can range from] 50–100 per year" ("Nonprofit Housing Provider Survey," 2007–2008).

[c] This nonprofit also identified at least one for-profit organization as a key network partner.

is to "improve the quality of life of its members, their families, and their communities by providing unparalleled solutions that focus on financial security, wellness and caring for others" (Thrivent Financial for Lutherans 2008, 1). Thrivent's business operations fuel its charitable outreach. As noted in its promotional materials, its "business success gives the organization a unique opportunity to promote member volunteerism, aid individuals and families in need, strengthen nonprofit organizations, and address critical community needs" (Thrivent Financial for Lutherans 2008, 1).

2. This categorization scheme is based on a factor analysis of collaborators indicating the presence of three different complexes. This is slightly different from the factor analysis presented in Chapter 7, which used only two categories of nonprofits: governmental and nongovernmental. This more refined classification results from running the factor analysis separately for the three types of collaborators.

3. The faith status of organizations was determined using a multifaceted approach. The faith status of the organizations that responded to the Nonprofit Housing Provider Survey was determined based on their responses to specific survey questions as well as confirmatory phone calls made while the survey contact list was developed. For organizations that were listed on the survey by other organizations but did not respond themselves, faith status was determined based on reviews of their websites and phone queries made directly to the organizations by members of the research team.

Governmental complex	
Local government	.90
State government	.69
Neighborhood complex	
Religious organizations	.81
Ethnic organizations	.69
Schools	.61
Neighborhood assoc.	.51
Social service and health complex	
Social service agencies	.52
Mental health agencies	.88
Hospitals	.56

4. Ten organizations, three of which are FBOs, identify the City of Detroit as a key network partner, and four nonprofits (one FBO) network with Wayne County. There are also network links to several government agencies in Detroit including the Detroit Housing Commission and Detroit Planning and Development. Eight organizations (two FBOs) identify MSHDA as central in their Detroit-area housing network, while two nonprofits (one secular, one faith based) identify the State of Michigan as a key partner and three secular nonprofits do so for HUD.

5. Habitat for Humanity Detroit is identified as a key network partner for two other FBOs. In addition, two FBOs—Neighborhood Centers and St. Ignatius Nonprofit Housing Corporation—identify numerous network ties to other organizations; these are all outreach efforts, however, with no agency reporting a tie back into them. Similarly, three secular nonprofits identify notably more network relationships than the other secular organizations: the Coalition on Temporary Shelter (COTS), Detroit Central City (DCC) Community Mental Health, and Bridging Communities (Figure 9.1).

6. Six of the twenty-three FBOs identified in the Detroit region are organizations initiating linkages with others, and the remaining seventeen are organizations identified as network partners by other organizations. Similarly, ten of the thirty-nine secular nonprofits identified in the Detroit network are initiators of partnerships highlighted in the network diagram. In addition, it is important to note that these numbers probably underestimate

actual collaborations, particularly for FBOs; when asked to identify specific collaborators, several organizations indicate that they collaborate with "too many congregations or
religious organizations to name, [it can range from] 50–100 per year" (Nonprofit Housing
Provider Survey 2007–2008).

7. Although Dwelling Place does not emerge from the network analysis as having substantial ties in the region, the MSHDA officials who were interviewed continuously stressed
the centrality of Dwelling Place to housing in the Grand Rapids region. Both Habitat for
Humanity of Kent County and the Inner City Christian Federation, located in Grand Rapids,
also partner with the Local Initiatives Support Corporation (LISC), a nonprofit committed
to sustainable community development, as do Dwelling Place of Grand Rapids, an FBO,
the Roosevelt Park Neighborhood Association in Grand Rapids, and the Neighborhood
Investment Corporation, a secular nonprofit located in Muskegon (Local Initiatives Support
Corporation 2009).

8. In 2009, Habitat for Humanity of Kent County was one of seventy-six independently
run local Habitat for Humanity affiliates in Michigan and one of over 1,700 local affiliates
in the United States; there were another 550 international affiliates (Habitat for Humanity
International 2009).

9. A few organizations might have the structural position of brokers in the other regions
as well; the data are not available, however, to confirm or dispute whether they are actually
playing that role. Examples include the Coalition on Temporary Shelter (COTS) and Bridging
Communities in the Detroit area (with betweenness centrality scores of 7 and 4, respectively);
as well as Neighborhoods of Battle Creek and the Community Action Agency of Southwest
Michigan (CAASCM) in South Central Michigan (both with betweenness centrality scores
of 3). In rural Northern Michigan only Northern Homes Community Development Corporation has a betweenness score greater than 0; its score is 1.

10. As for the Detroit network, the number of network collaborators, particularly FBOs,
denoted for Grand Rapids and later for rural Northern Michigan includes only those organizations specifically identified by organizations responding to the statewide housing
provider survey. In addition, of the organizations highlighted in the network map, ten FBOs
and eight secular nonprofits are identified by other organizations as key partners in their
local networks.

11. Although technically a nonprofit organization, Michigan State University is not
included in the count of secular nonprofits.

12. FHLBI is one of two for-profit financial institutions identified as a network partner by
housing nonprofits in Michigan. It is a key partner with four nonprofits in the rural Northern Michigan network and one in the Detroit-area network. FHLBI also emerged as a key
funding source for Michigan nonprofits engaged in housing in the 2003 and 2007 CEDAM
surveys (see discussion in Chapter 7). Northwestern Bank is the other financial institution
that emerges in the rural Northern Michigan network analysis (see Figures 9.1 and 9.3).

13. HomeStretch was founded in 1996 in response to an affordable housing crisis in the
Traverse City region of Michigan. The goal of the organization is to "serve as a clearing-
house for ideas and develop solutions to the [affordable housing] crisis." Since its inception, HomeStretch has focused on developing and sustaining "strategic partnerships among
agencies that don't have the resources to tackle the issue alone." In 2003, HomeStretch
became a community land trust, which allows the organization to retain ownership of land
and execute a ground lease with a home buyer at the time of purchase, typically for a period
of 99 years (HomeStretch n.d.).

14. For the state as a whole, MSHDA is named as a partner thirty-eight times, HUD is
named twenty-one times (three of which are attributed to local governments), USDA Rural
Development nine times, and the State of Michigan five times. The USDA emerged in the
network analysis as a partner largely in rural Northern Michigan. Interviews with USDA
officials highlight partnerships with several area nonprofits including Northeast Michigan

Affordable Housing (NEMAH), Goodwill, and Habitat for Humanity, all of which are FBOs and also identified through the network analysis. Ministerial Association is another FBO in the area that the USDA would like to develop a partnership with because of its focus on housing and home repairs. USDA officials also believe that Ministerial Association will provide an avenue to partner with many more FBOs in rural Northern Michigan. Interviews with USDA officials indicate that this agency is also active in the Grand Rapids area through partnerships with community action agencies, the Neighborhood Investment Corporation and the Inner City Christian Foundation.

15. The social network analysis of the Nonprofit Housing Provider Survey conducted by the authors revealed thirty-eight relationships between MSHDA and local nonprofits (Table 9.10). It is likely that some of these organizations overlap with the forty to fifty organizations referenced by a MSHDA representative as part of its core constituency group.

References

Borgatti, Stephen P. 2002. *NetDraw: Graph Visualization Software.* Harvard, MA: Analytic Technologies.

Borgatti, Stephen P., Martin G. Everett, and Linton C. Freeman. 2002. *UCINET for Windows: Software for Social Network Analysis* (Version 6.166). Harvard, MA: Analytic Technologies.

Dwelling Place. n.d. Providing Homes, Revitalizing Neighborhoods. www.dwellingplacegr. org.

Emirbayer, Mustafa, and Jeff Goodwin. 1994. Network Analysis, Culture, and the Problem of Agency. *The American Journal of Sociology* 99(6): 1411–1454.

Freeman, Linton C. 1979. Centrality in Social Networks: Conceptual Clarification. *Social Networks* 1:215–239.

Habitat for Humanity International. 2009. Habitat for Humanity: A Christian Ministry. www. habitat.org/how/christian.aspx.

Hawe, Penelope, Cynthia Webster, and Alan Shiell. 2004. A Glossary of Terms for Navigating the Field of Social Network Analysis. *Journal of Epidemiology and Community Health* 58:971–975.

HomeStretch. n.d. History. www.homestretchhousing.org/html/history.html.

Inner City Christian Federation. 2009. Programs and Services. www.iccf.org/programs/.

Keyes, Langley C., Alex Schwartz, Avis C. Vidal, and Rachel G. Bratt. 1996. *Networks and Nonprofits: Opportunities and Challenges in an Era of Federal Devolution.* Fannie Mae Foundation 7(2): 201–229.

Local Initiatives Support Corporation. 2009. *LISC Michigan: Partners-Community Development Corporations.* www.lisc.org/michigan/partners/corporations_4667.shtml.

Nieminen, J. 1974. On the Centrality of Graph Structure. *Scandinavian Journal of Psychology* 15:322–336.

Scott, John. 2000. *Social Network Analysis: A Handbook.* 2d ed. Thousand Oaks, CA: Sage.

Thrivent Financial for Lutherans. 2008. Who We Are. December 2. www.thrivent.com.

Wasserman, Stanley, and Katherine Faust. 1994. *Social Network Analysis: Methods and Applications.* Cambridge: Cambridge University Press.

10

Nature and Types of Collaboration

[T]hrough a variety of partnerships [the community housing development organization] created the first ever privately funded community renaissance zone. Through this partnership we re-focused all housing and revitalization efforts of all partners to one 12-block area, significantly changing the appearance and stability of the neighborhood. In addition to the partnership, we created the community house, a two-unit rental home where families were moved in and provided services to assist them to pay off debt, clean up credit, and become mortgage ready. At completion [of their time in the program], they then purchased one of the newly renovated or constructed homes in the neighborhood. As one family moved out another was moved in. A partnership with the County Regional Educational Service Agency (RESA) trained unemployed workers between the ages of 17 and 30 in the construction trade.

—From a response by a community services director to the 2007 CEDAM survey

Organizations can take several approaches to providing housing and related services, ranging from distinct and categorical to more integrative and holistic approaches (Figure 10.1). The framework behind the approach to service provision can also impact the types of and rationale for collaboration. It was quite common in the 1930s and 1960s to provide an array of social services in conjunction with housing (Bingham and Kirkpatrick 1975; Newman and Schnare 1992; Granruth and Smith 2001). In the early twenty-first century, integrative, holistic approaches once again became a preferred option of nonprofit organizations engaged in housing (e.g., Vidal 1992; National Congress for Community Economic Development 2005; Mayer and Temkin 2007; Bratt 2008). Enterprise Community Partners[1] and NeighborWorks America[2] are two examples of national nonprofit initiatives that employ a more integrative and holistic approach to providing housing and services.[3] This embodies the essence of the concept that Granruth and Smith (2001) identify as "housing *plus* services," a catch-all term that encompasses those housing programs and activities that serve any and all low-income populations. It is sufficiently broad to include rental and owned housing that is safe, decent, permanent, and linked to a variety of services.

It is important to note that housing plus services goes beyond social services to also include community and economic development as well as educational resources and job opportunities. Thus much of what has been observed in the Michigan nonprofit housing community is consistent with the housing plus services approach, though admittedly some organizations will still choose to engage in more distinct

Figure 10.1 **Approaches to Providing Housing and Related Services**

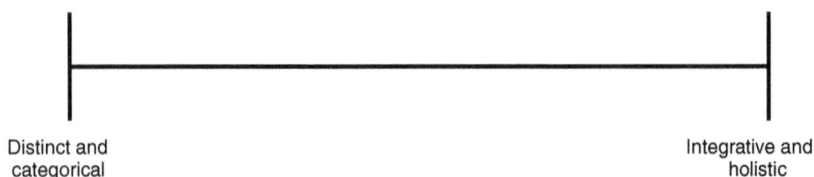

Distinct and
categorical

Integrative and
holistic

Figure 10.2 **Housing Plus Services Principles**

1. Housing is a basic human need, and all people have a right to safe, decent, afford-able, and permanent housing.
2. All people are valuable and capable of being valuable residents and valuable com-munity members. The basic human rights of residents must be respected.
3. Housing plus service programs should be integrated to enhance the social and economic well-being of the residents and to build healthy communities.
4. Residents, owners, property managers, and service providers should work together as a team in developing needed housing and community development programs and services.
5. Service design is based on sound research, which means that programs are based on an accurate assessment of the strengths and needs of the residents, evaluation is an integral part of program design, and modes of intervention are supported by research. Service evolves as the community changes.
6. Continuous strengthening and expansion of resident participation improves the community's capacity to create change.
7. Residents' participation in services is voluntary. However, outreach to the most vulnerable and isolated residents is a priority. Engagement of residents must take place in a context of strengths and needs.
8. Residents are members of the larger community in which the housing is located. Community development should be extended to the surrounding community and integration of residents with the larger community is a goal.
9. Assessment and intervention are multilevel—focusing on the individual and the collective—because the health of individuals and the health of neighborhoods are interdependent.
10. Service delivery maximizes the use of existing resources, avoids duplication, and expands the economic, social, and political resources available to residents.

Sources: Cohen and Phillips 1997; Tull 1998; Granruth and Smith 2001.
Note: The National Low-Income Housing Coalition added an 11th principle, namely that individuals who receive housing plus services should be fully integrated into the community in which they reside (Cohen et al. 2004).

and categorical operations by participating in brick-and-mortar projects or just one specific service. Granruth and Smith (2001, 15) argue that housing plus services that are designed utilizing a specific set of principles (see Figure 10.2) "will demonstrate their effectiveness and show that housing is more than bricks and mortar." As Bratt (2008, 100) notes, however, "not every nonprofit housing organization should offer housing plus services themselves. Rather, some organizations should develop referral relationships with other service providers." This underscores the importance of collaborative relationships among nonprofit housing providers and other service-related entities. The type of service being provided by nonprofit housing organizations will also shape the types and nature of collaborations and likely partners. For example, banks and other funders are likely to be less critical partners for organizations that provide home-ownership counseling services or related activities than for those organizations that engage in building new housing or rehabilitating existing housing.

Nonprofit organizations enter into collaborations and partnerships for a variety of reasons in order to fulfill their goal of providing housing services. Some use their ability to provide housing to seek additional services for their clients, thus improving the chances that the individuals and families they serve are more fully integrated into the fabric of the community (Rubin 1994; Evans 1998). Resource constraints can provide motivation for small and/or neighborhood-based nonprofits to collaborate with other organizations (Reese and Shields 2000). The potential to share or access funding, information, and additional clients through referrals are all noted as reasons why organizations collaborate. Not surprisingly, collaboration among nonprofits, the government, and for-profit organizations occurs at local, state, and national levels. Collaboration and coordinated networks become even more important for faith-based organizations (FBOs) and other nonprofit organizations as they face increased challenges in efforts to provide housing units and associated support services. By collaborating, organizations have the ability to increase their effectiveness and impact. Collaboration also provides an opportunity for organizations to share expertise and other resources, avoid duplication, create linkages to disenfranchised constituencies in their communities, and forge political alliances (Mitchell et al. 2002).

The With Whom and What For of Collaboration

The following discussion is based on data from the Nonprofit Housing Provider Survey and explores both the nature of collaboration—*what* organizations collaborate for—and types of organizational collaborators—*who* they work with. Specific differences in the types and nature of collaboration between faith-based and secular nonprofits are also examined. The most commonly cited reasons for collaboration among respondents are to provide housing or other services, receive funding, pool resources, and refer clients. This is consistent with the literature, where organizations collaborate in order to share expertise and resources (Mitchell et al. 2002). Field interviews reinforce the importance of collaboration if target households are to receive the range of needed services. Indeed, having a single organization providing a range of services may not be the most desirable way to operate. A leader of a faith-based nonprofit remarked:

> [B]y the time people got to us at the shelter all the wheels had fallen off the car. I mean they had multiple problems. Many times mental health issues, job issues, there were kids, just a number of things that were really difficult to handle and you had to have pretty much a long-term relationship with folks in order to really help them get back on the road. And at

least, that's what we thought at that time to be helpful. And so overseeing that transitional housing shelter, we kept people there or had people stay there for a couple years if they wanted to. But, I was starting to get a little disillusioned with the whole model, because I really didn't think that we needed to have people move into a shelter and stay there for two years in order for them to get services. And we started working as a larger group to see if there were better ways to serve people that become homeless.

Many organizations saw the value of collaborating to provide multifaceted services to the people they assisted. Table 10.1 highlights the reasons for collaboration, noting distinctions between service and policy rationales for collaboration. Most of the organizations indicate a level of comfort with and ease at collaborating in order to provide housing and other services to clients. Michigan nonprofits engaged in housing are less likely to cite anything policy related or to cite providing funding to others as explicit purposes for collaboration, however. This might suggest that these organizations do not forge political alliances. The nature of the correlations for collaboration between ethnic associations, advocacy organizations, neighborhood associations, and private organizations, noted earlier, suggests otherwise, however. One of this study's premises is that although organizations may not acknowledge collaboration for policy purposes or explicitly intend to do so (see Chapter 1, Figure 1.3), the patterns of their collaboration suggest that policy influence does occur. While the goal may be to collaborate for service delivery, the mere linkage to a certain organization may create an avenue for potential policy or political allegiances, or both.

Faith-based organizations report collaborating in order to provide housing services, engage in neighborhood development, pool resources, receive funding and, to some extent, to refer clients (Table 10.2). FBOs are less likely to report collaborating to receive housing services from other organizations or for any policy purpose. Similarly, secular organizations do not report collaborating to receive or provide policy advice. Nor do secular organizations report collaborating in order to provide funding for others. They primarily report collaborating for housing provision and other services and to some extent in order to receive funding. In comparison to secular organizations, faith-based organizations are significantly more likely to report collaborating in order to receive general services; this is the only area where the nature of collaboration is significantly different between the two types of organizations.

For the most part, organizations do not report collaborating for just one or two select purposes. An organization that is collaborating in order to provide housing services is also likely to collaborate for many other reasons including reciprocal client referral, pooling resources, or influencing state and local policy (Table 10.3). The correlations for FBOs essentially match those presented in Table 10.3 for the entire set of organizations, but there are no significant correlations for secular organizations.[4]

Nonprofit organizations report multiple reasons for collaboration. Identifying four conceptually different purposes, Table 10.4 presents a factor analysis of expressed reasons for collaborating: service delivery, policy influence, economic development, and organizational development. The latter includes items such as

Table 10.1

Purpose and Extent to Which Organizations Collaborate (in percent)

	Degree of collaboration	
Purpose of collaboration	Moderate/Large extent	Limited to none
Service collaboration		
Provide housing services	69.3	30.7
Provide other services	65.9	34.1
Receive housing services	47.6	52.3
Receive other services	43.0	56.9
Provide funding	32.2	67.8
Receive funding	65.9	34.1
Refer clients	62.8	37.2
Get referred clients	55.8	44.2
Pool resources	61.3	38.6
Policy collaboration		
Neighborhood development	55.2	44.8
Provide policy advice	38.6	61.4
Receive policy advice	29.4	70.6
Influence policy	38.3	61.7

bridge building, pooling resources, and reducing redundancies that, while clearly embracing service delivery, also strengthen general organizational capacities.

Figure 10.3 is a Venn diagram highlighting the nature of interactions between the different purposes for which organizations collaborate. Few organizations have just one reason for collaborating. As the diagram clearly suggests, the most common profile is for housing nonprofits to collaborate in multiple areas of activity: service delivery, policy influence, and organizational development.

Importance of and Rationale for Collaboration

The previous discussion focused on an organization's intent for collaboration. Specifically, are they collaborating for service delivery or for policy purposes?[5] Organizations were also asked to indicate what they hoped to achieve as a result of their collaboration—in other words, what goals were they trying to attain? Michigan nonprofits engaged in housing believe it is important to collaborate to enhance service or program delivery. Specifically, collaboration for program or service facilitation allows these organizations to: (1) increase efficiency by avoiding redundancy; (2) promote understanding across organizations and engage in bridge building; (3) engage in reciprocal referral arrangements; and (4) start new or expand existing programs. They also note the importance of collaborating to improve neighborhood conditions, advocate for underrepresented groups and influence state and local policy. This is consistent with the literature that notes that collaboration provides opportunities for organizations to avoid duplication, share expertise and other resources, and create linkages to disenfranchised constituencies

Table 10.2

Purpose and Extent of Collaboration by Faith-Based and Secular Organizations

		Moderate/ large extent (in %)	Mean[a]	t[b,c]	Significance
Service collaboration					
Provide housing services	Secular	67	1.95	−.48	.63
	Faith-based	74	1.84		
Provide other services	Secular	68	2.12	.08	.94
	Faith-based	61	2.14		
Receive housing services	Secular	45	2.63	−.83	.41
	Faith-based	53	2.43		
Receive other services	Secular	39	2.82	−1.95	.05**
	Faith-based	50	2.40		
Provide funding	Secular	29	2.91	−.92	.36
	Faith-based	39	2.68		
Receive funding	Secular	66	2.11	.23	.82
	Faith-based	67	2.17		
Refer clients	Secular	63	2.20	−.41	.68
	Faith-based	63	2.10		
Receive referrals	Secular	54	2.26	−.51	.61
	Faith-based	59	2.14		
Policy collaboration					
Neighborhood dev	Secular	45	2.41	−1.49	.14
	Faith-based	74	2.06		
Provide policy advice	Secular	37	2.68	−.03	.98
	Faith-based	42	2.68		
Receive policy advice	Secular	32	2.79	1.01	.32
	Faith-based	24	3.00		
Influence policy	Secular	41	2.71	.24	.80
	Faith-based	33	2.77		
Pool resources	Secular	58	2.25	−.24	.81
	Faith-based	68	2.19		

[a]This is the mean score based on a 1 to 4 Likert scale; where 1 indicates that an organization collaborates to a large extent and 4 indicates that the organization does not collaborate at all in order to achieve a specific purpose. Accordingly, a lower mean indicates more activity; the means range from 1.91 for collaborate for housing to 2.86 for receive policy advice.

[b]A negative value indicates that faith-based organizations collaborate more than secular organizations.

[c]Equal variances are not assumed.

**Significant at .05

(Mitchell et al. 2002). Michigan nonprofits engaged in housing are not concerned about promoting religion or religious principles through their collaboration. These trends hold for both faith-based and secular organizations, and there are no statistically significant differences between collaboration rationales for faith-based and secular organizations (Table 10.5).[6]

Table 10.3

Correlation between Collaboration to Provide Housing Services and Other Purposes of Collaboration

Purpose of collaboration	N	Correlation coefficient
Service collaboration		
Provide other services	85	.45***
Receive housing services	86	.50***
Receive other services	86	.39***
Provide funding	87	.37***
Receive funding	85	.27**
Refer clients	86	.39***
Receive referred clients	86	.50***
Policy collaboration		
Neighborhood development	87	.31***
Provide policy advice	88	.39***
Receive policy advice	85	.29***
Influence policy	86	.29***
Pool resources	88	.38***

Note: The dependent variable here is a single variable depicting whether an organization says they collaborate to provide housing.
***Significant at .01, **significant at .05

Table 10.4

Rotated Factor Matrix of Reasons for Collaborating

	Service activity	Organizational development	Policy activity	Economic development
Housing	.55	.00	.01	.25
Provide services	.72	.24	.05	.28
Receive housing services	.76	.13	.15	.03
Receive other services	.80	.18	.12	.00
Provide funding	.59	.12	.18	−.06
Receive funding	.35	.13	.09	.33
Refer clients	.66	.35	.01	.06
Receive referred clients	.64	.44	.01	.06
Pool resources	.64	.07	.23	.39
Avoid redundancy	.12	.77	.15	.07
Build bridges	.26	.77	.04	.11
Advocacy	.25	.77	.25	.01
New programming	.13	.70	.36	.24
Provide policy advice	.60	−.01	.67	.14
Receive policy advice	.55	.09	.71	.13
Influence policy	.50	.08	.74	.11
Influence state policy	.08	.28	.81	.04
Influence local policy	−.04	.39	.78	.11
Neighborhood development	.36	−.03	.02	.77
Fix neighborhoods	−.19	.32	.33	.69

Figure 10.3   **Collaboration Purposes for Nonprofits Actively Involved in Housing Construction and Renovation**

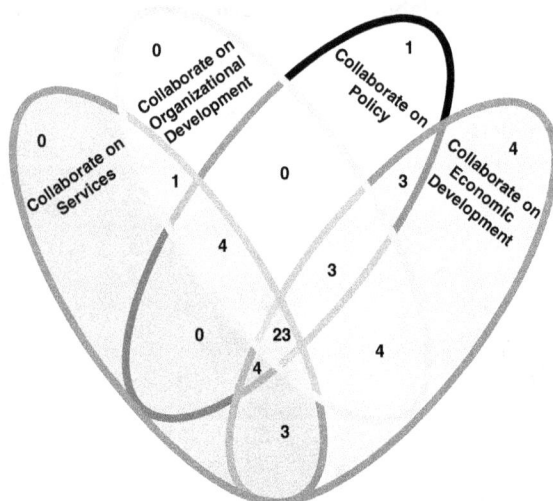

Note: Six nonprofits report no collaboration for any of these purposes.

Table 10.5

Goals the Organization Is Trying to Achieve through Collaboration

	Very/somewhat important (in %)			Mean[a]			
	All	Faith	Secular	Faith	Secular	t[b]	Sig.
Program/Service facilitation							
Avoid redundancy	92	97	90	1.34	1.51	−.86	0.39
Build bridges	90	93	88	1.37	1.58	−1.93	0.24
Receive referrals	88	93	86	1.72	1.68	.23	0.82
New programs	80	77	83	2.03	1.89	.63	0.53
Policy							
Advocate	67	80	61	1.97	2.14	−.69	0.49
Improve neighborhoods	89	93	86	1.47	1.58	−.63	0.53
Influence local policy	71	72	70	2.14	2.26	−.45	0.52
Influence state policy	60	62	60	2.31	2.49	−.65	0.52
Other							
Promote religion	5	11	02	3.61	4.39	−3.28	0.00***

[a]This is the mean score based on the 1 to 5 Likert scale; where 1 indicates that collaborating to achieve the specific goal is very important and 5 indicates that it is not at all important to achieve that goal. Accordingly, a lower mean indicates greater importance for collaborating to achieve a specific goal.

[b]A negative value indicates that collaborating to achieve a specific goal is more important to faith-based organizations.

***Significant at .01

Table 10.6

Collaboration Purposes and Goals

	Mean	Std. deviation	Min	Max
Purpose of collaboration				
Service collaboration: Any type	0.85	0.4	0	1
Service collaboration: Across all areas	4.39	3.0	0	9
Service collaboration only	0.44	0.5	0	1
Policy collaboration: Any type[a]	0.40	0.5	0	1
Policy collaboration: Across all areas	0.93	1.2	0	3
Policy collaboration only	0.00	0.0	0	0
Collaboration goals				
Any one goal associated with service delivery[b]	0.87	0.3	0	1
Multiple goals associated with service delivery	3.05	1.4	0	4
Only goals associated with service delivery	0.25	0.4	0	1
Any one goal associated with policy	0.62	0.5	0	1
Multiple goals associated with policy	1.14	0.9	0	2
Only goals associated with policy	0.00	0.0	0	0

[a]"Any type" of collaboration and "any one" goal represent those instances where an organization indicated that it collaborated for a specific purpose or goal, irrespective of how many purposes or goals it collaborated for. "Across all areas" denotes those instances where an organization indicated that it collaborated for all of the possible service delivery or policy purposes. "Multiple goals" indicates those instances where an organization collaborated in order to achieve more than one goal. "Only" represents those instances where an organization only indicated service delivery or policy purposes, or goals for collaboration, not both.

[b]This is also the mean for collaborating for both service delivery and policy purposes.

[c]This is also the mean for collaboration goals associated with both service delivery and policy involvement.

As noted earlier, the majority of organizations responding to the Nonprofit Housing Provider Survey collaborate for at least one, and, on most occasions, multiple service delivery purposes, including providing and receiving services related to housing or other services, and receiving and obtaining both funding and clients. Relatively few (11 percent), however, collaborate for all of these service delivery purposes. None of the organizations collaborate just for policy purposes; and across the range of options, there is less policy activity in comparison to service activity (Table 10.6). When it comes to the goals that organizations are trying to achieve through their collaborations, activities associated with both service delivery and policy are important. Most organizations are collaborating to achieve at least one service delivery–associated goal: avoiding redundancy and increasing efficiency, receiving and referring clients, and expanding existing programs or starting new ones. For over half of the organizations (61 percent), it is important to collaborate in order to meet all of these service delivery goals. Similarly, more than half the organizations (52 percent) collaborate in order to influence state and/or local policy (not shown in the table; this point is discussed more fully in Chapter 11).

Summary

Figures 10.4 through 10.7 highlight the key relationships between purposes (why the organizations are motivated to collaborate) and goals (what they hope to achieve) of collaboration for this set of organizations. These relationships are summarized as follows:

- Service provision, of housing and other services, and reciprocal client referrals are the major rationales for organizational collaboration (Figure 10.4).
- Nearly all of the organizations that collaborate for service-delivery purposes, including client referrals, do so in order to expand existing programs or create new ones, exchange clients, and increase efficiency while avoiding redundancies (Figure 10.4).
- The overwhelming majority of the organizations that collaborate to exchange clients and those that collaborate to provide and receive services also collaborate with the goal of influencing state housing policy specifically (Figure 10.5).
- Organizations that collaborate in order to influence local housing policy also collaborate in order to provide services other than housing and engage in reciprocal client referrals (Figure 10.6). Receiving services, housing or others, is not a key factor when the goal is to influence local policy.
- Organizations that collaborate to provide policy advice and influence public policy are intent on influencing both state and local policy. In comparison, organizations that collaborate in order to receive policy advice are only interested in influencing local policy (Figure 10.7).

There appear to be notable associations between what an organization is trying to achieve and the reasons underlying collaborations. Despite an apparent reluctance to claim policy involvement as a key component of organizational missions, nonprofits often become engaged in the policy fray through their collaborative relationships. Few, if any, collaborate simply to provide more and better services to clients. These findings are similar to Bratt and Rohe's (2004) claim that successful community development corporations are those that are able to take advantage of local partnerships that offer fiscal *and* policy support.

Collaboration and Primary Organizational Activities

Respondents to the Nonprofit Housing Provider Survey were asked to indicate the extent to which they engaged in six broad categories of activity: service delivery, economic development, political advocacy, community organizing, voter education, and community projects. Table 10.7 provides correlations between those activities (for context) and between each activity and the nature of and purposes for collaborators. Those organizations that are very involved in service delivery

Figure 10.4   **Overlapping Service Delivery Purposes and Goals for Collaboration**

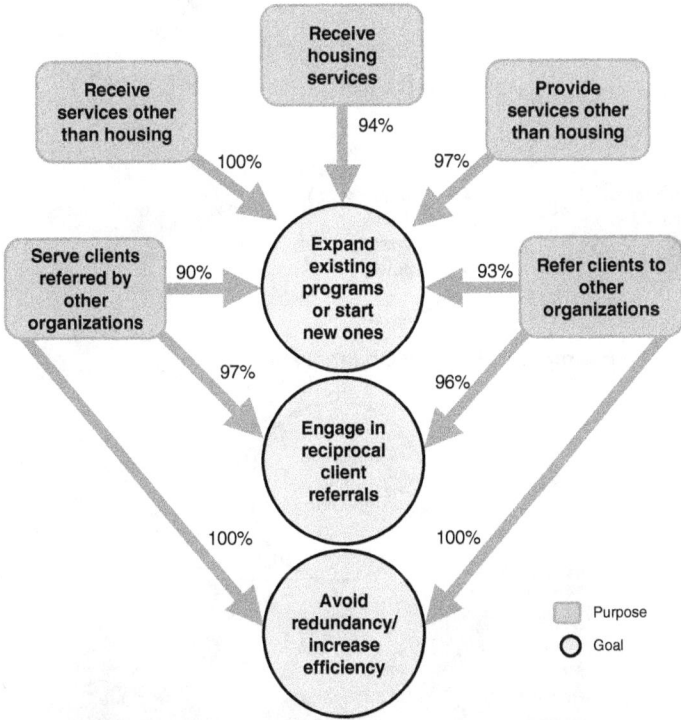

Figure 10.5   **Service Delivery Collaboration and Influencing State Housing Policy**

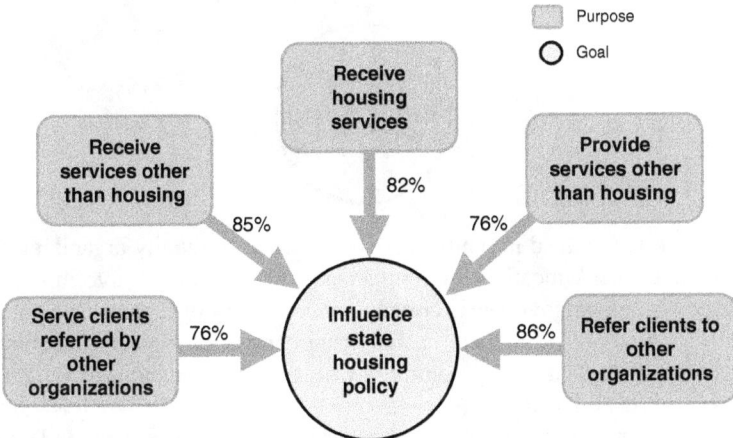

Figure 10.6   **Service Delivery Collaboration and Influencing Local Housing Policy**

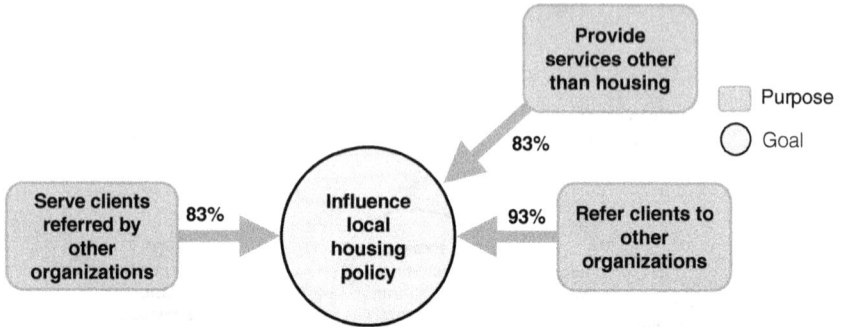

Figure 10.7   **Examples of Policy Collaboration**

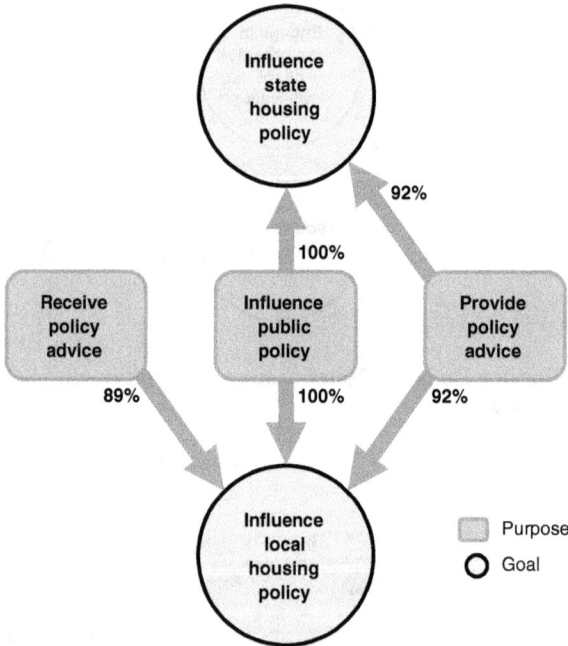

also tend to be involved in political advocacy and community organizing and to some extent voter education. In comparison, organizations active in economic development also get involved in community organizing or supporting community projects. Not surprisingly, there is significant correlation between organizations engaged in political advocacy, community organizing, voter education, and community projects (Table 10.7).[7]

As one might expect, the types of collaborators as well as purpose and rationale

Table 10.7

Correlation Matrix of Organizational Activities and Collaboration

	Deliver services	Economic development	Political advocacy	Community organizing	Voter education	Community projects
Types of organizational activities and changes in housing activity						
Deliver services	1.00					
Economic development	-.13	1.00				
Political advocacy	.25**	.08	1.00			
Community organizing	.25**	.38***	.28***	1.00		
Voter education	.19*	.14	.38***	.43***	1.00	
Community projects	.16	.42***	.27***	.64***	.34***	1.00
Types of organizational collaborators						
Social service	.34***	-.15	.38***	.24**	.26**	.05
Mental health	.40***	-.31***	.20*	.06	.30***	-.19
Local government	.11	.10	.24**	.21**	.13	.07
State government	.10	.19	.14	.14	.05	-.10
Civic	.14	-.15	.34**	.18	.02	.01
Neighborhood assoc.	.06	.21*	.05	.26**	.22**	.29***
Religious	.30***	-.14	.26	.24**	.23**	.19*
Ethnic	.29***	-.05	.06	.26**	.32***	.15
Schools	.30***	-.10	.22**	.34***	.28***	.14
Hospitals	.24**	.03	.30***	.31***	.44***	.20*
Advocacy organizations	.06	.05	.43***	.15	.30***	.11
Private sector	-.03	.17	.33***	.20*	.17	.14
Purpose of collaboration: Service						
Housing	.16	.00	.07	.20*	.10	.03
Provide service	.29***	.01	.26**	.37***	.35***	.20*
Receive housing service	.24**	-.01	.06	.24**	.20*	.21*

(continued)

Table 10.7 (continued)

	Deliver services	Economic development	Political advocacy	Community organizing	Voter education	Community projects
Types of organizational activities and changes in housing activity						
Receive service	.32***	-.10	.12	.23**	.20*	.16
Provide funds	.16	.05	.05	.18*	.13	.15
Receive funds	.34***	-.03	.28***	.16	.21*	.21*
Make referrals	.38***	-.16	.24**	.19*	.20*	.04
Receive referrals	.46***	-.19*	.20*	.25**	.17	.01
Purpose of collaboration: Policy						
Neighborhood develop	.15	.45***	.12	.56***	.19*	.41***
Give policy advice	.20*	.16	.41***	.30***	.24**	.24**
Receive policy advice	.19*	.07	.46***	.24**	.22**	.23**
Influence policy	.19*	.02	.50***	.20*	.31***	.18*
Pool resources	.12	.06	.15	.24**	.21*	.19*
Rationale for collaboration: Program/service facilitation						
Avoid redundancy	.38***	-.10	.22**	.24**	.20*	.10
Bridge building	.24**	-.02	.20*	.33***	.22**	.25**
Make and receive referrals	.18	-.18*	.24**	.06	.13	.03
New programs	.42***	.12	.39***	.26**	.15	.16
Rationale for collaboration: Policy Advocacy						
Improve neighborhoods	.30***	-.09	.27**	.32***	.23**	.16
Influence local policy	.07	.42***	.31***	.35***	.16	.38***
Influence state policy	.36***	.06	.56***	.12	.28**	.12
	.26**	.09	.46***	.11	.20	.15
Rationale for collaboration: Other						
Promote religion	.14	.02	.09	.12	.20*	.05

***Significant at the .01 level, **.05 level, *.10 level.

for collaboration vary based on primary organizational activities. In other words, why a nonprofit collaborates and with whom they collaborate depend on the activities pursued. Organizations actively involved in service delivery tend to collaborate with social service and mental health organizations, schools, and hospitals. They also collaborate with religious and ethnic organizations. They collaborate largely to achieve service goals by providing and receiving services, making and receiving client referrals, and obtaining funding. To a lesser extent, they also collaborate to achieve policy goals: giving and receiving policy advice and influencing policy. Their motivations for collaboration are both service and policy oriented. For example, organizations active in service delivery collaborate to avoid redundancies, to launch new programs, and to build bridges to and among other organizations. Advocacy and influencing state and local policy are also common rationales for service delivery organizations to collaborate (Table 10.7). In short, if a nonprofit has a service focus, it works with social service and health organizations in activities that primarily assist clients, although they are also concerned about the public policies that affect their clients.

Organizations focused primarily on economic development are less likely to collaborate in general. When they do, it is with neighborhood associations for the primary purpose of neighborhood development with the intent to improve neighborhoods. These organizations are less likely to take referrals from another organization, which stands to reason since they are singularly focused on a more narrow set of ends than more generalized housing service providers.

Schools, hospitals, and social service organizations are some of the common collaborators for organizations engaged in political advocacy, community organizing, and voter education. Organizations active in community organizing and voter education also collaborate with neighborhood associations, religious organizations, and ethnic associations. Organizations focused on voter education collaborate with mental health organizations. It is interesting to note that the only nonprofits that report collaborating with civic organizations, local governments, or the private sector are those with decidedly political purposes like political advocacy or community organizing. Similarly, the only organizations that report collaborating with advocacy organizations are those that are active in political advocacy and voter education. In summary, there appears to be a logical complex of collaboration for policy and political purposes. If these are the primary focus of the nonprofit (as opposed to housing services, for example), it collaborates with social and neighborhood organizations, as well as the government. Not surprisingly, the goals of collaboration are focused on increasing policy influence.

Logically, these more politically oriented organizations also collaborate to give and receive policy advice and to influence policy. They collaborate in varying degrees to provide and receive both services and referrals. Political advocacy organizations collaborate in order to receive funding, and community organizing nonprofits collaborate to pool resources and engage in neighborhood development. Common rationales for collaboration among this set of politically oriented organizations include advocacy, influencing state and local policy, improving neighborhoods, launching new programs, avoiding redundancy, and building bridges to other organizations. There is a slight tendency for organizations focused on voter education to collaborate in order to promote religion, as well (Table 10.7).

Organizations that participate in or otherwise support community projects collaborate almost exclusively with neighborhood associations and to a lesser extent with religious organizations and hospitals. While they may collaborate to receive funding, as well as to provide and receive services, their collaboration efforts are largely for policy purposes. These organizations collaborate for neighborhood development with the goal of improving neighborhoods. They also collaborate to give and receive advice as well as build bridges among organizations. To a lesser extent, organizations that participate in community projects also collaborate to pool resources and influence policy.

Summary

Most of the ties between activity focus and types of collaborators are quite logical; they represent coherence between purpose and partners:

- Organizations focused on the provision of social services tend to work with others that focus primarily on meeting service-related needs: social service and mental health agencies, schools, and hospitals. They collaborate to provide services and influence public policy.
- Nonprofits focusing on economic development or community projects are most likely to partner with neighborhood associations to affect policy and improve neighborhoods.
- Organizations emphasizing advocacy collaborate to receive policy advice and influence policy. They do this by working with a wide variety of actors that probably vary depending on the policy at hand.

Interactions among FBOs are in some instances notably different from those among secular organizations (see Appendix B, Tables B7 and B8). For example, there are no correlations between FBOs engaged in service delivery and FBOs active in any of the other areas. In comparison, secular organizations engaged in service delivery are also likely to be more active in political activities like political advocacy, community organizing, and voter education.

Like their secular counterparts, FBOs active in economic development are also likely to be active in community organizing and to participate in or otherwise support community projects. There is high correlation between secular organizations active in political advocacy, community organizing, voter education, and participation in community projects. In essence, engaging in one political activity enhances the chance that secular organizations will be active in other political activities. By comparison, FBOs are a bit more circumspect and selective in their political and service delivery activities. FBOs that are active in political advocacy also engage in voter education, while those active in community organizing are also active in voter education and community projects.

Collaboration Allows Nonprofits to Do More for Clients

Organizations responding to the Nonprofit Housing Provider Survey were also asked whether collaboration with other nonprofits allowed them to provide more and better housing to their clients. Eighty-two percent of the responding organizations agree that collaboration has enhanced both their productivity and effectiveness. There are no statistically significant differences between the views of faith-based and secular organizations on this issue. There are statistically significant correlations between nonprofits that believe collaboration allows them to provide better and more housing to their clients and collaboration to provide housing services, refer clients, receive funding, and pool resources (Table 10.8). The correlations are identical for secular nonprofits, but there are no significant correlations for FBOs. This suggests an interesting potential dynamic for secular organizations. Secular housing nonprofits tend to see collaboration as more effective if it brings tangible benefits in terms of resources and greater housing service capacity. They are also more positive about collaboration if they can use it to refer (potentially refer away) prospective clients. These benefits do not appear particularly important to how FBOs assess collaborative experiences.

Organizations that indicate that collaboration enhances their ability to serve their clients tend to believe it is important to collaborate in order to influence state and local policy (Table 10.9). Again, this is tied largely to secular organizations, as there are no significant correlations for faith-based organizations. Thus for secular nonprofits, collaborative experiences are seen as more effective if they are motivated to use them to influence housing policy. Taken together, these relationships suggest that collaboration for secular nonprofits is clearly the means to an end: providing more service or influencing policy, for example. FBOs, on the other hand, appear less instrumental in their collaboration, perhaps viewing working together as an end in itself.

Accuracy of Organizational Perceptions of Collaboration

One of the initial questions of the present study was the extent to which organizations' perception of their collaborations as indicated in respsonses to the Nonprofit Housing Provider Survey matched reality (see Chapter 1, Figure 1.3). Essentially, a two-by-two matrix was posited (Figure 10.8). The top left quadrant (A1) represents those organizations that indicated that they collaborated with any type of organization, and the data confirm the existence of collaboration. The top right quadrant (B1) represents those organizations that indicated that they collaborated, but there is no evidence of collaboration presented by the data. The bottom left

Table 10.8

Correlation between Beliefs That Collaboration Enhances Housing Service Provision and Purposes of Collaboration

Purpose of collaboration	N	Correlation coefficient
Service collaboration		
Provide housing services	84	.27**
Provide other services	82	.20
Receive housing services	82	.07
Receive other services	82	.11
Provide funding	83	.05
Receive funding	81	.35***
Refer clients	82	.30***
Receive referred clients	82	.16
Policy collaboration		
Neighborhood development	83	.04
Provide policy advice	84	−.03
Receive policy advice	82	−.03
Influence policy	82	.18
Pool resources	84	.30***

***Significant at .01, **significant at .05.

Table 10.9

Correlation between Beliefs That Collaboration Enhances Housing Service Provision and Rationales for Collaboration

Rational for collaboration	N	Correlation coefficient
Program/Service facilitation		
Avoid redundancy	82	.17
Bridge building	83	.17
Receive referrals	81	.17
New programs	83	.19
Policy		
Advocacy	82	.12
Improve neighborhoods	83	.05
Influence local policy	82	.33***
Influence state policy	82	.23**
Other		
Promote religion	80	.17

***Significant at .01, **significant at .05

quadrant (A2) represents organizations that reported no collaboration, but the data reveal that they did collaborate. Finally, the bottom right quadrant (B2) represents organizations that reported no collaboration, and the data confirm the absence of collaboration.

Because the survey questions did not directly ask whether the organization did

Figure 10.8   **Basic Test of Perception versus Reality for Collaboration Activity**

A1	**B1**
Perception and Reality Matched	Mismatch Between Perception and Reality
• Collaboration purported and existed	• Purported collaboration nonexistent
COLLABORATION	No Evidence of Collaboration
A2	**B2**
Mismatch Between Perception and Reality	Perception and Reality Matched
• Denied collaboration; however it exists	• Collaboration denied and nonexistent
Evidence of Collaboration	**NO COLLABORATION**

or did not collaborate, it would be difficult to assess the relationships diagrammed in Figure 10.8 at the most basic level. Instead, organizations were asked to indicate with whom they collaborated, and every organization indicated at least a limited extent of collaboration with some other organization. Indeed, all but three organizations had at least a moderate or large extent of collaboration with at least one other organization.

Another approach to assessing whether perception matches reality, however, is to look at the types of organizations that respondents collaborated with and their rationales for doing so. This leads to the more nuanced issues diagrammed in the conceptual model (see Chapter 1, Figure 1.3). This argument, implying a six-by-two matrix, is more viable, allowing examination of collaboration for specific activities (Figure 10.9). Boxes A1, A3, and A5 in Figure 10.9 represent those circumstances where data confirm the organizations' assertion that they collaborated for the purposes of service delivery only, political or policy reasons only, or both purposes. Similarly, boxes B2, B4, and B6 in Figure 10.9 represent those instances where organizations asserted that they did not collaborate solely for service delivery or political or policy purposes, nor for a combination of purposes, and this was confirmed by the data. These are the instances when perception matched reality.

There is also the possibility that organizations did not indicate that they were collaborating for a specific purpose, but the data cast serious doubts about this possibility. These perception mismatches could occur because of understating (Boxes A2, A4, A6, in Figure 10.9) or overstating the nature and purpose of collaboration (Figure 10.9, Boxes B1, B3, B5). For example, although organizations said they did not collaborate solely for service delivery, when asked to indicate their purpose for collaborating, the responses were exclusive to actions associated with service delivery. Additionally, the responses indicated that while collaboration facilitated service delivery; it did not impact political or policy-related activities (A2, in Figure 10.9). This would suggest that their collaboration was in fact for service delivery purposes only as opposed to service delivery and political or policy purposes.[8]

Similarly, some organizations indicated that they collaborated only for service delivery purposes, but there were no data to support this claim. When asked to indicate their intent or purpose for collaborating, none of the responses facilitated

Figure 10.9 **Perception versus Reality Based on Type of Collaboration Activity**

Purpose of Collaboration	Row	Column A	Column B
Service Delivery Only	1	Perception and Reality Matched • Service delivery collaboration purported and existed **COLLABORATION**	Perception and Reality Mismatch • Purported service delivery collaboration nonexistent No Evidence of Collaboration
	2	Perception and Reality Mismatch • Denied service delivery collaboration, but it exists Evidence of Collaboration	Perception and Reality Matched • Service delivery collaboration denied and nonexistent **NO COLLABORATION**
Political or Policy Purposes Only	3	Perception and Reality Matched • Political or policy collaboration purported and existed **COLLABORATION**	Perception and Reality Mismatch • Purported political or policy collaboration nonexistent No Evidence of Collaboration
	4	Perception and Reality Mismatch • Denied political or policy collaboration, but it exists Evidence of Collaboration	Perception and Reality Matched • Political or policy collaboration denied and nonexistent **NO COLLABORATION**
Service Delivery Purposes and Political or Policy Purposes	5	Perception and Reality Matched • Multipurpose collaboration purported and existed **COLLABORATION**	Perception and Reality Mismatch • Purported multipurpose collaboration nonexistent No Evidence of Collaboration
	6	Perception and Reality Mismatch • Denied multipurpose collaboration, but it exists Evidence of Collaboration	Perception and Reality Matched • Multipurpose collaboration denied and nonexistent **NO COLLABORATION**

service delivery (B1, in Figure 10.9). For example, the organizations reported that they collaborated to receive or provide services or clients, as opposed to receiving or providing policy advice or influencing policy. Collaborating to receive or provide referrals, expand or start new programs, or reduce duplication were not very important reasons for them to collaborate, however.

Before examining the degree of agreement between the organizations' purpose for collaboration and the goals they were trying to achieve by collaborating, it is useful to examine a few basic relationships between collaboration purposes and goals. Overall, 34 percent of the organizations responding to the housing provider survey indicated that they do not collaborate for service delivery, and approximately 85 percent indicated that they do not collaborate for policy or political reasons. Just over 50 percent of the organizations reported collaborating to achieve service delivery purposes exclusively, and 15 percent reported collaborating to achieve both service delivery and policy purposes. While some organizations collaborate for both policy and service delivery purposes, none reported collaborating for policy purposes exclusively. This strongly suggests that policy linkages happen in the course of making service-delivery linkages rather than as a specific and targeted strategy. Of the fifty-six organizations (65 percent) that collaborate for service delivery, the majority (77 percent) do so for service delivery reasons alone, while the remaining 23 percent collaborate to achieve both service and policy goals. In addition, although approximately one-half of the organizations report collaborating exclusively for service delivery purposes, when asked about the goals they were trying to achieve through collaboration, just over 25 percent identify goals unique to service delivery. What is more interesting is that a large majority of reporting nonprofits (84 percent) indicate that they did not feel it was necessary to collaborate for both service delivery and policy purposes to meet organizational goals. Even so, for over half of the organizations that said that it was not their intent to collaborate for multiple purposes, the goals that they were trying to achieve through collaboration addressed both service delivery and policy concerns (Table 10.10).

In short, most nonprofits collaborate to achieve their primary purpose-providing services. In addition, through the linkages and interactions required to fulfill service functions, nonprofits—both secular and faith-based—engage in activities that are policy related. Indeed, the fact that they underreport, or at the extreme deny, these policy-focused collaborations suggests a certain level of discomfort with a more political or governing role extending beyond services. Yet, the reality of nonprofit collaborations tells a story of *both* service and political activity, regardless of formal goals and intentions.

The instances where the data confirm organizational assertions of collaboration for the purposes of service delivery only, political or policy reasons only, or both purposes (Figure 10.10), are less interesting. Overall, 14 percent of the organizations collaborated exclusively for service delivery, just as they indicated it was their intent to do. The goals that were most important for them to accomplish through collaboration were all associated with components of service delivery. In addition,

Table 10.10

Associations between Purposes and Goals of Collaboration (in percent)

Purpose of collaboration		No (0)	Yes (1)	Chi Square χ^2	P
Goal: Service delivery only					
Service delivery only	No (0)	37.3	12.0	0.19	0.67
	Yes (1)	36.1	14.5		
Policy only	No (0)	73.5	26.5	n/a	
	Yes (1)	0.0	0.0		
Both service delivery and policy	No (0)	59.0	25.3	2.80	0.09
	Yes (1)	14.5	1.2		
Goal: Policy only					
Service delivery only	No (0)	49.6	0.0	n/a	
	Yes (1)	50.4	0.0		
Policy only	No (0)	100.0	0.0	n/a	
	Yes (1)	0.0	0.0		
Both service delivery and policy	No (0)	84.3	0.0	n/a	
	Yes (1)	15.7	0.0		
Goal: Service delivery and policy					
Service delivery only	No (0)	13.6	36.1	0.42	0.52
	Yes (1)	16.9	33.7		
Policy only	No (0)	30.1	69.9	n/a	
	Yes (1)	0.0	0.0		
Both service delivery and policy	No (0)	28.9	55.4	3.68	0.06
	Yes (1)	1.2	14.5		

another 14 percent of the organizations intended to collaborate for service delivery and political or policy purposes and did in fact do just that. The goals most important for them to achieve through their collaboration were both explicitly service delivery and politically or policy oriented. These were all instances where the nature of the collaboration was exactly as the organization had presented; that is, the purpose and goals of collaboration were perfectly aligned.

There were also instances where respondents said that they did not collaborate with other organizations solely for service delivery or political or policy purposes, nor for a combination of purposes, and this was confirmed by the data. For example, 37 percent of the organizations acknowledged that they collaborated for purposes beyond service delivery and that the goals that were important for them to achieve through collaboration also extended beyond service delivery. Similarly, 29 percent of the organizations denied collaborating to achieve both service delivery and policy purposes, and it was clear that the goals they were trying to achieve through collaboration were focused exclusively on one or the other areas (Figure 10.10). Again, these are the instances when perception matched reality.

Finally, there were cases when respondents indicated no collaboration for specific purposes, yet the data contradicted these assertions (Figure 10.10). For example, even though 12 percent reported not collaborating exclusively for service delivery,

Figure 10.10 Incidence of Collaboration Activity for Service Delivery, Political or Policy Purposes, or Both

Purpose of Collaboration	Row	Column A	Column B
Service Delivery Only $\chi^2 = 0.19$ $p = 0.67$	1	14.5% <u>Perception and Reality Matched</u> **Exclusive Service Delivery COLLABORATION**	36.1% Perception and Reality Mismatch No Evidence of Purported Exclusive Service Delivery Collaboration
	2	12.0% Perception and Reality Mismatch Evidence suggests that collaboration was for service delivery purposes exclusively even though organizations indicated it was not	37.3% <u>Perception and Reality Matched</u> **COLLABORATION is not for Service Delivery Purposes Exclusively**
Political or Policy Purposes Only No χ^2 statistic computed because no organizations report collaborating only for policy purposes	3	0% <u>Perception and Reality Matched</u> **Exclusive Political/Policy COLLABORATION**	0% Perception and Reality Mismatch No Evidence of Purported Exclusive Political/Policy Collaboration
	4	0% Perception and Reality Mismatch Evidence suggests that collaboration was for political/policy purposes exclusively even though organizations indicated it was not	100% <u>Perception and Reality Matched</u> **COLLABORATION is not for Political or Policy Purposes Exclusively**
Service Delivery Purposes and Political or Policy Purposes $\chi^2 = 3.68$ $p = 0.06$	5	14.5% <u>Perception and Reality Matched</u> **COLLABORATION for Service Delivery as well as Political/Policy Purposes**	1.2% Perception and Reality Mismatch No Evidence that the organizations collaborated for both service delivery and political/policy purposes
	6	55.4% Perception and Reality Mismatch Evidence suggests that collaboration was for both service and political/policy purposes even though organizations indicated it was not	28.9% <u>Perception and Reality Matched</u> **COLLABORATION is not to achieve a mix of Service Delivery and Political/Policy Goals**

service goals were the only ones that were mentioned. Similarly, 55 percent of the organizations collaborated to achieve both service delivery and policy goals, even though they indicated that they did not collaborate for multiple purposes (i.e., service delivery and policy). These again were instances where the organizations understated the nature of their collaboration. Overstating the nature of collaborations occurred somewhat less frequently than the tendency to not fully acknowledge the nature of collaborations. For example, the data did not support the assertion of 36 percent of the organizations that indicated that they only collaborated for service delivery purposes. This is because the goals that were important for them to achieve by collaborating extended beyond service delivery concerns and included explicit policy goals. Only 1 percent reported collaborating for both service delivery and policy purposes but failed to pursue multipurpose goals.

Housing nonprofits in Michigan tend not to collaborate exclusively for policy or political purposes. Rather, their primary motivation for working with other organizations is to provide service. Once those collaborative networks are in place, however, collaboration is broadened to include policy-related activity. In addition, even though a considerable number of nonprofits deny policy-related motivations behind their collaboration, they are clearly present.

Summary

Looking across the analyses presented in this chapter, it is clear that the motivations, purposes, and goals of collaboration are complex and do not necessarily match the reality of collaborative behavior. More specifically it appears that:

- The reality that most nonprofits embrace a housing plus services model means that collaboration is required to enhance capacity.
- Patterns of collaboration clearly indicate networks that enhance both the service and policy roles of nonprofits.
- Secular nonprofits tend to view collaboration as a means to an end, while faith-based nonprofits view working together as an end in itself.
- Whom a nonprofit collaborates with varies, depending on what the organization is trying to achieve, in a reasonably logical fashion.
- Housing nonprofits are more likely to indicate collaboration for service-related activities than for those related to policy.
- Service collaborations are tied to collaboration for broader policy or political purposes.
- There appears to be a tendency to understate the policy or political collaborations.

Overall, housing nonprofits emphasize their service delivery collaborations and appear somewhat ambivalent about policy-related networks. Despite this ambivalence, as the next chapter explores in more detail, the civic activities of nonprofits generally, and faith-based nonprofits in particular, define an important role for these organizations.

Notes

The quote in this chapter comes from a representative of a faith-based housing organization and is based on a personal interview conducted in 2009.

1. Inspired by the work of a faith-based organization affiliated with the Church of the Savior in Washington, DC, Enterprise Community Partners (formerly the Enterprise Foundation) was founded by real-estate developer Jim Rouse and his wife, Patty, in 1982 to help low-income individuals and families in the United States obtain affordable housing and move up and out of poverty. Enterprise Community Partners has a four-pronged focus: to partner, innovate, advocate, and finance housing and community development. As part of this, it collaborates with the government, community-based nonprofits, developers, investors, and other individuals and organizations in order to carry out its mission. The network of organizations connected to and through the national nonprofit, Enterprise Community Partners, spans communities in Vermont, New York, New Jersey, Pennsylvania, Ohio, Washington, D.C., Los Angeles, and Puerto Rico (Enterprise Community Partners 2009).

2. NeighborWorks America is a national nonprofit organization that was established by Congress in 1978 to improve distressed communities by providing financial support, technical assistance, and training for community-based revitalization efforts in the United States (Public Law 95–557). In addition to building and repairing houses and rental properties, the organization provides counseling and financial services to individuals and families. Between 2004 and 2008 an average of 88,245 families were assisted per year though the NeighborWorks network. In 2009, over 230 organizations in all fifty states were working with and through residents, government officials, banks, insurance companies, retailers, foundations, and other partners to achieve their collective goal of revitalizing communities (NeighborWorks America 2008a). Three Michigan organizations were active participants in the NeighborWorks campaign for home ownership between 1998 and 2007, with an investment of nearly 91 million dollars that resulted in almost 1,300 new home owners (NeighborWorks America 2003, 2007, 2008b).

3. Some of the more common terms for expressing this phenomenon include "service-enriched housing" and "service-enhanced housing." Another series of terms typically identifies programmatic thrusts aimed at specific subsets of low-income populations such as the elderly, the homeless, or individuals with HIV/AIDS; these include "support services," "supportive housing," and "congregate care." In an attempt to try to capture these approaches, the umbrella term "housing plus services" was proposed by the National Low Income Housing Coalition to reflect the myriad of services and programs that organizations provide alongside housing (Granruth and Smith 2001). Examples of federal programs that help nonprofit organizations provide housing plus services include Residential Opportunity and Self-Sufficiency (ROSS) and HOPE VI.

4. The only exception is that FBOs that collaborate to provide housing services do not collaborate to receive funding. Thus, most of the significant relationships noted in Table 10.3 are representative of faith-based organizations. Full correlation results for faith-based and secular nonprofits are available from the authors.

5. For ease of subsequent discussion and to reduce complexity, organizational development activities have been included with service activities, since the main purpose is to explore service versus policy and political collaborations.

6. One exception was the case of promoting religion, where not surprisingly there were statistically significant differences between faith-based and secular organizations ($\chi^2 = 13.648$,

$p = 0.009$). Even so, both types of organizations indicated that promoting religion was not an important rationale for collaborating.

7. With the exception of organizations heavily involved in economic development, all of the organizations experienced an increase in housing activity between 2003 and 2007.

8. Some of these organizations indicated that they collaborated to exchange funding, engage in neighborhood development, and/or pool resources. None of these actions are exclusively for service delivery or political or policy purposes. The nature of the analysis undertaken for this component of the study, however, isolated service delivery and political or policy purposes in order to assess the functionality of the collaborations.

References

Bingham, Richard D., and Samuel A. Kirkpatrick. 1975. Providing Social Services for the Urban Poor: An Analysis of Public Housing Authorities in Large American Cities. *Social Service Review* 49(1): 64–78.

Bratt, Rachel G. 2008. Viewing Housing Holistically: The Resident-Focused Component of the Housing-Plus Agenda. *Journal of the American Planning Association* 74(1): 100–110.

Bratt, Rachel G., and William M. Rohe. 2004. Organizational Changes among CDCs: Assessing the Impacts and Navigating the Challenges. *Journal of Urban Affairs* 26(2) 197–220.

Cohen, Carol S., Elizabeth Mulroy, Tanya Tull, Catherine White, and Sheila Crowley. 2004. Housing Plus Services: Supporting Vulnerable Families in Permanent Housing. *Child Welfare* 83(5): 509–528.

Cohen, Carol S., and M.H. Phillips. 1997. Building Community: Principles for Social Work Practice in Housing Settings. *Social Work* 2(5): 471–481.

Enterprise Community Partners. 2009. Enterprise. www.enterprisecommunity.org/.

Evans, Richard. 1998. Tackling Deprivation on Social Housing Estates in England: An Assessment of the Housing Plus Approach. *Housing Studies* 13(5): 713–726.

Granruth, Laura B., and Carla H. Smith. 2001. *Low Income Housing and Services Programs: Towards a New Perspective.* Washington, DC: National Low-income Housing Coalition.

Mayer, Neil, and Kenneth Temkin. 2007. *Housing Partnerships: The Work of Large-Scale Regional Non-Profits in Affordable Housing.* Washington, DC: Urban Institute.

Mitchell, Roger E., Paul Florin, and John F. Stevenson. 2002. Supporting Community-Based Prevention and Health Promotion Initiatives: Developing Effective Technical Assistance Systems. *Health Education and Behavior* 29(5): 620–639.

National Congress for Community Economic Development (NCCED). 2005. *Reaching New Heights: Trends and Achievements of Community-Based Development Organizations.* Washington, DC: 5th National Community Development Census. NCCED.

NeighborWorks America. 2003. NeighborWorks Campaign for Home Ownership 2002. http://www.nw.org/network/nwdata/documents/detailII.pdf.

———. 2007. NeighborWorks Campaign for Home Ownership 2003–2007. http://www.nw.org/network/nwdata/documents/detail.pdf.

———. 2008a. About Us. www.nw.org/network.

———. 2008b. Summary Report: NeighborWorks Main Production Indicators, First Quarter. http://www.nw.org/network/nwdata/documents/NetworkProductionIndicators.pdf.

Newman, Saundra J., and Ann B. Schnare. 1992. Beyond Bricks and Mortar: Reexamining the Purpose and Effects of Housing Assistance (Report No. 92–3). Washington, DC: Urban Institute Press.

Public Law. 95–557. Housing and Community Development Amendments of 1978.

Reese, Laura A., and Gary Shields. 2000. Faith-Based Economic Development: Characteristics of Active Churches. *Policy Studies Review* 17(2/3): 84–103.

Rubin, Herbert J. 1994. There Aren't Going to Be Any Bakeries Here If There Is No Money
to Afford Jellyrolls: The Organic Theory of Community-Based Development. *Social
Problems* 41(3): 401–424.

Tull, Tanya, ed. 1998. *Service Enriched Housing: Models and Methodologies.* 2d ed. Los
Angeles: Beyond Shelter.

Vidal, Avis C. 1992. *Rebuilding Communities: A National Study of Urban Community
Development Corporations.* New York: New School for Social Research, Community
Development Research Center.

11

Political Activity and
Policy Involvement

A central question driving this project is: does the provision of low-income housing lead nonprofits into public policy-making networks that may, over time, give them access to the broader governing regime? Some critics of public funding for faith-based nonprofits fear that one outcome of such funding would be a blurring of boundaries between church and state (Goetz 1992; Chaves et al. 2004). Others argue that faith-based nonprofits limit their activities to the provision of services and do not venture into policy or political arenas. While it is certainly plausible that faith-based organizations (FBOs) will use their service function to gain greater access to, and power in, policy and politics relating not only to housing services, but also to the larger urban governing system, there is surprisingly little empirical evidence about whether this actually occurs. Work by a number of scholars has examined the governing role of community-based organizations generally but not of FBOs specifically (e.g., Smith and Evans 2001; LeRoux 2007; Silverman 2008), suggesting that there is a place for nonprofits in local governing regimes, particularly in the areas of housing policy, social justice issues, and community development. This chapter focuses on the political and policy-related activities of nonprofit housing providers, to explore the extent to which their efforts extend beyond the provision of housing and related services, and explicitly examines potential differences between faith-based and secular nonprofits.

The Nonprofit Housing Provider Survey was expressly designed to measure broader policy-related activity of nonprofits. There was some attention in the two surveys by the Community Economic Development Association of Michigan (CEDAM) to policy or political activity, and these are also explored when available. As in the other chapters, these data are supplemented with the findings from a series of field interviews.

CEDAM Surveys: 2003 and 2007

The 2003 CEDAM survey only included two questions that related to broader policy or political activity: whether the organization conducted voter registration drives and whether it conducted advocacy activities. Only a handful of housing nonprofits engage in voter registration efforts, it was found, and there is no difference between secular and faith-based organizations in this regard. Secular nonprofits are significantly more likely ($t = -0.05$, $p < 0.05$) than their faith-based counterparts to perceive themselves as acting in an advocacy capacity (29 percent as opposed to 10 percent are active in this area).[1] While what constitutes voter registration activities is relatively clear, this is not the case for "advocacy." The survey did not provide any description of what advocacy activities might include, so it is somewhat difficult to interpret this result.

The 2007 CEDAM survey included a number of questions more directly related to political and policy-related activity. Three questions ask about the extent of organizational participation in local, state, and federal policy making. The questions do not specifically ask about housing policy, so it can be assumed that respondents are talking about more generalized policy activity. There are no significant differences between faith-based and secular nonprofits in their reported levels of participation in policy making at any level. Secular nonprofits have slightly more interaction with local policy making (53 percent have substantial involvement in local policy, as opposed to 35 percent of FBOs with substantial involvement). FBOs, on the other hand, have slightly more interaction with state policy making than their secular counterparts (27 percent for FBOs and 19 percent for secular nonprofits). Neither type of nonprofit has much involvement in federal policy making (9 percent for secular nonprofits and 5 percent for FBOs). Two other questions ask about the extent of relationships with local and state (but not federal) elected officials and policy makers. Again there are no significant differences between secular and faith-based nonprofits in these relationships. FBOs appear to have more relationships with local officials (46 percent say they have substantial relationships, compared to 37 percent of secular nonprofits) but their interactions with state level officials are identical, at 32 percent.

The five policy questions are highly interrelated, as shown in the correlation matrix presented in Table 11.1 and the factor analysis in Table 11.2. Both suggest that if an organization has substantial activity in one aspect of policy, it is active in all aspects. Thus there appears to be a single policy activity complex among the nonprofits responding to the CEDAM survey. A single policy activity index was constructed from the five questions using factor scores generated by the factor analysis reported in Table 11.2. This index serves as the dependent variable for the correlation analysis shown in Table 11.3. Policy-related activity is correlated with a number of organizational characteristics. Nonprofits most engaged in policy activity are generally those that have greater resources: larger boards, budgets, investments, and full- and part-time employees. They are more likely to be receiving funding from public sources, banking institutions, and profit-making resources such as endowments or earned income from business entities. Politically active housing organizations have significantly fewer contract employees. They are less likely to be serving rural communities, the homeless, and individuals with disabilities. They are also less likely to be involved in local planning processes and transportation projects. It is important to note that chi-squares were used to test these relationships due to the nominal nature of a

Table 11.1

Correlation Matrix Political Activities (CEDAM 2007)

	Local policy	Local officials	State policy	State officials	Federal policy
Local policy	1.00				
Local officials	.49**	1.00			
State policy	.56**	.50**	1.00		
State officials	.44**	.60**	.66**	1.00	
Federal policy	.33**	.38**	.71**	.52**	1.00

***Difference significant at the .01 level, **.05 level.

Table 11.2

Rotated Factor Matrix for Political Activity (CEDAM 2007)

	Political activity
Level of participation in local policy	.70
Relationship with local elected officials	.76
Level of participation in state policy	.88
Relationship with state elected officials	.83
Level of participation in federal policy	.76

number of survey questions and thus do not show the direction of correlations. A visual inspection of the crosstab distribution (not shown) indicates that all of these correlations are negative. Despite their greater resources, nonprofits more involved in policy activity are also more likely to have considered dissolution.

In general, the policy activities that an organization undertakes are related to a variety of factors, including characteristics of the organization (e.g., staffing, age, budget, faith status), funding sources, population served, engagement in local service issues, location, the types of collaborators (governmental, for-profit, nonprofit), and reasons for collaboration (service delivery and/or policy).[2] A multiple regression model is constructed to estimate the independent impact of each of these factors:

Policy-Related Activity = **F** (**O**rganizational **C**haracteristics, **F**unding **S**ources, **P**opulation **S**erved, **L**ocal **S**ervice **E**ngagement, **L**ocation, **C**ollaboration)

$$Y = \alpha + \beta_1 OC_{1i} + \beta_2 FS_{2i} + \beta_3 PS_{3i} + \beta_4 LSE_{4i} + \beta_5 L_{5i} + \beta_6 C_{6i} + \varepsilon_i$$

Where: Policy-related activity is the index of an organization's connectedness to policy makers combined with the extent of their involvement in local, state, and federal policy;

Table 11.3

Policy Activity and Organizational Attributes (CEDAM 2007)

	Political activity index
Faith nature[a]	3.24
Number on board	.26**
Annual operating budget	.43***
Public funding	.60***
Bank funding	.33***
Faith-based funding	−.07
Nonprofit funding	.19
Profit funding	.46***
Annual investment in projects	.31**
Full-time employees	.51***
Volunteers	.12
Part-time employees	.41***
Contract employees	−.26**
501 (c) (3)[a]	4.97
CHDO status[a]	2.01
Serve urban community[a]	.85
Serve suburban community[a]	4.21
Serve rural community[a]	7.52**
Offer health insurance[a]	3.19
Part of local coalition[a]	.95
Have a neighborhood plan[a]	1.58
Part of local planning process[a]	10.14**
Engaged with local schools[a]	1.31
Engaged with transportation issues[a]	26.72***
Have partners to accomplish projects[a]	1.42
Have considered merger[a]	.41
Have considered dissolution[a]	10.48***
Serve low income[a]	1.50
Serve moderate income[a]	.86
Serve market rate[a]	1.07
Serve seniors[a]	.57
Serve children/youth[a]	1.16
Serve homeless[a]	6.26**
Serve those with disabilities[a]	7.32**
Serve those with HIV/AIDS[a]	2.15
Serve jobless[a]	2.43

[a]Chi square.
***Significant at .01, **significant at .05.

Local service engagement is measured in the 2007 CEDAM survey by involvement with city or regional planning, transportation, and education issues;

Location is measured in the 2007 CEDAM survey as serving rural or urban communities; and

Collaboration is not measured for the 2007 CEDAM survey.

Of the correlates noted in Table 11.3, only one remains significantly related to policy activity in multiple regression: involvement in local service issues. Nonprofits not involved in transportation projects are more likely to engage in policy activities, perhaps because resources can be expended on other policy areas (Table 11.4). Thus, the analysis tells us more about what types of organizations do not engage in policy activity than anything about those that do. The resource index comes close to significance, suggesting that more resources do provide support for greater policy activity.[3]

Nonprofit Housing Provider Survey

The Nonprofit Housing Provider Survey includes a number of questions focused on political and policy activity. Figure 11.1 presents agreement with a number of attitudinal statements about policy activity. These questions address the values, attitudes, and political biases of nonprofit respondents that may impact the organizational approach toward policy-related activity. The highest levels of agreement are with three statements:

1. It is appropriate for housing providers to help frame public policy (38 percent).
2. It is important for housing providers to be active in the design and implementation of government-funded housing programs (38 percent).
3. Working with public officials provides a way to make sure that the organization has its views represented in public policy decisions (34 percent).

There is widespread agreement among directors of housing nonprofits that providing housing services is an effective and appropriate way to become involved in the larger policy-making process. At the same time, these nonprofit leaders do not appear to feel that their organizations have been particularly successful in these roles: only 7 percent indicate that they strongly agree that their organization has a say in the creation of state and local housing policy. At least one state housing official agrees with this sentiment, noting that while some housing nonprofits do engage in advocacy activities, "often it's only as it affects their neighborhood, not so much about the big picture of municipal policy or urban policy at the state level. They tend to be very project focused, getting these houses done because that's how they keep their staff paid, by continuing to produce [housing]." While these nonprofits and some state agency officials may not see or feel the immediate impacts of their policy efforts, state legislators and representatives of ethnic associations and policy organizations note that local service providers are indeed useful sources of information for state legislators (Jackson-Elmoore 2005). Even so, 23 percent are in strong agreement that too many strings come with public funding, indicating that there is still concern about this issue, although most organizations accept government support.

Table 11.4

Political Activity Regression (CEDAM 2007)

	B	Standard error	Beta	Significance
Organizational characteristics				
Resource index	.19	.12	.19	.12
Contract employees	−.12	.26	−.05	.63
Considered dissolution	.09	.42	.02	.83
Population served				
Serve homeless/Disabilities	−.06	.11	−.06	.58
Location				
Serve rural areas	−.08	.24	−.04	.75
Engagement in local service issues				
Part of local planning	−.17	.19	−.10	.38
Engaged with transportation issues	−1.27	.24	−.63	.00
Constant	2.11	1.01		.05

Multiple $R^2 = .64$

Figures 11.2 and 11.3 present visual representations of how individual organizations engage the political process. Clearly the most common individual policy-related activity is community organizing (24 percent), followed by general political advocacy and trying to influence local housing policy (15 percent) (Figure 11.2). As with the CEDAM surveys, very few organizations report voter education activities (2 percent). In the area of collaborative activities, nonprofits are most likely to engage in collaboration to provide policy advice to public officials and organizations (14 percent). Figure 11.3 presents the percentages of organizations that are "always" involved in specific political or policy efforts, or who view collaboration for specific purposes as being "very important." Participating in collaborative networks for the purposes of advocacy for underrepresented groups (40 percent) and to influence state (24 percent) and local (31 percent) housing policy are viewed as the most important activities. Political activity (1 percent) and voter education programs (2 percent) are very uncommon, and activity in the areas of environmental (2 percent) and social (9 percent) justice is also relatively rare. Thus, it seems clear that respondents place a great value on the importance of networks for policy-related activity but do not necessarily engage in such activities on an individual basis.

Statistically significant differences between secular and faith-based organizations in these activities and attitudes are presented in Table 11.5.[4] Leaders of secular nonprofits are more likely to agree that working with public officials is a good way to get the views of the organization represented in policy decisions. Faith-based nonprofits are more likely to engage in community organizing and social justice programs. Not surprisingly, FBOs are more likely to feel that government officials need to be more sensitive to values held by religious organizations active in the area of low-income housing.

Table 11.5

Political and Policy Activity (Nonprofit Housing Provider Survey) (in percent)

Focused on community organizing**

	Very involved	Somewhat involved	Not very involved	Not involved at all
Secular	.23	.26	.34	.16
Faith-based	.26	.49	.20	.06

Social justice programs*

	Always	Often	Sometimes	Seldom	Never
Secular	.05	.10	.14	.25	.46
Faith-based	.15	.09	.30	.06	.39

	Strongly agree	Agree	Neutral	Disagree	Strongly disagree
Working with public officials provides a way to make sure that the organization has its views represented in public policy decisions* Secular	.21	.56	.23	.00	.00
Faith-based	.17	.47	.23	.13	.00
Government officials need to be more sensitive to values held by religious organizations active in the area of low-income housing*** Secular	.04	.09	.66	.09	.13
Faith-based	.17	.43	.33	.07	.00

***Difference significant at the .01 level, **.05 level, *.10 level based on difference in means tests.

Figure 11.1 **Percent Strongly Agree with Statements about Policy Activity**

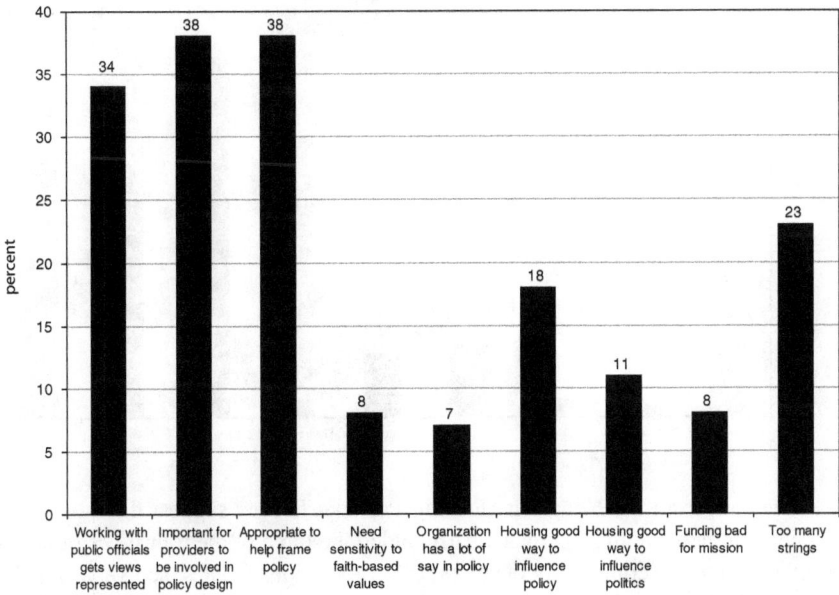

Figure 11.2 **Percent Very Involved in Policy or Political Activity**

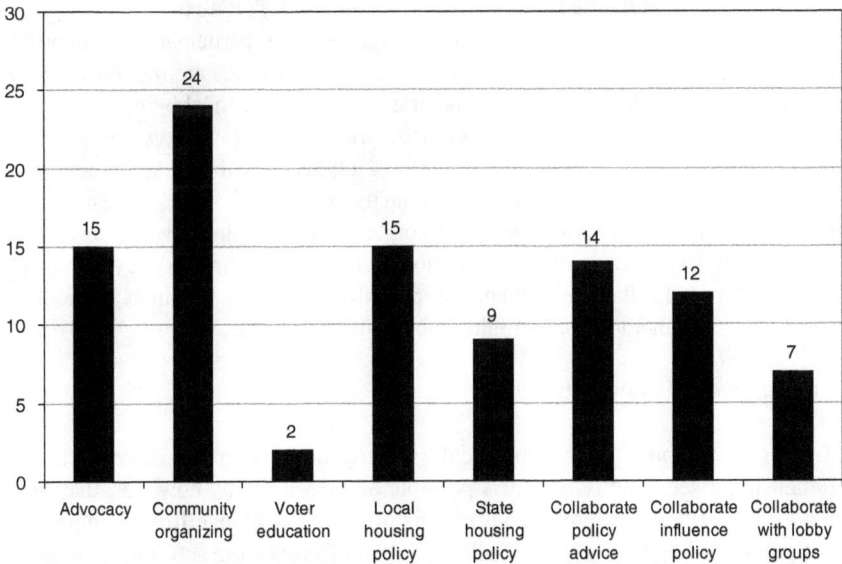

Figure 11.3   **Percent Always Engaging in Policy or Political Activity**

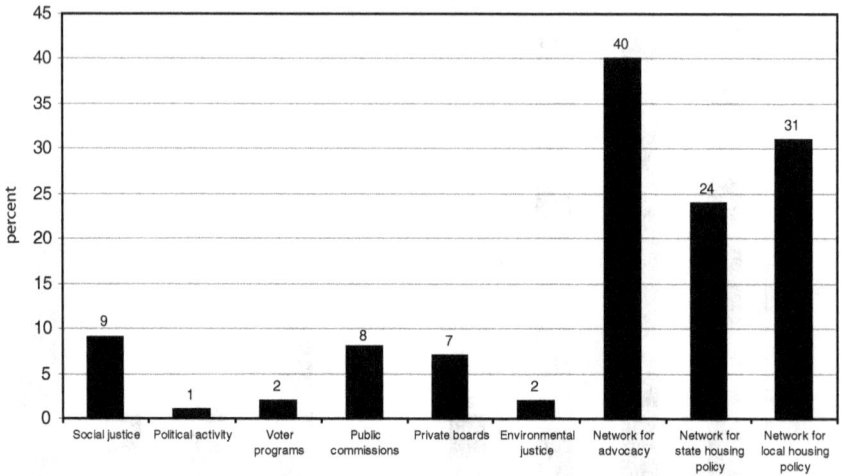

The data from the Nonprofit Housing Provider Survey suggest that nonprofits engaged in housing in Michigan clearly undertake three of the four types of advocacy attributed to community development corporations (CDCs; see Table 2.7) by Goetz (1992). First, they engage in externally based advocacy through their efforts to influence state and local policy makers. To the extent that they are successful in these endeavors, the entire community is empowered by enhanced access to decision makers and the resources that they control. By engaging in community organizing, housing nonprofits also undertake internally based advocacy, which can result in the empowerment of individual members of the community. To the extent that nonprofits are involved in social justice and related programs, they participate in community interest advocacy that can help ensure that community needs are met (see Figures 11.1 through 11.3). It is likely that collaborative activities with lobbying groups may also enable nonprofits to engage, even if by proxy, in the fourth type of advocacy common among CDCs, organizational survival advocacy. In this instance, nonprofits can secure their organizational position within the community and stabilize resources, if they lobby for programs to support their organization, housing development activities, or both. Even when nonprofits are not intentional in their advocacy efforts, the mere existence of collaborative relationships with lobbying organizations, particularly CEDAM, gives them the opportunity to be politically active.

The Nature of Policy Activity

To this point "policy" and "political" activity have been presented as a one-dimensional set of activities. It is possible and even likely, however, that these represent distinctly different kinds of pursuits. For example, efforts to impact the design of housing policy may be substantively different from activities to increase voter registration and participation among underrepresented groups. To explore the nature of policy and political activity further, the policy and political questions just discussed were entered into a factor analysis to determine whether there are conceptually different types of activities. Three distinct factors emerge (Table 11.6). Eight questions or activities load on the same factor: engaging in policy advocacy; influencing local and state policy; collaborating to influence local and state policy; perceiving that it is important for service providers to be involved in policy design; perceiving that it is appropriate for such organizations to help frame policy; and perceiving that the particular organization has a say in policy design. All focus on influencing the nature of housing and other public policies.

The activities loading on the second factor are more focused on direct political or electoral action and include: voter education, registration, and turnout programs, and social and environmental justice programs. They focus on assisting individuals in making the political system work for them and emphasize fairness and equity. The focus on electoral politics implies a greater comfort level with political competition, whereas the policy-related activity in the other factor is likely to be focused on lobbying or influencing legislation once political officials are in place. Two of the questions load on a third factor: agreement that housing provision leads to greater influence in housing policy and in other policy areas. This reveals an explicit belief that participating in housing can lead to influence or power in the larger policy or governing system. The survey questions loading on each of the factors were combined to create three separate indexes of policy and political activity. Respondent scores on each index were calculated using standardized scores (f-scores).

Although they represent three conceptually different foci, two of the three factors are significantly correlated (Table 11.7). Nonprofits high on policy-related activity are also significantly more likely to engage in political activity and have leaders that believe that service provision can lead to policy power. There is no significant correlation between political activity and perceptions that housing can lead to policy influence, however. Thus, while policy and political activity are clearly related, they still represent two conceptually different emphases.

Correlates for each type of policy and political activity are shown in Table 11.8. While the general pattern of correlates is similar across types of policy and political activity, there are also some important differences. Most of the similarities relate to the collaborative relationships of nonprofits high on the policy and political indexes. Thus, the collaborative networks are similar for these two types of activities, yet their other correlates differ.

Policy Activity

Policy-related activity is significantly correlated with both foundation and corporate funding; organizations with such funding are significantly more engaged in policy-related activity. Nonprofits focused on policy input are significantly more likely

Table 11.6

Rotated Factor Matrix Political/Policy Activity
(Nonprofit Housing Provider Survey)

	Policy activity	Political activity	Housing is power
Involved in policy advocacy	**.58**	.41	.17
Involved in influencing local policy	**.84**	8.912E-6	.03
Involved in influencing state policy	**.79**	.05	.13
Goal of collaboration is influence local policy	**.79**	−.07	.32
Goal of collaboration is influence state policy	**.77**	.04	.17
Important for providers to be involved in design and implementation of housing programs	**.73**	.22	.08
Appropriate for housing providers to help frame public policy	**.68**	.33	.09
Organization has a say in creation of state/local housing policy[a]	**.59**	.02	.52
Involved in voter education programs	.04	**.86**	.08
Involved in political activity programs	.29	**.50**	−.02
Involved in social justice programs	.24	**.67**	−.10
Involved in voter registration/turnout programs	.01	**.93**	.09
Involved in environmental justice programs	−.02	.19	−.08
Housing provision leads to housing influence	.16	.12	**.91**
Housing provision leads to general influence	.18	.10	**.92**

[a]While this statement loads on two factors, the stronger relationship is with policy activity. Further, it more logically goes with questions about the organization itself rather than with the more philosophical views about whether housing can lead to power and influence.

Table 11.7

Correlation Matrix for Alternative Political Activities

	Policy activity	Political activity	Housing is power
Policy activity	1.00		
Political activity	.31**	1.00	
Housing is power	.41**	.12	1.00

**Significant at 0.05 level.

to serve senior citizens, families, and low-income individuals on a citywide basis. Also, they increased their housing activity between 2003 and 2007. Nonprofits more engaged in policy activity are significantly more likely to collaborate with all types of organizations, from mental health agencies to those organizations in the private sector. They also collaborate on a broad spectrum of activities, including service provision and organizational and neighborhood development.

In addition to policy activity, these nonprofits are significantly more engaged in associated housing services, ownership services, housing construction and

Table 11.8

Correlation Matrix (Nonprofit Housing Provider Survey)

	Policy activity	Political activity	Housing is power
Organizational characteristics			
Faith/secular[a]	−4.02	−1.91	−1.67
Older age	.03	.33***	−.02
Resources	.46***	.25	.24
Funding source			
Religious	.16	.24**	.17
Donations	.15	.13	−.02
Foundation	.24**	.18	.09
Corporate	.24**	.05	.00
Government	.13	.10	−.04
Bank	.05	−.04	−.12
Population served			
Own members	.14	.31***	−.04
Senior citizens	.43***	.23**	.14
Inner-city	.08	.30***	.04
Families	.35***	.03	.11
City-wide	.28**	−.06	.04
Regional	.15	.09	.18
Neighborhood	.11	.26**	−.16
Specific race	.00	.37***	−.37***
Low income	.36***	.17	.17
Religion	−.03	.20	−.30**
Locations[a]			
Region 2: Northern	−1.18	−2.10	−.14
Region 3: Southwest	−3.35	−.03	−.94
Region 4: Central	−.34	−3.28	−2.78
Region 5: Southeast	−.44	−.50	−.80
Region 6: Detroit	−.53	−11.47***	−2.57
Types of housing services and changes in housing activity			
Housing activity change	.40*	.30***	.30***
Associated housing services	.34***	.21	.31***
Ownership services	.30***	−.05	.02
Build housing	.31***	.04	−.02
Multifamily housing	.34***	.12	.39***
Types of community (nonhousing) activities			
Social services	.42***	.47***	.26**
Youth services	.17	.69***	.06
Economic development services	−.24*	.10	−.21
Land development	−.23*	.04	.02
Collaborate with			
Social service organizations	.54***	.33***	.25**
Mental health organizations	.41***	.29***	.31***
Local government	.34***	.15	.18

(continued)

Table 11.8 *(continued)*

	Policy activity	Political activity	Housing is power
State government	.41***	.04	.21
Civic organizations	.25**	.09	−.10
Neighborhood	.23**	.25**	.04
Religious organizations	.23**	.28**	.09
Ethnic organizations	.23**	.38**	.15
Schools	.27**	.37***	.09
Hospitals	.31***	.47***	.22
Private sector	.46***	.26**	.17
Collaborates for			
Services	.52***	.33***	.32***
Organizational development	.45***	.33***	.27**
Neighborhood development	.26**	.24**	.04

[a]Chi squares are used to determine the relationship between this variable or set of variables and the policy indexes because the independent variables are dichotomous. Scores on the indexes are collapsed into low, medium, and high activity in thirds.
   ***Difference significant at the .01 level, **.05 level

renovation, multifamily housing, and social service provision. They are less likely to be engaged in economic development services and land development. Not surprisingly, nonprofits more engaged in policy activity have higher levels of resources in the form of budget, staff, and volunteers, probably allowing them to engage in a greater range of service activities.[5] This analysis again asserts that policy-related activities are a function of the type and nature of the organization, its funding sources, the population it serves and local service issues it engages in, the location of the organization, and the nature of collaborations that it participates in. The relative importance of these individual types of factors is measured in the following regression model:

Policy-Related Activity = **F** (**Organizational Characteristics, Funding Sources, Population Served, Local Service Engagement, Location, Collaboration**)

$$Y = \alpha + \beta_1 OC_{1i} + \beta_2 FS_{2i} + \beta_3 PS_{3i} + \beta_4 LSE_{4i} + \beta_5 L_{5i} + \beta_6 C_{6i} + \varepsilon_i$$

Where: Policy activity measures the organization's involvement, broadly, in policy advocacy at the state and local levels (see the policy activity factor in Table 11.6);
   Local service engagement is measured in the 2007–2009 Nonprofit Housing Provider Survey by involvement with a set of housing activities and a set of community (nonhousing) activities; and
   Collaboration includes both the type of collaborator and reason for collaboring.

Table 11.9

Regression: Policy Activity

	B	S.E.	Beta	Significance
Organizational characteristics				
Resources	.18	.12	.17	.11
Funding source				
Funding from nongovt sources	−.09	.10	−.09	.38
Population served				
Serves seniors	.14	.10	.15	.14
Serves citywide	.05	.07	.06	.52
Serves poor/families	.09	.10	.09	.36
Type of housing services				
Associated housing services	−.11	.12	−.12	.37
Build housing	.13	.11	.13	.24
Build multifamily housing	.09	.09	.10	.31
Ownership services	.03	.10	.03	.81
Housing activity change	.17	.08	.20	.03
Type of community activities				
Social services	−.08	.13	−.09	.54
Economic development services	−.10	.09	−.11	.27
Land development services	−.21	.10	−.23	.04
Type of collaborator				
Government collaborators	.20	.09	.21	.03
Neighborhood collaborators	.05	.10	.05	.63
Health collaborators	−.10	.13	−.11	.45
Reason for collaboration				
Collaborate for services	.17	.11	.18	.12
Collaborate for organizational dev	−.01	.11	−.02	.89
Collaborate for neighborhood dev	.08	.09	.08	.40
Constant	−.76	.27		.01
Multiple R^2 = .54				
N = 96				

A similar model is posited for political activity, where the dependent variable is a factor score generated by a factor analysis of voter education efforts, registration and turnout programs, political activity programs, social justice programs, and environmental justice programs (see Table 11.6). Again, only those variables significantly correlated with the dependent variables in bivariate analysis were included in the regression.

Most of the relationships noted in Table 11.8 for policy activity disappear in multiple regression analysis. Those that remain are associated with housing activity (Table 11.9). Only higher levels of housing construction and renovation, less land development activity, and collaborating with government actors remain significantly correlated to policy activity in multiple regression. This suggests that the most critical determinants of policy-related activity for these organizations are higher levels of housing activity, specifically related to brick-and-mortar projects as opposed to services. Taken together, all of the independent variables account for 54 percent of the variation in policy activity.

Table 11.10

Regression: Political Activity

	B	S.E.	Beta	Significance
Organizational characteristics				
Age	.10	.00	.27	.00
Funding source				
Religious	−.20	.15	−.11	.17
Population served				
Serves own members/seniors	.06	.09	.06	.48
Serves inner-city residents	.07	.07	.10	.28
Serves specific neighborhood	.00	.10	.00	.99
Location				
Region 6-Detroit	.41	.19	.21	.01
Housing activity involvement				
Housing activity change	.08	.07	.08	.28
Type of community activities				
Social services	−.21	.12	−.20	.08
Youth services	.56	.09	.55	.00
Reason for collaboration				
Collaborate for services	−.02	.10	−.02	.81
Collaborate for organizational dev	.13	.09	.13	.15
Collaborate for neighborhood dev	.13	.09	.13	.14
Type of collaborator				
Neighborhood collaborators	.06	.10	.05	.58
Health collaborators	.08	.11	.08	.47
Constant	−.61	.56		.28
Multiple R^2 = .63				
N = 98				

Political Activity

Organizations engaged in more political activity are significantly more likely to be in the city of Detroit. They tend to serve their own members, seniors, inner-city residents, specific neighborhoods, and specific races. Thus, compared to those nonprofits engaging in policy-related activity, the more politically oriented nonprofits are more insular and local in their client base. These organizations also increased their housing services between 2003 and 2007, and tend to be older, better established nonprofits.

Organizations focusing on political activity are more likely to collaborate with all types of organizations, except local and state government and civic organizations. This suggests that their relationship with government may be more adversarial than is the case for the more policy-focused nonprofits. When they do collaborate, they do so for services, organizational development, and neighborhood development. Nonprofits focused on political activity do not engage in as broad an array of other activities. They are, however, more likely to provide social and youth services. Age, location in Detroit, and the provision of youth services remain significantly

Table 11.11

Regression: Housing Is Power

	B	S.E.	Beta	Significance
Population served				
Serves specific race	−.21	.09	−.23	.02
Serves specific religion	−.36	.14	−.25	.01
Housing activity involvement				
Housing activity change	.20	.08	.22	.02
Type of community activities				
Social services	−.05	.15	−.05	.77
Type of collaborators				
Social service collaborators	−.03	.14	−.03	.81
Mental health collaborators	−.01	.11	−.02	.90
Associated housing services	.07	.13	.09	.50
Multifamily housing	.20	.10	.21	.04
Reason for collaboration				
Services	.25	.13	.24	.06
Organizational dev	.06	.11	.06	.57
Constant	1.63	.65		.01
Multiple R^2 = .35				
N = 95				

related to political activity in a multiple regression model (Table 11.10); the entire model accounts for 63 percent of the variation in political activity.

Perceptions of Housing as Power

Perceptions that housing service provision can lead to political power are related to relatively few organizational variables. Respondents from nonprofits that serve a single race or religion are less likely to feel that housing provision can lead to political influence. This may be due in part to the organization's marginalization (perceived or real). Increasing housing provision, however, increases perceptions that housing is power. Respondents who feel that providing housing leads to policy influence come from organizations that are more likely to collaborate with social service organizations and mental health agencies and to collaborate for services and organizational development. These organizations are more engaged in associated housing services, multifamily housing, and social services.

Table 11.11 reports a regression analysis in which the dependent variable is the perception that involvement in housing services provides an avenue for influencing policy. Four variables remain significantly correlated with the dependent variable, all related to populations served or housing activity involvement. Nonprofits not serving a specific race or religion and those with increasing housing activity and more multifamily housing tend to have respondents who think that housing can lead to policy influence. The complete model accounts for 35 percent of the variation in the dependent variable.

Modeling Policy and Political Activity

As noted earlier, the aim of this chapter is to test the theories and models presented in Chapter 1. Specifically, the goal is to determine whether service-related activity by nonprofit organizations is an avenue to participation in the policy networks and governing regime of cities, regions, and states. By receiving public funding to provide housing services, do nonprofits gain membership in service networks that translates into political power within larger governing circles? The analysis in this chapter indicates that there are conceptually different aspects to governing or engagement within the policy apparatus. There is activity directed at affecting public policy and activity directed at impacting the composition of governing bodies—hence the distinction between policy and more expressly political activities of nonprofits. Data from the statewide survey of nonprofit housing providers clearly show that there are few significant differences between secular and faith-based organizations in the state of Michigan for most of these policy and political activities. Indeed, faith status is not included in any of the multiple regressions explaining policy or political activity. Hence, the following discussion focuses on all nonprofits without distinction between faith or secular status.

Figure 11.4 presents a detailed listing of indicators used to test the models presented in Chapter 1. Specifically, two models are posited: the first hypothesizes that faith-based nonprofits deliver services only, and the second outlines a process by which faith-based nonprofits gain access to the larger political system *because* of their service activities. The analysis that has been presented to this point does not support any claim that faith-based and secular nonprofits engage the political system in different ways. This does not address the issue of whether nonprofits in general use access to public funding as a path to broader political participation. Based on the analysis presented over several chapters, it seems clear that there are important connections between the nature of nonprofits, their service roles, the types of networks in which they participate, and their ultimate policy and political activities.

Central concepts employed to understand these connections include: organizational traits, services, linkages, and governing activity (see Figure 11.4). Organizational traits available for analysis include: faith or secular nature, region of location, resources (staff, budget, volunteers), nature of funding (public sector, traditional banks, or "other" sources), age of organization, and the types of clients served (neighborhoods, poor families, seniors, or larger regions). The service indexes include four types of primary housing services (associated services, construction and renovation, ownership services, and multifamily construction and management) as well as a number of ancillary services (general social services, youth services, economic development, and land development). While many types of organizations are involved in networks with nonprofit housing providers, factor analysis was used to reduce that number to three primary linkage complexes: the community complex, including neighborhood, civic, and educational organizations; the

Figure 11.4 **Theoretical Model**

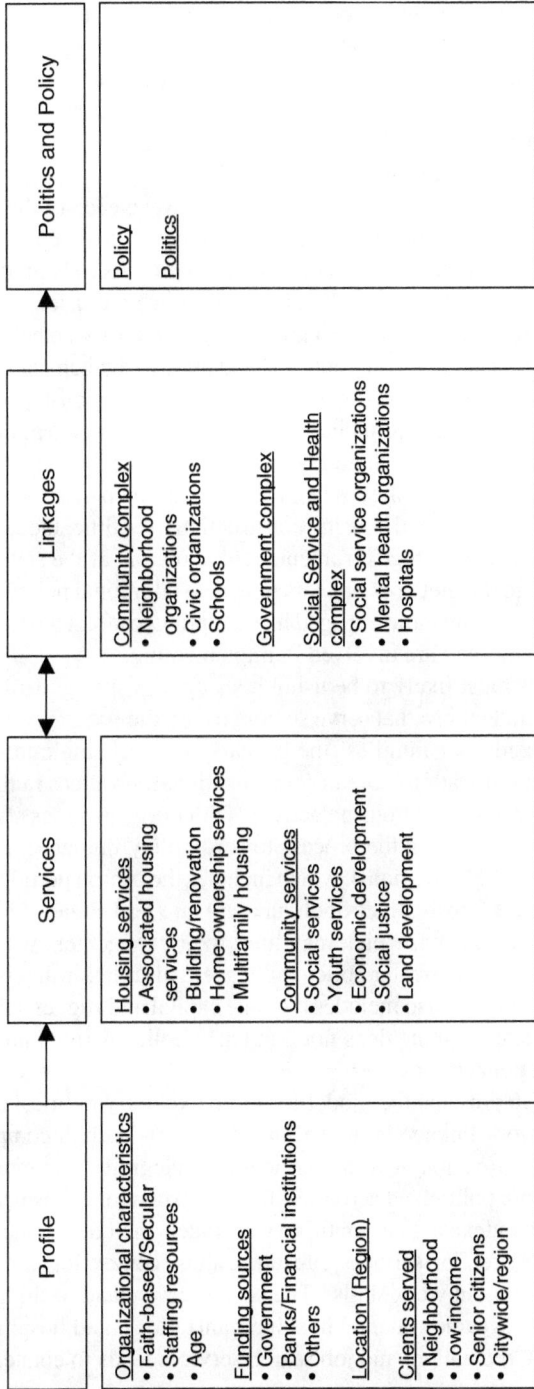

Profile	Services	Linkages	Politics and Policy

Profile

Organizational characteristics
• Faith-based/Secular
• Staffing resources
• Age

Funding sources
• Government
• Banks/Financial institutions
• Others

Location (Region)

Clients served
• Neighborhood
• Low-income
• Senior citizens
• Citywide/region

Services

Housing services
• Associated housing services
• Building/renovation
• Home-ownership services
• Multifamily housing

Community services
• Social services
• Youth services
• Economic development
• Social justice
• Land development

Linkages

Community complex
• Neighborhood organizations
• Civic organizations
• Schools

Government complex

Social Service and Health complex
• Social service organizations
• Mental health organizations
• Hospitals

Politics and Policy

Policy

Politics

government complex; and a social services and health complex including mental health agencies, hospitals, and general social service organizations.[6] Finally, the primary governance variables are the policy and political activity indexes described earlier in this chapter. Since the power index is primarily perceptual, based on how respondents see the effects of their policy activities, it is not used as a central outcome variable in this analysis.

Earlier chapters have explored linkages between each of the major conceptual variables. Here, an effort first is made to identify possible associations between organizational traits and particular service activities. As a result of engagement with the public sector in the form of funding and service provision, broader service and policy linkages are identified. Finally, the question of whether such services and policy linkages lead to greater political and policy engagement is explored. Figure 11.5 presents the model portraying the significant relationships for policy-related activity. All nonprofits are included, since there is no indication that faith-based and secular organizations should be analyzed separately due to variations in their behavior.[7] The path to policy-related activity on the part of nonprofits appears to operate through increased housing construction over time. Indeed, this brings non-profits into contact with governmental collaborators at the state and local levels. Involvement in that network appears to lead to additional policy-related activities, as nonprofits become more engaged in attempting to affect the state and local housing policies that they are involved in implementing.

Nonprofits most likely to be using housing as a springboard to general policy influence include those that serve seniors (often the focus of multifamily housing complexes) and poor families (the primary focus of single-family housing construction and renovation). Greater organizational resources in the form of budget and staff allow for more housing activity. Older organizations also are more active in housing, thus starting the process toward policy influence. Finally, nonprofits located in CEDAM's Region 4, which includes the central portion of the state (most prominently the Lansing metropolitan area), are less engaged in the construction of multifamily housing, which may limit their engagement with the government networks that lead to greater policy influence. This relationship is somewhat ironic given that the region also includes the state capital and suggests that physical proximity to legislators alone does not guarantee policy activity absent other service and network connections.

Figure 11.6 presents the model for more explicitly political activity. Here, the primary network linkage is the social services and health complex. Not surprisingly, it is the provision of youth services that integrates a nonprofit into a network leading to more politicized activities. It is important to reconsider what is included in these two indexes. The youth service index includes: educational activities, provision of recreation services, substance abuse counseling, assistance in locating jobs, and training in work skills.[8] The social service and health network includes: social service agencies, mental health organizations, and hospitals. Thus, a focus on education, recreation, and job search services leads to connections with social

Figure 11.5 **Policy Activity**

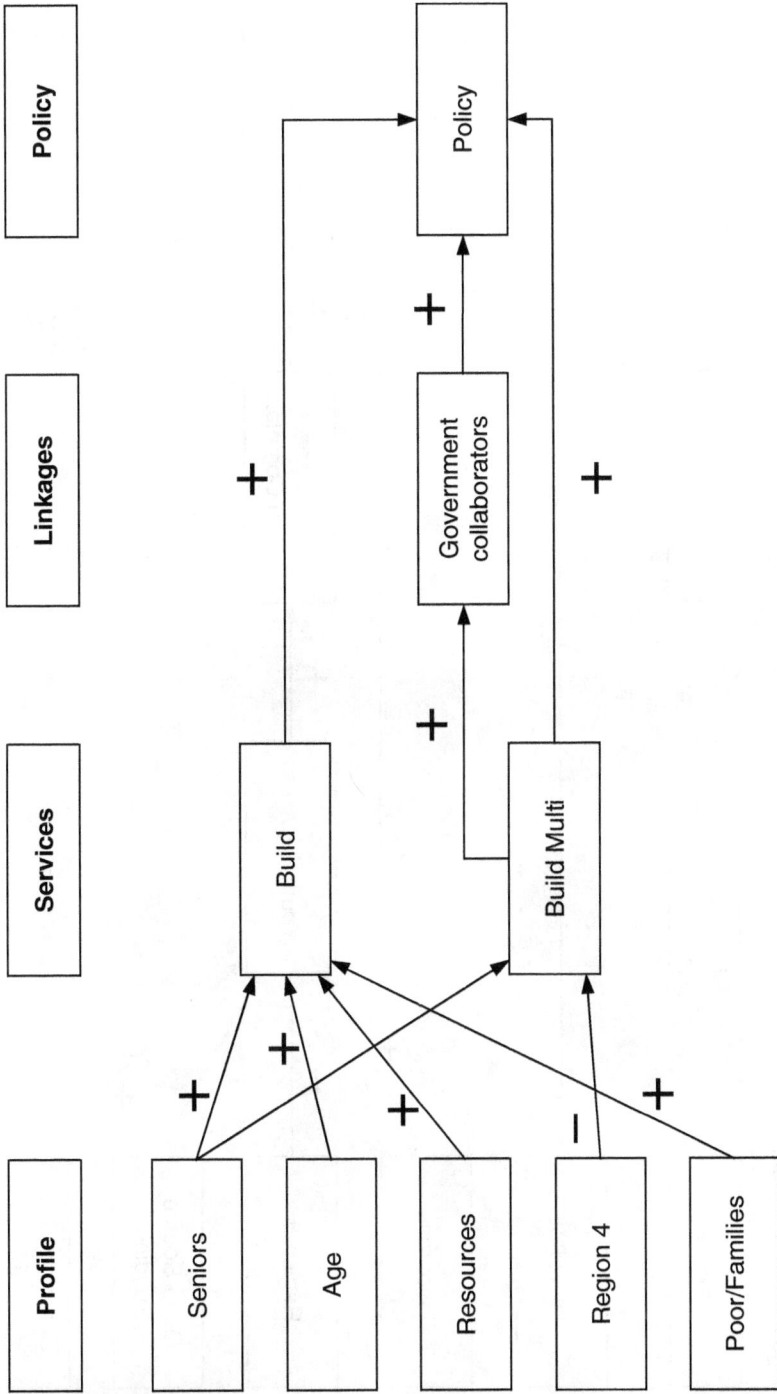

302

Figure 11.6 **Political Activity**

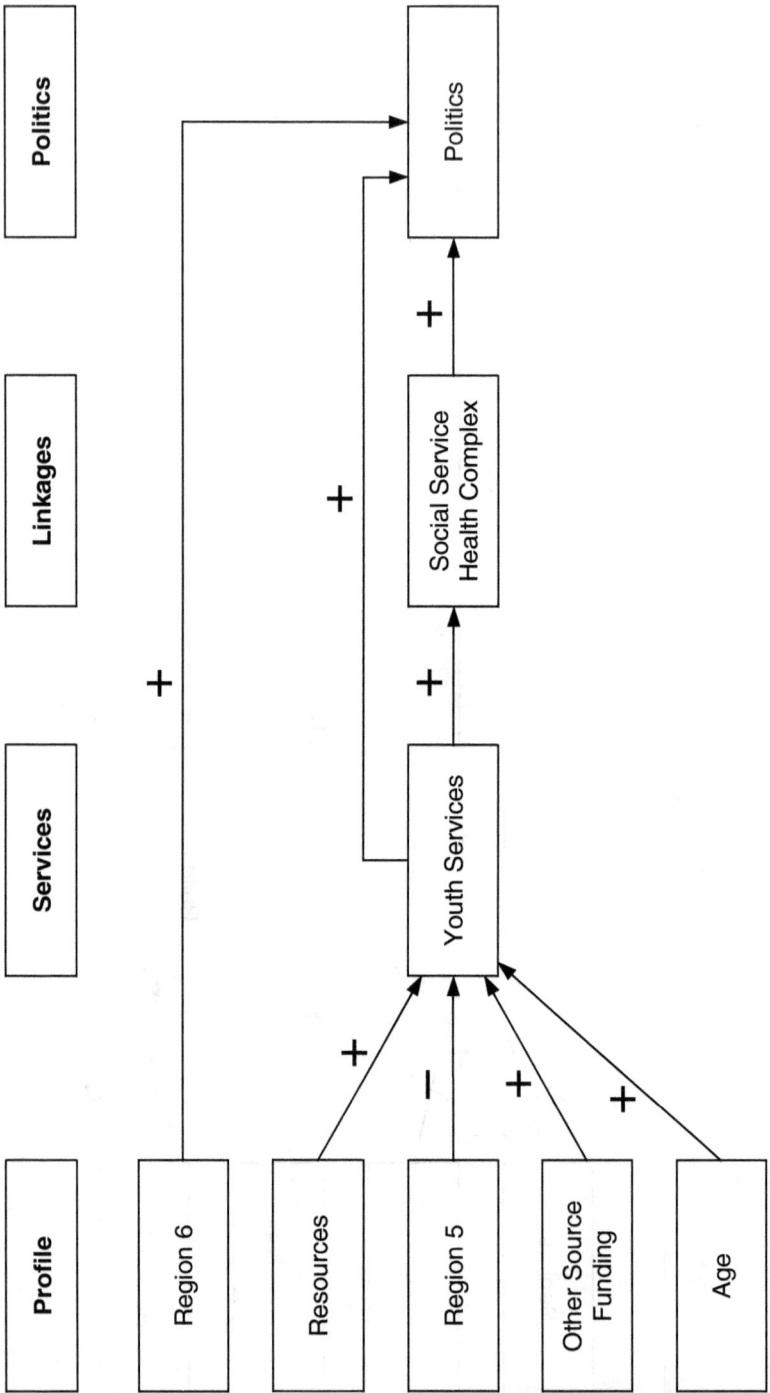

| **Profile** | **Services** | **Linkages** | **Politics** |

services agencies, while a focus on substance abuse logically places nonprofits in mental health and hospital networks.

The profile of nonprofits most likely to be engaged with the provision of youth services includes those with greater resources and those that have been in existence longer, characteristics that are also important for policy-related activity. Having sources of funding not dependent on the public sector is a central trait of nonprofits providing youth services, as well. These sources include individual donations, foundations, religious support, and corporations. Nonprofits in Region 5, which includes southeastern Michigan, excluding the city of Detroit, provide lower levels of service to youth. Finally, it should be noted that nonprofits located within the city of Detroit are more likely to be engaging in political activity. This is a direct relationship, not dependent on either services or networks.[9] While the faith nature of nonprofits does not appear critical to these relationships, it is useful to note that Detroit has the largest contingent of faith-based nonprofits in the state. The network analyses presented in Chapter 9 clearly show the important role of faith-based nonprofits in that city. It can be posited that the political traditions of many black churches and the nonprofits they establish can be seen in the greater political focus of nonprofits in Detroit (Brown and Brown 2003; Wald 2003; Hula et al. 2007). These traditions, apart from particular service provision roles, may be leading to greater political engagement.

Overall, service provision and governing network linkages are important in the ultimate policy and political activities of nonprofits. Different activities and networks are important for policy-related and more directly political activities, however. Housing provision and ties to public sector networks are essential to the larger policy activities of nonprofits. For political activity, the provision of broader youth-related services as opposed to housing activity and linkages to networks involved in those services appear to lead to greater politicization on the parts of nonprofits. In both cases, organizational resources and time in existence as well as regional location appear to drive the service provision process. For policy activity, the nature of clients served is important, and for political activity, the funding source is an important driver.

Summary

The most critical finding from the analysis of policy and political activity in this chapter and in the preceding chapter on collaboration is that service provision does indeed appear to provide nonprofits an entrée into the larger civil society. Clearly housing-related activities and services remain the primary focus of nonprofits. Furthermore, their primary collaborative relationships are directed toward enhancing their capacity to serve clients and communities. Yet despite some apparent hesitation to report collaboration for more political purposes, nonprofits do engage in policy-related and governing activities. With the exception of nonprofits in Detroit, there are no apparent differences in civic activity between secular and faith-based nonprofits in these respects. Thus, service delivery is not a path toward membership in governing regimes solely for FBOs; rather it is a mechanism for nonprofits of all types to gain greater access to the political system for both the organization and its clients. The case of Detroit suggests that in large cities, with many African American FBOs, service delivery may represent a particularly potent mechanism for faith-based organizations to gain a seat at the governing table.

More specific findings from this chapter include:

- Civic or governing activity has two conceptually different components: efforts to influence public policy and those directed at affecting who is elected to political office. The former is more common among nonprofits in Michigan than the latter.
- Once a nonprofit engages in one or two types of governing activities, it tends to embrace a full array of policy and political activity.
- Resources appear particularly important in affecting the level of civil activity; political and policy activity seem to be the purview of nonprofits with higher capacity levels.
- Relatively large numbers of nonprofit respondents believe that it is important and appropriate for their organizations to be involved in the design of policy, but they are cautious about the strings associated with public financing and question their effectiveness in influencing policy.
- Participation in networks of organizations to attempt to influence public policy is more common than individual nonprofit activity.
- More activity in housing construction appears to lead to greater effort to influence housing policy.
- A focus on youth-related services appears particularly important in generating greater political activity among nonprofits.
- Providing service to senior citizens and poor families appears to contribute to increased policy activity.
- Collaboration with public sector actors is important in policy-related activity, while working with social service and health organizations is related to political activity.

The final chapter summarizes findings, revisits initial theories and research questions, and summarizes the conditions under which the faith nature of the nonprofit does make a difference. Most importantly, it provides conclusions and forecasts about the current and future roles of nonprofit organizations in service delivery and governing the civil society.

Notes

1. Indicates t-test computed with group variance not assumed to be equal across groups, based on result of Levene's Test for Equality of Variances.
2. The 2007 CEDAM survey did not assess collaboration. Therefore this factor is not

included in the current analysis for policy activity; it is, however, taken into consideration for the Nonprofit Housing Provider Survey. For the 2007 CEDAM survey only, an assessment of organizational structural considerations is also included under organizational characteristics and is a measure of whether the organization considered a merger or dissolution.

3. The various measures of organizational resources are highly intercorrelated. Factor analysis indicates that the following are part of a single concept describing "organizational resources":

Factor Loading	
Budget	.96
Full-time staff	.97
Part-time staff	.84

Funding sources are not included in the regression analysis here because all are highly correlated with the resource index. To reduce multicollinearity, only the resource index is used.

4. Respondents from secular and faith-based nonprofits are significantly different on only four of the 29 items on the survey related to policy.

5. These variables are included in the resource index described in Chapter 7, which includes budget, staff, and volunteers.

6. Linkage factors used here include:

Governmental complex	Local government	.90
	State government	.69
Neighborhood complex	Religious organizations	.81
	Ethnic organizations	.69
Social service and health complex	Schools	.61
	Neighborhood associations	.51
	Social service agencies	.50
	Mental health agencies	.88
	Hospitals	.56

7. These models do not represent linear regressions per se. The linear regression analysis yielded models that were far too complex and obscured the more critical relationships in the data based on theory and prior analysis. Thus the models used here were created as follows: the multiple regression results for policy and political activity were used to identify the central correlates of those two dependent variables, and those variables or indexes were included in the model. The bivariate correlates of the linkage and service variables were also then included. Complete linear regression results are available from the authors upon request, but we are confident that the models presented here include all critical relationships. The directions of the relationships were based on correlation coefficients or crosstabs from previous analyses already presented.

8. Prior analyses include voter registration activities in this index as well; however, it is excluded from the analysis in this chapter, since it is reflected in the political activity index used here.

9. This finding is consistent with a great body of literature that describes Detroit politics as highly polarized and fragmented (See Rich 1989; Widick 1989; Digaetano and Klemanski 1999; Jelier and Hula 1999; Farley et al. 2000).

References

Brown, R.Khari, and Ronald E. Brown. 2003. "Faith and Works: Church-Based Social Capital Resources and African-American Political Activism." *Social Forces* 82(2): 617–641.

Chaves, M., L. Stephens, and J. Galaskiewicz, 2004. Does Government Funding Suppress Nonprofits' Political Activity? *American Sociological Review* 69(2): 292–316.

Digaetano, Alan, and John S. Klemanski. 1999. *Power and City Governance: Comparative Perspectives on Urban Development.* Minneapolis: University of Minnesota Press.

Farley, Reynolds, Sheldon Danziger, and Harry J. Holzer. 2000. *Detroit Divided.* New York: Russell Sage Foundation.

Goetz, Edward G. 1992. Local Government Support for Nonprofit Housing: A Survey of U.S. Cities. *Urban Affairs Quarterly* 27(3): 420–435.

Hula, Richard C., Cynthia Jackson-Elmoore, and Laura A. Reese. 2007. Mixing God's Work and the Public Business: A Framework for the Analysis of Faith-Based Service Delivery. *Review of Policy Research* 24(1): 67–89.

Jackson-Elmoore, Cynthia. 2005. Informing State Policymakers: Opportunities for Social Workers. *Social Work* 50(3): 251–261.

Jelier, Richard W., and Richard C. Hula. 1999. A House Divided: Community Politics and Education Reform in Detroit. *Urban Review* 31:3–29.

LeRoux, Kelly. 2007. Nonprofits as Civic Intermediaries: The Role of Community-Based Organizations in Promoting Political Participation. *Urban Affairs Review* 42(3): 410–422.

Rich, Wilbur C. 1989. *Coleman Young and Detroit Politics: From Social Activist to Power Broker.* Detroit: Wayne State University Press.

Silverman, Robert Mark. 2008. The Influence of Nonprofit Networks on Local Affordable Housing Funding: Findings from a National Survey of Local Public Administrators. *Urban Affairs Review* 44(1): 126–141.

Smith, Steven Rathgeb, and Daniel J. Evans. 2001. Nonprofit Organizations in Urban Politics and Policy. *Policy Studies Review* 18(4): 7–26.

Wald, Kenneth D. 2003. *Religion and Politics in the United States,* 4th ed. Lanham, MD: Rowman and Littlefield.

Widick, B.J. 1989. *Detroit: City of Race and Class Violence.* Detroit: Wayne State University Press.

12

Nonprofits, Service Provision, and Governing the Civil Society

Nonprofit organizations involved in the provision of housing operate in a complex network of relationships and collaborations. Overall, the service delivery roles of nonprofits bring them inexorably in contact with governing political institutions. Even those organizations eschewing public financing must deal with rules and regulations established by federal, state, and local governments. No nonprofit provides services in a vacuum. Capacity constraints force most nonprofits to interact with other organizations—public, private for-profit, and nonprofit—to provide services, respond to clients, enhance resources, and ultimately to engage the policy and political processes. While the faith nature of nonprofits clearly matters in how nonprofits provide services and interact with the public sector, the impact of faith orientation is rarely simple or straightforward. Generally, the nature of other organizations within collaborative networks is more important than the faith status of an individual nonprofit. The role of faith in service provision is more complex, and perhaps more limited, than much of the extant literature has suggested.[1] This chapter will proceed with a summary of findings and then explicitly revisit research questions posed in Chapter 1. The alternative models of the role of faith-based nonprofits will also be explored.

Summary of Major Findings

Past research on faith-based nonprofits shows that they fulfill important service and community development roles. Their success is often seen to be a function of the fact that they tend to be present in the neediest communities, have long histories of providing support and services for the downtrodden, and offer the potential power of faith to motivate their activities. Nonprofits in general are seen as a viable and even preferable option to inefficient and expensive public institutions. Yet their full potential as service providers may be limited by deficits in budgets, professional staff, skills, and experience. Faith-based nonprofits (FBOs) in particular must thus engage a broad array of other organizations. Partners include funders such as banks, foundations, government, and a host of other entities that can range from other faith-based and secular nonprofits to educational institutions, social service agencies, and health care providers.

Faith-based and secular nonprofits differ in how they interact with the public sector and levels and quality of services provided. Faith-based nonprofits are more likely to embrace a holistic approach to their service provision, treating many aspects of individual and family circumstances rather than a narrow set of goals. Moreover, they focus on those communities and individuals most in need of services. Those FBOs that are publicly funded limit the amount of faith incorporated into their service provision. FBOs seldom operate alone; there have been significant ties between faith-based and secular nonprofits and the public sector in service provision going back decades.

Since the late 1800s, nonprofits have had important roles in the creation and maintenance of low and moderate-income housing. Clearly, nonprofit involvement in the provision of such housing is not a new event. Yet the service role of nonprofits and faith-based nonprofits in particular has broadened over time. The perceived legitimate scope of such services has expanded with an increasing commitment to the housing plus services model. In addition, faith-based initiatives of the Bush administration (subsequently supported by the Obama administration) have expanded the pool of public resources available to nonprofit organizations. Indeed, many nonprofits have now become dependent on such public financing to realize their service roles. Interactions between the public and nonprofit sectors go far beyond what is still relatively limited public funding, however. Efforts to provide low- and moderate-income housing interact to form a complex system that includes federal, state, and local political institutions, private sector actors, and a wide array of nonprofit organizations.

The review of Michigan nonprofits reveals that low-income housing and assistance, housing renovation, owner-occupied housing, and home-ownership counseling are the most common housing services provided. While most nonprofits do not provide a single service but focus on several housing-related activities or service components, there appears to be a significant specialization among nonprofits in the nature of housing services provided. Differences between organizations often fall along a build-versus-service continuum. Better resourced (specifically monetarily) nonprofits tend to focus on bricks and mortar, either building or renovating housing and housing units. Nonprofits with less capacity focus on services related to housing, such as home-ownership counseling.

Many aspects of nonprofits are significantly correlated with the type and amount of housing activities pursued. When such associations are tested in a multivariate regression model, however, the relationships often disappear. Resources in the form of budget and collaboration with other organizations to marshal resources are most consistently related to the provision of housing services. The only exception is for the provision of home-ownership services, which tend to be less costly. The primary variable driving the provision of home-ownership services is the need of clients, particularly the poor and families with children.

While the nonprofits included in this study were targeted because of their focus on housing, these organizations also engage in a number of other community-based social service and economic development activities. The provision of direct assistance to individuals and families is a common activity complementing housing efforts. Other activities include education, assisting other organizations or agencies, and working with public bodies on service provision. Emergency assistance and loans are also common. Fewer nonprofits report regularly engaging in political activities, service to immigrants, or environmental justice activities. The scope of nonhousing services provided by these organizations is again primarily a function of resources and the need to collaborate to gain additional resources. Resource issues are particularly critical to the provision of social services, social justice activities, and economic development. Collaboration for the purpose of influencing policy is particularly important to social justice and land development activities. Collaboration with the government is critical to social service provision. Issues related to resources, collaboration, and the nature of clients served tend to be more important than faith in variation in service type and level.

Numerous entities participate in the planning and provision of affordable housing, including state and local governments, community development corporations, faith-based entities, neighborhood associations, and other nonprofit and for-profit organizations. A key issue is how coordination and collaboration occur across and among this diverse set of stakeholders. Examples of some of the activities for which these organizations collaborate include brick-and-mortar projects like building or renovating single-family homes and rental property, as well as support services like home-ownership counseling and training, emergency assistance and temporary housing, and providing financial assistance to renters and home owners. On average, regardless of the task undertaken, nonprofits in the housing arena engage in a great deal of collaboration with social service organizations and local and state governments. Very few housing nonprofits collaborate with religious, advocacy, or civic organizations, however.

Two critical points regarding the nature of housing collaboration emerge: (1) almost all nonprofits, faith-based and secular, collaborate with other organizations and the public sector to provide services; and (2) the nature of these collaborative networks is diverse and complex but appears to vary by region of the state. Thus, the question is not whether nonprofits collaborate to provide service but rather with whom, how much, and for what purposes. With the exception of targeted partnerships with state and federal agencies, most of the collaboration for the delivery of housing services occurs at the local or regional level. Exploration of housing networks by region indicates three distinct models. In Detroit, city government is a partner with several faith-based organizations. In the Grand Rapids area, faith-based organizations partner more readily with the state housing authority, secular nonprofits, and other FBOs, rather than with the local government. In rural Northern Michigan, there are fewer faith-based organizations engaged in housing; those present, however, partner with other organizations to provide housing and related services. Regardless of the network, collaboration to provide services is more common than collaboration to influence policy or the political system, at least as a primary goal of the collaborative effort. Yet much more collaboration in these latter two areas is present than many nonprofits are willing to admit. While they seem more comfortable talking about collaboration for service purposes, their involvement in housing networks brings them into contact with larger efforts to influence the policy process and the decision makers who control it.

Housing nonprofits agree that providing housing services is an effective and appropriate way to become involved in the larger policy-making process. At the same time, these nonprofit leaders do not feel that their organizations have been particularly successful in these roles. The most common individual policy-related activity is community organizing, followed by general political advocacy and trying to influence local housing policy. Respondents place a great value on the importance of networks for policy-related activity, but do not necessarily engage in such activities on an individual basis. It is clear that there are important connections among the nature of nonprofits, their service roles, the types of networks in which they participate, and their ultimate policy and political activities.

Nonprofits that serve seniors and poor families are more likely to be using housing as a springboard to general policy influence than are other organizations. Greater organizational resources in the form of budget and staff allow for more housing activity. Older organizations are also more active in housing, thus starting the process toward policy influence. Overall, service provision and governing network linkages are important in the ultimate policy and political activities of nonprofits. Different activities and networks are important for policy-related and more directly political activities, however. Housing provision and ties to public sector networks are essential to the larger policy activities of nonprofits. For more political activity, the provision of broader youth-related services, as opposed to housing activity, and linkages to networks involved in those services lead to greater politicization on the parts of nonprofits. In both cases, organizational resources and time in existence as well as regional location drive the service provision process. For policy activity, the nature of clients served is important and for political activity, funding source is an important driver. Resources are particularly important in affecting the level of civil activity; political and policy activity are the purview of nonprofits with higher capacity levels. Collaboration with public sector actors is important in policy-related activity, while working with social service and health organizations is related to political activity.

Does Faith Matter?

The faith nature of the nonprofit has relatively little impact on the organization's behavior in the housing arena, at least in the state of Michigan. This finding is surprising given the extant literature and the enormous public debate.[2] In terms of organizational profiles—age, staff, volunteers, budget, funding sources, and client capacity—there are few differences among nonprofits based on their faith status. Yet there are still important and interesting variations depending on the variable of faith. FBOs have more volunteers and receive more of their funding from banks, corporations, individual donations, and religious bodies; secular nonprofits get more public funding. Although funding sources are different, overall capacity in terms of budget and staff is not significantly different. The number of clients served is similar. Faith-based nonprofits report needing more support in the technical aspects of housing provision and have more difficulties interacting with public agencies. FBOs also experience more problems with political and bureaucratic processes and barriers; they are particularly sensitive to the amount of red tape that often accompanies public funding. Secular nonprofits may be in a better position to interact with government, at least in the short run. On the other hand, because FBOs draw funding from a wider array of sources, often beyond government, they may be in a better position to withstand changes in the larger economy. Indeed, faith-based nonprofits are planning significantly greater housing provision activities in the future than is the case for secular nonprofits. For both types of nonprofits, there are many with resources constraints and a few with significant capacities for service provision. There is wide variation among nonprofits in their levels of capacity and resources, but very little of that variation appears related to faith.

FBOs report significantly more activity in the areas of new single-family, owner-occupied, and special needs housing. They also provide greater maintenance training and home-ownership counseling services and are more likely to engage in housing renovation. In short, where there are significant differences, faith-based nonprofits indicate higher levels of service. There are greater differences in the housing activities of faith-based and secular nonprofits than in the other types of activities in which they engage. Although not reaching statistical significance, there are relatively large differences between faith-based and secular nonprofits in food banks or community nutrition programs and after-school programs; faith-based nonprofits are more likely to provide all of these services, as well. Nonprofits are significantly different (at the .05 level) only for the development of microenterprises (secular) and business district development (faith-based). Faith nature of the nonprofit is also related to social service provision and social justice activities (with FBOs being more active). Receiving funding from religious sources is important in providing social services and social justice, and donations are important to land development activities. These correlations do not tend to hold up in multivariate regression, however, suggesting that variables other than faith are more important in explaining the amount and type of housing and housing services produced. For example, the nature of clients (poor families) is more important than faith in predicting levels of housing-related services. For multifamily housing, resources levels are more critical. There may be interactions between these variables and faith, however. FBOs are more likely to serve the poor and families and thus may be particularly driven to provide housing services to clients most in need.

While the differences in service provision between secular and faith-based nonprofits are quite modest, they do serve somewhat different client groups; specifically, FBOs are more likely to be providing housing and broader community services to inner-city residents, families with children, and low-income groups or individuals. This is extremely important because it supports past research suggesting that faith-based entities are more likely to serve those most in need. In light of the connections between service provision and policy and political input, this also implies that FBOs may be providing a critical link between poor communities and political authorities. The result could be an enfranchising of these communities. General trends over time suggest that while faith-based nonprofits tend to provide more social services, the social service activities of secular nonprofits are increasing, while FBOs appear to be shifting somewhat to economic development activities and investment in poor communities.

In comparison to secular organizations, FBOs are significantly more likely to collaborate with other religious organizations and neighborhood associations. For FBOs, social service agencies, private organizations, and advocacy organizations are most frequently noted as collaborators. For secular nonprofits, social service agencies have the most significant collaborations. Based on the above, it appears that a broader and more complex set of collaborations surround faith-based nonprofits. Perhaps related to this, faith-based nonprofits are more likely to view collaboration as a good in and of itself, while secular nonprofits very clearly view collaboration as a means to an end, typically to increase capacity or gain policy influence.

Faith-based nonprofits are significantly more likely to engage in community-organizing and social justice programs than are secular housing nonprofits. Not surprisingly, FBOs are also more likely to feel that government officials need to be more sensitive to values held by religious organizations active in the area of low-income housing. Leaders of secular nonprofits are significantly more likely to agree that working with public officials is a good way to get the views of the organization represented in policy decisions. Other than these differences, data from the statewide survey of nonprofit housing providers show few significant differences between faith-based and secular organizations for most policy and political activities. Indeed, faith status is not included in any of the multiple regressions explaining policy or political activity.

To provide a summary of the primary differences between faith-based and secular housing nonprofits, research questions posited in Chapter 1 specifically related to the faith nature of nonprofits are reintroduced next.

How do faith-based and secular nonprofit social service efforts compare, complement each other, and interact? What types of housing and community development activities are faith-based institutions pursuing?

Based on the Community Economic Development Association of Michigan (CE-DAM) surveys discussed in previous chapters, FBOs are more active in foreclosure prevention and counseling, and secular nonprofits are more active in land trusts, although this is not a major area of focus for either type of organization. Other areas of relatively large differences include single-family-ownership housing, individual development accounts (IDAs), and multifamily-ownership housing (FBOs are more active in all cases). Indeed, FBOs are more active in twelve of the twenty housing service areas included on the CEDAM surveys. Along with the FBOs' more ambitious future housing plans, these findings suggest that there may be an increase in the proportion of housing and housing services provided by faith-based nonprofits that appear to be slightly more stable or even expansive in their service activities. In the nonprofit housing provider survey, FBOs reported significantly more activity in the areas of new single-family, owner-occupied housing and special needs housing. They also report more maintenance training and home-ownership counseling services and are more likely to engage in renovation. Again, where there are significant differences, faith-based nonprofits are indicating higher levels of service. It seems clear, then, that faith-based nonprofits have a critical current and future role in the provision of housing services. Because of their propensity to participate in collaborations with other organizations to provide services and their tendency to view such collaboration as a good in and of itself, they have an important place in the complex of actors and activities necessary to provide the housing service safety net.

A somewhat different picture emerges for broader community development activities, however. According to the CEDAM surveys, there are no significant differences among faith-based and secular nonprofits in the broader types of social service and community development programs offered. Arts programming comes closest to statistical significance, with faith-based nonprofits being more likely to offer such services. With the exception of crime prevention and cultural programs, FBOs are slightly more likely to offer social services. FBOs are more likely to operate for-profit businesses and are more involved in the formation and operation of business districts or main street development projects. Secular nonprofits are significantly more likely to develop microenterprises and appear more focused on crime-related activities. When prisoner reentry programs were added in the 2007 survey, it became clear that secular nonprofits are more likely to be offering such services. The general increases in social service and community development activity between the two CEDAM surveys appear to be the result of activity increases among secular organizations. In the Nonprofit Housing Provider Survey, there was only one significant difference between faith-based and secular nonprofits: FBOs are more involved in the delivery of general services; nevertheless, faith-based and secular organizations are not significantly different in the frequency with which they provide any individual service. These findings together suggest that there are more differences in the nature of housing services between faith-based and secular nonprofits than there are for broader community development or social services.

Secular and faith-based nonprofits do have distinctly different client bases, suggesting that they are complementary service providers with different missions. Specifically, FBOs are more likely to be providing housing and broader community services to inner-city residents, families with children, and low-income groups or individuals. Although only significant at the .10 level and not common among secular or faith-based nonprofits, FBOs report offering more services to religiously based groups. Thus, as has been suggested in some of the literature, it seems that FBOs may be filling a public service gap by providing services to individuals most in need.

How are faith-based services financed and organized? What is the extent of public sector funding? How does it affect the nature and extent of service activities?

Secular nonprofits receive more public funding, while faith-based nonprofits are more likely to be getting funding from a greater variety of sources. Overall, their staffing and budget profiles are very similar. Receiving more funding from the government is positively associated with the provision of general social services and associated housing services, but is not related to policy or political activity. As a general rule, the amount of funding from sources other than the government is more strongly related to services and policy activity than public funding per se.

What is the extent of collaboration between faith-based organizations, other nonprofits, and local governmental institutions in service provision?

There is extensive collaboration between faith-based and secular organizations and between both types of nonprofits and government entities. FBOs do not appear to be particularly insular in their linkages, and networks include faith-based and secular organizations. FBOs do work with religious and ethnic organizations more often than their secular colleagues, however. There are no differences in their propensities to collaborate with public sector agencies or governments.

Does the provision of public services appear to correlate with or lead to greater integration of FBOs in local governing processes?

The answer to this question is "yes," but these connections do not differ between faith-based and secular nonprofits. Providing housing and other social services brings faith-based nonprofits in contact with the civil society in ways that include policy-related and more expressly political activities.

Testing Alternative Models

The overall purpose of this project was to test two theoretical positions about faith-based public service provision: (1) that FBOs represent additional, potentially more effective, capacities for providing services than secular organizations, and that they would focus on that role without further integration into the political or governing system; and (2) that the service provision role of faith-based nonprofits would provide an avenue into the larger policy and political system, thus opening the possibility that FBOs would become integrated into governing regimes in the civil society. A corollary of this model is that FBOs would indeed take this opportunity to become involved in the governing system. If the latter theory is more realistic, then the public service provision role of faith-based entities and nonprofits potentially raises questions about the separation of church and state.

As described in Figures 1 and 2 in Chapter 1, both theoretical models begin with the same set of assumptions or relationship paths. First, it is hypothesized that the organizational profile and capacities will affect the quantity and quality of services provided by a nonprofit. This is clearly supported by the Michigan case. The most important organizational traits in determining the nature of housing and other community services appear to be, not surprisingly, resources. Those nonprofits with greater budgets and paid staff (volunteers cannot substitute for these factors) are able to provide a wider array of services and are more likely to move beyond housing provision to larger community services, as well as political and policy activity. Budget is more important for the construction of housing projects, while staffing is vital for the more labor-intensive services associated with housing support. Geographic location is also important, with location in the city of Detroit most influential in both service and policy activity. Age of the nonprofit also enhances services, since it provides more experience, resources, and capacities for service provision. Finally, the nature of the primary clients served by the nonprofits—which could be interpreted as mission—is also consistently related to the extent and nature of services provided. Focusing on the poor, families with children, and senior citizens is most likely to define the types of services provided and indeed the nature of policy and political activity.

As noted, the faith nature of the nonprofit is not particularly important in affecting services. Yet there are some interesting differences. The primary differences between faith-based and secular nonprofits appear to be: (1) in the clients they serve—FBOs tend to focus on the most needy populations; (2) funding sources—secular nonprofits are most likely to rely on government funding, while FBOs have a more diverse set of funding sources; (3) capacity needs—FBOs appear to have greater problems in dealing with government regulations and processes; and (4) plans for future housing activity—FBOs envision greater housing activity and also appear to be moving into larger economic and community development activities. Overall, where there are service differences, it is the faith-based nonprofits that most often provide the higher level of services, although differences tend not to rise to statistical significance. The variation between faith-based and secular nonprofits thus suggests that there is current, and probably future, untapped capacity within FBOs for the provision of public services, but that they are not fully integrated into public funding systems and face greater challenges in dealing with governmental processes, rules, and regulations.

The next step in both Figures 1.1 and 1.2 predicts that activity in public housing provision will lead nonprofits to form collaborative linkages with other organizations. The logic here is simple: individual nonprofits are unlikely to have sufficient capacities to meet their public service goals, whether those are related to housing services, the construction of housing, or broader community and policy initiatives. Nonprofits will thus be motivated to collaborate with other organizations to meet their particular goals and missions. Because client base seems so important, it is likely that nonprofits consider the needs of their clients in conjunction with their own capacities and determine what aspects are lacking: monetary resources, service capacity, skills, political connections, and so on. These capacity deficits then cause the nonprofit to seek partners or a network of partners to accomplish their mission. Such partners would include the government, but also other nonprofits, social service agencies, schools, churches, health care providers, and so on.

As Chapters 9 and 10 clearly revealed, there are high levels of collaborative linkages among nonprofits in Michigan. All of the nonprofits collaborate with at least one other organization to meet their goals. Further, the general pattern is to collaborate with a number of other organizations, rather than just one or two, suggesting that collaborative networks are more prevalent than random incidences of linkage. Most organizations are collaborating to achieve at least one of these service delivery–associated goals: avoiding redundancy and increasing efficiency, receiving and referring clients, and expanding existing programs or starting new ones. And, as suggested in the figures, the nature of services is correlated with the purposes of collaboration and the nature of collaborators in primarily logical fashions. Thus, for example, organizations focused on the provision of social services tend to work with others that focus primarily on meeting service-related needs: social service and mental health agencies, schools, and hospitals. They collaborate to provide services and influence public policy. Nonprofits with community development missions tend to collaborate with neighborhood groups and community development corporations.

Collaborative networks have significant regional variations. While there are many faith-based nonprofits involved in the housing provision network in Detroit, there appears to be little coordination among them. Much like the city's political process, the system appears to be highly fragmented. Although the city government clearly has a significant role in the network, no single organization acts as a coordinator. The linkage system in the Grand Rapids area is quite different. There are fewer faith-based nonprofits in the service provision system, but two central FBOs act as pivotal coordinators for the other nonprofits and local government, which has a smaller role than in Detroit. Service provision linkages in northern Michigan again reflect the nature of the region. Because the area is more rural, government agencies such as the USDA become important actors in the housing network. Fewer faith-based nonprofits are involved in the provision of housing, and secular nonprofits and the public sector have a larger role. This regional variation appears to have much to do with the rural or urban nature of the environment, the number of faith-based nonprofits, and the larger governing culture of the area. The fragmented and competitive Detroit political environment appears to spill over into the linkage system of nonprofits. In Grand Rapids, the more homogeneous and conservative environment appears to encourage the development of a well-organized or more systematic network with connections through a small number of very well-established faith-based nonprofits. Whether the Detroit system, with more numerous but fragmented FBOs, or the Grand Rapids system, with fewer but more organized FBOs, leads to more political or governing influence for faith-based entities is an important question that will be discussed shortly.

A central theoretical question asked whether collaborative linkages reported by nonprofit respondents did, in fact, exist. In general, respondents are relatively accurate in their reporting of collaboration. In most cases, those that report greater need for collaboration do collaborate at higher levels. The most important inconsistency, however, was an underreporting of collaborations for the purposes of affecting public policy and influencing electoral officials. It appears that while nonprofits are uncomfortable with collaboration to achieve public policy influence, they are actively engaging in it. There is very little difference between faith-based and secular nonprofits in this regard.

The final, and most critical, aspect of the theoretical models, and the primary difference between models 1 and 2, is whether or not existing service delivery linkages are tied to broader policy and political involvement. The findings indicate that the primary motivation for working with other organizations is to provide service. Once networks are in place, however, collaboration is broadened to include policy-related activity. In other words, while policy or political activity is clearly not the central mission or motivating force for service nonprofits, many engage in such activity as an outgrowth of their public service roles and the linkages formed through the provision of services. Hence Figure 1.1, "The Anti-FBO Argument: Service Delivery Activity Leads to Political or Policy Engagement by FBOs," represents the prevailing model in the state of Michigan. The most common policy-related activities are community organizing, political advocacy, and trying to influence local housing policy. Nonprofits are most likely to engage in collaboration to provide policy advice to public officials and organizations. Participating in collaborative networks for the purposes of advocacy for underrepresented groups and to influence local housing policy are also viewed as important.

Efforts to influence the nature of public policy, particularly related to housing and general community organizing activities, are more common than more explicitly political efforts to register individuals to vote or promote social or environmental justice. Faith-based nonprofits are more likely to engage in community organizing and social justice programs than are secular housing nonprofits, however. This suggests that FBOs are more politicized. This appears to be particularly the case for Detroit-based FBOs. Indeed, there is also a significant correlation between receiving funding from religious organizations and political activity. While this could be related to the governing environment in Detroit, it could also be a function of the greater prevalence of African American FBOs in that city. Because the survey did not ask about the racial composition of nonprofit membership or clients, however, this suggestion is only speculative.

The building of housing (as opposed to housing-related services) and collaboration with housing and social service organizations are particularly important in bringing nonprofits into the policy system. A focus on youth services—such as educational activities, provision of recreation services, substance abuse counseling, assistance in locating jobs and job search, and training in work skills—and collaborations with mental health and service organizations are related to more expressly political activities. Again, these latter connections are strongest for Detroit nonprofits.

It is clear that there are important connections among the services provided by nonprofits, the collaborative networks they create, and policy and political activities as suggested in Figure 1.1. It should be noted, however, that while the models are presented as linear, causal directionality is ultimately unclear. The relationship between services and linkages is particularly complex. Why an organization chooses to collaborate, what other organizations they collaborate with, and what services are provided are difficult to identify sequentially. Do nonprofits decide they want to provide housing services, realize they need additional resources or capacities available in other actors, select their partners, and through those partnerships, work to affect housing policy? Or, are service and policy activity determined conterminously as a function of the need for collaboration and the particular set of organizations collaborating? The Michigan case argues that collaborations developed for the primary purpose of enabling service provision often lead nonprofits into greater contact with the political system, increasing their influence because of the importance of their service roles and the power of their collaborative networks.

Revisiting Central Research Questions

In addition to testing the two theoretical models, a number of other research questions were presented in Chapter 1. Each of these is now revisited.

Are the same types of organizations active in housing and community development activities?

While most nonprofits do not appear to specialize in just housing services or particular housing services, there are a few significant correlations between housing activities and broader community development services and activities. Nonprofits that provide more associated housing services and build more housing are more likely to be providing social services generally. Those providing more associated housing services also provide more youth-related training and education services. Finally, nonprofits more actively engaged in building and renovating housing are more likely to engage in land development activities. In short, there is variability in the types of organizations active in housing and community development.

Do capacity and funding attributes affect the propensity of service nonprofits to move into or strengthen their public policy roles?

There are several important links between the capacity, particularly in terms of budgetary resources, of nonprofits and their public policy activities. Nonprofits with larger budgets and more staff engage in more policy-related activities. Receiving more funding from corporations and foundations also appears to enhance policy activity. Serving senior citizens and low-income families is positively associated with policy activity, while a focus on inner-city neighborhoods and specific races is positively associated with political activity. This may say something about the dynamics of the more politicized nonprofits in Detroit. Again, racial composition in the local environment and of the nonprofit itself may impact political activity. The historical-political traditions of many African American churches and congregations may be enhancing the governing role of faith-based nonprofits in the Detroit environment.

How important are collaborative networks in making the service–policy influence connections? Do specific types of networks enhance the civic and policy roles of nonprofits?

Collaborative networks are critically important for nonprofits. Linkages forged as a result of capacity needs for housing provision appear to spill over into policy-related activity. A mission to serve the housing needs of poor families through the construction and renovation of housing leads organizations into networks with other housing and social service organizations. These linkages then appear to enhance activity in influencing housing policy and organizing communities and residents. A greater focus on education, training, and counseling promotes linkages with mental health and social service organizations and is connected to more expressly political activities, such as voter registration drives and efforts to promote social and environmental justice. Again, specific and varied networks provide nonprofit organizations with access to civic and policy roles.

Are particular types of nonprofits more prone to become active in policy arenas? Or are particular service profiles, for example housing plus services, more likely to enhance engagement with the policy process?

While both the nature of the nonprofit organization and its service profile are related to policy activity, multivariate analysis shows that the type of services provided is a more reliable predictor of policy activity. Housing construction is most important in promoting policy-related activity, while the provision of youth services is most strongly related to political activity. In short, services matter.

Are there differences between faith-based and secular nonprofits in their desire for and success in translating service activity into political and policy influence?

There are some significant differences between faith-based and secular nonprofits in their political activities and in their attitudes about engaging the larger political system. Faith-based nonprofits are more likely to engage in community organizing and social justice programs. FBOs are also more likely to feel that government officials need to be more sensitive to values held by religious organizations active in the area of low-income housing. Leaders of secular nonprofits more often agree that working with public officials is a good way to get the views of the organization represented in policy decisions, implying that they view their efforts in this regard as being more successful. While such differences are present when specific aspects of policy or political activity are considered, when indexes of activities are used, the relationships between faith nature and policy activity disappear. This implies that the services provided and the linkages and collaborations developed are more important than the faith nature per se in determining the governing role of nonprofits.

Do the service activities of faith-based nonprofits provide access to the local civic arena, giving them a place in urban governing regimes?

The answer to this question is "yes," but the access is not specific to faith-based nonprofits; it also applies to secular nonprofits. Providing public services brings nonprofits into the policy and governing arena. To the extent that the role of faith-based nonprofits in the civil society is of particular concern, then the reality that service provision leads to policy and political activity is of importance.

Nonprofits and the Civil Society

Perhaps the most striking finding reported here is the similarity of faith-based and secular nonprofits. While important differences have, of course, been noted, there seem not to be as many as conventional wisdom would lead us to expect. Does this imply that faith simply does not make much of a difference? The Michigan case counsels caution and provides evidence that the distinction between secular and faith based is, in fact, important. Consider three critical areas where faith does matter: clients served, expectations for future service levels, and the value placed on collaboration. If faith-based nonprofits serve those most in need in terms of both housing and potentially larger political representation, represent an increasing service force, and place higher value on working with other organizations, the relative long-term growth potential of faith-based nonprofits may be significant. Just how much FBOs might be able to expand their service output, and whether the government can facilitate that expansion, are critical policy questions. Increased capacity for faith-based nonprofits may lead to more service to those most in need and hardest to serve. Such an expansion in service delivery may also enhance the governing role of faith-based nonprofits. The result may be an expansion of the debate about the appropriate role of faith-based organizations in a predominately private housing sector.

Comparing the roles of secular and faith-based nonprofits leads to another critical policy issue. What can one say about the relative quantity and quality of housing services provided by secular and faith-based organizations? While self-reported data on output and personal assessments of outcomes were included in the surveys reported here, matching these perceptions to reality would provide a useful check, as well as allowing for the comparison of faith-based and secular service quality. Use of comprehensive state housing data, grant information, and client surveys and interviews would greatly enhance understanding of the role of nonprofits in the housing sector.

There remains much to learn about faith-based organizations in the American political process. What is clear, however, is that these organizations play an important role in the design and delivery of publicly financed goods and services. Moreover, there is strong evidence that such organizations will play an increasingly important role in American civil society. Whether this expansion is something to be nurtured and supported or actively constrained defines one of the complex challenges in contemporary American politics.

Notes

1. Of course, efforts to generalize to all nonprofits on the basis of housing activists must be viewed with caution. This study did not include large FBOs that are most well known for service provision outside of housing. For example, Catholic Charities, Lutheran Social Services, and the Salvation Army were largely ignored. Services provided by congregations or congregational networks have also not been included.

2. Once again, it is important to note the limitations of the study. This study did not include large FBOs that are most well known for service provision outside of housing. In addition, a number of religiously affiliated organizations active in efforts to address homelessness were excluded.

Appendix A
Methodology Appendix

Appendix A1. 2003 CEDAM Survey

CEDAM

Present

mittac
Michigan Training &
Technical Assistance Collaborative

Michigan CDC Accomplishments Survey 2003

Community Economic Development Association of Michigan in partnership with the Michigan Training and Technical Assistance Collaborative asks that you PLEASE take the time to answer all questions on this survey that apply to your organization. Please skip any questions that are not relevant to your organization.

We understand that you are very busy, and for this reason, we have combined questions that pertain to services and interests of all organizations in the MITTAC Collaborative so that we are sure not to overburden you with multiple surveys this year. This survey aims to collect accurate and complete information in order to produce a report that demonstrates the accomplishments of community development organizations across Michigan. In addition, information collected from this survey will assist us in determining the need for training and technical assistance. Thank you very much in advance for your participation.

Confidentiality: We will not reveal any information in this report that identifies the name of the organization without first obtaining permission to do so.

Return Instructions: Please complete this survey and mail, fax or email as an attachment by **the extended deadline of Friday, December 19, 2003 to:**

CEDAM
Attn: Sage Hales
1000 South Washington Avenue, Suite 101
Lansing, MI 48910
Phone: (517) 485–3588 • Fax: (517) 485–3043
hales@cedam.info

Follow-up calls: CEDAM staff may also contact you to set up an appointment to complete this survey over the telephone. If you would prefer to do the survey over the phone, please contact Sage Hales at (517) 485–3588 x141 to set up a time to do so.

Electronic Version: Electronic versions of this survey (both pdf and word files) are available online at www.mittac.org if you need additional copies or if you prefer to fill the survey out in word. You may email completed surveys to hales@cedam.info.

Questions? If you have any questions regarding the survey please do not hesitate to contact Sage Hales at (517) 485–3588 x141.

Drawing: Each organization that completes and returns this survey will automatically be entered into a drawing to win a $100 gift certificate to Home Depot!

Resulting Report on Data Collected: An electronic version of the resulting report will be sent to each organization that completes and returns the survey.

Thank you! We appreciate your work in community development and your participation

CEDAM CDC Survey 2003

Organization Name: _____

Executive Director: _____

Name of the person filling out survey: _____

Title: _____

Address: _____

City: _____ State: _____ Zip: _____ County: _____

Email: _____ Phone: _____ Fax: _____

Section I: General Organization questions

1) Organization year of inception: _____

2) Is your organization: 501 (c) (3)   other (please list): _____

3) What is your annual budget: $ _____

4) Has your organization received CHDO status?   ☐ Yes   ☐ No   ☐ In the process of obtaining

5) Please list all names, titles and hours of each of your current staff people (attach another sheet of paper if necessary):

Name	Title	Full or Part Time?		Receiving Benefits?	
		☐ Full	☐ Part	☐ Yes	☐ No
		☐ Full	☐ Part	☐ Yes	☐ No
		☐ Full	☐ Part	☐ Yes	☐ No
		☐ Full	☐ Part	☐ Yes	☐ No

6) What hurdles do you face as a non-profit in the housing arena in building capacity and growing? (i.e. operating dollars, staff turnover, land costs etc.)

_____

_____

_____

_____

7) What financing institutions do you use?

8) What types of funding sources, if any, are you having trouble accessing?

9) When participating in the local planning process, what barriers have you encountered in relation to your development projects (i.e. lot size requirements, etc.)?

Section II: Legal Questions

1) What percentage (out of 100%) of the legal services rendered to your organization have been provided by each of the following?

- Private attorney paid market rate _____ %
- Private attorney paid reduced rate _____ %
- Legal services provided free of charge _____ %

2) What is your annual budget for legal services? $_____

3) For the legal services that were provided free of charge, please list the service provided and the name of the attorney, firm or organization that provided the services:

Legal Services Provided: _____ Attorney, Firm or Organization Providing free Legal Services:

_____

_____

_____

_____

Section III: Training and Technical Assistance Questions

1) What types of Technical Assistance do you need in the area(s) of:

- Housing development? _____

- Community or neighborhood planning? _____

- Commercial development? _____

- Commercial strip revitalization? _____

2) What barriers are you encountering in obtaining assistance? _____

3) How much do you typically spend each year on technical assistance for planning and development activities? $ _____

4) What type of training do you need in the areas of:

- Housing development? _____

- Community or neighborhood planning? _____

- Commercial development? _____

- Commercial strip revitalization? _____

5) What barriers are you encountering in obtaining assistance? _____

6) How much do you typically spend each year on training for planning and development activities? $ _____

7) Please list the name of any consultants that you have used within the past 2 years and what types of assistance they have provided:

Consultant Name / Organization	Type of assistance provided	Satisfied?
		☐ Yes ☐ No
		☐ Yes ☐ No
		☐ Yes ☐ No
		☐ Yes ☐ No

8) Please check the areas in which you would like to see a Certification Program established in Michigan:

☐ Board & Staff Development   ☐ Asset Management   ☐ Financial Management
☐ Housing Development   ☐ Human Capital & Community Building   ☐ Fund Development
☐ Commercial, Industrial, & Public Facilities Dev   ☐ Strategic & Business Planning

9) How often do you visit the Michigan Training and Technical Assistance Collaborative (MITTAC) website at www.mittac.org? Please check one:

☐ Weekly   ☐ Monthly   ☐ Once a quarter   ☐ Never

10) Please list suggestions to improve the MITTAC website:

Section V: Programs or Activities

1) Please check the programs or activities in which your organization is currently involved:

Housing Development	Business Development	Social Services	Other
☐ Rental Housing	☐ Commercial Development	☐ Day Care	☐ Mixed use development
☐ Cooperative Housing	☐ Industrial Development Incubator	☐ Summer Camp Youth Programs	☐ Energy Conservation
☐ Home Ownership	Development		☐ Community Reinvestment Act (CRA)
		☐ Drug Abuse Counseling	☐ Other (please write in):
☐ SRO Housing	☐ Operate a Business	Teen/Parent Counseling	
☐ Elderly Housing	☐ Brownfield Redevelopment	☐ Landlord/Tenant Mediation	
☐ Housing for people w/AIDS	☐ Small Business Loan Program	☐ Crime Prevention	
☐ Housing for people with disabilities	☐ Small Business Technical Assistance		
☐ Single Family Housing	☐ Micro Enterprise Development	☐ Cultural Programs/Centers	
☐ Small Residential	Business District/Main Street Revitalization	☐ Arts Programs	
☐ Large Residential		☐ Voter Registration	
☐ Scattered Site		☐ Advocacy	
☐ Land Trust		☐ Homeownership	
		☐ Counseling	
☐ HOPE VI		☐ Leadership Training Job	
☐ Lead Paint Abatement		Counseling/Job Training	
☐ Asbestos Removal			
☐ Condos for lease to own			

Section VI: Production Numbers

Please complete the following tables that apply to your organization. The "existing" tables request information on the most recent development that your organization has completed. The "future" tables request information on any development projects that your organization is currently in the process of producing.

Table 1: Existing Housing Development / Current Portfolio

Project Name	# Units	Sq. Ft.	Year Dev.	Total Dev. Cost $	Construction Type (New, Acquisition/ Rehab)	Type of Housing (Single Family, Multi Family)	Target Population	Major Financing Sources

Table 2: Future Housing Development (in the process of production)

Project Name	# Units	Sq. Ft.	Year Anti-cipated	Proj. Dev. Cost $	Status	Construction Type (New, Acquisition/ Rehab)	Type of Housing (Single Family, Multi Family)	Potential Financing Source(s)	Partners/ Collaborators	Target Population

Table 3: Existing Commercial, Industrial & Community Facility Development

Project Name	# Units	Gross Sq. Ft.	Year Dev.	# Tenants	# Perm. Jobs	Total Dev. Cost $	Type of Development	Financing Source(s)

Table 4: Future Commercial, Industrial & Community Facility Development

Project Name	# Units	Status	Year Anti-cipated	Proj. Dev. Cost $	Type	Gross Sq. Ft.	# Comm. Tenants	# Perm. Jobs	Potential Financing Source(s)	Partners/ Collaborators	Target Population

Table 5: Existing Mixed Use Development

Project Name	Year Dev.	Proj. Dev. Costs $	Const. Type	# Resid. Units	Gross Sq. Ft. Comm. Space	# Comm. Tenants	Descrip. Non-Resid.	Descrip. Resid. Space	Financing Source(s)	Collaborators

Table 6: Future Mixed Use Development

Project Name	Status	Year Anti-cipated	Proj. Dev. Costs $	Const. Type	Type of Develop.	# Resid. Units	# Comm. Tenants	# Perm. Jobs	Descrip. Resid. Space	Potential Financing Source(s)	Partners/ Collaborators

Table 7: Open Space Development (e.g. Parks, Playgrounds, Community Gardens, Greenways, etc.)

Site Location	Type of Space	Year Dev.	Sq. Ft./acres	Financing Sources

Table 8: Future Open Space Development

Site Location	Type of Space	Year Anticipated	Sq. Ft./acres	Potential Financing Sources

Please complete the following tables based upon your organization's activity within the past year.

Table 9: Home Improvement Loans

# Loans	Total $s Loaned	Total Units Improved	During What Year?

Table 10: Micro Business Development

# Businesses Provided Training	# Businesses Provided T.A.	# Loans	Total $s Loans	# Loans to Women / Minorities	During What Year?

Table 11: Small Business Development

# Businesses Provided Training	# Businesses Provided T.A.	# Loans	Total $s Loans	# Loans to Women / Minorities	During What Year?

Table 12: Housing Services-People Served Since Program Inception

# Received Landlord/ Tenant Mediation	# Received 1st Time Home Busy Pre-purchase Counseling	# Received 1st Time Home Busy Post-purchase Counseling	# Units Deleaded	Property Management

Table 13: Employment & Community Services-People Served Since Program Inception

# Received Job Counseling	# Received Job Training	# Job Linkages	# Youth received Services	# Received Daycare / After School	# Received Elder Services	# participated in Arts Program	# participated in Cultural Programs & Neighborhood Festivals

Appendix A2. 2007 CEDAM Survey

CEDAM

COMMUNITY ECONOMIC DEVELOPMENT ASSOCIATION OF MICHIGAN

UNITING PARTNERS TO REBUILD OUR COMMUNITIES

CEDAM INDUSTRY SURVEY
Asking the Community Economic Development
Industry to Stand Up and Be Counted!

This survey aims to collect accurate and complete information in order to produce a report that demonstrates the accomplishments of CEDAM members across Michigan. PLEASE take the time to answer all the questions on this survey that apply to your organization. Please skip any questions that are not relevant to you. Thank you very much in advance for your participation.

Where specific data is requested, the answer should reflect your Organization's activities in **2006 and 2007** (two years). Please provide your best estimate for any question for which you are unsure of an exact number.

CONFIDENTIALITY: CEDAM will not reveal any information from this survey that identifies the name of the organization without first obtaining permission to do so. All survey results will be presented in aggregate form.

RETURN INSTRUCTIONS and DEADLINE: Please complete this survey and mail, fax, or email to CEDAM by **AUGUST 31, 2007. Each organization that completes and returns this survey by the deadline will automatically be entered into a drawing to win a $100 gift certificate to a home improvement superstore!**

Return completed survey to:

CEDAM
Attn: Emily Doerr
1000 S. Washington Ave., Suite 101
Lansing, MI 48910
Phone 517.485.3588 • Fax 517.485.3043 • doerr@cedam.info

PLEASE COMPLETE THIS SURVEY AND RETURN IT TO
CEDAM NO LATER THAN
FRIDAY, AUGUST 31, 2007

ELECTRONIC VERSION OF SURVEY: If you need a clean copy or prefer to fill out the survey electronically, electronic versions (both Survey Monkey and .pdf files) are available online at www.cedam.info/IndustryReport2007. You may fax completed surveys to 517-485-3043.

FOLLOW UP CALLS: We need every one of CEDAM's community development corporation members to complete this survey and be counted! CEDAM staff will contact organizations that have not yet completed the survey to set up an appointment to complete this survey over the phone. If you would prefer to do the survey over the phone, please contact Emily Doerr at 517.485.3588.

RESULTING SURVEY REPORT: The resulting community economic development industry survey report will be sent to each organization that completes and returns this survey. In addition, CEDAM will use this report to advocate for the community economic development industry with policy makers, funders and others. We also hope it will help YOU to tell the vital story of the community economic development industry in Michigan.

CEDAM Industry Survey
Stand Up and Be Counted!

GENERAL ORGANIZATION QUESTIONS

Organization Name: _____

Executive Director: _____
How long has the Executive Director served the Organization in this capacity? _____

Name of Person Completing This Survey: _____

Title of Person Completing This Survey: _____

Address of Organization: _____

City: State: Zip: County:

Phone: Fax:

Web: E-mail:

Organization Year of Inception: _____

Is Your Organization   ❏ 501(c)(3)   ❏ Other (please list)

Has Your Organization received CHDO status? ❏ Yes   ❏ No   ❏ In the process of obtaining?

How would you characterize the community your Organization serves?
❏ Urban   ❏ Suburban   ❏ Rural

How many people currently serve on your Organization's Board of Directors? _____

What is your Organization's annual operating budget? $_____

Approximately how much money did your Organization invest in projects in 2006–2007? $

* Please provide an estimate for any number for which you are unsure of an exact number.

EMPLOYEES AND EMPLOYEE BENEFITS

How many <u>full-time</u> employees does your Organization employ today? _____

How many <u>part-time</u> employees does your Organization employ today? _____

Does your Organization employ <u>consultants/contract workers</u>?   ❐ Yes   ❐ No

    If so, approximately how many consultants/contractors does your Organization engage
    each year? _____

Does your Organization use <u>volunteers</u> (not including board members)?   ❐ Yes   ❐ No

    If "Yes," approximately how many volunteers each year? _____

Does your Organization provide <u>health insurance</u> for its full-time employees?   ❐ Yes   ❐ No

POLICY ADVOCACY

How would you describe your Organization's level of participation in <u>local</u> policy discussions?
❐ None   ❐ Rare, for specific activities   ❐ Some, a few times a year
❐ Substantial, active throughout the year

How would you describe your Organization's relationship with <u>local elected officials</u> and policymakers?
❐ None   ❐ Weak   ❐ Satisfactory   ❐ Strong

How would you describe your Organization's level of participation in <u>statewide</u> policy discussions?
❐ None   ❐ Rare, for specific activities   ❐ Some, a few times a year
❐ Substantial, active throughout the year

How would you describe your Organization's relationship with your <u>state elected officials</u> (e.g., state senators,
state representatives) and policymakers (e.g., MSHDA, DLEG, DHS, etc.)?
❐ None   ❐ Weak   ❐ Satisfactory   ❐ Strong

How would you describe your Organization's level of participation in <u>federal</u> policy discussions?
❐ None   ❐ Rare, for specific activities   ❐ Some, a few times a year
❐ Substantial, active throughout the year

* Please provide an estimate for any number for which you are unsure of an exact number.

PLANNING, SCHOOLS, TRANSPORTATION, AND ORGANIZATIONAL CHANGE

Is your Organization part of <u>a local (or regional) coalition or trade association</u> of similar organizations?
  ❏ Yes   ❏ No

Has your Organization <u>prepared a neighborhood plan</u> for the area you are working in?
  ❏ Yes   ❏ No   ❏ Working on one now

Has your Organization been <u>part of a local planning process</u> such as the development of your city's master plan?
  ❏ Yes   ❏ No   ❏ Working on one now

Has your Organization engaged in activities related to <u>local schools and/or the education system</u>?
  ❏ Yes   ❏ No

Has your Organization engaged in activities related to <u>transportation issues</u> in your community?
  ❏ Yes   ❏ No

Has your Organization engaged in a <u>partnership</u> to accomplish one or more of its projects?
  ❏ Yes   ❏ No

Has your Organization considered <u>merger and/or consolidation</u> with another organization?
  ❏ Yes   ❏ No

Has your Organization considered <u>dissolution</u>?   ❏ Yes   ❏ No

  If "Yes," why?   ❏ Funding   ❏ Staffing   ❏ No longer needed

  ❏ Other (please specify) _____

* Please provide an estimate for any number for which you are unsure of an exact number.

FUNDING SOURCES

Please check below any funding source from which your Organization has received funds in 2006 or 2007 (over the past TWO years). For those funding sources checked, please mark whether you receive operating and/or project funding from the source; whether the funding is a "substantial" (more than 20%) part of your annual budget; and whether your receipts from this funding source have increased or decreased since 2000.

Received Funding in 2006-2007	Funding Source	Type of Funding		Substantial (>20%) Source of Organization's Funding?	Support Organization has Received from Funding Source Since 2000		
		Operating?	Project?		Increased	Stayed the Same	Decreased
☐	Financial Institutions/Banks	☐	☐	☐	☐	☐	☐
☐	MSHDA	☐	☐	☐	☐	☐	☐
☐	Federal Home Loan Bank	☐	☐	☐	☐	☐	☐
☐	Federal Government/HUD	☐	☐	☐	☐	☐	☐
☐	City Government	☐	☐	☐	☐	☐	☐
☐	USC	☐	☐	☐	☐	☐	☐
☐	MI Interfaith Trust Fund	☐	☐	☐	☐	☐	☐
☐	Great Lakes Capital Fund	☐	☐	☐	☐	☐	☐
☐	Foundations	☐	☐	☐	☐	☐	☐
☐	Private Donors	☐	☐	☐	☐	☐	☐
☐	USDA	☐	☐	☐	☐	☐	☐
☐	CDBG	☐	☐	☐	☐	☐	☐
☐	UHTC	☐	☐	☐	☐	☐	☐
☐	HOME	☐	☐	☐	☐	☐	☐
☐	Earned Income from Business Entity(ies)	☐	☐	☐	☐	☐	☐
☐	Endowment	☐	☐	☐	☐	☐	☐
☐	Religious Institution(s)	☐	☐	☐	☐	☐	☐
☐	Other (Please Specify):	☐	☐	☐	☐	☐	☐
☐	Other (Please Specify):	☐	☐	☐	☐	☐	☐
☐	Other (Please Specify):	☐	☐	☐	☐	☐	☐

SERVICES PROVIDED AND RESULTS PRODUCED

Please mark any of the services/products listed below that your Organization provided or produced in **2006 and 2007 (over the past TWO years).** For those services/products marked, please complete the request for additional information about the provision of service and/or production numbers. (Where exact numbers are not available, please estimate.)

Housing Produced

	Home Ownership (For Sale Housing)	# of units '06-'07	Total Cost of Development
☐	Single Family		$
☐	Multi Family		$
☐	Other		$

	Rental Housing	# of units '06-'07	Total Cost of Development
☐	Single Family		$
☐	Multi Family		$
☐	Other		$

		# of units '06-'07	Total Cost of Development
☐	Cooperative Housing		$

		# of units '06-'07	Total Cost of Development
☐	SRO Housing		$

		# of units '06-'07	Total Cost of Development
☐	Senior Housing		$

		# of units '06-'07	Total Cost of Development
☐	Housing for People w/AIDS		$

		# of units '06-'07	Total Cost of Development
☐	Housing for People w/Disabilities		$

		# of units '06-'07	Total Cost of Development
☐	Land Trust		$

		# of units '06-'07	Total Cost of Development
☐	HOPE IV		$

		# of units '06-'07	Total Cost of Development
☐	LIHTC		$

* Please check the box if you engaged in any of these services/activities in 2006 or 2007. Please provide an estimate for any number for which you are unsure of an exact number. The number should represent your Organization's activities in 2006 and 2007 (two years).

Housing-Related Services Provided

		# of units assisted '06-'07	Total Cost of Assistance
☐	**Lead Paint Abatement**		$

		# of units assisted '06-'07	Total Cost of Assistance
☐	**Asbestos Removal**		$

		# of units assisted '06-'07	Total Cost of Assistance
☐	**Home Repair**		$

		# of individuals assisted '06-'07	Total Cost of Assistance
☐	**Homebuying Counseling/Training**		$

		# of individuals assisted '06-'07	Total Cost of Assistance
☐	**Homeownership Counseling/Training**		$

		# of individuals assisted '06-'07	Total Cost of Assistance
☐	**Foreclosure Prevention Counseling/Training**		$

		# of individuals assisted '06-'07	Total Cost of Assistance
☐	**Landlord-Tenant Mediation**		$

		# of individuals assisted '06-'07	Total Cost of Assistance	Total Amount Saved in IDAs
☐	**Asset Building/Individual Development Accounts (IDAs)**		$	$

* Please check the box if you engaged in any of these services/activities in 2006 or 2007. Please provide an estimate for any number for which you are unsure of an exact number. The number should represent your Organization's activities in 2006 and 2007 (two years).

Business/Commercial Development

		# of sq. ft. developed	Total Cost of Development	Jobs Created
☐	Business District/Main Street Revitalization		$	

		# of sq. ft. developed	Total Cost of Development	Jobs Created
☐	Commercial/Retail Development		$	

		# of sq. ft. developed	Total Cost of Development	Jobs Created
☐	Industrial Development		$	

		# of businesses improved	Total Cost of Program	
☐	Façade Improvement Program		$	

Business/Commercial Development Services

		# of businesses assisted	Total Cost of Assistance	
☐	Small Business Incubator		$	

		# of businesses assisted	Total Cost of Assistance	Total Amount of Loans
☐	Small Business Loan or Microloan Program		$	$

		# of businesses assisted	Total Cost of Assistance	
☐	Small Business Technical Assistance		$	

		Annual Revenue	# of people employed	
☐	Organization Operates a For-Profit Business			

Other Development

		# of sq. ft. developed	Total Cost of Development
☐	**Mixed-Use Development**		$

		# of sq. ft. developed	Total Cost of Development
☐	**Brownfield Development**		$

* Please check the box if you engaged in any of these services/activities in 2006 or 2007. Please provide an estimate for any number for which you are unsure of an exact number. The number should represent your Organization's activities in 2006 and 2007 (two years).

CEDAM Industry Survey
Stand Up and Be Counted!

		# of sq. ft. developed	Total Cost of Development
❏	**Greenspace/Park Development**		$

		# of sq. ft. farmed	Total Cost of Development
❏	**Urban Agriculture/Food Systems**		$

		# of sq. ft. produced	Total Cost of Development
❏	**Green Building**		$

		# of sq. ft. developed	Total Cost of Development
❏	**Other (Please specify)**		$

Youth Programs

		# of youth in program '06-'07	Total Cost of Program
❏	**Day Care**		$

		# of youth in program '06-'07	Total Cost of Program
❏	**After School Program**		$

		# of youth in program '06-'07	Total Cost of Program
❏	**Summer Camp**		$

		# of youth in program '06-'07	Total Cost of Program
❏	**Head Start**		$

		# of youth in program '06-'07	Total Cost of Program
❏	**School Readiness**		$

		# of youth in program '06-'07	Total Cost of Program
❏	**Other Youth Programs**		$

* Please check the box if you engaged in any of these services/activities in 2006 or 2007. Please
provide an estimate for any number for which you are unsure of an exact number. The number should represent
your Organization's activities in 2006 and 2007 (two years).

Social Services/Training

		# of individuals assisted	Total Cost of Assistance
☐	**Drug Abuse Counseling**		$

		# of individuals assisted	Total Cost of Assistance
☐	**Teen/Parent Counseling**		$

		# of individuals assisted	Total Cost of Assistance
☐	**Literacy Program**		$

		# of individuals assisted	Total Cost of Assistance
☐	**Tax Preparation Assistance**		$

		Total Cost of Program
☐	**Crime Prevention/Neighborhood Watch**	$

		Total Cost of Program
☐	**Cultural/Arts Program**	$

		# of individuals assisted	Total Cost of Assistance
☐	**Community Center**		$

		Total Cost of Program
☐	**Voter Registration**	$

		# of individuals served	Total Cost of Program
☐	**Food Bank or Community Nutrition**		$

		# of individuals assisted	Total Cost of Assistance
☐	**Homeless Services**		$

		# of individuals served	Total Cost of Program
☐	**Energy Conservation Training/Services**		$

* Please check the box if you engaged in any of these services/activities in 2006 or 2007. Please provide an estimate for any number for which you are unsure of an exact number. The number should represent your Organization's activities in 2006 and 2007 (two years).

		# of individuals assisted	Total cost of assistance
☐	**Job Counseling/Job Training**		$

		# of individuals assisted	Total cost of assistance
☐	**Prisoner Re-entry**		$

		Total cost of program	
☐	**Community Organizing**	$	

TOP 3 Activities

Of the activities listed above, what are the TOP 3 for your organization?

_____
_____
_____

Aspirational Activities

Of the Activities listed above, what 3 activities does your Organization aspire to add in the coming years?

_____
_____
_____

* Please check the box if you engaged in any of these services/activities in 2006 or 2007. Please provide an estimate for any number for which you are unsure of an exact number. The number should represent your Organization's activities in 2006 and 2007 (two years).

Individuals Served

Please check the box next to the type of individuals your Organization serves.

❑ Low Income
❑ Moderate Income
❑ Market Rate
❑ Seniors
❑ Children/Youth
❑ Homeless
❑ People w/Disabilities or Special Needs
❑ People Living w/AIDS
❑ Jobless

Case Studies in Community Development

Please outline one or more stories about your Organization's work that you would like CEDAM to consider for future newsletter articles or in-depth case studies. We want to tell the story of community development in Michigan!

_____
_____
_____
_____

Innovation in Community Development

Are there any systems leaps or new strategies that your Organization has employed that are innovative and important to share? Please take a moment to tell us about them.

_____
_____
_____
_____

* Please check the box if you engaged in any of these services/activities in 2006 or 2007. Please provide an estimate for any number for which you are unsure of an exact number. The number should represent your Organization's activities in 2006 and 2007 (two years).

Appendix A3. 2007 Nonprofit Housing Provider Survey

HOUSING SERVICE
PROVIDER *Survey*

GLOBAL URBAN
STUDIES PROGRAM
MICHIGAN STATE
UNIVERSITY

Researchers affiliated with the Global Urban Studies Program at Michigan State University are examining the role of nongovernmental agencies in providing housing and related services in local communities. The survey is being sent to public, for-profit and nonprofit organizations involved in housing services. Your participation in this study will contribute to a greater understanding of how political and organizational forces can be aligned to strengthen and develop community and institutional assets; particularly with regards to housing.

The information will be reported in various publications; however we will not reveal any data that identify individuals or organizations without first obtaining permission to do. The survey does include an identifying code for record keeping purposes only.

If you feel uncomfortable answering any items, feel free to skip them. This survey should take about 25-30 minutes to complete. You indicate your voluntary agreement to participate by completing and returning this survey. To avoid additional mailings, please complete this questionnaire and return it <u>within</u> *three weeks* to the address below:

Global Urban Studies Program
Michigan State University
College of Social Science
447 Berkey Hall
East Lansing, MI 48824

Thank you in advance for completing the survey. If you would like a copy of the results, there is a place at the end of the survey to provide your email address so that you can receive a summary.

Marking Instructions:
- *Use black or blue pen or a number 2 pencil.*
- *Make dark marks that fill the response completely.*
- *Do not use pens with ink that soaks through the paper.*
- *Make no stray marks.*

Correct Mark ●   Incorrect Marks ✓ ⊗ ◑ ⊙

Section 1. Nature of the Housing Provider:

First we would like to know some background information about your organization.

1. Which of the following best describes your organization? *(Please mark only one)*
   - ○ Independent religious congregation
   - ○ Congregation that is part of a larger denomination
     Denomination _____
   - ○ Collaborative of individual congregations or religious organizations
   - ○ Non-congregational organization based on religious principles
   - ○ Not a religious organization but cooperates with religious organizations
     Examples of collaborators _____
     _____

   - ○ Not a religious organization and not related to religious organizations or based on religious values

2. What is the primary purpose of your organization? *(Please mark only one)*
   - ○ Housing
   - ○ Social Services
   - ○ Economic Development
   - ○ Neighborhood Development
   - ○ Other _____

3. In what year was your organization founded?

   YEAR
   ⓪⓪⓪⓪
   ①①①①
   ②②②②
   ③③③③
   ④④④④
   ⑤⑤⑤⑤
   ⑥⑥⑥⑥
   ⑦⑦⑦⑦
   ⑧⑧⑧⑧
   ⑨⑨⑨⑨

4. How many full time staff are employed at your organization?
   - ○ 0
   - ○ 1-5
   - ○ 6-10
   - ○ 11-24
   - ○ 25-49
   - ○ 50-99
   - ○ 100 or more

5. How many part-time staff are employed at your organization?
   - ○ 0
   - ○ 1-5
   - ○ 6-10
   - ○ 11-24
   - ○ 25-49
   - ○ 50-99
   - ○ 100 or more

6. In a "typical week," how many individuals volunteer at your organization?
   - ○ 0
   - ○ 1-5
   - ○ 6-10
   - ○ 11-24
   - ○ 25-49
   - ○ 50-99
   - ○ 100 or more

7. To what extent does your organization receive funding from the following sources (based on percent of overall budget)?

	Great Extent (60-100%)	Moderate Extent (26-59%)	Some Extent (up to 25%)	None
a. Religious bodies	○	○	○	○
b. Individual donations/offerings	○	○	○	○
c. Foundations	○	○	○	○
d. Corporations	○	○	○	○
e. Government	○	○	○	○
f. Banks/Financial Institutions	○	○	○	○

PLEASE DO NOT WRITE IN THIS AREA
◫○○○○○○○○○○○○○○○○○○○○○○○○○○○

Page 2

8. We are interested in getting a sense of the size of your organization's budget relative to other housing service providers. Please indicate the category your budget falls into (total budget from all sources):

- ○ $0 - $100,000
- ○ $100,001 - $250,000
- ○ $250,001 - $500,000
- ○ $500,001 - $1,000,000

- ○ $1,000,001 - $1,500,000
- ○ $1,500,001 - $2,000,000
- ○ $2,000,001 - $2,500,000
- ○ $2,500,001 - $3,000,000

- ○ $3,000,001 - $3,500,000
- ○ $3,500,001 - $4,000,000
- ○ $4,000,001 and above

9. If you receive NO government funding, please indicate the extent to which you agree that each of the following statements is a reason for the lack of government funding:

	Strongly agree	Agree	Neutral	Disagree	Strongly disagree
a. Organization is not eligible	○	○	○	○	○
b. Organization has a policy against receiving funds from government	○	○	○	○	○
c. Organization has applied for government funding but has not received it	○	○	○	○	○
d. Funding is not available for our activities	○	○	○	○	○
e. Do not need public funding, sufficient revenue from other sources	○	○	○	○	○
f. Too many strings/restrictions come with public funding	○	○	○	○	○
g. Public financing changes organizational values/mission	○	○	○	○	○

Section 2. Service Detail:

We are generally interested in the activities and nature of services provided by this organization. In addition, we are specifically interested in the nature and number of housing and related service activities that your organization is engaged in. Please answer the following questions about these services.

10. To what extent is your organization involved in each of the following activities?

	Very involved	Somewhat involved	Not very involved	Not at all involved
a. Delivery of services	○	○	○	○
b. Community and/or economic development	○	○	○	○
c. Policy advocacy	○	○	○	○
d. Community organizing	○	○	○	○
e. Voter education	○	○	○	○
f. Participation in/support of community projects	○	○	○	○

11. To what extent do your organizations' programs serve the following types of clients?

	Large extent	Moderate extent	Limited extent	None
a. Your own organization members	○	○	○	○
b. Senior citizens	○	○	○	○
c. Inner-city residents	○	○	○	○
d. Families with children	○	○	○	○
e. City-wide clients	○	○	○	○
f. Regional clients	○	○	○	○
g. Specific community neighborhood [identify _____]	○	○	○	○
h. Specific racial or ethnic communities [identify _____]	○	○	○	○
i. Low-income individuals and families	○	○	○	○
j. Religious communities [identify _____]	○	○	○	○
k. Other [identify _____]	○	○	○	○

12. How frequently does your organization engage in the following activities?

	Always	Often	Sometimes	Seldom	Never
a. Direct assistance to the needy	○	○	○	○	○
b. Programs in cooperation with a general-purpose social service agency such as St. Vincent De Paul, Catholic Social Services, Lutheran Social Services, United Way, Red Cross, etc.	○	○	○	○	○
c. Programs focused on physical health needs	○	○	○	○	○
d. Programs focused on mental health needs	○	○	○	○	○
e. Programs with educational purposes not including religious education and mentoring	○	○	○	○	○
f. Programs directed at immigrants, migrants, or refugees, including English as a Second Language classes	○	○	○	○	○
g. Programs focused on recreation	○	○	○	○	○
h. Programs focused on crime prevention, crime victims, or police and fire departments	○	○	○	○	○
i. Programs explicitly providing only short-term emergency or temporary assistance	○	○	○	○	○
j. Substance abuse programs	○	○	○	○	○
k. Programs to help people obtain jobs	○	○	○	○	○
l. Programs to train people in work skills or job-seeking skills	○	○	○	○	○
m. Programs giving or loaning money to individuals or organizations	○	○	○	○	○
n. Business incubation / Incubator development	○	○	○	○	○
o. Small business technical assistance	○	○	○	○	○
p. Brownfield redevelopment	○	○	○	○	○
q. Mixed-used development	○	○	○	○	○
r. Business district/main street development	○	○	○	○	○
s. Community Reinvestment Act (CRA)	○	○	○	○	○
t. Programs focused on social justice	○	○	○	○	○
u. Programs focused on political activity	○	○	○	○	○
v. Voter registration, voter turnout	○	○	○	○	○
w. Membership on public commissions/boards/advisory panels	○	○	○	○	○
x. Membership on private advisory boards/boards of directors	○	○	○	○	○
y. Environmental justice	○	○	○	○	○
z. Other _____	○	○	○	○	○

13. To what extent does your organization provide each of the following aspects of housing services or housing related activities?

	Large extent	Moderate extent	Limited extent	None
a. Builds new single-family housing	○	○	○	○
b. Builds new multi-family housing	○	○	○	○
c. Renovates housing	○	○	○	○
d. Builds or renovates rental housing	○	○	○	○
e. Builds or renovates owner-occupied housing	○	○	○	○
f. Builds or renovates low income housing	○	○	○	○
g. Builds or renovates market rate housing	○	○	○	○
h. Provides assistance with utility payments	○	○	○	○
i. Provides rental assistance	○	○	○	○
j. Provides assistance with furniture and/or household items	○	○	○	○
k. Provides credit counseling	○	○	○	○
l. Provides home ownership counseling	○	○	○	○
m. Provides home maintenance training	○	○	○	○
n. Provides landlord/tenant mediation	○	○	○	○
o. Runs programs directed at the homeless or transients (including temporary shelters and day sheltering)	○	○	○	○
p. Provides transitional housing	○	○	○	○
q. Provides special needs housing [indicate type _____]	○	○	○	○
r. Provides referrals to other housing programs	○	○	○	○
s. Influences local housing policy	○	○	○	○
t. Influences state housing policy	○	○	○	○
u. Other _____	○	○	○	○

14. Please list and describe the two most important housing activities your organization is engaged in. (Examples: Housing assistance programs, housing renovation programs, housing rental, housing construction, utility assistance, homeownership training, etc.)

a. Activity 1:

_____

_____

_____

_____

b. Activity 2:

_____

_____

_____

_____

15. With what other organizations does your organization collaborate on these programs? If you do not collaborate with a particular type of organization, leave this section blank.

a. Activity 1:

Type of Collaborator (Please mark *all* that apply)	Name of Collaborator (Please list *all* that apply for <u>each</u> type of collaborator)
○ Government collaborator	_____
○ Non-profit collaborator (not congregations or religious organizations)	_____
○ Congregations or Religious Organizations	_____
○ Neighborhood organization partner	_____
○ Other (Specify type below)	_____

6. Activity 2:

Type of Collaborator (Please mark *all* that apply)	Name of Collaborator (Please list *all* that apply for <u>each</u> type of collaborator)

○ Government collaborator _____

○ Non-profit collaborator (not congregations or religious organizations) _____

○ Congregations or Religious Organizations _____

○ Neighborhood organization partner _____

○ Other (Specify type below) _____

16. **How many individuals has your organization served (for housing-related services) over the past three years?**

○ 0   ○ 26-50   ○ 100-249   ○ 500-999
○ 1-25   ○ 51-99   ○ 250-499   ○ 1000 or more

17. **Please indicate the number of each type of housing unit your organization has built and/or renovated over the past three years:**

New
Number of each housing type.

Single Family	Multi-Family	Total

Renovated
Number of each housing type.

Single Family	Multi-Family	Total

New
Number of each housing type.

Rental	Owner-Occupied	Total

Renovated
Number of each housing type.

Rental	Owner-Occupied	Total

New
Number of each housing type.

Low-Income	Market Rate	Total

Renovated
Number of each housing type.

Low-Income	Market Rate	Total

New
Number of each housing type.

Senior	Special Needs	Family	Total

Renovated
Number of each housing type.

Senior	Special Needs	Family	Total

18. How has the level of your organization's involvement in housing activity changed over the past <u>five</u> years?

○ Large increase
○ Moderate increase
○ Same level
○ Moderate decrease
○ Large decrease

19. **What percent of the organization's budget is spent in the following areas?**

    Budget Category

    ○ a. Development Activities   ○ b. Housing Projects,   ○ c. Management & Related   ○ d. Other
                                 Programs, Services   Expenses

% Spending	% Spending	% Spending	% Spending

Section 3. Collaborations/Networks:

20. **To what extent does your organization collaborate with other organizations for each of the following purposes?**

	Large extent	Moderate extent	Limited extent	None
a. To provide housing services	○	○	○	○
b. To provide other services	○	○	○	○
c. To receive services related to housing	○	○	○	○
d. To receive other services	○	○	○	○
e. To provide funding	○	○	○	○
f. To receive funding	○	○	○	○
g. To refer clients	○	○	○	○
h. To provide services to clients referred from other organizations	○	○	○	○
i. To engage in neighborhood development	○	○	○	○
j. To provide policy advice	○	○	○	○
k. To receive policy advice	○	○	○	○
l. To influence public policy	○	○	○	○
m. To pool resources or otherwise create partnerships	○	○	○	○

21. **How important are each of the following goals to your organization in decisions to create networks with other organizations?**

	Very important	Somewhat important	Neither: Neutral	Not very important	Not important at all
a. Avoid redundancy/increase efficiency	○	○	○	○	○
b. Promote bridge-building/understanding	○	○	○	○	○
c. Receive referrals to/from other groups	○	○	○	○	○
d. Advocacy for underrepresented groups	○	○	○	○	○
e. Expand/start new programs	○	○	○	○	○
f. Improve neighborhood conditions	○	○	○	○	○
g. Promote religious identity	○	○	○	○	○
h. Influence state housing policy	○	○	○	○	○
i. Influence local housing policy	○	○	○	○	○

22. In planning and implementing your housing programs, do you have any colleagues in other organizations in the area that you rely on for information and advice?

○ Yes   ○ No   ○ Don't know

(If yes), Please list the organizations they are affiliated with: _____

_____

_____

_____

_____

_____

23. In planning and implementing your housing programs, are there other organizations that you cooperate with in either service planning or provision?

○ Yes   ○ No   ○ Don't know

(If yes), Please list them: _____

_____

_____

_____

_____

_____

24. To what extent does your organization currently collaborate with the following types of groups or organizations?

	Large extent	Moderate extent	Limited extent	None
a. Social/community service organizations	○	○	○	○
b. Mental health agencies	○	○	○	○
c. Local government agencies	○	○	○	○
d. State agencies	○	○	○	○
e. Civic organizations (e.g. historical society, Lions club, Jr. League, Kiwanis, Little League, Rotary)	○	○	○	○
f. Neighborhood associations	○	○	○	○
g. Religious organizations	○	○	○	○
h. Ethnic organizations	○	○	○	○
i. Schools/child-care providers	○	○	○	○
j. Hospitals/health agencies	○	○	○	○
k. Advocacy/lobby groups	○	○	○	○
l. Private sector organizations	○	○	○	○
m. Other_____	○	○	○	○

25. Over the last five years, what has been your organization's pattern of collaboration
   with the following types of groups or organizations? Collaboration has...

	Increased greatly	Increased somewhat	Remained the same	Decreased somewhat	Decreased greatly
a. Social/community service organizations	○	○	○	○	○
b. Mental health agencies	○	○	○	○	○
c. Local government agencies	○	○	○	○	○
d. State agencies	○	○	○	○	○
e. Civic organizations (e.g. historical society, Lions club, Jr. League, Kiwanis, Little League, Rotary)	○	○	○	○	○
f. Neighborhood associations	○	○	○	○	○
g. Religious organizations	○	○	○	○	○
h. Ethnic organizations	○	○	○	○	○
i. Schools/child-care providers	○	○	○	○	○
j. Hospitals/health agencies	○	○	○	○	○
k. Advocacy/lobby groups	○	○	○	○	○
l. Private sector organizations	○	○	○	○	○
m. Other _____	○	○	○	○	○

26. We are trying to make sure that we have a complete list of housing providers in the State. Please identify
   three to five of the most prominent housing providers in this community.

_____

_____

_____

_____

_____

Section 4. Engagement and Impact:

27. For each of the following statements please indicate whether you strongly agree, agree, disagree, or
   strongly disagree with the statement posed.

	Strongly agree	Agree	Neutral	Disagree	Strongly disagree
a. Collaboration with other nonprofit organizations has allowed this organization to provide more and better housing to clients.	○	○	○	○	○
b. Public funding can sometimes interfere with the mission of the organization.	○	○	○	○	○
c. Working with public officials provides a way to make sure that the organization has its views represented in public policy decisions.	○	○	○	○	○
d. It is important for housing providers to be active in the design and implementation of government funded housing programs.	○	○	○	○	○
e. It is appropriate for housing providers to help frame public policy.	○	○	○	○	○
f. Government officials need to be more sensitive to values held by religious organizations active in the area of low-income housing.	○	○	○	○	○
g. This organization has a say in the creation of state and local housing policy.	○	○	○	○	○
h. Providing housing is a good way to influence the political process related to housing.	○	○	○	○	○
i. Providing housing is a good way to influence the political process in general.	○	○	○	○	○
j. Our housing programs have made a significant impact on low income housing needs in our community.	○	○	○	○	○

28. Please indicate how satisfied you are with your organization's accomplishments in each of the following areas.

	Very satisfied	Satisfied	Neutral	Dissatisfied	Strongly dissatisfied
a. How satisfied are you with the organization's accomplishments in amount of housing it provides?	○	○	○	○	○
b. How satisfied are you with the quality of housing provided by the organization?	○	○	○	○	○
c. How satisfied are you with the organization's ability to meet its goals and objectives?	○	○	○	○	○

Section 5. Organizational Leadership

Finally, we would like some background information about the organization's leadership and advisory board or board of directors.

29. Organization Name _____

30. Executive Director/President/CEO _____

31. Title of person filling out survey _____

Please provide the following information about the <u>organization's leader</u>.

32. Number of years with the organization:

YEARS

⓪⓪
①①
②②
③③
④④
⑤⑤
⑥⑥
⑦⑦
⑧⑧
⑨⑨

33. Year Born:

YEAR

⓪⓪⓪⓪
①①①①
②②②②
③③③③
④④④④
⑤⑤⑤⑤
⑥⑥⑥⑥
⑦⑦⑦⑦
⑧⑧⑧⑧
⑨⑨⑨⑨

34. Highest level of education completed *(Please mark only one).*

   ○ Less than 8th grade
   ○ 8th grade through 11th grade
   ○ High school graduate or GED
   ○ Technical / Junior college graduate
   ○ Some college
   ○ College graduate
   ○ Some post graduate
   ○ Graduate degree

358   APPENDIX A: METHODOLOGY APPENDIX

> Please provide the following information about the **organization's leader**. (continued)

35. Ethnicity:
Of Hispanic, Latino, or Spanish origin?

○ Yes
○ No

36. Race

○ American Indian or Alaska Native.
○ Asian.
○ Black or African American.
○ Hispanic or Latino.
○ Native Hawaiian or Other Pacific Islander.
○ White.

37. Gender:

○ Male
○ Female

38. Please provide the following information about the members of your advisory board or board of directors.

Name   Home Organization

_____   _____
_____   _____
_____   _____
_____   _____
_____   _____
_____   _____
_____   _____

39. Provide an email address if you would like a summary of the study results. (Print please)

_____

Appendix A4. Survey Target Populations

CEDAM Surveys: 2003 and 2007

The 2003 survey population was composed of members of the Community Economic Development Association of Michigan (CEDAM) and the Michigan Training and Technical Assistance Collaborative (MITTAC). CEDAM's membership is comprised of community development corporations (CDCs), community housing development organizations (CHDOs), financial institutions, city governments, state agencies, consultants, national intermediaries, community action agencies, and various Habitat for Humanity affiliates around the state. MITTAC is composed of organizations and agencies providing training and technical assistance to Michigan nonprofit organizations and local units of government engaged in sponsoring, producing, and/or operating affordable housing and other community development activities.

It cannot be suggested that this population included *all* nonprofit housing providers in the state, but because CEDAM and MITTAC represent the primary professional organizations for such entities, it can be assumed that most active housing nonprofits were included. The CEDAM survey collected information on the impact of CDCs in Michigan's neighborhoods and communities. Although it was possible that there were CEDAM members that provided no housing or housing-related services, only twenty-three of the survey respondents produced no housing units, and only thirteen respondents provided no housing-related services. The 2007 CEDAM survey population consisted of members of CEDAM only.

Nonprofit Housing Provider Survey

Since there was no preexisting list of housing service providers in the state (and this is probably the case in most states) significant effort was devoted to creating a list of such providers that represented, as closely as possible, the population of nonprofit housing providers. The survey was electronically scannable to reduce errors in coding. Several surveys (fewer than ten) received very late in the process were hand coded. Research staff checked the coding of every fifth scanned survey for validity and to identify any possible problems with questions or responses.

At the outset, it should be clear that there is no way to be certain that the ultimate list includes every element of the potential population. Indeed, it is unrealistic, if not impossible, to identify all housing and community development service providers; identifying faith-based providers is particularly problematic (see Reese 2004 for a discussion of this). Yet after employing a variety of methods to attain as accurate a list as possible, there is confidence that most nonprofits with any significant role in housing are included. The initial basis for the population list was drawn from the membership of the CEDAM and MITTAC. A total of 176 organizations came from these membership lists. To this membership base, 212 more housing providers were added. These were identified by using membership lists from the Community Development Advocates of Detroit and the Local Initiatives Support Corporation in Michigan (LISC). Community Development Advocates of Detroit (CDAD) is a trade association to provide a citywide voice for community development organizations (CDOs) in Detroit. Representing approximately fifty-five CDO and thirty-five technical service providers, CDAD currently has over ninety members and supporting member organizations. CDAD provides training and technical assistance, advocates on behalf of CDOs, facilitates common action on issues of concern, and assists in expanding financial resources available for CDO projects and programs. CDAD members share a commitment to community-based sustainable development projects.

The following description of LISC comes from the organization's website:

> LISC helps resident-led, community-based development organizations transform distressed communities and neighborhoods into healthy ones—good places to live, do business, work and raise families. By providing capital, technical expertise, training and information, LISC supports the development of local leadership and the creation of affordable housing, commercial, industrial and community facilities, businesses and jobs. (Local Initiatives Support Program, 2010)

Finally, another sixty nonprofit housing providers were identified by snowball sampling (Patton 1990). The survey sent to the initial list of 388 housing nonprofits included a question asking respondents to identify the five most prominent housing providers in their local community. Any organizations so identified and not in the original database were sent surveys. Finally, any organization that was listed on a survey response as a "partner" in service provision or other activities was also added to the list. Ultimately, 495 organizations received surveys and thus constitute the population of nonprofit housing providers for the study. While 495 organizations initially received surveys, follow-up phone calls indicated that a number were no longer in operation, some turned out to have no connection to housing or community development, and some redundancies were noted. These organizations were purged from the population list, leaving 386 valid organizations in the population.

References

Local Initiatives Support Program. 2010. About Us. www.lisc.org/section/aboutus/.
Patton, Michael. 1990. *Qualitative Evaluation and Research Methods.* Newbury Park, CA: Sage.
Reese, Laura A. 2004. A Matter of Faith: Urban Congregations and Economic Development. *Economic Development Quarterly* 18(1):50–66.

Appendix A5. Individuals Interviewed

Michigan State Housing Development Authority	SE Michigan development director, executive director, community development director, housing voucher manager
Department of Housing and Urban Development	Detroit and Grand Rapids field office directors
Habitat for Humanity	Executive director, Grand Rapids
U. S. Department of Agriculture	Director, single-family housing program
Community Economic Development Association of Michigan	Chief executive officer
Inner City Christian Federation	Executive director

Appendix A6. Interview Schedule

1. Please identify the organizations most involved in providing housing or housing services in (the Grand Rapids area OR the Detroit area OR the Traverse City area):
   a. Identify secular nonprofits.
   b. Identify faith-based organizations.

2. Assessment of organization's abilities:
   a. Do you think the secular nonprofits providing housing/housing services in (the Grand Rapids area OR the Detroit area OR the Traverse City area) are doing a good job? Why or why not?
   b. Do you think the faith-based organizations providing housing/housing services in (the Grand Rapids area OR the Detroit area OR the Traverse City area) are doing a good job? Why or why not?

3. Assessment of organizational capacity:
   a. Do you think secular nonprofits in (the Grand Rapids area OR the Detroit area OR the Traverse City area) have sufficient capacity to continue providing the current levels of housing and/or housing services? Could they provide a higher level of service given current resources? Why or why not?
   b. Do you think faith-based organizations in (the Grand Rapids area OR the Detroit area OR the Traverse City area) have sufficient capacity to continue providing the current levels of housing and/or housing services? Could they provide a higher level of service given current resources? Why or why not?

4. About what proportion of the city's total housing services are being provided by secular nonprofits? What proportion by faith-based organizations? [Provide examples of housing services, e.g., home ownership counseling, repair/rehab.]

5. How important do you think (secular nonprofits, faith-based organizations) are in the total housing market in (the Grand Rapids area OR the Detroit area OR the Traverse City area)?

6. To what extent do secular nonprofits cooperate with local and state government in providing housing? Please give some examples of cooperation. Please give some examples of where efforts to cooperate have failed. What other types of entities/organizations do these secular nonprofits cooperate with?

7. To what extent do faith-based organizations cooperate with local and state government in providing housing? Please give some examples of cooperation. Please give some examples of where efforts to cooperate have failed. What other types of entities/organizations do these faith-based organizations cooperate with?

8. Do you have a sense that private/nonprofit actors that provide housing and housing services have become more active in (the Grand Rapids area OR the Detroit area OR the Traverse City area) over the last five years? If yes:
   a. Is there more involvement by secular nonprofits or faith-based organizations, or is the level of increased activity comparable?
   b. Has this been the result of a reduced role of the public sector in housing?
   c. Has this increase caused the public sector to reduce its housing services?

9. Do you think that the relationships between secular nonprofit and faith-based providers have become more cooperative, more competitive, or stayed the same during the last five years? Why do you think this is so?

10. Do FBOs in this community seem to have cooperative or conflictual relationships with community groups? Other nonprofits? Other private providers?

11. Do you think that there is a relationship between the housing construction and housing service roles of faith-based organizations and their political activism? In other words, have housing activities led to increased political participation and influence beyond the housing arena?

12. Do you think local faith-based organizations are more or less politically powerful in (the Grand Rapids area OR the Detroit area OR the Traverse City area) compared to other areas of the state?

13. How has the religious community in general been active in the politics and policy making of (the Grand Rapids area OR the Detroit area OR the Traverse City area)? On what particular issues do they participate? Do they focus on morality-related issues? On services? Give examples.

Nonprofits Only

1. Please describe the kinds of political or electoral activities your organization is involved in.
   a. If none: You do not engage in activities such as get-out-the-vote drives, candidate appearances, recommend slates, demonstrations, petitions, etc.?

2. Please describe the kinds of community activities in which you are involved outside this organization. (Examples: community boards, public advisory boards, electoral politics, campaign activity, etc.)
   a. How about policy activities such as working with elected and appointed public officials?
   b. How about political or electoral activities?

3. Do you see your service roles as separate from your policy and political activity? Does the service provision role complement or enhance your policy activity? Your political activity?

4. Is your organization formally involved in public policy making? In what way?

Appendix B

Supplemental Tables,

Figure, and Map

Figure B1   Barriers to Citizen Participation in Community-Based Housing Organizations (CBHOs)

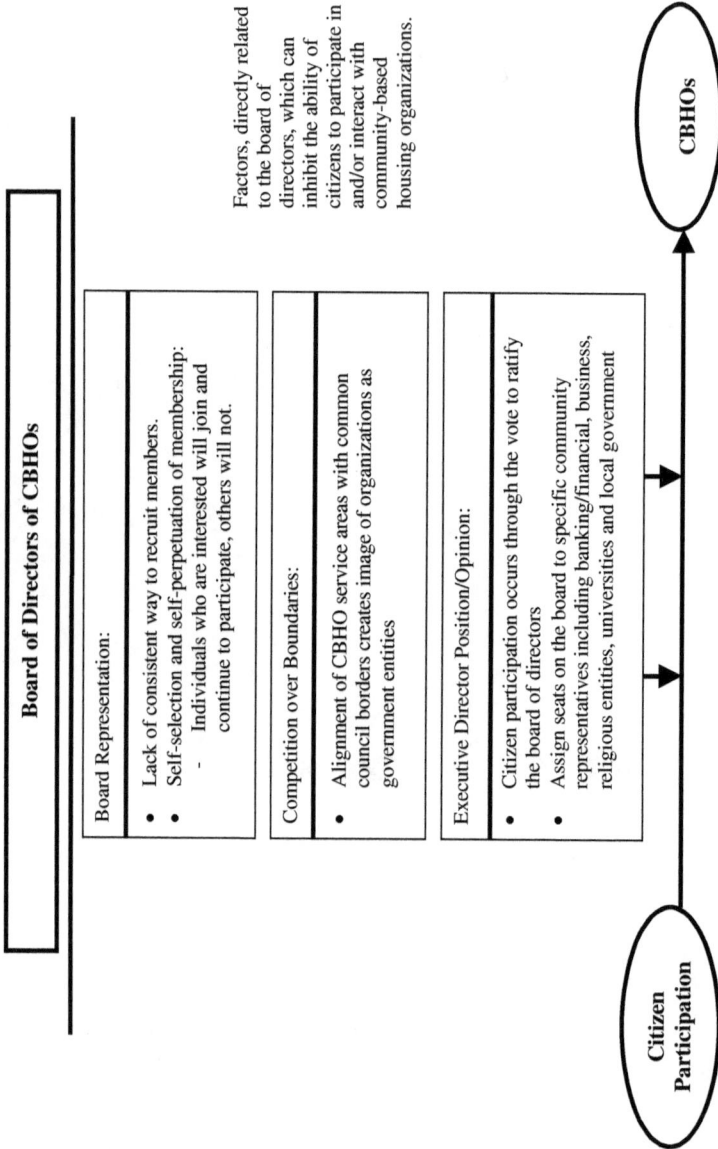

Board of Directors of CBHOs

Board Representation:

- Lack of consistent way to recruit members.
- Self-selection and self-perpetuation of membership:
  - Individuals who are interested will join and continue to participate, others will not.

Competition over Boundaries:

- Alignment of CBHO service areas with common council borders creates image of organizations as government entities

Executive Director Position/Opinion:

- Citizen participation occurs through the vote to ratify the board of directors
- Assign seats on the board to specific community representatives including banking/financial, business, religious entities, universities and local government

Factors, directly related to the board of directors, which can inhibit the ability of citizens to participate in and/or interact with community-based housing organizations.

Citizen Participation

CBHOs

Source: Silverman (2009).

Note: Supplemental material for Chapter 6, "Structure and Capacity of Housing Nonprofits." Data drawn from fifteen interviews conducted in 2004 with CBHO executive directors, who were asked to describe how citizen participation was viewed and incorporated within their nonprofit.

Map B1   **MSHDA County Locations**

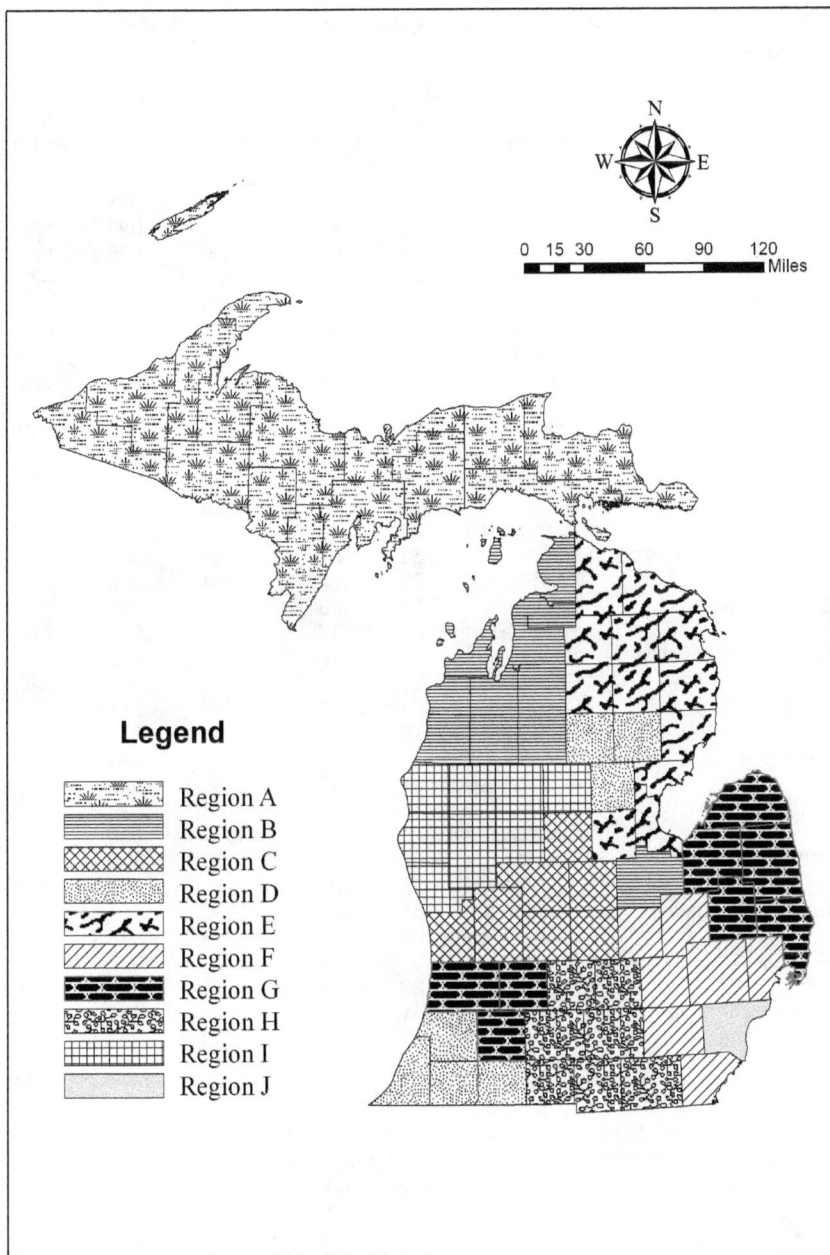

Legend

Region A
Region B
Region C
Region D
Region E
Region F
Region G
Region H
Region I
Region J

Note: Supplementary material for Chapter 9.

Table B1

Housing Development Activities of CEDAM Secular and Faith-Based Nonprofit Organizations 2003

	Organization type	N	Proportion Yes	Std. deviation	Std. error mean	t-test significance
Rental Housing	Secular	51	.53	.504	.071	
	Faith-based	29	.62	.494	.092	.435
Cooperative Housing	Secular	51	.00	.000	.000	
	Faith-based	29	.00	.000	.000	—[a]
Home-ownership	Secular	51	.67	.476	.067	
	Faith-based	29	.66	.484	.090	.918
SRO Housing	Secular	51	.06	.238	.033	
	Faith-based	29	.07	.258	.048	.859
Elderly Housing	Secular	51	.24	.428	.060	
	Faith-based	29	.24	.435	.081	.952
AIDS Housing	Secular	51	.12	.325	.046	
	Faith-based	29	.14	.351	.065	.795
Disability Housing[b]	Secular	51	.24	.428	.060	
	Faith-based	29	.10	.310	.058	.117
Single-Family Housing	Secular	51	.69	.469	.066	
	Faith-based	29	.62	.494	.092	.557
Small Residential[b]	Secular	51	.29	.460	.064	
	Faith-based	29	.17	.384	.071	.210
Large Residential	Secular	51	.16	.367	.051	
	Faith-based	29	.14	.351	.065	.822
Scattered Site	Secular	51	.51	.505	.071	
	Faith-based	29	.48	.509	.094	.819
Land Trust	Secular	51	.10	.300	.042	
	Faith-based	29	.07	.258	.048	.663
Hope VI	Secular	51	.02	.140	.020	
	Faith-based	29	.00	.000	.000	.454
Lead Paint Abatement	Secular	51	.24	.428	.060	
	Faith-based	29	.24	.435	.081	.952
Asbestos Removal	Secular	51	.04	.196	.027	
	Faith-based	29	.07	.258	.048	.563
Condos to lease to own	Secular	51	.04	.196	.027	
	Faith-based	29	.03	.186	.034	.094*
Home-ownership counseling	Secular	51	49	.505	.071	
	Faith-based	29	48	.509	.094	.95

Notes: Supplemental material for Chapter 7, "Housing Provision: Context by Sectors and Trends Over Time."

[a] t cannot be computed because the standard deviations of both groups are 0.

[b] Indicates t-test computed with group variance not assumed to be equal across groups. Otherwise equal variance assumed. Assumption used based on result of Levene's Test for Equality of Variances.

*Significant at the 0.10 level.

Table B2

Housing Development Activities of CEDAM Secular and Faith-Based Nonprofit Organizations 2007

	Organization type	N	Proportion Yes	Std. deviation	Std. error mean	t-test significance
Home buying training	Secular	36	.47	.51	.08	
	Faith-based	14	.64	.51	.13	.29
Home repair	Secular	40	.55	.50	.08	
	Faith-based	14	.43	.51	.14	.44
Home-ownership training	Secular	38	.47	.51	.08	
	Faith-based	14	.57	.51	.14	.54
Single-family ownership	Secular	60	.45	.50	.07	
	Faith-based	22	.64	.49	.11	.14
Foreclosure prevention	Secular	38	.37	.49	.08	
	Faith-based	14	.64	.50	.13	.08*
Multifamily rental	Secular	34	.35	.49	.08	
	Faith-based	13	.54	.52	.14	.26
Lead paint removal[a]	Secular	38	.40	.50	.08	
	Faith-based	13	.23	.44	.12	.27
IDAs	Secular	30	.23	.43	.08	
	Faith-based	10	.50	.53	.17	.12
LIHTC	Secular	32	.31	.47	.08	
	Faith-based	14	.29	.47	.13	.86
Disability	Secular	35	.29	.46	.08	
	Faith-based	13	.23	.44	.12	.71
Senior[a]	Secular	32	.19	.40	.07	
	Faith-based	14	.36	.50	.13	.27
Single-family rental[a]	Secular	34	.27	.45	.08	
	Faith-based	09	.11	.33	.11	.27
Landlord–tenant mediation	Secular	35	.14	.36	.06	
	Faith-based	12	.17	.39	.11	.84
Multifamily ownership[a]	Secular	28	.04	.19	.04	
	Faith-based	09	.33	.50	.11	.12
SRO	Secular	27	.07	.27	.05	
	Faith-based	11	.09	.30	.09	.87
AIDS	Secular	31	.07	.25	.05	
	Faith-based	13	.08	.28	.08	.89
Asbestos removal	Secular	31	.07	.25	.05	
	Faith-based	12	.08	.29	.08	.83
Land trusts[a]	Secular	30	.10	.31	.06	
	Faith-based	12	.00	.00	.00	.08*
Cooperative housing	Secular	29	.03	.19	.03	
	Faith-based	12	.00	.00	.00	.53
HOPE VI	Secular	30	.00	.00	.00	
	Faith-based	12	.00	.00	.00	na

Notes: Supplemental material for Chapter 7, "Housing Provision: Context by Sectors and Trends Over Time."

[a]Indicates *t*-test computed with group variance not assumed to be equal across groups. Otherwise equal variance assumed. Assumption used based on result of Levene's Test for Equality of Variances.

*Significant at the 0.10 level.

Table B3

Correlation Matrix of Housing Service Indexes

	Associated services	Home ownership services	Build and renovate	Build multifam-ily, special needs	Change in housing activity
Types of housing services and changes in housing activity					
Associated services	1.00				
Home-ownership services	.25**	1.00			
Build and renovate	.19	.51***	1.00		
Build multifamily, special needs	.42***	.05	.31***	1.00	
Housing activity change	.23**	.07	.05	.28**	1.00
Organizational characteristics					
Faith-based+	2.75	6.11*	1.68	11.03**	5.57
Full time staff	.57***	.07	.26**	.38***	.30***
Part-time staff	.51***	.08	.20	.35***	.18
Volunteers	.26**	.23	.10	.10	.18
Budget	.47***	.09	.26**	.33***	.27**
Organization age	.21	−.03	.22**	.15	−.06
Funding sources					
Religious funds	.34***	.19	−.13	.19	.24**
Donations	.28***	.26**	−.07	.01	.13
Foundation funds	.21	.09	−.04	.08	.21
Corporate funds	.13	.18	−.06	.18	.08
Govt funds	.30***	−.04	.03	−.07	.02
Bank funds	−.02	.18	.10	.07	.11
Population served					
Own members	−.02	−.02	.04	.20	.21
Seniors	.21	.11	.36***	.21	.26**
Inner-city	−.08	.08	.12	.06	.06
Families	.20	.42***	.29***	−.01	.02
City-wide	.13	.22**	.12	.08	.01
Region	.01	.08	.01	.10	.07
Neighborhood	−.05	.08	.22	−.19	−.03
Specific race	.01	.03	.24	−.03	.05
Low income	.28***	.28***	.30***	.08	.04
Religion	.17	.10	.11	.08	.21
Location					
Region+	4.94	6.00	3.84	10.95	25.92
Northern	.41	.08	.42	.81	5.14
Southwest	.73	1.69	.54	.36	4.79
Central	.67	.05	1.79	6.20**	4.80
Southeast	3.15	3.50	1.35	1.97	4.69
Detroit	1.18	2.26	.68	4.46	13.45**
Collaborates with					
Social service	.43***	.19	.04	.19	.17
Mental health	.57***	−.16	−.06	.42***	.23**

Local gov't	.12	.12	.06	−.02	.06
State gov't	.26**	.26**	.11	.20	.08
Civic orgs	.02	.04	−.21	−.19	.16
Neighborhoods	−.03	.18	.24**	.09	.00
Religious	.30***	.42***	.09	.15	.14
Ethnic	.25**	.16	.16	.16	.14
Schools	.37***	.13	−.08	.17	.05
Hospitals	.34***	−.06	−.04	.30***	.28**
Advocacy	.12	−.09	.06	.28**	.29***
Private sector	.01	.25**	.03	.04	.20
Collaborates for					
Housing	.37***	.21	.26**	.18	.14
Provide service	.49***	.07	.01	.18	.17
Receive service	.49***	.21	.16	−.08	.11
Provide funds	.18	.10	.18	.15	.15
Receive funds	.28**	.20	.27**	.28**	.13
Make referrals	.58***	.28***	.08	.10	.04
Neighborhood dev	−.02	.26**	.23**	.03	.19
Give policy advice	.27**	.11	.19	.08	.20
Receive policy advice	.26**	.05	.13	.10	.15
Pool resources	.27**	.23**	.13	.08	.17
Avoid redundancy	.26**	.15	.09	.17	.14
Bridge building	.15	.13	−.02	.06	.21
Receive referrals	.34***	.11	.11	.12	.10
Influence state housing policy	.24**	.29***	.20	.30***	.36***
Influence local housing policy	.20	.26**	.18	.22	.29*

Notes: Supplemental material for Chapter 7, "Housing Provision: Context by Sectors and Trends Over Time."

+Chi square statistic is used in the analysis and presented in the table for the regional and faith-based variables because they are nominal. Region and faith-based versus secular are the only nominal variables included in the analysis. Region is coded 1 if a respondent is in a particular region, 0 if they are not. To calculate the chi square for the relationship between region and score on each of the indexes, the indexes were recoded into ordinal variables representing low, medium, and high levels of service. Faith-based is coded 2 if respondent is a faith-based organization and 1 if they are not.

***Significant at the .01 level, **.05 level, *.10 level

Table B4

Correlations with Satisfaction Index

	Satisfaction
Types of housing services and changes in housing activity	
Associated services	.09
Home-ownership services	.06
Build and renovate	.25**
Build multifamily	.20
Housing activity change	.18
Organizational characteristics	
Faith-based+	3.01
Full time staff	−.28**
Part-time staff	−.12
Volunteers	.13
Budget	−.33**
Organization age	−.14
Funding sources	
Religious funds	.05
Donations	−.13
Foundation funds	−.25**
Corporate funds	.01
Govt funds	−.03
Bank funds	.06
Population served	
Own members	−.04
Seniors	.13
Inner-city	−.09
Families	.06
City-wide	.19
Region	.05
Neighborhood	−.17
Specific race	−.14
Low income	.07
Religion	−.09
Location	
Northern+	4.89
Southwest+	.21
Central+	3.88
Southeast+	3.02
Detroit+	3.32
Collaborates with	
Social service	.01
Mental health	.25**
Local government	−.09
State government	.07
Civic orgs	.11
Neighborhoods	−.11
Religious	−.03
Ethnic	.14

Schools	−.06
Hospitals	.09
Advocacy	.05
Private sector	−.07
Collaborates for	
Collaborate for services	.00
Collaborate for organizational development	.16
Collaborate for policy input	−.03
Collaborate for neighborhood development	.04
Respondent characteristics	
Years with organization	−.11
Education	.03
Race+	.44
Gender+	.20

Notes: Supplementary material for Chapter 7, "Housing Provision: Context by Sectors and Trends Over Time."

+ Chi square statistic is used in the analysis and presented in the table for these variables because there are nominal.

**Significant at the .05 level

Table B5

Correlations for the Collaborating Organizations for Secular Organizations Engaged in the MI Housing Arena

	Social service	Religious	Ethnic	Mental health	Schools	Hospitals	Local gov't	State gov't	Advocacy	Civic	Neighborhood	Private	Other
Social service	1.00												
Religious	.42***	1.00											
Ethnic	.37***	.68***	1.00										
Mental health	.52***	.36***	.26	1.00									
Schools	.34**	.50***	.37***	.34**	1.00								
Hospitals	.29**	.54***	.44***	.53***	.53***	1.00							
Local gov't	.41***	.28**	.22	.25	.14	.23	1.00						
State gov't	.38***	.25	.17	.26	.27**	.21	.56***	1.00					
Advocacy	.50***	.26	.26	.28**	.25	.15	.12	.22	1.00				
Civic	.25	.19	.09	.26	.27**	.28**	.31**	.19	-.05	1.00			
Neighborhood	.21	.39***	.29**	-0.1	.12	.11	.36***	.14	.12	-.17	1.00		
Private	.35**	.32**	.28**	.04	.41***	.32**	.06	.33**	.52**	.21	.01	1.00	
Other	.38**	.08	-.14	-.04	-.07	-.23	-.38	-.32	.89***	-.21	.13	.68**	1.00
Total significant collaborations	10	8	6	5	8	7	5	4	4	3	3	8	3

Notes: Supplementary material for Chapter 9, "Collaborations and Partnerships: Networks for Housing Service Delivery."

[a]"Collaboration is measured on a four point scale ranging from "large extent' to "not at all."

***Significant at .01, **significant at .05

Table B6

Correlations for the Collaborating Organizations for FBOs Engaged in the MI Housing Arena

	Social service	Religious	Ethnic	Mental health	Schools	Hospitals	Local gov't	State gov't	Advo-cacy	Civic	Neighbor-hood	Private	Other
Social service	1.00												
Religious	0.35	1.00											
Ethnic	.36**	.37**	1.00										
Mental health	.65***	0.06	.52**	1.00									
Schools	.55***	.54***	0.36	.37**	1.00								
Hospitals	.58***	0.17	.62***	.57***	.49***	1.00							
Local gov't	.48**	0.12	0.13	0.25	0.28	0.25	1.00						
State gov't	.57***	0.32	0.23	0.31	0.19	.41**	.66***	1.00					
Advocacy	.53***	0.19	.61***	.69***	.36**	.61***	.38***	.46***	1.00				
Civic	.36**	0.12	-0.15	0.25	0.30	0.22	0.07	0.12	0.18	1.00			
Neighborhood	0.07	0.12	0.32	0.19	0.19	0.15	.39**	0.09	0.30	-0.29	1.00		
Private	.40**	.53***	.38**	.37**	.61***	.51***	0.23	0.21	.47***	.43**	.36***	1.00	
Other	0.66	0.59	0.65	0.54	0.53	.76**	0.16	0.21	0.34	0.18	.68**	.78**	1.00
Total significant collaborations	9	3	6	6	6	7	4	4	8	2	3	10	3

Notes: Supplementary material for Chapter 9, "Collaborations and Partnerships: Networks for Housing Service Delivery."

[a] Collaboration is measured on a four-point scale ranging from "large extent" to "not at all."

***Significant at .01, **significant at .05

Table B7

Correlation Matrix of Organizational Activities and Collaboration for Secular Organizations

	Deliver services	Economic development	Political advocacy	Community organizing	Voter education	Community projects	Change in housing activity
Types of organizational activities and changes in housing activity							
Deliver services	1.00						
Economic development	-.09	1.00					
Political advocacy	.40***	.03	1.00				
Community organizing	.27**	.40***	.32**	1.00			
Voter education	.31**	.11	.37***	.39***	1.00		
Community projects	.16	.49***	.36***	.69***	.39***	1.00	
Types of organizational collaborators							
Social service	.39***	-.24*	.45***	.17	.28**	.10	
Mental health	.48***	-.52***	.25*	-.06	.34**	-.24	
Local government	.24*	-.07	.21	.30**	.13	.13	
State government	.25*	.06	.10	.10	.01	-.05	
Civic orgs	.27**	-.06	.32**	.31**	.14	.06	
Neighborhoods	.08	.14	.03	.26**	.26*	.36***	
Religious	.36***	-.06	.23*	.28**	.44***	.34***	
Ethnic	.30**	-.08	.30**	.20	.41***	.20	
Schools	.32**	.01	.27**	.42***	.36***	.13	
Hospitals	.34**	-.06	.35***	.26*	.50***	.20	
Advocacy Organizations	.11	.04	.48***	.04	.15	.24*	
Private sector	-.02	.37***	.33**	.22	.20	.16	

Purpose of collaboration:
Service

Housing	.14	-.04	.11	.10	.066	.044
Provide service	.32**	-.01	.34***	.39***	.283**	.273**
Receive housing service	.22	.01	.22	.21	.169	.247*
Receive service	.23*	-.11	.25*	.26*	.185	.195
Provide funds	.18	-.02	.24*	.08	.124	.148
Receive funds	.36***	.01	.48***	.20	.300**	.253*
Make referrals	.40***	-.24	.38***	.15	.192	.069
Receive referrals	.50***	-.28**	.35***	.24*	.161	.068

Purpose of collaboration: Policy

Neighborhood develop	.12	.47***	.16	.53***	.18	.50***
Give policy advice	.27**	.09	.48***	.28**	.18	.30**
Receive policy advice	.23*	.00	.50***	.26*	.18	.30**
Influence policy	.26**	.01	.50***	.18	.27**	.26*
Pool resources	.08	.04	.21	.20	.20	.21

Rationale for collaboration:
Program/Service facilitation

Avoid redundancy	.40***	-.09	.30**	.19	.18	.07
Bridge building	.27**	.06	.36***	.34***	.21	.29**
Make and receive referrals	.16	-.26*	.35***	.05	.23*	.01
New programs	.57***	.05	.47***	.31**	.17	.19

Rationale for collaboration: Policy

Advocacy	.38***	-.10	.40***	.36***	.32**	.18
Improve neighborhoods	.12	.44***	.35***	.42***	.17	.43***
Influence local policy	.55***	-.14	.54***	.08	.33**	.12
Influence state policy	.38***	.01	.42***	.04	.19	.21

Rationale for collaboration: Other

Promote religion	.08	.12	.14	.00	.26*	-.01

Notes: Supplemental material for Chapter 10, "Nature and Types of Collaboration."
***Significant at the .01 level, **.05 level, *.10 level

Table B8

Correlation Matrix of Organizational Activities and Collaboration for FBOs

	Deliver services	Economic development	Political advocacy	Community organizing	Voter education	Community projects
Types of organizational activities and changes in housing activity						
Deliver services	1.00					
Economic development	-.21	1.00				
Political advocacy	-.19	.18	1.00			
Community organizing	.04	.42**	.20	1.00		
Voter education	-.14	.20	.41**	.49**	1.00	
Community projects	.05	.35**	.01	.46***	.23	1.00
Types of organizational collaborators						
Social service	.19	.03	.25	.35**	.23	-.10
Mental health	.14	.03	.11	.27	.24	-.06
Local government	-.18	.36**	.28	.08	.15	-.08
State government	-.23	.36**	.19	.26	.13	-.22
Civic orgs	-.1	-.28	.38**	-.04	-.15	-.10
Neighborhoods	-.06	.33*	.10	.21	.16	.13
Religious	-.05	-.19	-.24	.03	-.06	-.05
Ethnic	.12	.05	-.29	.28	.17	.07
Schools	.18	-.24	.13	.11	.12	.17
Hospitals	-.13	.20	.23	.39**	.33*	.22
Advocacy Organizations	-.10	.08	.35*	.33*	.52***	-.17
Private sector	-.08	-.16	.35*	.14	.11	.08

Purpose of collaboration:					
Service					
Housing	.21	.09	.00	.42**	.17	-.03
Provide service	.25	.03	.08	.33*	.42**	-.05
Receive housing service	.30	-.01	-.31*	.29	.28	.09
Receive service	.52***	-.03	-.18	.09	.23	.01
Provide funds	.26	.18	-.29	.35*	.12	.15
Receive funds	.36*	-.09	-.13	.10	.05	.08
Make referrals	.30	.00	-.11	.31*	.22	-.08
Receive referrals	.35*	-.02	-.16	.278	.19	-.18
Purpose of collaboration: Policy					
Neighborhood develop	.13	.49***	.06	.58***	.20	.15
Give policy advice	.04	.28	.26	.37**	.39**	.07
Receive policy advice	.24	.16	.36*	.21	.41**	.00
Influence policy	.02	.02	.49***	.26	.41**	-.06
Pool resources	.30	.12	-.02	.36**	.22	.12
Rationale for collaboration:					
Program/service facilitation					
Avoid redundancy	.26	-.12	.01	.41**	.28	.27
Bridge building	.05	-.14	-.21	.24	.23	.09
Receive referrals	.27	-.05	-.06	.09	-.09	.09
New programs	.14	.22	.23	.20	.13	.13
Rationale for collaboration:					
Policy					
Advocacy	.045	.191	-.038	.198	.039	.099
Improve neighborhoods	-.133	.416**	.225	.141	.144	.221
Influence local policy	-.321	.446**	.632***	.215	.160	.108
Influence state policy	-.190	.292	.566***	.250	.211	-.046
Rationale for collaboration:					
Other					
Promote religion	.111	.003	.022	.214	.121	.260

Notes: Supplemental material for Chapter 10, "Nature and Types of Collaboration."
***Significant at the .01 level, **.05 level, *.10 level

Reference

Silverman, Robert Mark. 2009. Sandwiched between Patronage and Bureaucracy: The Plight of Citizen Participation in Community-based Housing Organizations in the US. *Urban Studies* 46(1): 3–25.

Index

Single-family housing, 103, 161, 166
Smith, Carla H., 256
"Social justice" factor and activities, 186,
    202, 204, 207, 211, 214, 215, *216,*
    217, *218*
Social network analysis, 85–88, 223–224,
    234–236, *237–240,* 241–244, *245,*
    246–247, *247, 248*
Social services activities. *See* Community-
    based social services
Social welfare activities, 56, *57,* 58, *60,*
    61, 62, 73. *See also* Community-
    based social services
Special Impact Amendment (1966), 22
Special needs housing, 51, 101, 174,
    176–177, *176*
SPSS 17 database, 89
Staffing
    community development corporations,
        31, 124
    faith-based organizations, 31–32,
        124–125
State and federal housing network, *239,* 242
State and local housing programs, 98,
    See also Michigan; *specific program
    name*
State government, 54, *See also* Michigan
Structural capacity, 123–125
Subsidized housing units, 101, *102*
Success markers, faith-based
    organizations, 38–39, *39*

Target population surveys, 79–80, 359–360
Tax Reform Act (1986), 101
Technical assistance, 34–35, 135, 137–138,
    138, 139, *140, 142*
Title IV of Community Services Act, 22
Title VI of Housing and Community
    Development Amendments, 22, 24
Tocqueville, Alexis de, 55
Training needs, 142, *143,* 144–145
Twombly, Eric, 34

UCINET Version 6.166, 86–88, 235
Unrotated factors, 89
Urban Institute report (2008), 55
U.S. Conference of Mayors survey (2001),
    22
U.S. Department of Agriculture (USDA),
    98, 103, 224, 244
U.S. Department of Housing and Urban
    Development (HUD), 21, 98, 103,
    105, 224
U.S. Supreme Court ruling on FBOs
    (1988), 21

Varimax rotation, 89
Vietnam War (1970s), 4
Voicu, Ioan, 27
Voluntary organizations, 55–56, *57,* 58–62,
    59, 60, 61, 62, 63, 64, 73

Walker, Christopher, 153
War on Poverty (1960s), 4
Washtenaw Affordable Housing
    Corporation, 179
Wylde, Kathryn, 20

Youth services activities, 186, 202, 204,
    211, 214, 215, *216,* 217

About the Authors

Cynthia Jackson-Elmoore is professor and dean of the Honors College at Michigan State University; she is affiliated with the School of Social Work, department of political science, and the Global Urban Studies Program. Her research and teaching interests and publications focus broadly on urban politics, public policy processes, and public services. She conducted evaluations on community health care reform and managed a multi state study. She is senior associate editor of the *Journal of Urban Affairs* (2010–2015) and editor-in-chief of the *Red Cedar Undergraduate Research Journal (ReCUR)*.

Richard C. Hula is professor and chair of the department of political science at Michigan State University. His research and teaching interests include environmental policy and urban politics. Current projects include changing state and local environmental policy, the impact of faith-based organizations on public service delivery, and the political consequences of state-level interventions into local policy arenas. He has served as president of the Policy Studies Association (1997–1998) and was selected as a Distinguished Scholar Teacher by the University Maryland (1987).

Laura A. Reese is professor of political science and director of the Global Urban Studies Program at Michigan State University. Her research and teaching areas include urban politics and policy, economic development, and local governance in Canada and the United States. She has conducted large-scale evaluations for the Economic Development Administration and substate economic development programs. She has written several books and numerous articles in these areas. She is the editor-in-chief of the *Journal of Urban Affairs*.

For Product Safety Concerns and Information please contact our EU
representative GPSR@taylorandfrancis.com
Taylor & Francis Verlag GmbH, Kaufingerstraße 24, 80331 München, Germany